Colección Támesis
SERIE A: MONOGRAFÍAS, 234

# A COMPANION TO US LATINO LITERATURES

This volume, documenting the linguistic and cultural diversity of Latino literary output in the United States, offers an exciting introduction for non-specialist readers. Unique in its scope and perspective, it focuses on various literary genres, and cinema, related to Latinos. Each essay considers not only Latino writers who were born or raised in the United States, but also Latin American writers who took up residence in the United States but may also be considered part of the literary scene of their countries of origin. Rather than follow one specific mode of organization and presentation, each contributor has offered his or her original perspective on the subject matter or theme. The result is an inclusive spectrum of the voices of the US Latin American diaspora, illuminating the rich and complex culture of Latinos.

*Tamesis*

*Founding Editor*
J. E. Varey

*General Editor*
Stephen M. Hart

*Editorial Board*
Alan Deyermond
Julian Weiss
Charles Davis

# A COMPANION TO
# US LATINO LITERATURES

Edited by

Carlota Caulfield
Darién J. Davis

**TAMESIS**

© Editors and Contributors 2007

*All Rights Reserved*. Except as permitted under current legislation no part
of this work may be photocopied, stored in a retrieval system,
published, performed in public, adapted, broadcast,
transmitted, recorded or reproduced in any form or by any means,
without the prior permission of the copyright owner

First published 2007
by Tamesis, Woodbridge
Paperback edition 2010

Transferred to digital printing

ISBN 978-1-85566-139-4 hardback
ISBN 978-1-85566-216-2 paperback

Tamesis is an imprint of Boydell & Brewer Ltd
PO Box 9, Woodbridge, Suffolk IP12 3DF, UK
and of Boydell & Brewer Inc.
668 Mt Hope Avenue, Rochester, NY 14620, USA
website: www.boydellandbrewer.com

A CiP catalogue record for this book is available
from the British Library

This publication is printed on acid-free paper

# CONTENTS

List of Contributors     vii

Acknowledgements     xi

Introduction: Pluralism in US Latino Literature: A Historical Perspective     1
    CARLOTA CAULFIELD and DARIÉN J. DAVIS

1   Resistance, Revolution, and Recuperation: The Literary Production of     12
    the Mestizo/Mexican-American/Chicano
    ELIZABETH COONROD MARTÍNEZ

2   The Importance of Being Sandra (Cisneros)     37
    EVA PAULINO BUENO

3   The Island as Mainland and the Revolving Door Motif: Contemporary     51
    Puerto Rican Literature of the United States
    PATRICIA M. MONTILLA

4   Am I Who I Am? Identity Games in US Cuban Literature     67
    JORGE FEBLES

5   Afro-Cuban Identity in the Theater of the Diaspora     88
    ARMANDO GONZÁLEZ-PÉREZ

6   Between the Island and the Tenements: New Directions in     101
    Dominican-American Literature
    ELIZABETH COONROD MARTÍNEZ

7   Three Central American Writers: Alone Between Two Cultures     120
    VINCENT SPINA

8   American Dream, *Jeitinho Brasileiro*: On the Crossroads of Cultural     140
    Identities in Brazilian-American Literature
    ANTONIO LUCIANO DE ANDRADE TOSTA

9   Argentine Writers in the US: Writing South, Living North     158
    SERGIO WAISMAN

10  A Balancing Act: Latin American Jewish Literature in the United States (or Towards a Jewish-Latino Literature)  177
    LYDIA M. GIL

11  US Latina Caribbean Women Poets: An Overview  191
    CARLOTA CAULFIELD

12  The Latino Film Experience in History: A Dialogue Among Texts and Collaborators  208
    DARIÉN J. DAVIS

Further Reading  227

Index  231

# LIST OF CONTRIBUTORS

**Eva Paulino Bueno** is a professor in the Languages Department at St Mary's University, San Antonio, Texas, where she teaches Latin American literature, Spanish, and Portuguese. She is the author of *Resisting Boundaries* (1995), and *O Artista do Povo, Mazzaropi no cinema do Brasil* (2000), and the co-editor of several books, including *Imagination Beyond Nation* (1999), *Naming the Father* (2000), and *I Wouldn't Want Anybody to Know: Native English Teaching in Japan* (2002). She has also published essays in periodicals in the US, Brazil, and France.

**Jorge Febles** is a graduate of the University of Iowa. He teaches Spanish American Literature and Culture at the University of North Florida. Although he has written numerous essays on diverse subjects pertaining to Spain and Latin America, the bulk of his publications center on Cuban and US Cuban literature and particularly on Matías Montes-Huidobro, Roberto G. Fernández, José Martí, and Alfonso Hernández Catá. Along with Armando González-Pérez, he co-edits the literary and cultural journal *Caribe*.

**Lydia M. Gil** received her Ph.D. at the University of Texas at Austin. She has contributed critical essays on Jewish literature of Latin America to *Jewish Writers of the Twentieth Century*, *The Oxford Encyclopedia of Latinos and Latinas in the US*, and *Latin American Theatre Review*, among others. She is an independent scholar.

**Armando González-Pérez** is Professor of Medieval and Renaissance Spanish Literature as well as Afro-Hispanic Literature at Marquette University in Milwaukee, Wisconsin. He is the author of *Presencia Negra: Teatro Cubano de la Diáspora* (1999). He is also co-editor of the literary and cultural journal *Caribe*.

**Elizabeth Coonrod Martínez** holds a joint appointment in Spanish/Latin American Literature, and the Department of Chicano and Latino Studies, where she is department Chair, at Sonoma State University. Her articles have appeared in academic journals and in the United Nations-sponsored *Americas* magazine. She has published four books on Mexican-Americans with the Millbrook Press, in 2001, a book of literary criticism, *Before the Boom: Latin American Revolutionary Novels of the 1920s*, and, in 2005, *'Lilus Kikus' and Other Stories by Elena Poniatowska* (translation and Introduction).

**Patricia M. Montilla** has a doctoral degree from the University of Chicago, where she specialized in contemporary Spanish American poetry and US Latino literature and culture. She is currently an Assistant Professor at Western Michigan University. She has authored papers and articles on the poetry of Oliverio Girondo, as well as a book on the poetics of parody in the writings of this Argentine poet. Montilla has also published articles and book reviews on the works of Matías Montes Huidobro, Judith Ortiz Cofer, Carlota Caulfield, Mariano Brull, and Eugenio Florit.

**Vincent Spina** has a doctoral degree from New York University. He has published articles on José María Arguedas, Laura Esquivel, and Eunice Odio. He is the author of *El Modo Épico de José María Arguedas* (Pliegos). He teaches at Clarion College.

**Antonio Luciano de Andrade Tosta** has a Ph.D. in Comparative Literature from Brown University. He is currently Assistant Professor of Brazilian literature and culture at the University of Illinois Urbana-Champagne. He also has a Master's degree in Portuguese and Brazilian Studies from Brown University and a Master's degree in Comparative Literature from the State University of New York at Buffalo, where he was a Fulbright Scholar. His essays on Brazilian literature and culture and foreign language teaching have appeared in several academic journals and as book chapters in the United States and Brazil.

**Sergio Waisman** was born in New York to Argentine parents in 1967. He is currently Associate Professor of Spanish at the George Washington University. He received his Ph.D. from UC Berkeley in 2000, and an MA in Creative Writing from CU Boulder in 1995. His translation of *The Absent City* (Duke University Press) by Ricardo Piglia received an NEA Translation Fellowship Award in 2000. His first book of literary criticism, *Borges and Translation: The Irreverence of the Periphery*, was published in 2005. *Leaving*, his first novel, was also published in 2005.

*The Editors*

**Carlota Caulfield** is a Cuban poet and critic. She is also a Latina Caribbean, Latina, Hispanic, and Latin American writer. She holds a Ph.D. from Tulane University. Caulfield is the author of a number of poetry books, written in Spanish and English, including *Autorretrato en ojo ajeno*, *The Book of Giulio Camillo (a model for a theater of memory)* and *Movimientos metálicos para juguetes abandonados*, which won the 2002 First Hispanoamerican Poetry Prize 'Dulce María Loynaz'. She is the editor of *From the Forbidden Garden. Letters from Alejandra Pizarnik to Antonio Beneyto*, *Voces viajeras: Poetisas cubanas de hoy* and *The Other Poetry of Barcelona. Spanish and Spanish-American Women Poets*. Her research interests include the avant-garde and interdisciplinary approaches to poetry and art. Her poems, essays, and reviews have appeared in newspapers and journals in Europe, Latin America, and the United States. She is Professor of Spanish and Spanish-American Studies at Mills College, California.

**Darién J. Davis** received his doctoral degree from Tulane University in 1992. He is currently Associate Professor of History at Middlebury College, Middlebury, Vermont where he specializes in Latin American intellectual, cultural, and social history. He is the author of *Avoiding the Dark: Race and the Forging of National Consciousness in Brazil* (1999) and *Afro-Brasileiros Hoje* (2000). He is also the editor of two volumes on the African contribution to Latin American societies. He has published numerous essays and articles on early Brazilian immigrants to the United States, and on Latino, and Latin American cultural production, including work in the fields of intellectual history, film, and music.

# ACKNOWLEDGEMENTS

The editors wish to extend their thanks to the editorial team of Boydell & Brewer, and especially to Ellie Ferguson and Vanda Andrews for their help with preparing this book for publication. We are also grateful to Stacy McKenna for her assistance in the editing process and to Ashley Kerr for her help in creating the Latino timeline as well as her feedback as a potential reader of this volume. Our thanks also go to the contributors to this volume for their knowledge and forbearance. A Summer Research Fellowship from Mills College supported part of the project. We especially want to thank Dr Stephen Hart, Professor of Hispanic Studies at University College London, for his enthusiasm about this *Companion* and his invaluable suggestions.

# Introduction

# Pluralism in US Latino Literature: A Historical Perspective

### CARLOTA CAULFIELD and DARIÉN J. DAVIS

For any student interested in Latino history and culture in the United States, one fact becomes evident: Latinos are a culturally diverse group whose composition has changed over time. Like most identity labels, 'Latino' has political, economic, and social meanings nuanced and shaped by relationships to power. Some Latinos are descendants of Iberian *conquistadores* who once constituted an elite in the southwestern US or the region we now call Latin America. Others are descendants of conquered natives or Africans forced to adopt the dominant Iberian cultural values and language. Many more are the linguistic and cultural products of centuries of multiple stages of hybridization that not only included African, native, Portuguese, and Spanish influences, but also contributions from a host of immigrant and religious groups from around the globe. Not surprisingly, Latino literature and culture in the US reflect this diversity.

Latino populations are comprised of immigrant populations from all over Latin America who have made the US their home, but they also include the descendants of those immigrants. Some immigrants from Spain and their descendants also consider themselves Latinos. However, the oldest roots of the contemporary Latino populations were present in the US prior to the arrival of English-speaking settlers, when the southwestern part of the US constituted a part of the Spanish viceroyalty of New Spain with its center of power in Mexico City.

According to the 2000 US census reports, Mexicans or people claiming Mexican ancestry comprised almost 60 per cent of the Latino population, some 20.6 million. Puerto Ricans made up 9.6 per cent while Cubans accounted for 3.5 per cent. Almost 30 per cent claimed heritage or ancestry from one or more Latin American countries, or Spain.[1] As Cherríe Moraga reminds us, US Latinos represent the whole spectrum of color and class and political position,

---

[1] See http://www.predec.org/summaries/hispanics/hispanics.html Overview of Race and Hispanic Origin (C2KBR/01–1)14]; http://www.census.gov/prod/2001pubs/e2kbr01-1.pdf 'The Hispanic Population' (C2KBR/01–3)]; http://www.census.gov/prod/2001pubs/e2kbr01-3.pdf

including those who firmly believe they can integrate into the mainstream of North American life.² Indeed, throughout US history many *have* integrated into mainstream life, depending on how one defines mainstream. At the beginning of the twenty-first century, many North American cities boast presses, newspapers, and television and radio stations that cater to Spanish and bilingual audiences. Americans have elected Latinos to state, local, and national legislatures. Since Latino writers have made bestseller lists across the country and many musicians and artists have become household names, many argue that some of Latino culture is 'mainstream' in certain parts of the US. Nonetheless, many Latinos continue to suffer exclusion and discrimination, and have remained culturally and economically on the margins.

Latina and Latino poets, dramatists, novelists, short story writers, essayists, and filmmakers have been instrumental in the articulation of Latino aesthetic and ethical issues in the US. They have played roles as cultural interlocutors, interpreters, and recorders of their own cultural past as well as the real or imagined past of the countries that many have left behind. As Nicolás Kanellos puts it:

> Since before the United States was even founded, Hispanics have imagined themselves through literature and have provided a record of their culture in North America. And within the United States, Hispanics have written and published their works since the early days of the Republic. From the mid-19th-century on, Hispanics have written in English as well as Spanish. The literary heritage is continuous and unbroken . . .³

Kanellos's comments highlight the place of language in the creation of Latino/Hispanic identities and literatures, but his examples can be expanded. While many writers utilize the terms 'Hispanic' and 'Latino' interchangeably as categories of differences compared to 'white', 'black', or 'Anglo', for example, the term 'Latino' has won more widespread acceptance for a number of reasons. As Alvina E. Quintana explains, 'Latino' 'allows for a recognition of the cultural hybridization created by the European fusion with Indigenous, Asian, or African peoples'.⁴ On the other hand, while it is true that Latino writers historically published in either English or Spanish, since the 1970s, Spanglish has also gained acceptance in the mainstream press and in cinema. These developments give further testament to the cultural hybridization that has been recognized as a fundamental force in Latin American and Latino history.

The term 'Latino' has also gained currency among Brazilians in the US who do not see themselves as 'Hispanic'. Although Brazilians helped shaped perceptions of the Latino (then called Latin) populations in the early twentieth century,

---

[2] Cherríe Moraga, 'Art in America con Acento', in Diana Taylor and Juan Villegas (eds.), *Negotiating Performance: Gender, Sexuality and Theatricality in Latin America* (Durham, North Carolina: Duke University Press, 1994), 32.

[3] See N. Kanellos, *The Hispanic Literary Companion* (Detroit: Visible Ink, 1997), xvii.

[4] Alvina E. Quintana (ed.), *Reading US Latina Writers. Remapping American Literature* (New York: Palgrave Macmillian, 2003), 3–4.

until the 1980s their demographic and literary impact was negligible. Since then, Brazilian immigrants and a second generation of Brazilian-Americans have begun to dialogue more vigorously with other Latino groups. Brazilian literary texts have appeared in Portuguese and English, and in some cases in a hybrid of English and Portuguese. Brazilians have also begun to speak and write in Portañol, a type of Portuguese-Spanish idiom, which has developed in many communities where Portuguese and Spanish speakers interface.

## Conceptualization and organization of this book

Conceived as a part of the Tamesis Companion Series, the *Companion to US Latino Literatures* attempts to document the linguistic and cultural diversity of the Latino literary output in the United States for non-specialist readers. We have attempted to create a useful and exciting introduction to that output rather than an exhaustive or all-inclusive oeuvre. This *Companion* is unique in its scope and perspective. It focuses on various literary genres and cinema related to Latinos in the US. All the chapters included here are related not only to Latino writers who were born or raised in the United States, but also to Latin American writers who took up residence in the US and may also be considered part of the literary scene of their countries of origins. Rather than follow one specific mode of organization and presentation, each critic has contributed his or her original perspective on the subject matter or theme. We have attempted to assemble an inclusive spectrum of voices of the US Latin American Diaspora that we hope will provide windows into the rich and complex writings of Latinos.

Our different research interests and backgrounds have shaped the assembly and organization of this work, and we hope that they have helped to provide a unique and fresh perspective on US Latino writing and cultural texts. One of us (Carlota) is a Cuban poet and literary critic of Irish and Sephardic-Catalan heritage and the other (Darién), of Bahamian and Panamanian parentage, is a cultural and social historian of Latin America. We met at Tulane University in 1990 during a graduate student seminar taught by Juan Gelpí, an important scholar and mentor to both of us. Professor Gelpí gave us an in-depth guide into the role of Puerto Rican literature on the mainland and on the island, and showed us how Caribbean and Latin American intellectuals negotiated identities, status, and relations to power. The ideas discussed in that seminar helped us conceptualize the relationships between literature, society, and history, particularly as they relate to Diaspora studies. However, it was a conference in 1994, organized by Evelina Félicité-Maurice in the Department of Spanish at Middlebury College, that first afforded us the space to contemplate, think, speak, and write about Latinos in the US. Entitled 'Latinos in the United States: Nuestra Honra y Nuestra Cultura' ('Our Honor and Our Culture'), the conference allowed us to discuss numerous questions about the nature of Latino writings and identity with Julia Alvarez, Nicholasa Mohr, Dolores Prida, William Luis, José Piedra, and others. We emerged from those intense days of exchanges, conversations, and readings with new challenges and questions. The present work has been directly influenced by the Middlebury conference.

We have elected to organize and present the majority of the chapters largely on the basis of national origin, well aware of the limitations of such a decision. For example, some Latino and Latina writers hail from more than one national background. Other writers – including North Americans from many backgrounds, Europeans, and African Americans – have influenced Latino writers. It is important to remember that how we define 'Latino' remains in flux. Hybridization occurs on multiple levels that complicate the desire to group and define. Despite the contributions of transnational, border, and exile studies, which illustrate the duality and conflicts of place and identity in many Latino texts, we believe that the nation-state still exerts one of the most powerful forces on the way that individuals conceptualize and define themselves, and that these influences are manifested in the production of cultural texts. 'Latino' cultural texts do not only represent organic expressions of a given people; they also negotiate their position within the prevailing cultural landscape through a host of differences and similarities with other cultural texts.

Six of the contributions in this volume fall under the category of what Gustavo Pérez-Firmat calls the hyphenated-American (two on Mexican-Americans, two on Cuban-Americans, one on Puerto Ricans, and one on Dominican-Americans). Three others comment on writers from national communities that do not have long traditions in the US (Argentines, Central Americans, and Brazilians). In these chapters, memories and relationships to 'home' become central to the literary discourse. We conclude the volume with three contributions that cross national boundaries and look at pan-Latino identities from the perspective of religion, gender, and film, respectively. These chapters provide evidence of the dialogue between Latinos across national groupings, based on other important frameworks of analysis.

Finally, it is important to reiterate that the Latino community, like any other group is, to borrow from Benedict Anderson, an imagined community. But it is a community imagined across time and space, often fragmented regionally, economically, racially, and socially. As María Ávila suggests in Earl Shorris's moving biography of the Latino community when she asks Shorris to 'just tell them who we are and that we are not all alike', sometimes it is easier to explain what Latinos are not than who they are.

## The chapters

In Chapter 1, 'Resistance, Revolution, and Recuperation: The Literary Production of the Mestizo/Mexican-American/Chicano', Elizabeth Coonrod Martínez analyzes how the hybridity of the Mexican-American culture came into being. Contrary to the literature produced in the US by writers who have emigrated from their original nations and considered by many critics under the terms of Diaspora, exile, or immigration literature, Mexican-American and/or Chicano literature is concerned with the production of a people who have long resided in an area that now forms part of the United States. Although this *mestizaje* was not democratically induced and often does not explicitly account for influences such as the African or Asian, Mexican-American literature officially recognizes its *mestizo* nature.

For the most part, Mexican-American cultural production is the product of merged ethnicities – the indigenous or native to North America with the Spanish and other European. Mexican-American literature can be transcultural and transnational as well as American in nature. Contemporary US Latino literature often falls into categories of 'native North American' writers (those born in the US), but also includes permanent and temporary US immigrants and residents in exile from their original nations. Mexican-American literature has an additional category, a focus on the recovery of works that were produced in the US before its origin and ethnicity was recognized. A further differentiating factor from other US Latino literature is that it is produced not only in English, Spanish or bilingual form, but often includes words and phrases from indigenous languages, such as Nahuatl and Maya and incorporates indigenous practices, myths, history, and language.[5]

The 1984 publication by Arte Público Press of Sandra Cisneros's *The House on Mango Street* signaled the 'crossing over' of US Latino literature into the awareness of the general American reader. Thus, we have dedicated one chapter to Cisneros. In Chapter 2, 'The Importance of Being Sandra (Cisneros)', Eva Paulino Bueno discusses not only the importance of Cisneros's novel, but also how it is possible to understand her work within the history of the feminist movement, the Black feminist movement, and the Chicana movement. Furthermore, for Bueno, it is impossible to understand the existence of a Chicana movement if one does not take into consideration the broader struggles for civil and human rights that became crucial in the 1960s. In addition to *The House on Mango Street*, Bueno analyzes Cisneros's *Woman Hollering Creek*, and some of the writer's short stories. For Bueno, Cisneros's characters bring to the forefront of the literature of the US a necessary awareness of borders.

Chapter 3, Patricia M. Montilla's 'The Island as Mainland and the Revolving Door Motif: Contemporary Puerto Rican Literature of the United States', focuses on the literary works of the second largest Latino national population group in the US. Montilla offers a panoramic scope although it is not an all-encompassing analysis of contemporary Puerto Rican literature in the US. Her essay highlights two prominent characteristics in recent US Puerto Rican literary production: the depiction of the island on the mainland, or rather its presence as a primary geographic and literary space, and the leitmotif of the Revolving Door. It examines these concepts in the poetry, autobiographical writings, and fiction of US Puerto Rican authors in the last twenty-five years, with a

---

[5] The employment of indigenous language and customs is not unique to Mexican-American writers, however. Central American writers in the US also employ them, as do other Latino writers who come from areas where indigenous influences are prevalent, including the Andes, parts of Brazil, and Chile.

particular emphasis on the works of Puerto Rican women writers; among them are Carmen de Monteflores, Nicholasa Mohr, Judith Ortiz Cofer, and Esmeralda Santiago. In identifying both the island of Puerto Rico and the Revolving Door as prominent motifs in contemporary Puerto Rican literature of the US, Montilla discusses how these recurring literary trends vary between authors and texts and how they reflect the diverse realities and experiences of Puerto Ricans living in the US.

Chapters 4 and 5 focus on Cuban-Americans, the third largest Latino population group in the US. Contrary to popular belief, the modern Cuban presence in the US did not begin with the Castro revolution of 1959 but can be documented as far back as the early nineteenth century. In Chapter 4, 'Am I Who I Am? Identity Games in US Cuban Literature', Jorge Febles defines the identity quest of the Cuban-American writers as a fertile trope that has produced a vast literary corpus. Febles focuses 'somewhat arbitrarily', as he himself states, on selected authors and texts that evince discovery games founded on the 'Am I who I Am?' theme. Throughout his chapter, the author argues that the identity meta-narrative formulated or augmented by specific writers of Cuban descent, who view themselves explicitly or implicitly as part of a transnational continuum, evolves to a substantial degree from their ludic instinct, that is to say, from a desire to play in a most sacred sphere: the realm of ego-centered imagination.

Chapter 5 continues the discussion on Cuban Diasporic Literature with Armando González-Pérez's 'Afro-Cuban Identity in the Theater of the Diaspora', where he considers that Cuban playwrights and artists in exile continue to examine carefully the African influence in all aspects of Cuban culture and life. Through their works, Cubans express their most intimate feelings as they rediscover their roots and search for their national identity in a foreign land. Direct African influences remained salient in Cuba longer than any other Spanish-speaking country. The illegal slave trade continued well into the latter half of the nineteenth century and abolition did not come to the island until 1886. Cuban scholars such as Fernando Ortiz and Lydia Cabrera have documented these influences on the island. Ortiz used the term 'transculturation' to explain the transference of African cultural influences to the New World. Given the ubiquity of African influences on the island, it follows that many Cubans who left the island for the US would carry those influences within them. González-Pérez studies the Afro-Cuban influence in the theater from colonial times to the present and discusses how, in the theater of the Diaspora, various playwrights and artists such as Matías Montes Huidobro, José Triana, Raúl de Cárdenas, José Corrales, Manuel Pereiras García, Pedro R. Monge-Rafuls, Manuel Martín Jr, Héctor Santiago, Dolores Prida, Caridad Svich, and Leandro Soto have been inspired by Afro-Cuban religion and folklore. All of them incorporate, in one way or another, the African influence with its rich repertoire of songs, dances, choral prayers, pantomimes, and dialogues.

Elizabeth Coonrod Martínez is once again present in these pages in Chapter 6 with 'Between the Island and the Tenements: New Directions in Dominican-American Literature', where she discusses the important presence of Dominican-

American Literature in the US. Here, the author presents a panoramic view of Dominican-American literature from the nineteenth century until the present. If, fifteen years ago, the only known author of Dominican heritage writing in English was Julia Alvarez, these days a new generation of Dominican-American novelists already has a place in US Latino literature. This new generation includes Junot Díaz, Loida Maritza Pérez, Nelly Rosario, and Angie Cruz. Looking at the publishing market, Coonrod-Martínez notices that not only have most of their novels been published in Spanish translation, but that many Dominican poets from the island are being discovered in English translation in journals and bilingual anthologies in the US.

Chapter 7 is dedicated to Central American literature, offering us only a glimpse of the complex cultural and literary tradition of the isthmus. Central Americans do not have a long tradition of settlement in the US although Central American history is deeply intertwined with North American economic and political history. Only since the 1980s, after the bloody civil wars unleashed brutal and corrupt military dictatorships, did significant numbers of Nicaraguans, Salvadorans, and Guatemalans establish communities in states such as Florida, California, and Illinois. Although Central Americans share a political and economic history since independence from Mexico in the early nineteenth century, those commonalities did not necessarily translate into cultural bonds among the national groups. Indeed, the diversity within and between the Central American states is impressive: the English-speaking Belizians, hundreds of native populations, Afro-indigenous communities such as the Garifuna in Honduras, Caribbean immigrants, the Meskita in Nicaragua, and the descendants of Spaniards, Germans, Japanese, Chinese and other nationalities from Panama to Guatemala.

Vincent Spina's 'Three Central American Writers: Alone Between Two Cultures' discusses the works of Conny Palacios (Nicaragua), Rima de Vallbona (Costa Rica) and Omar Castañeda (Guatemala). Their work represents three different genres (poetry, novel, and short story, respectively) and three different moments in the process of adaptation, or lack of adaptation, to living in the US. Spina discusses the complexities that always arise when analyzing Central American writers.

In Chapter 8, 'American Dream, *Jeitinho Brasileiro*: On the Crossroads of Cultural Identities in Brazilian-American Literature', Antonio Luciano de Andrade Tosta offers the reader a panoramic essay on Brazilian-American (*Brazuca*) texts. Brazilians in the US represent a small group relative to their national population but their numbers have been growing in recent decades. With this growth, literature and data on Brazilians and Brazilian-Americans have also grown. According to Tosta, whether fictionalized or not, most Brazilian-American texts remain highly based on personal experience. *Brazuca* works discuss Brazil and the United States, and what it means to be Brazilian and North American. Oftentimes this discussion of national identity and cultural traits happens by way of a comparison (implicit or explicit) between the Brazilian '*jeito de ser*', 'way of being' – the so-called *jeitinho brasileiro*, which is a mark of national identity that emphasizes a happy, cordial, relaxed, and sensual attitude – and the American lifestyle, revealing how Brazilian-ness fits within the North American standard of living. Whereas this cultural encounter on occasion points to Brazilians' admiration of a number of American values, such as organization, practicality, and independence, these same features – and numerous others – are equally shown as incompatible with Brazilian culture.

Chapter 9, 'Argentine Writers in the US: Writing South, Living North', by Sergio Waisman, discusses a number of Argentine writers who have spent significant portions of their careers living and writing, primarily in Spanish, in the US and questions if they really belong in a volume on US Latino literature or not. Indeed, this question is relevant to many writers from Latin America who reside in the US but who do not yet consider themselves Latino. According to Waisman, if US Latino literary identity includes a movement towards writing mostly in English from a Latin American heritage, then the Argentine writers discussed here will seem out of place. But issues of identity and language in US Latino literature are considerably more complex than this, while the category of the US Latino itself can still be said to be in a process of formation. Waisman believes that there is much to be gained by expanding the dialogue between the fields of US Latino and Latin American literary and critical studies, and that such a dialogue could offer important contributions to both fields.

The Argentine writers whom Waisman discusses in his essay are a heterogeneous group who come from different places and represent different literary generations. Argentine writers living in the US write in different genres and styles, with different degrees of success and, without a doubt, with different objectives and skills. Waisman discusses a number of issues central to both Latin American and US Latino literatures in relation to issues of language, translation, exile, tradition, and identity.

Chapter 10, 'A Balancing Act: Latin American Jewish Literature in the United States (or Towards a Jewish-Latino Literature)', by Lydia M. Gil, studies the works of Marjorie Agosín, Ruth Behar, Isaac Goldemberg, and José Kozer. Sufficiently aware of *such* a threat, these Jewish-Latin American writers in the US have devised a series of narrative and poetic strategies to circumvent the autoethnographic trap while still alluding to their Jewish and Latin American cultural traditions. Humor, irony, parody, and sarcasm are among the tools most often used by these writers when reconstructing the past for their creative texts, for they allow allusions to a national past and to a national literary tradition while simultaneously disrupting its official posture and pretensions of continuity and homogeneity.

Autobiographical texts present yet another narrative strategy that instills a critical posture in the reconstruction of the past even while highlighting their subjective character: an insistence on the unreliability of memory and the relevance of the cultural and historical context of the act of remembering. Gil argues that, by attempting to reconstruct the past, not only from a temporal but also a geographic distance, these writers successfully disrupt the unidirectional official discourse of their former countries by inserting a forking narrative: the narrative of exile, 'where' the remembering takes place.

In Chapter 11, 'US Latina Caribbean Women Poets: An Overview', Carlota Caulfield presents a panorama of some of the most important Caribbean women poets writing in the US. Among them are Sandra María Esteves and Judith Ortiz Cofer (Nuyorican/Puerto Rican), Magali Alabau and Carolina Hospital (Cuban-American), and Julia Alvarez (Dominican-American). The poetry of Latina women in the US incorporates a great variety of voices that speak in a great diversity of registers on crucial themes such as identity, borders, memory, and exile, to mention just a few of the most important themes that their poetry presents. Caulfield's text is a guide meant to be of use to the readers of this *Companion* rather than an exhaustive critical essay about Latina Caribbean poetry.

This volume concludes with Chapter 12, 'The Latino Film Experience in History: A Dialogue Among Text and Collaborators', by Darién J. Davis. This chapter discusses the complexity of the Latino experience, which has yet to be aptly explored in film. Davis points out that, like Latino literary texts, most themes and characters in Latino films have emerged from the sensibilities of national communities' insertion into the North American reality. From these national experiences, filmmakers have been able to explore issues relevant to the broadly constructed 'Latino' community. Davis divides his contribution into three parts: the early construction of *Latinidad*, 1910–1950, civil rights and social dramas from 1950 to the 1990s, and the celebration of Latino literature, culture, and icons from the 1980s to the present.

Contemporary 'Latino films', which emerge from the Latino community in the US, are a relatively new phenomenon, and a result of Latino empowerment and shifting paradigms of representation of the American cultural industry. The Latino presence in North American films dates back to the early twentieth century, however. This representation, like that of other ethnic films, must be understood in its proper historical context. Although non-Latino directors and producers often constructed their Latino *mise en scène* based on stereotypical and one-dimensional representations of *Latinidad*, the talent of early Latino actors within the industry nonetheless paved the way for more nuanced representations later on. This chapter explores the changes and development of filmic representation of the Latino experience from the 1910s to the present day by focusing on themes that dialogue with those present in the published literary texts.

## Conclusion

The essays presented in this text explore a number of themes about Latino literature and culture in the US. We would need tomes if we attempted accurately to reflect and represent all of the Latino and Latina authors and genres. Yet it is important to recognize several other growing Latino national groups and the importance of many other writers not present in this volume. The number of South American immigrants, particularly from Venezuela and Colombia, has grown in the last two decades and among them are many talented writers. While

Chileans do not constitute a major portion of South Americans in the US, figures such as Isabel Allende, who writes in English and Spanish, should be recognized. Peruvian- American writers such as Eduardo González Viaña and Daniel Alarcón also represent two of many important Latino voices who did not make it into this volume. Many of the short stories in Alarcón's *War By Candlelight* and in Viaña's *American Dreams* reflect and dialogue with other Latino texts. In Alarcón's short story 'Absence', for example, the author writes about the difference between 'leaving one's country' and 'staying away'. These chapters may be included in subsequent editions as scholars begin to pay more attention to South American authors in the US in the future.

This volume, in our view, provides a window into the vibrancy of contemporary Latino literature in the US. As William Luis has pointed out, the literary movement represented by the Latino writers born or raised in the US is not only 'at the vanguard', but 'has opened up a new field in literary history and criticism'.[6] This extraordinary literature is not a new phenomenon, however. It has been developing in the US since the foundation of the nation at the end of the eighteenth century.

## Historical timeline[7]

1492: Columbus arrives in the New World.
1846–48: Mexican-American War and the annexation of Texas under the Treaty of Guadalupe Hidalgo.
1898: Spanish American Cuban War. The Treaty of Paris ends the war and Puerto Rico becomes a US protectorate.
1910: Mexican Revolution. An estimated 500,000 Mexicans enter the US legally.
1917 (2 March): President Woodrow Wilson signs the Jones Act, granting Puerto Ricans US citizenship.
1930s: More than 500,000 Mexicans are deported from the US, in part as a reaction to tight labor markets during the Great Depression.
1935: Dennis Chavez elected the first Latino senator as the Democratic senator of New Mexico, 1935–62.
1939: Carmen Miranda arrives in the US from Brazil and rides a wave of Latin themed musicals until her death in 1954.
1943: Zoot Suit riots in Los Angeles.

---

[6] An important and theoretical analysis of the importance and proliferation of US Latino literature, and in particular of Latino Caribbean literature, appears in William Luis's *Dance Between Two Cultures* (Nashville: Vanderbilt University Press, 1997), ix–xxii.

[7] This timeline was organized with the help of Ashley Kerr, Middlebury College. Sources included *Hispanic America: The Last 100 Years*. http://www.hispaniconline.com/hh/timeline/index.html; and Himilce Novas in *Everything You Need to Know About Latino History* (New York: Plume Books, 1994, new edn, 2003).

1944: The Texas legislature passes the Caucasian Race Resolution, which declares all Mexican-Americans white.
1940–50: The Puerto Rican population in the US increases by 500,000 people.
1951: The Cuban Desi Arnaz becomes the first Latino to star in his own US television show.
1952: Puerto Ricans vote to become a Commonwealth of the US and are granted the right to write their own constitution.
1959: Cuban Revolution. Cuban refugees flee to the US in thousands.
1960: Creation of the Political Association of Spanish Speaking Organizations, led by Albert Peña.
1960s: Political and economic instability in the Dominican Republic leads to increased US immigration.
1961: Univisión, currently the fifth largest television network in the US, is founded.
1961: *West Side Story*, the musical written by Leonard Bernstein, is released.
1962: Cuban missile crisis.
1970: Salvador Allende's Popular Unity government elected to power in Chile; some Chileans emigrate to the US. 'Hispanic' is used in the US census for the first time.
1973: Pinochet coup in Chile. Many Chileans forced into exile.
1976–83: Argentine 'Dirty War' sends many Argentines into exile.
1978: Sandinista coup and guerilla civil war cause many Nicaraguans to flee to the US.
1980: The category 'Hispanic' appears for the first time on the US Census that goes out to all households.
1980s–90s: Civil war in El Salvador.
1980: The *Mariel* exodus. Thousands of Cubans leave the island and arrive in the US.
1983: *El Norte* released. The film documents the experiences of Central Americans fleeing to the US to escape civil war.
2000: First Latin Grammy Awards broadcast nationally.
2001: Start of the Argentine economic crisis. Many Argentines, especially professionals, emigrate to the US. The continued political crisis in Colombia and Venezuela also leads to emigration from those countries.
2003: Latinos, who are of many races, are named the nation's largest minority group after new Census figures are released showing the US Hispanic population at 37.1 million in July 2001.

# 1

# Resistance, Revolution, and Recuperation: The Literary Production of the Mestizo/Mexican-American/Chicano

ELIZABETH COONROD MARTÍNEZ

As the Spanish *conquistadores* and their colonial descendants – often of mixed Indian and Spanish blood – traveled into the northern reaches of their new domain, their settlements and experiences helped establish a future hybrid culture, which in the contemporary era would be called 'Mexican-American'. While the Spaniards considered the Americas their 'New World', the original residents were virtually wiped out,[1] and their traditions, stories, and philosophies were submerged, often combined with those of the invaders, to re-emerge in safer times. Subsequent cultural expression, in the invaders' language, would recount a centuries'-old heritage. New immigrants added to and helped portray the newly conceived culture, and when the region became the United States, the evolving cultural production would often be expressed in the English language.

Literature produced by groups in the US who have emigrated from their original nations tends to fall under the terms of *Diaspora*, exile, or immigration literature. Mexican-American or Chicano literature, however, possesses the additional sense of occupation, an experience of evidencing the production of a people who have long resided in an area that has come to be called 'America' and the United States. It is moreover the cultural production of merged ethnicities – the indigenous or native to this continent with the Spanish and other Europeans – rendering a unique *mestizo* or *raza* consciousness.[2] Thus, Mexican-American literature can be transcultural and transnational as well as North

---

[1] The indigenous or native population is estimated at between 10 million and 18 million for North America (the US and Canada), which was reduced to half a million by the late 1800s, according to contemporary sources. The Western Hemisphere held 90 to 112 million, or more than the population of Europe at the end of the fifteenth century. But in the first 130 years of contact, nearly 95 percent died, a majority from European-origin diseases. For a recent article on estimated populations, see '1491' (cover story) by Charles C. Mann, *Atlantic Monthly*, 289:3 (March 2002), 41–53.

[2] Terms applied to contemporary theory/philosophy by Chicana writer Gloria Anzaldúa and Mexican philosopher José Vasconcelos, respectively.

American in nature.³ Contemporary US Latino literature can fall into categories of 'native' writers – those born in the US – as well as those who compose in the country, in exile from their original nations. Mexican-American literature has an additional category, a focus on the *recovery* of works that were produced in the US *before* its origin and ethnicity was recognized.

Mexican-American literature also varies from other US Latino literature not only in that it is produced in English, Spanish or bilingual form but also in that it often includes words and phrases from indigenous languages, such as Nahuatl and Maya. It resists the greater US hegemony by incorporating indigenous practices, myth, history, and language. Chicano literature will often adapt terms of Nahuatl origin such as *Anáhuac* for 'North America', or *Flor y Canto* as the title of a journal or cultural organization (the words in Spanish for *Xochitlcuícatl*, indicating poetry or literature).⁴

Thus, the process of discovering the origins of this cultural production is ongoing. Its study promulgates three different stages or markers. Initially, Chicano literature was connected to the civil rights movement of the 1960s. Then the focus was broadened to an inception point of 1848, when California and the greater Southwest became part of the US, placing a new layer over what were previously Spanish and Indian. Now, the marker is often given as 1542, indicating first Spanish arrival in the region, or the beginning of merging native heritage with that of European-origin people.

The geographic area now called Mexico and the US is a zone of continuous mobility for a people whose history traverses Aztec (1325–1521), as well as many prior and simultaneous indigenous civilizations, the Spanish colonial (1521–1821), the brief, early Mexican (1821–48), and US (1848–present) nationalities. Regularly crossing borders, not in the physical but in a cultural sense, is an action that has deeper roots than one nation's history can explain. Chicana critic and theorist Gloria Anzaldúa called the US–Mexican border an 'open wound where the Third World grates against the first and bleeds',⁵ creating a 'lifeblood' that has formed what is now called the borderlands or border culture. Anzaldúa referred to this psychological border as an 'open cut'

---

[3] For the purposes of this chapter, 'American' will be used to denote 'US resident', which is contemporary practice although inaccurate. In all countries south of the US, 'American' is a term that denotes a person of this continent. Therefore, all peoples in this hemisphere are American, in addition to their nationalities of particular countries.

[4] The term *Chicano* is derived from the Nahuatl pronunciation of the word Mexica (*meshica*), the name of the indigenous group that had prominence in the valley of Mexico at the time of the arrival of the Spanish. In the US, the term is more political than the term Mexican-American. A Chicano or Chicana, born or raised in the US, is one who exhibits political consciousness about being both of the US and of mixed Indian-Spanish background, whereas a Mexican-American is simply one who immigrated to the US or was born to parents who immigrated.

[5] Gloria Anzaldúa, *Borderlands / La Frontera: The New Mestiza*. San Francisco: Spinster/Aunt Lute Press, 1987, xxx.

that is never healed. Such a wound could also be said to expose the inner depths that a superficial *reality* can never reach.

The written accounts by Spaniards (often called *Relaciones*), documenting indigenous customs and life in the Southwest, are now credited as the earliest *Hispanic* record for this region. A foremost and extraordinary piece of long narrative is the travel/exploratory account by a shipwrecked Spanish soldier, Álvar Núñez Cabeza de Vaca. His journey across 1,500 miles – from the central Texas coast west to the Gulf of Baja California, as well as an additional 1,300 miles south to Mexico City – reveals many cultural details (and the extensive populations) of a region now utterly changed. Cabeza de Vaca's intriguing story of seven years of residence among native peoples, first as a captive, then as a spiritual healer, is a fascinating read. But it also demonstrates early merging of cultural practices and linguistic adaptation to a new hegemony. Cabeza de Vaca was an immigrant who had to accept the rules of the society in which he was lost, and eventually find a way to overcome his hardships. Juan Bruce-Novoa says he developed intercultural and inter-linguistic ability, and calls him a border merchant who crossed back and forth between indigenous groups facilitating as a connecting link between them. Cabeza de Vaca's book, first published in 1542, can represent a *first* example of border or hybrid culture.

Another early Spanish record is that of Gaspar Pérez de Villagrá, who set out to record the travel, subjugation of native peoples, and settlement, in what is now the US Southwest, accompanying the *conquistador* Juan de Oñate and five hundred colonists. His account is often cited for documenting the actual first *Thanksgiving* (predating Plymouth Rock) on what is now US soil – celebrated in 1598 near what is currently the city of El Paso. A classical scholar, Pérez de Villagrá wrote in the literary style popular in that era – long, epic verse. His extensive cultural analysis, published in 1610, is titled *Historia de la Nueva México*. It relates the legend of the pilgrimage of the Aztecs to the Mexican central valley, where they were to found their city on an island where they would see an eagle perched on a cactus, devouring a serpent. Villagrá's account includes other Aztec myths, descriptions of the region, of its residents, and of their great skill in hunting bison or buffalo, including the processing of its skins for clothing, tents, and household goods (the first descriptions of Indian skill that the Spanish dubbed *vaquero*, later called cowboy). His epic poem also relates Spanish conquest of villages, their resistance and revolts, and the chilling account of the Spanish destruction of Acoma after this village's uprising.

The purpose of his account was to inform the Spanish king of the conquest of 'New' Mexico (the Southwest), but Pérez de Villagrá's contribution is definitely a literary work. Eminent critic Luis Leal calls Pérez de Villagrá 'ahead of his time', and credits his work as equivalent to the historical novel of the nineteenth century. His epic poem (consisting of thirty-four *cantos*) is often compared to Alonso Ercilla y Zúñiga's epic poem, *La araucana*, about northern Chile and the Mapuche. For three hundred years before the founding of the US, Spanish-language accounts, mostly in narrative form, document the changing social base of California and the Southwest. Some cite lifestyle and economic pursuits;

others, often by Catholic priests and scribes, relate the religious and cultural traditions of various Indian groups. Another example of engaging writing style that transcends the tedious chronicle-writing of many Spanish scribes is the recently recovered, quasi-anthropological text by Fray Gerónimo Boscana, a San Juan Capistrano mission priest, which portrays songs, dances, and oral tales.

## The legacy of 1848

With the signing of the Treaty of Guadalupe Hidalgo in 1848, the Southwest and California become part of the US. The original residents' poetry and short prose remained invisible to the US public, but Spanish-language newspapers flourished even after governments changed. Recent academic research projects have sought to recuperate early – in terms of US domain – newspaper writing, often in Spanish but also in English, of people of Mexican ancestry. Such records are being reevaluated, first in a pivotal study by Luis Leal, and recently by scholars such as Genaro Padilla, for their continuity of reflection on a people now known as Mexican-American.

The Mexican *corrido* (a ballad or story told in song) has continued an oral tradition of relating the stories of a people and the travails of their heroes. *Corridos* of the nineteenth century often relate how their people's land was suddenly taken from them, as in the case of Joaquín Murrieta, a miner in northern California who decries the English-speaking bandits who in 1850 killed his wife and brother and stole his mine during the gold rush. Murrieta becomes a bandit himself in order to seek justice and revenge. 'Legal' actions against Spanish-speaking people caught suddenly as underdogs in a new power structure also occurred in Texas, where eminent Chicano scholar Américo Paredes memorialized the famous *corrido* about Gregorio Cortez in his study *With His Pistol in His Hand* (1958). Paredes, hired by the University of Texas in Austin in 1951, is considered one of the earliest contemporary scholars in folklore for his efforts documenting cultural practices and stories in Texas. His dissertation influenced many new scholars of Chicano literature and folklore, and his account was converted to film in the 1980s, a marvelous production starring Edward James Olmos as Gregorio Cortez.

*Corrido* ballads are oral historical records; many relate the lives and archetypes of women in Mexican-American culture, often not included in written narratives. A landmark study by María Herrera-Sobek collects some three thousand *corridos* that portray the plight of women in the complex society of the nineteenth and early twentieth centuries.

Various projects of recovery and recuperation of manuscripts and oral histories since the late 1980s include items from the California Bancroft collection, the New Mexico and Arizona Works Progress Administration Federal Writers' Projects, and from oral folk tales and stories. Researchers seek to restore a connection to earliest literary production with publications such as the series of volumes published by Arte Público Press, 'Recovering the US Hispanic Literary Heritage', or a recovery of women's stories, such as *Las mujeres hablan: An*

*Anthology of Nueva Mexicana Writers* (1988), edited by Tey Diana Rebolledo, as well as her collection, *Nuestras Mujeres: Hispanas of New Mexico, their images and their lives, 1532–1992* (1992). Books such as these recuperate records from early diaries and other records kept by people on their travels and lives in the remote corners of New Spain, far from its headquarters in Mexico City, where sources of publication and distribution resided. Mainstream historical records, whether in Spanish or English, have overlooked or given scant mention to women's roles, and studies such as Rebolledo's restore women's perspectives to this history. Texts published officially by the Spanish colony seldom included mention of significant female roles of indigenous origin, such as those of *curandera*, healer, and *bruja*, witch, for women who possessed respected spiritual powers. Mythic and cultural figures, such as La larga and La Llorona, are found only in diaries and the records kept in remote areas, but reappear in contemporary literature. Modern scholars have studied these connections, many examples of which Rebolledo documented in her book, *Women Singing in the Snow* (1995).

Late nineteenth- and early twentieth-century literary production included several women writers, who often composed stories and novels in English. Known as early Chicana writers by contemporary scholars, their creative works are an excellent documentation of political changes, cultural traditions maintained in a shift of governments, and the era's social life. Several university presses have recently reissued their out-of-print novels. María Amparo Ruíz de Burton, a *Californio* (as the Spanish residents of California were called), born in 1832, published two of the earliest known novels, *Who Would Have Thought It?* (1872), and *The Squatter and the Don* (1885). The second novel critically denounces violence and fraud committed on the *Californios* as the Anglo-Americans stripped them of their land holdings and businesses by means of a newly implanted US legal system.

María Cristina Mena, born in 1893 in Mexico City, grew up in an aristocratic family during the waning years of the Porfirio Díaz dictatorship. She was sent to New York City in 1907, where she remained the rest of her life. Mena wrote in English, publishing short stories and non-fiction articles between 1913 and 1916, all of which take place in Mexico and involve Mexican society. Although these are principally love stories, her female characters – drawn in somewhat stereotypical fashion – appear to resist the inferior social position designated to women. Rebolledo (*Women Singing*) notes her incorporation of humor and irony to undermine images of women as objects of beauty. Her stories include Aztec legends and significant figures and cultural symbols, such as the Virgin of Guadalupe, and the shawl or *rebozo* worn by women. Once she married, Mena published no other stories with the exception of one in 1931, depicting revolutionaries and Porfiristas. Between 1942 and 1953 (after her husband's death), Mena published five books for children that introduce Mexican history and culture. In 1977, her short stories were recovered and published by Arte Público Press. While the Californian Ruíz de Burton criticized Euro-American injustices in her novels, Mena is notable as the only writer with a non-racist perspective on

Mexican culture publishing in New York magazines. Each, however, writes from an aristocratic Mexican point of view, in contrast to Chicano movement writers of the 1970s.

## The Mexican Revolution of 1910

Josefina Niggli, born in Monterrey, northern Mexico, in 1910, is a very different writer from Mena in that the focus of her narrative is not a love story, but instead feelings of both euphoria and alienation in a rapidly changing society. While she is better known as a playwright, Niggli published two extensive novels in 1945 and 1947. *Mexican Village* and *Step Down, Elder Brother* depict life in or near Monterrey between 1920 and 1930 and in the early 1940s, respectively. Her third novel, *A Miracle for Mexico* (1964), tells the story of the appearance of the Virgin of Guadalupe. It is the first full-length novel on Mexico's patron saint.

Niggli began her creative activity – by writing poetry and creating radio and Spanish-tradition festival plays – in San Antonio, Texas, where her parents had relocated during the unrest of the Mexican Revolution, and where she completed high school and her bachelor's degree. In 1931 she was invited to pursue a master's degree in play-writing in North Carolina. It is here, on the East Coast, that Niggli wrote and produced the first Mexican folk plays in English. Three decades before the Teatro Campesino was launched in California, Niggli provided in English what was not even available in Spanish.[6] She published five of her one-act plays in 1938 in a book titled, *Mexican Folk Plays*; several others can be found in various anthologies. One of her most intriguing plays is *Soldadera*, based on women soldiers during the Mexican Revolution. Her characters model the emergence of the peasant *mestiza* woman, who disregarded European rules for female behavior. The lead character is named *Adelita*, which is the title of a popular Mexican *corrido*. In 1936, Niggli put into words the story of women's involvement in this significant social revolution. It is the first written creative description of the valiant Mexican woman of the early twentieth century, otherwise revealed only in oral song and historical photographs.

In contemporary literature, the *Adelita* figure is a symbol of women's stuggle and accomplishment. For contemporary Chicana writers, 'Adelita' equals 'Chicana', a revolutionary figure who resists powers that limit and control her. Niggli's excellent plays, explaining the Mexican ethos in English, served as a first step in her creative production by evaluating societal and cultural issues, including indigenous legends. She elaborated on these issues in her longer narrative, with more complex characters. Throughout Niggli's plays and her three novels, the importance of indigenous roots in Mexican identity and the foundation of a *mestizo* society is evident as a constant and strong element.

---

[6] This declaration was made by the eminent Mexican playwright, Rodolfo Usigli, who wrote the Foreword to Niggli's book, *Mexican Folk Plays* (Durham: University of North Carolina Press, 1938).

While Mena was in New York and Niggli in North Carolina, Jovita González found her way to graduate school and research in Texas. She was born in 1904, not in Mexico but on the US side of the border, and she predates Paredes as a specialist in Texas folklore. She did not write about the new post-Revolution society in Mexico as Niggli did, but instead focused on life for Mexican-Americans in Texas. She collected folk tales and centers her stories on the border, portraying the social effects of Anglo domination on Texas Mexicans. She published articles in Texas magazines, presented papers at the Texas Folklore Society, and wrote two novels, *Caballero: An Historical Novel* and *Dew on the Thorn*, which were not published in her lifetime, but recently appeared in edited versions (1996 and 1997, respectively). González first worked as a high school teacher, but she was awarded a full scholarship to pursue her MA at the University of Texas (thus entering this institution two decades before Paredes). Her thesis was on the social life of three South Texas border counties. She received a Rockefeller grant in 1934 (Niggli received Rockefeller fellowships in 1936 and 1938). From 1939 on, González lived in Corpus Christi, where she and her husband (a grade-school teacher) collaborated on creating two books to teach basic Spanish, and struggled against racial prejudice throughout their teaching careers. A large wave of Anglo-Americans from the Midwest, seeking cheap land and exploitable labor, moved into south Texas early in the twentieth century, changing the political tone and peace of 'Mexicans' and Anglos living side by side that had existed in the nineteenth century. This experience, together with her research in various counties, informs González's novels. Written in the 1930s and 1940s, *Dew on the Thorn* is a rich portrait of the Olivares family clan and their ranch life in south Texas. It focuses on the cultural traditions of Texas Mexicans and changing societal pressures, which led to the class and race divisions that would mark twentieth-century Texas.

Fabiola Cabeza de Baca Gilbert was born in New Mexico in 1893 but did not publish her novel, *We Fed Them Cactus*, until 1954. This depicts a sense of alienation from mainstream society, in terms of both language and culture. She describes the livelihood, social life, and customs of residents of northern New Mexico at the turn of the century, including buffalo hunting, rodeos, and raids by Indians and bandits, but also a domestic life composed of mixed Indian and Spanish traditions. This novel was reissued in the 1990s with a critical introduction. Another New Mexican, Nina Otero-Warren, published a book of similar tone in 1936, *Old Spain in Our Southwest*, but it has received little attention. The literary accomplishment and cultural revelations of these women writers are comparable to African-American writer Zora Neale Hurston, who published her novel, *Their Eyes were Watching God*, in 1936, and likewise received no critical attention until decades later.

Paredes, mentioned above, also completed a novel in the early twentieth century, during his years as a journalist and before he entered the University of Texas. Titled *George Washington Gómez*, it concerns the political handicap of being 'Mexican' under a US government. A historical novel about free agency and ethnic conflict, it focuses on the activities of one family in southeastern

Texas. The grandson (and title character of the novel) of a man killed by the Texas Rangers grows up in a US system that pays him to betray his own people when he becomes a Texas Ranger, or *rinche,* as these prairie police are commonly called by Texas Mexican-Americans. The novel explores considerations of class (position in society for those who speak English well and are light-skinned) as well as gender: the lead character's sisters are not allowed to receive an eduation like their brother, and one is severely beaten by her mother when she becomes pregnant out of wedlock. The full force of the novel demonstrates an attack by the hegemony – whether Mexican or Anglo – on the Mexican/Indian tradition of collective communities. Written between 1936 and 1940, this novel remained unpublished until 1990, when it was released by Arte Público Press.

## Farm workers and the inception of the Chicano movement

The US sought workers for the construction of irrigation projects in the Southwest. Following the Newlands Reclamation Act in 1902, US job agents recruited workers, traveling by railroad into Mexico between 1910 and the 1920s, and charged Mexicans a fee for the jobs they got them, primarily fieldwork. Workers were supposed to be fed, housed, and given medical care while they worked on a farm. But they were often required to live crammed together in rundown buildings with no heat, an outhouse for a toilet and a stream for a shower. In some cases entire families traveled across the border for these jobs, with children working in the fields and women cleaning houses and doing laundry for their employers. Migrants often joined communities where those of similar culture resided, but ensuing waves of migrants did not always find an easy welcome.

Tomás Rivera's novel, *Y no se lo tragó la tierra* (1971; *And the Earth Did Not Devour Him*, 1987) vividly depicts some of these experiences. Born in Texas in 1935, Rivera joined his migrant worker parents in the fields as a child, and presents the experience of children – shipped to or following the harvest far north into the US – who must spend months of time away from school. The protagonist of this incipient and influential Chicano novel strongly desires to continue his education. He studies by candlelight in the evenings, and builds his identity (alone and far from his family) by reconstructing anecdotes and family stories, and reflecting on the collective spiritual strength of his people as well as his society's view of the Mexican-American. Rivera's poetic narrative captures the language of the migrant worker. This protagonist evokes both a personal and collective identity – a narrative strategy that would occur repeatedly as Chicano literature emerged. *Y no se lo tragó la tierra* is one of the first outstanding novels to emerge in what would later be dubbed the Chicano Renaissance. Severo Pérez, in his artistic film representation of Rivera's novel, expertly captures a significant image at the end of the book, where the young character has climbed a tree, and sees another person in a tree in the distance, to whom he waves. Is the character seeing his double, his future; does it represent an element of hope or reflection? It is a provocative ending to a story on a young migrant worker seeking his future identity.

Political backlash against the migrant workers and their families – and any person who appeared to be Mexican – helped foment Chicano involvement in the social revolution of the 1960s, which increased the visibility of a Mexican-ethnic people, many of whom were also US citizens. Chicano awareness would then help launch new poetry, novels, and drama. In the decades following World War II, the need for agricultural and factory workers fluctuated, with society putting pressure on them to leave but also pulling them back when greater labor was needed. The US government-enacted *Bracero* program ran from 1942 to 1964. Through the years, agricultural workers' wages never increased, nor were improvements made in their living conditions. This situation incited action on the part of César Chávez (born in Arizona in 1927), who called for a strike in 1965, and inspired the creation of an innovative community theater called Teatro Campesino. It would be ten years after the strike inspired by Chávez before contracts were signed to give farm workers better wages.

Concurrent with the *huelga* activities, Luis Valdez (born in 1940 in California) founded his theatrical company on acreage in central California in 1967, providing residence and jobs to many workers, and staging plays for protest events. Teatro Campesino's works evoke religious *pastorelas* and plays created for special occasions in the colonial Spanish era, as well as indigenous dramatic presentations in song and dance. Valdez produced his first play while at San José State College and then studied propaganda theater and Italian Commedia dell'arte in San Francisco. In the late 1960s, he moved his theater from unionizing efforts to various theatrical genres, with a focus on Amerindian roots and the place of the Chicano in US society, using techniques ranging from Lope de Vega to Bertolt Brecht. *Bernabé* (1970), based in an East Los Angeles *barrio*, employs Aztec mythology and symbols; other plays incorporated Mayan concepts. One critic has designated Valdez's *Teatro* as homegrown as *chile* and *frijoles* (beans, chili, and corn form a complete nutritional diet and have been for centuries the mainstay of Indian culture).[7] His best-known play, *Zoot Suit* (1977) – which was performed on Broadway in New York and released as a film – depicts the so-called 'zoot suit riots' of the 1940s in Los Angeles, and the actions of police, sailors, and judges against Mexican-Americans.

Native, indigenous roots became a principal identity factor of the Chicano movement. Poetry written and performed by members of the political movement served as manifestos for a new generation. The epic poem *Yo soy Joaquín*, performed by Rodolfo 'Corky' González, who launched his Crusade for Justice campaign in Denver in 1967 (filmed by Luis Valdez), called attention to the disenfranchised 'Mexican' aspect of the American. His poem cites various Mexican-Indian ethnicities and calls attention to leaders and heroes, such as Cuauhtémoc, Benito Juárez, and Emiliano Zapata. The lyrical voice in this poem

---

[7] Carlos Morton, 'La Serpiente Sheds its Skin, The Teatro Campesino', *Theatre Drama Review* 18:4 (Indigenous Theatre Issue), 71–6.

invokes Joaquín Murrieta and nineteenth-century injustice, and calls out as an anonymous Chicano everyman – who picks crops or dies on the fields of Korea and Vietnam – to demonstrate his invisibility in twentieth-century US society.

Another movement poet, Alurista (Alberto Baltasar Urista), was born in Mexico and came to live in San Diego when he was thirteen. Like Luis Valdez, Alurista's ancestors were of the northern Yaqui indigenous, and he salutes them in his political poetry book, *Floricanto en Aztlán* (1971). His verse is often multilingual, in Spanish, English, Nahuatl, and the Chicano *caló* dialect,[8] an incorporation of street slang, Spanish and words from the Mesoamerican language of Nahuatl. Aztlán is the fabled lost paradise of the Aztecs, and it featured in literature as well as in Chicano dialogue as the term for the homeland or origin of the Mexican-American, said to be located in northern Mesoamerica, therefore in what is now the US.

Miguel Méndez's novel *Peregrinos de Aztlán* of 1974 is a work in Spanish, using various linguistic registers, from archaic, baroque Spanish to that of northern Mexico to *caló*. This novel, with a hero embarking on a long journey in the style of old literature, has been critically acclaimed in Mexico and Spain for many years. It was not translated into English until 1992. Rivera, Alurista, and Méndez each have doctoral degrees and have been employed as professors (and Rivera as Chancellor of UC Irvine) since early in their writing lives.

José Antonio Villarreal's novel, *Pocho* (1959), was originally touted as the first novel of Chicano literature. It would take another three decades to bring attention to the fact that novels and short stories written in English by people of Mexican ancestry residing in the US had been published previously. *Pocho* is a term applied to a man of obvious Indian or *mestizo* appearance who cannot speak standard Spanish well, and it is often applied to Chicanos when they visit Mexico. But it is also used by Chicanos to represent their double inferiority since they are criticized in the US for not speaking English correctly. Villarreal's coming-of-age novel depicts the conflicts of being 'Mexican' in the US through his character, Richard Rubio, who grows up in 1930s' Los Angeles. Villarreal himself was born in Los Angeles in 1924, and his novel is saluted for its masterly portrayal of the Mexican-American identity crisis – a sense of belonging neither here nor there – in the modern era.

Rivera's novel and Rudolfo Anaya's *Bless me, Última* (1972), are considered the two classic, early Chicano-era novels. Anaya's novel was the first Chicano bestseller. Anaya wrote it between 1963 and 1970, as he completed two master's degrees. He describes the ranch land of northern New Mexico, where 'Spanish' people have lived for centuries and speak a mixture of English and archaic Spanish. In 1974 the University of New Mexico appointed Anaya as a professor of creative writing. He has published many other novels, but the first continues to be taught in university classes as an introduction to Chicano literature. It is a

---

[8] For an excellent sociolinguistic study on *caló*, see Leticia Galindo's *Speaking Chicana: Voice, Power & Identity* (Tucson: University of Arizona Press, 1999).

coming-of-age story, as is Anaya's more recent novel, *Alburquerque* (1992), although the latter has a more urban setting. Texan Rolando Hinojosa joins Rivera and Anaya as one of the earliest creators of Chicano novels, and the three were the first recipients of the Quinto Sol literary award established in the late 1960s.[9]

The fourth recipient of this award was Estela Portillo-Trambley, who is recognized as one of the first women writers of the Chicano movement. Born in El Paso in 1927, Portillo-Trambley was not only active politically; she began writing stories and plays, and also composed a novel, *Trini* (although it was not published until 1986), during the 1970s. Like Anaya's, it is a coming-of-age story for Chicana identity. The protagonist is a *mestiza*, raised in Tarahumara land in northern Mexico, who eventually crosses the US border to live outside of El Paso. At the opening of the novel, an artist paints her (and foreshadows her role) as a brown-skinned woman whose feet and limbs seem to emerge from the earth. She carries seeds with her during her several relocations – to a mining town, to the city of Chihuahua, to Ciudad Juárez, and to El Paso – until she can plant them in her own land. She also crosses spiritual borders, trading her worship of Tonantzín for the Virgin Guadalupe in the chapel she visits on the US side of the border. Her Indian *self* becomes increasingly Westernized with each of her moves, necessitated by economic hardship.

Portillo-Trambley emerged on the literary scene with her play, *The Day of the Swallows*, which focuses on the collective will of a culture that denies women voice and any role but that of submission in marriage. Later, Portillo-Trambley became the first Chicana writer to adapt the seventeenth-century nun of colonial Mexico as a model of intellectual aspiration, in her play *Sor Juana*. Her short stories, published as *Rain of Scorpions* (1975), portray the female struggle to live autonomous lives, the most radical being that of a character in *The Paris Gown*. Although deserving of further study, Portillo-Trambley's works have received little critical attention; in the case of her novel, this is most likely because it was overshadowed by the publication of Sandra Cisneros's *House on Mango Street* two years earlier.

Also born in El Paso in 1938, Arturo Islas arrived as a tenure-track professor at Stanford in 1970. He completed a novel that first carried the title of 'Día de los muertos', based on the Mexican-American community in El Paso, which helped him win tenure in 1976. He was not able to publish it until 1984 and by then had changed the title to *The Rain God*. As in Portillo-Trambley's case, this novel reveals a spiritual connection to the land and to nature, as well as the difficulties of being a minority within a Southwest Mexican-American community, that of being gay. Islas's deep and humanistic psychological portrayal of a Texas

---

[9] *Quinto Sol*, or Fifth Sun, is the term used by the Aztecs for the new and final generation of their people, which emerged with the arrival of the Spaniards. The phrase 'The Quinto Sol Generation', first used by Francisco Lomelí (1976) and subsequently by other Chicano critics, indicates the literary generation that emerged between 1959 and the early 1970s.

family makes this and his later novel, *Migrant Souls* (1990), representative of a new perspective in Chicano literature.

Some writers from the 1930s wove their own personal biographies and experiences, both in the Chicano movement and prior to its inception, into the works they published. Mary Helen Ponce first published short stories during the 1980s, and received greater attention with her autobiography/novel, *Hoyt Street* (1993), where she describes life in mid-twentieth-century East Los Angeles. Oscar 'Zeta' Acosta, who was a lawyer and a sidekick of Hunter S. Thompson, published two books, *The Autobiography of a Brown Buffalo* (1972) and *The Revolt of the Cockroach People* (1973), which focus on the idea of Chicanismo and document the late 1960s and early 1970s.

## The contemporary era

The political issues and identity themes that arose out of the 1960s movement inspired a plethora of writers born in the 1940s who soon flowered into the pages of literary history. In Texas, Tino Villanueva, born to migrant field workers, lived in one place during the school year but worked in the fields each summer, returning weeks after school started once the crops were finished. His desire to attend college remained strong after completing high school and working in a furniture store for three years while he read and increased his vocabulary to make up for a poor education in high school. In 1963 Villanueva was drafted into the US Army. Years later, with a Texas bachelor's degree, he accepted a fellowship at the State University of New York at Buffalo, where he completed an MA. His first book of poems, *Hay Otra Voz* (1972), embraces the Chicano Movement. In 1981 he received his Ph.D. from Boston University. Villanueva's poetry has been saluted for its exacting language and themes of time, death, and silence, on personal and societal levels. His recent work is a series of seventeen poems titled *Scene from the Movie "Giant"* (1993), which trace the transformation of a silent 'Mexican' teenager in the back of the movie house into an empowered poet. The original 1956 Hollywood film captured Anglo-American life and society in Texas through two generations, and Villanueva revisits its impact to reveal the Mexican-American *gaze*.

Pat Mora is a prolific writer and poet who has the broadest audience of any Latino poets in the US. Her poems are often included in elementary, middle, and high school textbooks. She writes children's books that depict Mexican folk tales, themes of women in the Southwest desert terrain, and uses frequent metaphors of borders, both as a vantage point for personal assessment and for representing a position of power or authority. She earned bachelor's and master's degrees in Texas, and has published more than twenty books, most collections of poetry. Mora's early work, including *Chants* (1984) and *Borders* (1986), demonstrates an interest in shamanism (*curanderas* and *abuelitas* with magical powers) – a connection to Indian heritage – and biculturalism, identifying with the desert as mother creator. Mora's belief is that poetry provides hope and healing, as revealed in her acclaimed collection of essays blended with poetry, also mixing political and personal thought, *Nepantla: Essays from the Land in the Middle* (1993).

Norma Elia Cantú provides a mid-twentieth-century portrait of Mexican-American families in south Texas in her coming-of-age story, *Canícula, Snapshots of a Girlhood en La Frontera* (1995). This book is a collage of photographs, fiction, and autobiography, with descriptions demonstrating how social and cultural factors influence young women, including the dresses they wear and standards for proper conduct. As Chicano writers receive greater critical attention, their works defy simple categorizations.

While Mora salutes the Maya female spirit, called *Ixtabai* (cited in one of Niggli's early novels), Lucha Corpi casts a positive light on the maligned Indian woman of the Spanish conquest, *La Malinche*.[10] Her work vividly depicts an Indian mother heritage in her best-known 'Marina poems', where she develops her as a person. Born in Mexico, Corpi arrived in California as a new bride in the mid-1960s, and has published poetry since 1976. During the 1990s, she turned to writing mystery novels as well as a children's book in English, while her considerable poetry is always in bilingual form. The 'lost *viejos*' invoked in many of her poems calls attention to the need for present generations to connect to the oracular elders and heed their wisdom and guidance.

In the Southwest, significant fiction was also published in Spanish. Margarita Cota-Cárdenas's novel *Puppet* (1985) creatively depicts a mental breakdown by the principal character of her novel. The protagonist attempts to continue her life as role model, citizen, professor, wife, and mother, while her psyche deals with feelings about the shooting death of a young Mexican-American by a police officer in Phoenix, and the conflict of her status as a member of the social class *outside* the Mexican community. Her mind eventually equates her with the infamous *Malinche* figure.

Erlinda Gonzáles-Berry, who principally writes literary criticism and serves as a member of the editorial board for the federally funded 'Recovering the US Hispanic Literary Heritage' project of the Arte Público Press, received her Ph.D. from the University of New Mexico. In 1991, she published an extraordinary short novel that dialogues with Mexican intellectuals and youth on politics and racial differences, serving as an exploration of Chicano historical and cultural roots. *Paletitas de guayaba* has been celebrated for its rich linguistic repertoire and lively prose. It captures the Mexican and Chicano Spanish, which is different from that of other Spanish speakers, and creates a female discourse by scandalously placing in female dialogue sexually charged words only used by

---

[10] This historical figure's name was Malinalli or Malintzín; she had been sold into slavery by her mother, and was a young adult when she and a group of other women were provided as a gift to Spanish *conquistador* Hernán Cortés. Having learned several languages in the time she had traveled with a caravan of merchants, she quickly became instrumental to Cortés. The Spaniards called her Doña Marina, and the Mexicans of the colonial era, *La Malinche*, indicating that she was a traitor to the indigenous, essentially selling them out by serving as interpreter for Cortés.

males. The novel also relates a breathtaking trip – in a dream sequence – to the ancient city of Tenochtitlán to encounter the Indian Lady Malintzín.

Denise Chávez is a member of the very noticeable phenomenon of Chicana writers publishing since the late 1980s. Like several of these writers, however, her writing activity began in the 1970s. Chávez wrote nineteen plays from 1973 to 1987, based on Mexican religious observances, social, and existential issues. Like other Chicano writers who compose juvenile books, Chávez has written children's plays, such as *The Flying Tortilla Man* (1975). Her recent novels capture southern New Mexico landscapes as well as specific cultural elements in small Mexican-American communities. *The Last of the Menu Girls* (1986) relates a teenage girl's coming-of-age experiences as a hospital volunteer and later in college. *Face of an Angel* (1994) reads as a waitressing manual, incorporating family histories and passages from college term papers as well as dialogue between various characters. *Loving Pedro Infante* (2001) is a very amusing read, which joins the lives of the members of a Pedro Infante fan club and the dreams of one member, who works as a teacher's aide and thinks her relationship with a married man has a future. Chávez, who has received several literary awards, including the American Book Award in 1995, is adept at portraying the inner psyche of her characters.

The son of prominent writers born in California, Victor Villaseñor is notable for expertly weaving his family's biography into his extensive fiction. Villaseñor grew up on a ranch where his parents worked as permanent field hands. He dropped out during his first year in college and lived in Mexico for a few years until his parents convinced him to return and face his identity as Mexican-American. During a ten-year period, while working in construction, Villaseñor wrote nine novels and 65 short stories, and was rejected by publishers 260 times until the publication of his novel *Macho!* in 1973. This poetic, raw and powerful coming-of-age story takes a young man from Michoacán to field work in California to the agriculture strikes under César Chávez.

Villaseñor wrote the screenplay – adapted from Paredes' dissertation – for the film *The Ballad of Gregorio Cortéz*, released in 1982. *Rain of Gold* (1991) is his best-known work, and its process to publication also has a history. Villaseñor had written this saga spanning several generations to tell his family's story from before the Mexican Revolution to their immigration to California, material he researched for years, which also includes myths and oral traditions of Mexican culture. When a New York publisher wanted to change its title and describe it as fiction, Villaseñor canceled his contract and withdrew the manuscript, later publishing it with Arte Público Press.

Alma Luz Villanueva, who was raised by her grandmother in the Mission District of the city of San Francisco, began publishing poetry in the 1970s. By the mid-1980s Villanueva had switched to narrative, and has published several extensive and richly constructed novels. The daughter of a Yaqui healer and visionary, her remarkable grandmother related traditional Mexican stories and educated her in the ways of *curanderas*. After her grandmother's death, Villanueva (who became pregnant at 15) married young and – her husband being overseas with the US marines – raised children and lived in poverty for several years. Later on, she stayed for four years in the Sierra Nevada mountain range of California, where she tells that she connected with the rhythms of nature and came to understand the processes of life and death, and womanhood, which are central themes in her work. She completed an MFA in her late thirties. Her poem 'La Chingada' (the violated woman) published in 1985 analyzes the condition of the Chicana woman in a world of masculine values. In many of her works, the individual being participates in a communion with matter and spirit by participating in life.

Alejandro Morales published his first novel in 1975. *Caras viejas y vino nuevo* was written in Spanish as Rivera and Hinojosa had done with their first novels. With a BA from UCLA, he then completed an MA in Spanish in 1971 at Rutgers University. His many novels sprawl across decades, even centuries, to reveal a continuity of Chicano concerns as well as the chaos of a mixed-heritage identity. *Reto en el paraíso* (1983) contrasts the Spanish and Anglo presence in California with contemporary politics and the impact of Manifest Destiny. Morales's early novels were written in Spanish, but most have been translated into English. His literary device is often metafiction, incorporating political observations by the author in the fictional story.

The nationalist Chicano movement originally considered cultural heritage only in terms of Aztec mythology and tradition, but writers since the 1980s have additionally depicted Mayan symbology. The metaphor of corn or maize as the basis of human life and sustenance (prevalent in Mexican and Central American novels) assists in defining Indian image and philosophy. Juan Felipe Herrera's *Mayan Drifter: Chicano Poet in the Lowlands of America* (1997) is a collage of travel diary, memoir, poetry, and a play. Although the text is written in English, Herrera uses several words in Spanish and Maya, and includes a glossary of definitions. The account represents a need for nourishment of the poet's mind and soul, not just nutritionally. When he purchases thick, Mayan-style tortillas from a 'small Indian woman' in the *zócalo* or main square, he walks chewing and meditating on the corn paste in his mouth. While some dissolves, the rest knots together and remains clogged in his throat, 'forcing me, against my will, to spit everything out. Most of all it wanted me to spit myself out' (39). Here maize serves to begin a soul-searching connection to Herrera's Mayan roots. At the end of his book, he calls Chicano 'a half-step between Ladino and Indian, a jump start from apathy into commitment on the edge of a contemplation between Mexican, American, *campesino*, and Maya' (258). His works express not only how culture is translated but also what occurs when its basic philosophy is disregarded.

Herrera is one of the most innovative contemporary Chicano poets, his works placed technically and thematically in the vanguard. He began writing poetry in the early 1970s, composing *Rebozos* as his first publication. He not only incorporates pre-Hispanic themes and motifs, but also a sense of oral story-telling that by the 1980s would interweave narrative and poetry. The son of migrant workers, Herrera earned an MA from Stanford in 1980, and received fellowships from the National Endowment for the Arts (NEA) in 1980 and 1985. Herrera's work, including the book *Face Games*, which received the American Book Award in 1987, has influenced, and dialogues with, many Mexican-American writers outside of the Chicano movement, including more nationally known writers such as Sandra Cisneros and Ana Castillo.

## Beyond the Chicano movement: prominent writers born since the 1950s

Sandra Cisneros is often celebrated for her first novel, *The House on Mango Street* (1984), which was developed at the Iowa Writer's Workshop in 1978 (see Chapter 2 below). She wrote about growing up in the Mexican *barrios* of Chicago (although *barrio* is a pejorative term used in English, its literal meaning is 'neighborhood'). Cisneros described where she and many other Latinos grow up, and related the female experience, including games little girls play, children's speech, and a *gaze* toward the roles awaiting them – that of being locked in, with no opportunity or permission to fulfill one's own aspirations. In the novel that made her famous, the principal character leaves the *barrio* to find her own space and her own role in life, but she also takes the neighborhood with her figuratively in that she reveals their stories in all of her published works. Her subsequent short stories, in the collection *Woman Hollering Creek* (1991), depict Mexican legends (such as that of La Llorona, a 'hollering' woman), and again the need for women to be safe in a society where men make the rules. Her recent novel, *Caramelo* (2002), launches a summer trip on the part of three connected families, from Chicago to Mexico, and in the process traverses family history, focused through the women, whose stories, like their *rebozos*, are handed down through the generations.

Ana Castillo, also born in Chicago, earned her college degrees in Illinois, also publishing poetry in the 1970s. After a year as poet-in-residence for Urban Gateways of Chicago, Castillo lived in San Francisco and served as a founding editor of Third Woman Press. Her first novel, *The Mixquiahuala Letters* (1986), explored woman's desire for identity and sexuality, and dialogues with a male-dominant Mexican society and the Catholic Church. A second novel, *Sapogonia* (1990), features a male anti-hero and takes place in a fictitious Central American country and Spain. While her poetry evokes the voices of the downtrodden, Castillo's third novel, *So Far from God* (1993), is a feminist appraisal of the limited choices permitted women in US society and a beautiful rendition of New Mexico Indian and Hispanic cultures. Male critics who called the novel melodramatic and sentimental failed to recognize the non-Western traditional voice of a strong matriarchy. Castillo has also published excellent collections of essays, *Massacre of the Dreamers* (from her dissertation work), and *Goddess of the Americas* (on the Virgin Guadalupe), both of which have been translated into Spanish.

In California, Helena María Viramontes is recognized for a collection, *The Moths and Other Stories* (1985), but her stories – which exhibit strong political and sociological awareness – are scattered over three decades. 'Growing' is frequently anthologized for its classic portrayal of the rite of passage for girls, as well as 'Cariboo Café', one of her most complex stories, which contrasts the experience of Salvadoran refugees fleeing terror in their nation with the lives of Mexican-Americans. Another collection, *Paris Rats in East L.A.* (1993), and a novel, *Under the Feet of Jesus* (1995), are attracting new critical attention. The latter work is a haunting and sensitive portrayal of the lives of migrant workers and a female version comparable to Tomás Rivera's novel. Issues of gender, ethnicity, and social injustice interplay in this occasionally anguished novel, as characters are beset by pregnancy, illness, and starvation.

Gary Soto was born in Fresno, as were his parents, but they grew up doing field and factory work in the San Joaquín Valley, which figured in the title of Soto's first book of poetry in 1977. As he completed his BA, he blossomed into a poet and earned an MFA two years later. He has received a Guggenheim Fellowship (1979), an NEA Fellowship (1981), the prestigious Levinson Award for poetry (1984), and the American Book Award in 1985 for *Living Up the Street: Narrative Recollections*. In his first book, Soto takes the four universal elements (the key to balance and the cosmos in indigenous thought) of earth, air, water, and fire and translates them into the particular sights, smells, and labors of this rich agricultural valley. Much of his work in both poetry and prose engages a personal tone and a strong sense of humanity. Issues of poverty, childhood, nature, and faith resound, with an acute sense of ethnicity that transcends into the universal. In Soto's poetry the Chicano condition becomes one of the forms of the human condition. His great depth of meaning has earned him an undisputed place in American letters. Soto published thirty-five books in twenty years, some of which are used in public education.

Cherríe Moraga is not only a poet and playwright; she has helped open doors for women's writing by calling for women to explore their own ideas about life and creativity. She has participated with Gloria Anzaldúa (born in 1942 in Texas) in the publication of several edited volumes of essays and poetry by Latinas. In 1983 she published *Loving in the War Years*, a collage of essays, stories, and poems describing the intersections of culture, gender, and sexuality through reflection and political analysis. Although their texts are different, this book and Anzaldúa's *Borderlands* are similar in the way they mix genres, as well as political and personal contemplations, but Moraga's is more overt in its depiction of lesbian thought. Her ongoing analysis is of women called *vendidas* (traitors, those who sell-out). Moraga cites *La Malinche*, as Chicanas often do, but focuses on the Indian woman's mother, who is said to have sold her into slavery upon remarrying. Moraga's *La Malinche* does not blame her mother when she encounters her later in life. Moraga posits that women should emulate *La Malinche* and not her mother, by not selling out to institutional heterosexuality. She also reviews the roles of the iconic Virgin of Guadalupe and mystical La Llorona – both mother images – and reconsiders their influence on contemporary Mexican-American women.

In Moraga's play, *Heart of the Earth: A Popul Vuh Story* (2001), she takes the ancient Mayan tale that relates the antics of the hero-twins and how the gods created humankind from corn, but her version has a twist. During the play the male gods – 'Grandfather' and 'Cucumatz' – try to create humans first from clay and then from wood, while the female god is in the kitchen preparing food for them. When their second attempt fails, they retreat to think longer about their project. While the 'Grandmother' is preparing the corn dough for *tortillas*, she is the one who discovers that this is the essence of the new creation. Thus, in the Mayan Popol Vuh the 'gods' create humans from corn, in Moraga's play the woman, owing to her work in the kitchen, is the one who figures it out.

An American Book Award recipient in 1996, Victor Martínez's *Parrot in the Oven* explodes with intense emotions and violence. A portrait of *barrio* life, this novel depicts the family father's struggles with alcoholism and unemployment, and even incarceration. Born in Fresno like Soto, Martínez attended Stanford University and worked as a field laborer, truck driver, and teacher as he developed his poetry and novels.

Alicia Gaspar de Alba, born in Texas, first published her poetry with two other Chicanas in *Three Times a Woman* (1989). She completed an MA in Creative Writing at the University of Texas, El Paso, worked for many years as a teacher and translator, and received a Ford Foundation fellowship. In 1994 she received a Ph.D. from the University of New Mexico, and was appointed a professor at UCLA. Her extensive novel, *Sor Juana's Second Dream* (1999), is a fictional version of the life of the famous seventeenth-century nun and intellectual in colonial Mexico, a prolific writer punished by the Catholic Church for daring, as a woman, to publish her work. Gaspar de Alba's recent work is on the murder and disappearance of hundreds of women in the Juárez area across the border from El Paso; her book *Desert Blood: The Juárez Murders* was released in 2005 by Arte Público Press.

Her sister contributor in *Three Times a Woman*, Demetria Martínez, was born in New Mexico in 1960. She is a journalist and poet who published one novel, *Mother Tongue* (1994), a hard-hitting, short account that explores the lives and reasons for fear of both a Central American refugee and a young Chicana. Her lyrical prose alternates with excerpts from poetry and newspaper clippings, passionate excitement, and meditative introspection. While Martínez's 'mother tongue' is English, this book explores the Latino's desire to express one's heritage, including the Spanish language. This book won the Western States Book Award for fiction that year. Martínez's poems also evoke powerful messages and feelings about abortion, divorce, trauma, and violence, as well as a spirituality connected to the earth and nature.

In recent years, one of youngest and most widely produced Latina playwrights is Josefina López, whose 1992 play *Real Women Have Curves* (which concerns immigration and garment factory work as well as women's self-esteem) was converted to film (with a slightly different story) in 2003. Born in 1969 in Mexico, López came to California at the age of five. She stands out as the next generation of Chicana playwrights after Josefina Niggli and Estela Portillo-Trambley.

López's plays, which are often humorous, depict the desires of young adults to attain greater meaning from life, but her *Unconquered Spirits* (1997), recreates the Mexican and Chicano legend of the wailing woman, La Llorona, found in many Chicano works. She is the indigenous spirit ever present in the Chicano ethos. Having produced her first play at 18, López is quite prolific. She participated in the Young Playwrights Lab at the Los Angeles Theater Center from 1985 to 1988, then spent two years in New York studying playwriting, then at UC San Diego. She then completed a BA in film and screen writing at Columbia College in Chicago followed by a comedy-writing workshop with Warner Brothers in 1993. A Spanish-language version of her best-known play, *Las Mujeres de Verdad Tienen Curvas*, premièred in New York City in 1994. Among her recent work is *Confessions of Women from East L.A.* (1997), where women talk about their relationships with men, citing physical abuse and invisibility in both societies.

Chicano literature is no longer simply a *minority* literature in the US; it is the *American* voice of the native or indigenous in the Western Hemisphere, whose traditions and philosophies have merged with the Spanish and English-speaking people who settled upon and among them. Their culture has found ways to resist, recuperate, and *hybridize* as their production continues, centuries later. While at times revolutionary in nature, its evolution has brought forceful, highly noticeable creativity to US letters. In a recent study, Teresa McKenna sees Chicano literature developing out of social conflict and as a reaction to political events, while other critics have found its true spirit in those early records uncovered by new scholarly endeavors.[11] Manuel Martín-Rodríguez calls for attention to the discontinuities as well as the connectors, which have kept Chicano literature alive through the years, because ignoring those 'fissures' would distort other critical strategies.[12] José F. Aranda sees a binational literary history; he advocates placing Chicano novels alongside those of Europe-origin Americans in a re-telling of US culture. These contemporary critics stress that such sociopolitical issues as school desegregation, linguistic marginalization, and affirmative action strongly influence cultural production.

A decade and a half ago, Ramón Saldívar's proposal for a dialectics of difference (1990) posited Chicano literature as challenging the notion that categorizes it as a regional or immigrant literature. Instead, Saldívar saw Chicano authors creating a cultural imaginary that confronted the exclusionary practices of the Chicano nationalist political movement. For him, resistance occurs in the broad identification as *la raza*, an Indian/Native conscious people, and for many US Chicana writers it is resistance against patriarchy and institutional heterosexuality.[13] Resistance to hegemonic forces, desire for the preservation of native cultural traditions, and absorption of US and Spanish influences have shaped a centuries-old and unique Mexican-American literary production.

---

[11] Teresa McKenna, *Migrant Song: Politics and Process in Contemporary Chicano Literature* (Austin: University of Texas Press, 1997).

[12] *Life in Search of Readers* (Albuquerque: University of New Mexico Press, 2003), 155–6.

[13] See the article by Angie Chabrám-Dernersian, 'I Throw Punches for My Race, but I Don't Want to Be a Man: Writing Us – Chican-nos (Girl, Us)/Chican*as* – into the Movement Script', in Lawrence Grossberg, Cary Nelson, and Paula A. Treichler (eds.), *Cultural Studies* (New York: Routledge, 1992), 81–95.

## Works Cited

Acosta, Oscar 'Zeta'. *The Autobiography of a Brown Buffalo.* New York: Random House, 1972.
—— *The Revolt of the Cockroach People.* New York: Knopf, 1973.
Alurista. *Floricanto en Aztlán.* Los Angeles: Chicano Studies Center-University of California Press, 1971.
Anaya, Rudolfo. *Alburquerque.* New York: Warner Books, 1992.
—— *Bless me, Última.* 1972. New York: Warner Books, 1993.
Anzaldúa, Gloria. *Borderlands / La Frontera, The New Mestiza.* San Francisco: Aunt Lute Book Co., 1987.
—— (ed.). *Making Face, Making Soul / Haciendo Caras: Creative and Critical Perspectives by Women of Color.* San Francisco: Aunt Lute Foundation, 1990.
—— and Cherríe Moraga (eds.). 1981. *This Bridge Called my Back: Writings by Radical Women of Color.* New York: Kitchen Table, 1983.
Aranda, José F, Jr. *When We Arrive: A New Literary History of Mexican America.* Tucson: University of Arizona Press, 2003.
Arteaga, Alfred. *Chicano Poetics, Heterotexts and Hybridities.* Harvard: Cambridge University Press, 1997.
Boscana, Fray Gerónimo. *Chinigchinich*, trans. Alfred Robinson. Santa Ana, California: Fine Arts Press, 1933.
Bruce-Novoa, Juan. *Chicano Poetry: A Response to Chaos.* Austin: University of Texas Press, 1982.
—— 'Shipwrecked in the Seas of Signification: Cabeza de Vaca's *La Relación* and Chicano Literature', in *Reconstructing a Chicano/a Literary Heritage, Hispanic Colonial Literature of the Southwest.* Tucson: University of Arizona Press, 1993, 3–23.
Cabeza de Baca Gilbert, Fabiola. *We Fed Them Cactus.* Albuquerque: University of New Mexico Press, 1954. Reprinted with Introduction by Tey Diana Rebolledo, 1994.
Cabeza de Vaca, Álvar Núñez. 1542. *The Narrative of Cabeza de Vaca*, trans. Rolena Adorno and Patrick Charles Pautz, 3 vols. Lincoln and London: University of Nebraska Press, 1999.
Cantú, Norma Elia. *Canícula, Snapshots of a Girlhood en la Frontera.* Albuquerque: University of New Mexico Press, 1995.
Castillo, Ana (ed.). *Goddess of the Americas: Writings on the Virgin of Guadalupe.* New York: Riverhead Press, 1996; also published as *La Diosa de la Américas*, 2000.
—— *Massacre of the Dreamers: Essays on Xicanisma.* New York: Plume, 1994.
—— *Sapogonia: An Anti-Romance in 3/8 Meter.* Tempe, Arizona: Bilingual Review Press, 1990.
—— *So Far from God.* New York: Plume, 1993.
—— *The Mixquiahuala Letters.* 1986. New York: Doubleday, 1992.
Chabrám-Dernersian, Angie. 'I Throw Punches for My Race, but I Don't Want to Be a Man: Writing Us – Chican-nos (Girl, Us)/Chicanas – into the Movement Script', in Lawrence Grossberg, Cary Nelson, and Paula A. Treichler (eds.), *Cultural Studies*, New York: Routledge, 1992, 81–95.
Chávez, Denise. *Face of an Angel.* New York: Warner Books, 1994.
—— *Loving Pedro Infante.* New York: Pocket Books, 2001.

——— *The Flying Tortilla Man*. Española, New Mexico: Northern New Mexico Community College, 1975.
——— *The Last of the Menu Girls*. Houston: Arte Público Press, 1986.
Cisneros, Sandra. *Caramelo*. New York: Vintage Books, 2002.
——— *The House on Mango Street*. 1984. New York: Vintage Books, 1991.
——— *Woman Hollering Creek and Other Stories*. New York: Vintage Books, 1991.
Corpi, Lucha. *Delia's Song*. Houston: Arte Público Press, 1989.
——— *Eulogy for a Brown Angel*. Houston: Arte Público Press, 1992.
Cota-Cárdenas, Margarita. *Puppet*. 1985. Albuquerque: University of New Mexico Press, 2000.
Covey, Cyclone (trans.). *Cabeza de Vaca's Adventures in the Unknown Interior of America*. Albuquerque: University of New Mexico Press, 1961.
De Foor Fay, Julia. '(Re)Claiming the Race of the Mother: Cherríe Moraga's *Shadow of a Man, Giving Up the Ghost* and *Heroes and Saints*', in Elizabeth Brown-Guillory (ed.), *Women of Color: Mother–Daughter Relationships in Twentieth-Century Literature*. Austin: University of Texas Press, 1996, 95–116.
Eysturoy, Annie O. *Daughters of Self-Creation: The Contemporary Chicana Novel*. Albuquerque: University of New Mexico Press, 1996.
Galindo, Leticia. *Speaking Chicana: Voice, Power & Identity*. Tucson: University of Arizona Press, 1999.
Gaspar de Alba, Alicia. *Desert Blood: The Juárez Murders*. Houston: Arte Público Press, 2005.
——— *Sor Juana's Second Dream*. Albuquerque: University of New Mexico Press, 1999.
——— María Herrera-Sobek, and Demetria Martínez. *Three Times a Woman, Chicana Poetry*. Tempe, Arizona: Bilingual Press, 1989.
Gonzales, Rodolfo 'Corky'. *I Am Joaquin*. No place: no publisher, 1967.
Gonzáles-Berry, Erlinda. *Paletitas de guayaba*. Albuquerque: El Norte Publications, 1991.
——— and Chuck Tatum (eds.). *Recovering the U.S. Hispanic Literary Heritage*, vol. II. Houston: Arte Público Press, 1996.
González, Jovita. *Caballero: An Historical Novel*, eds. José E. Limón and María Cotera. College Station: Texas A&M University Press, 1996.
——— *Dew on the Thorn*, ed. José E. Limón. Houston: Arte Público Press, 1997.
Gutiérrez, Ramón and Genaro Padilla. *Recovering the US Hispanic Literary Heritage*. Houston: Arte Público Press, 1993.
Herrera, Juan Felipe. *Mayan Drifter, Chicano Poet in the Lowlands of America*. Philadelphia: Temple University Press, 1997.
Herrera-Sobek, María (ed.). *Beyond Stereotypes: The Critical Analysis of Chicana Literature*. Binghamton, New York: Bilingual Press, 1985.
——— *Reconstructing a Chicano/a Literary Heritage, Hispanic Colonial Literature of the Southwest*. Tucson: University of Arizona Press, 1993.
——— *The Mexican Corrido, A Feminist Analysis*. Bloomington: Indiana University Press, 1990.
Hinojosa, Rolando. *Estampas del Valle*. Berkeley, California: Quinto Sol, 1973.
——— *Klail City y sus alrededores*. La Habana: Casa de las Américas, 1976; published in English as *Klail City*. Houston: Arte Público Press, 1987.
——— *Mi querido Rafa*. Houston: Arte Público Press, 1981; published in English as *Dear Rafe*. Houston: Arte Público Press, 1985.

―――― *This Migrant Earth*. Houston: Arte Público Press, 1987.
Islas, Arturo. *Migrant Souls*. New York: William Morrow & Co., 1990.
―――― *The Rain God*. New York: Avon, 1984.
Kanellos, Nicolás (ed.). *En otra voz: Antología de la literatura hispana de los Estados Unidos*. Houston: Arte Público Press, 2002.
―――― and Helvetia Martell (eds.). *Hispanic Periodicals in the United States, Origins to 1960*. Houston: Arte Público Press, 2000.
Leal, Luis. 'Mexican-American Literature: A Historical Perspective', *Revista Chicano-Riqueña* 1.1 (1973), 32–44.
―――― 'Poetic Discourse in Pérez de Villagrá's *Historia de la Nueva México*', in María Herrera-Sobek (ed.). *Reconstructing a Chicano/a Literary Heritage, Hispanic Colonial Literature of the Southwest*. Tucson: University of Arizona Press, 1993, 95–117.
Lomelí, Francisco A. (ed.). *Handbook of Hispanic Cultures in the United States*. Houston: Arte Público Press, 1993.
―――― and Donaldo W. Urioste (eds.). *Chicano Perspectives in Literature: A Critical and Annotated Bibliography*. Albuquerque: Pajarito Publications, 1976.
López, Josefina. *Confessions of Women from East L.A.: A Comedy*. Woodstock, Illinois: Dramatic Publishing, 1997.
―――― *Real Women Have Curves*. Seattle: Rain City Projects, 1992.
―――― *Unconquered Spirits: A Historical Play*. Woodstock, Illinois: Dramatic Publishing, 1997.
Mann, Charles C. '1491', *Atlantic Monthly*, 289:3 (March 2002), 41–53.
Martín-Rodríguez, Manuel. *Life in Search of Readers: Reading (in) Chicano/a Literature*. Albuquerque, University of New Mexico Press, 2003.
Martínez, Demetria. *Breathing Between the Lines*. Tucson: University of Arizona Press, 1997.
―――― *Mother Tongue*. Tempe, Arizona: Bilingual Press, 1994.
―――― *Three Times a Woman, Chicana Poetry*, by Demetria Martínez, Alica Gaspar de Alba, and María Herrera-Sobek. Tempe, Arizona: Bilingual Press, 1989.
Martínez, Elizabeth Coonrod. 'Crossing Gender Borders: Sexual Relations and Chicana Artistic Identity'. *MELUS*, 27:1 (Spring 2002), 131–48.
―――― 'La historia *antes* del viaje al otro lado: La novela *Trini* de Estela Portillo-Trambley', in Manuel F. Medina et al. (eds.). *Pensamiento y Crítica: Los discursos de la cultura hoy*. México D.F.: Universidad Autónoma Mexicana (2000), 360–73.
―――― 'Nuevas Voces Salvadoreñas: Sandra Benítez y Demetria Martínez', in Priscilla Gac-Artigas (ed.). *Reflexiones: Ensayos sobre escritoras hispanoamericanas contemporáneas* I. Fair Haven, New Jersey: Ediciones Nuevo Espacio, Colección Academia (2002), 109–19.
―――― 'Recreating the Macho: Erlinda Gonzalez-Berry's *Paletitas de guayaba*'. *VOCES: A Journal of Chicana/Latina Studies*, 3:1 (Summer 2001), 47–67.
―――― 'The Cultural Significance of Maya Themes in US Latino/Chicano Literature', *Community College Humanities Review*, 22:1, Special Issue on the Maya (Fall 2001), 114–30.
―――― 'The Sexual Metaphor in Artistic Creation: Alma Villanueva's "The Ripening"', in José Villarino and Arturo Ramírez (eds.). *Aztlán: Chicano Culture and Folklore*. San Diego: McGraw-Hill (1997; 2nd edn 1999, 3rd edn 2002), 137–40.

Martínez, Victor. *Caring for a House*. San Jose, California: Chusma House Publications, 1992.
—— *Parrot in the Oven: Mi Vida*. New York: HarperCollins, 1996.
McKenna, Teresa. *Migrant Song: Politics and Process in Contemporary Chicano Literature*. Austin: University of Texas Press, 1997.
Mena, María Cristina. *The Collected Stories of María Cristina Mena*, ed. Amy Doherty. Houston: Arte Público Press, 1997.
Méndez, Miguel. *Peregrinos de Aztlán*. 1974. Tempe, Arizona: Bilingual Review Press, 1991.
—— *Pilgrims of Aztlán*, trans. David W. Foster. Tempe: Bilingual Review Press, 1992.
Mora, Pat. *Borders*. Houston: Arte Público Press, 1986.
—— *Chants*. Houston: Arte Público Press, 1984.
—— *Nepantla: Essays from the Land in the Middle*. Albuquerque: University of New Mexico Press, 1993.
Moraga, Cherríe L. *Loving in the War Years: lo que nunca pasó por sus labios*. Boston: South End Press, 1983.
—— *The Hungry Woman: A Mexican Medea* (and) *Heart of the Earth: A Popul Vuh Story*. Albuquerque: West End Press, 2001.
—— and Gloria Anzaldúa (eds.). 1981. *This Bridge Called my Back: Writings by Radical Women of Color*. New York: Kitchen Table, 1983.
Morales, Alejandro. *Caras viejas y vino nuevo*. Mexico City: Joaquín Mortiz, 1975.
—— *Reto en el paraíso*. Ypsilantí, Michigan: Bilingual Review/Press, 1983.
Morton, Carlos. 'La Serpiente Sheds its Skin, The Teatro Campesino', *Theatre Drama Review: TDR* 18:4, Indigenous Theatre Issue (1974), 71–76.
Niggli, Josefina. *Mexican Folk Plays*. Durham: University of North Carolina Press, 1938. Reprinted Arno, 1976.
—— *Mexican Village*. University of North Carolina Press, 1945. Reprinted University of New Mexico Press, 1994, with Introduction by Maria Herrera-Sobek.
—— *A Miracle for Mexico*. New York: New York Graphic Society, 1964.
—— *Step Down, Elder Brother*. New York: Rinehart, 1947.
Otero-Warren, Nina. *Old Spain in our Southwest*. New York: Harcourt, Brace & Co., 1936.
Padilla, Genaro. 'Imprisoned Narrative? Or Lies, Secrets, and Silence in New Mexico Women's Autobiography'. *Criticism in the Borderlands: Studies in Chicano Literature, Culture, and Ideology*, eds. Hector Calderón and José David Saldívar. Durham: Duke University Press, 1991.
—— and Ramón Gutiérrez. *Recovering the US Hispanic Literary Heritage*. Houston: Arte Público Press, 1993.
Paredes, Américo. *George Washington Gómez: A Mexicotexan Novel*. Houston: Arte Público Press, 1990.
—— *With His Pistol in His Hand: A Border Ballad and its Hero*. Austin: University of Texas Press, 1958.
Pérez de Villagrá, Gaspar. *Historia de la Nueva México*, eds. Miguel Encinias, Alfred Rodríguez, and Joseph P. Sánchez. Albuquerque: University of New Mexico Press, 1992.
Ponce, Mary Helen. *Hoyt Street*. New York: Anchor, 1993.
Portillo-Trambley, Estela. *Rain of Scorpions*. Berkeley: Tonatiuh International, 1975.
—— *Sor Juana and Other Plays*. Ypsilanti, Michigan: Bilingual Press, 1983.

—— *Trini*. Binghamton, New York: Bilingual Press, 1986.
Rebolledo, Tey Diana (ed.) *Las muejeres hablan: An Anthology of Nueva Mexicana Writers*. Houston: Arte Público Press, 1988.
—— *Nuestras Mujeres: Hispanas of New Mexico, their images and their lives, 1532–1992*. Albuquerque: El Norte Publications/Academia, 1992.
—— *Women Singing in the Snow: A Cultural Analysis of Chicana Literature*. Tucson: University of Arizona Press, 1995.
—— *Women's Tales from the New Mexico WPA, La Diabla a Pie*. Houston: Arte Público Press, 2000.
Rivera, Tomás. *Y no se lo tragó la tierra*. Berkeley: Quinto Sol Publications, 1971. *And the Earth Did Not Devour Him*, trans. Evangelina Vigil-Pinon. Houston: Arte Público Press, 1987.
Ruíz de Burton, María Amparo. *The Squatter and the Don*, eds. Rosaura Sánchez and Beatrice Pita. Houston: Arte Público Press, 1992.
—— *Who Would Have Thought It?* Houston: Arte Público Press, 1995.
Saldívar, José David. *Border Matters, Remapping American Cultural Studies*. Berkeley: University of California Press, 1997.
Saldívar, Ramón. *Chicano Narrative: The Dialectics of Difference*. Madison: University of Wisconsin Press, 1990.
Sánchez, Rosaura. 'Discourses of Gender, Ethnicity and Class in Chicano Literature', *The Americas Review* 20:2 (1992), 72–88.
Soto, Gary. *Baseball in April*. San Diego: Harcourt Brace Jovanovich, 1990.
—— *Black Hair*. Pittsburgh: University of Pittsburgh Press, 1985.
—— *Chato's Kitchen*. New York: Putnam, 1995.
—— *Living Up the Street: Narrative Recollections*. San Francisco: Strawberry Hill, 1985.
—— *The Elements of San Joaquín*. Pittsburgh: University of Pittsburgh Press, 1977.
—— *Too Many Tamales*. New York: Putnam, 1993.
Valdez, Luis. *Early Works*. Houston: Arte Público Press, 1990.
Villagrá, Gaspar Pérez de, 1610. *Historia de la Nueva México*, trans. and ed. Miguel Encinias, Alfred Rodríguez, and Joseph P. Sánchez. Albuqueque: University of New Mexico Press, 1992.
Villanueva, Alma Luz. *Bloodroot*. Austin, Texas: Place of Herons Press, 1982.
—— *Desire*. Tempe, Arizona: Bilingual Press, 1998.
—— *Life Span*. Austin, Texas: Place of Herons Press, 1985.
—— *Mother, May I?* Pittsburgh: Motheroot, 1978.
—— *Naked Ladies*. Tempe, Arizona: Bilingual Press, 1994.
—— *Planet*. Tempe, Arizona: Bilingual Press, 1993.
—— *The Ultraviolet Sky*. Tempe, Arizona: Bilingual Press, 1988.
—— *Weeping Woman, La Llorona and Other Stories*. Tempe, Arizona: Bilingual Press, 1994.
Villanueva, Tino. *Hay Otra Voz: Poems*. Staten Island, New York: Editorial Mensaje, 1972.
—— *Scene from the Movie "Giant"*. Willimantic, Connecticut: Curbstone Press, 1993.
Villarreal, José Antonio. *Pocho*. Garden City, New York: Doubleday, 1959.
Villaseñor, Victor. *Macho!* 1973. New York: Bantam Books, 1973.
—— *Rain of Gold*. Houston: Arte Público Press, 1991.

Viramontes, Helena María. *Paris Rats in East L.A.* Houston: Arte Público Press, 1993.
—— *The Moths and Other Stories.* Houston: Arte Público Press, 1985.
—— *Their Dogs Came with Them.* (forthcoming).
—— *Under the Feet of Jesus.* 1995. New York: Plume, 1996.
Zimmerman, Marc. *US Latino Literature: An Essay and Annotated Bibliography.* Chicago: March/Abrazo Press, 1992.

# 2

# The Importance of Being Sandra (Cisneros)

### EVA PAULINO BUENO

Just as her character Esperanza, of *The House on Mango Street*, is the result of energies of her *barrio* and its evolving dynamics, the work of Sandra Cisneros can only be understood within the history of the feminist movement, of the Black feminist movement, and of the Chicana movement. Furthermore, it is impossible to understand the existence of a Chicana movement if one does not take into consideration the Chicano movement in the United States, and what it has represented in the struggle for human rights that gained urgency in the 1960s. As Marc Zimmerman writes in *U.S. Latino Literature*:

> (T)he emergent Latino literatures of the 1960s attempted to serve as laboratories for the expression and then reconstruction of the transformed Latin American and US Southwest Hispano-Indian peoples into 'Mexican-Americans' or 'Chicanos', into 'Nuyoricans' or other Ricans, and, ultimately, into the problematic and questionable aggregate we know today as 'Hispanics' or 'Latinos'. (10)

The process of creation and recognition of this literature was gradual. From these laboratories of Latino consciousness that accelerated in the 1960s, 'it took the first relatively large scale wave of Latino students in US universities, in the context of the overall civil rights movement and the emergence of an anti-establishment, anti-Vietnam War counter-culture, to produce both the writers and readers of these new literatures' (Zimmerman, 10). Zimmerman asks, how can a 'marginal, subcultural enterprise' (10) achieve national recognition when the literary production of its members only finds publishing outlets in small publications and small ethnic studies programs?

The recognition of this body of work, we believe, comes not just from the growing number of potential readers, but from the increasing presence of literate and politically active Latinos in several sectors of society. The 'demands for multi-cultural curriculum' did not spring from the wider society, but rather from the increasing demands of the Latinos themselves, who were at once attending university in large numbers, and also in search of a literature that reflected their own reality, struggles, and needs. As Paul Guajardo writes in *Chicano Controversy*, 'much of the early literature was a form of social protest' (4). And yet, even in its first moments, the Latino experience is far from homogeneous.

In her contribution to *Breaking Boundaries*, Ellen McCracken details how Cisneros's first novel, as late as 1989, was still excluded from the canon, even though it was well known among Chicano critics. The book was, then, 'difficult to find in most libraries and bookstores', and 'virtually unheard of in larger academic and critical circles' (63). McCracken contrasts the situation of Cisneros's novel with the fact that 'major publishing houses are quick to capitalize on a Richard Rodríguez whose widely distributed and reviewed *Hunger of Memory* (1982) does not depart ideologically and semantically from the dominant discourse' (63).

This double standard accorded two male writers in contrast with one of the most prominent Chicana writers in the beginning of her career is a result, McCracken argues, 'of the fact that Cisneros's novel "speaks another language altogether", one to which the critics of the literary establishment "remain blind" ' (63).

What is the language of *The House on Mango Street*? And why would this language make the novel's initial reception so restricted? One reading of the novel will show that the language *itself* is very simple, and the chapters consist of forty-four brief stories of varying length. Myrna-Yamil Gonzáles, contributing to *U.S. Latino Literature*, calls the writing 'finely crafted' (102), whereas Julián Olivares in *Bloom's Guides* says that 'Cisneros employs her imagery as a poetics of space' (77), and Ellen McCracken points out that, '(I)n opposition to the complex, hermetic language of many canonical works, *The House on Mango Street* recuperates the simplicity of children's speech, paralleling the autobiographical protagonist's chronological age in the book' (64). The seeming simplicity of the language, which renders it as a form of prose poetry, is nevertheless used to convey deep truths both about the life of Esperanza, the narrator, and of other people in her *barrio* on Mango Street.

At the beginning of the novel, Esperanza reveals her discomfort with her name, which she inherited from her great-grandmother, 'a wild horse of a woman' who did not want to get married, but had to when Esperanza's 'great-grandfather threw a sack over her head and carried her off', and then had to spend the rest of her life looking out of the window, 'the way so many women sit their sadness on an elbow' (*House*, 11). This initial connection with a great-grandmother she did not know, whose name in English means 'hope', 'sadness', 'waiting', and in Spanish 'means too many letters' (10) provides two of the major energies of the book: a link to a Mexican past represented in a female ancestor, and her desire to obtain a new, more Anglo name such as 'Lisandra or Maritza or Zeze the X' (11). The fact that Esperanza vows not to have her great-grandmother's destiny, and wants to acquire a different non-Hispanic name, connects her to her roots as well as showing that she is aware of the wider 'Anglo' world around her. In his discussion about this section of the novel, Juan Daniel Busch reads the matter of Esperanza's name in a different way. He argues in the journal *Mester* that:

(t)he section 'My Name' may seem like an allusion to the history of Esperanza's family, but it represents a label imposed from one 'world', not necessarily by the matrilineal past, onto another where two 'worlds', the family's past and present, overlap and inform each other. Names not only remind you who you are in your family context, but when your name originates from a seemingly 'foreign' language it also reminds you of your 'foreign' status. (128)

One important detail is that Esperanza's last name, 'Cordero', means sheep. Here there is a clear sign that Cisneros is both using this family name (her own mother's name is Elvira Cordero Anguiano, as we learn from the dedication in *Caramelo*), and also making reference to that which is expected of women: to be meek as a sheep and, by allusion to the Christian religion, to be ready to be sacrificed for the benefit of others. It is this destiny that Esperanza rejects. As she says clearly, she does not want to become a revised version of her grandmother, even though her name may be a reminder of the ancestor and her destiny.[1]

## Crossing the border back and forth

In the next fictional work, *Woman Hollering Creek* (1991), a collection of short stories once again of varying lengths as in the chapters of *The House on Mango Street*, Cisneros revisits some of the themes present in *House*. In *Women*, however, Cisneros opens up the lens and gives a wider scope to the complex reality of Chicano life. Alexandra Fitts writes that '(t)he topics of the stories range from the confusions of a bicultural and bilingual childhood to the struggles of a dark-skinned woman to recognize her own beauty in the land of Barbie dolls and blond beauty queens' (11). The stories are organized in three separate parts: 'My Lucy Friend Who Smells Like Corn', 'One Holy Night', and 'There Was a Man, There Was a Woman'. Each of the parts is introduced by lyrics from Francisco Gabilondo Soler, Bobby Capó, and Tomás Méndes Sosa, respectively. Each of these lyrics provides a motto for the stories that will be told in the chapter.

The two most discussed stories in *Woman Hollering Creek* are the title story, 'Woman Hollering Creek', and 'Never Marry a Mexican', both of the last part. These two are stories that advance the theme of *la frontera* – the borderland – and how to cross it can mean, on the one hand, the entrance in a strange world where 'the towns ... are built so that you have to depend on husbands', and, on another, a place where a mother can tell her daughter never to marry a Mexican, even though she herself was a Mexican too. But the category 'Mexican' is anything but simple, because the narrator's mother 'was born here in the US, and (the father) was born there, and it's *not* the same, you know' (68, italics in

---

[1] The *Cordero* of her name can be seen as a way Cisneros finds to pay homage to her mother – who gave her 'the fierce language' with which she is going to narrate the story. See the dedication in *Caramelo*.

original). The *frontera*, then, is both a real, political division between the US and Mexico, and a more fluid one, as illustrated especially in 'Never Marry a Mexican'. 'Woman Hollering Creek', as Jacqueline Doyle writes, 'charts psychological, linguistic, and spiritual border crossings' (103).

The crossing of the political frontier can also represent a moment *just before* geopolitical considerations, as we see in, for instance, 'My Lucy Friend Who Smells Like Corn', a story in which the universe of childhood is at the center, and a child asks the other, 'Have you ever eated dog food?' (3). Here we have the language of childhood, the language of play, as well as the syntax of bilingual children normalizing the irregular verb 'to eat' into a regular one following the pattern of the regular verbs. The girls in the story register their surroundings, call the grandmother 'Abuelita', but are not aware of their ethnic background, because they do not deal directly with the wider, 'Anglo' world. In 'Eleven', the narrator is Rachel, who is turning eleven, but who is bullied by her teacher into putting on somebody's sweater, and that just ruins her day. She muses at the end, with surprising maturity, 'I'm eleven, ten, nine, eight, seven, six, five, four, three, two, and one, but I wish I was one hundred and two' (9). What she wishes for is to be heard, to be believed, and, as long as she is only eleven, that is not possible. She foresees a time when she is older, more secure, more assertive, when she will be able to speak up and affirm her truth.

It is in the next story, 'Salvador Late or Early', that the text begins to disclose how the self is constructed within the ethnic environment. The protagonist, Salvador, is a boy

> with eyes the color of caterpillar, Salvador of the crooked hair and crooked teeth, Salvador whose name the teacher cannot remember . . . (he) lives behind a raw wood doorway, shakes the sleepy brothers awake, ties their shoes, combs their hair with water, feeds them milk and corn flakes from a tin cup . . . (11)

Here Cisneros describes the reality of a boy who has to become the guardian of his younger brothers. He is a representative of a reality in the poor families, where very young children are given responsibilities, even though their bodies are a 'geography of scars' (10). How were these scars acquired? Did he break his arms like Meme Ortiz of *House*? Was he beaten by his parents? Did he fight with other boys? The text does not clarify, and just requires that the reader fill in the blank with his or her own knowledge of how these scars are obtained.

A contrast is provided between this story and 'Mexican Movies', in which the family gathers at the theater to see a movie, and the narrator registers the delight of families enjoying themselves while watching a Mexican musical. The children fall asleep in the theater, are carried out to the car, and then to their own beds, where the parents 'take off (their) shoes and clothes, and cover (them), so when (they) wake up, it's Sunday already, and (they)'re in (their) beds and happy' (13). What this story does in the collection is show a happy family situation, in which the children are loved and looked after, and do not have to take care of the others beyond their own capabilities, as is the case with Salvador.

The second part of the book, under the title 'One Holy Night', presents two female protagonists who are older than those who appear in the first part. The subject matter changes, and the language also acquires more complexity. The title story tells a story of seduction of a young girl by a man who tells her he is called Chaq Uxmal Paloquín, 'of an ancient line of Mayan kings' (27). She is seduced both by him as a man and by the stories he tells. When the story opens, she says that she doesn't know 'how many girls have gone bad from selling cucumbers' (27–8), but she knows she is not the first. 'My mother took the crooked walk too, I'm told, and I'm sure my Abuelita has her own story, but it's not my place to ask' (28). Chaq Uxmal Poloquín in time is revealed to be not a Mayan king, not even a Maya, but just Boy Baby, a thirty-seven-year-old man named Chato, born 'on a street with no name in a town called Miseria' (33).

After this revelation, the narrator, pregnant, is sent to Mexico, to *dar a luz*, while her *abuelita* and her uncle argue whose fault it is: 'Uncle Lalo says if they never left Mexico in the first place, shame enough would have kept a girl from doing evil things' (28). When Boy Baby comes looking for the girl, the grandmother runs after him with a broom, and he later is seen in newspaper clippings, '(a) picture of him looking very much like stone, police hooked on either arm . . . on the road to Las Grutas de Xtacumbilxuna, the Caves of *the Hidden Girl* . . . *eleven female bodies . . . the last seven years* . . .' (34). It is not clear from the text whether Boy Baby really killed the eleven women. He may as well be the victim of police persecution because he is a Mexican man. As far as the narrator is concerned, her encounter with Chaq Uxmal Poloquín at once shatters her innocence and unites her destiny with that of other women like her mother and even her grandmother.

The story poses the question whether the most important aspect is the exploitation of the narrator because she is a young, inexperienced woman in the hands of a much older man, or whether the treatment of a Mexican living in the US is a determining factor of the way he acts. Since he fabricates for himself a lineage going back to the Mayan kings, it means that he has knowledge of the plight of the Indians in Mexico. However, the very fact that he claims to come from a submitted people should have determined that he did not take advantage of an innocent girl, who was left to her destiny, with an 'animal stirring inside', a 'ghost inside' her, that 'will not let (her) rest' (34). And yet, it may well be that, indeed, she carried within her all the ghosts that Boy Baby represents because like his, hers is also a story of innocence and submission. The question here, then, is whether gender trumps ethnic affiliation.

In the last part of the book, 'There Was a Man, There Was a Woman', there are two much-discussed stories, 'Woman Hollering Creek', and 'Never Marry a Mexican'. In the first one is the story of Cleófilas Enriqueta DeLeón Hernández, a Mexican woman who marries Juan Pedro Martínez Sánchez with the permission of her father, Don Serafin, and comes across the border to live in Seguín, Texas. What seemed at first the happy ending of a *telenovela* becomes a nightmare when Juan Pedro becomes violent because, 'when a man and a woman love each other, sometimes that love sours' (43). Cleófilas finds herself trapped in the marriage, and surprised that, when he slapped her the first time, 'she didn't cry out or try to defend herself. She had always said she would strike back if a man, any man, were to strike her' (47). In fact, Cleófilas does not fight back, and does not 'run away as she imagined she might when she saw such things in the telenovelas' (47).

In a classic example of domestic violence, she says nothing, and ends up stroking 'the dark curls of the man who wept and would weep like a child, his tears of repentance and shame, this time and each' (48). The situation deteriorates for Cleófilas as the husband becomes more violent, and spends more time with other men at the ice house. Two women, Felice and Graciela, arrange to help Cleófilas escape, and Felice gives her a ride to the bus station, where she will get a bus to Mexico to return to her father's house. On the way to the bus station, 'when they drove across the arroyo, the driver opened her mouth and let out a yell as loud as any mariachi' (55). The arroyo called La Gritona, whose presence has been a constant throughout the story, reminds Cleófilas of the story of La Llorona, a mythical female figure, who is condemned to roam the rivers forever, as punishment for drowning her children. Once in Mexico, back in her father's house, Cleófilas – who avoided the destiny of a martyr her name evokes – tells her father and brothers about Felice's yelling 'like crazy' (56).

Cleófilas is surprised by Felice's reaction when they cross the arroyo because she, like so many women, has been taught that women who do not obey their husbands will end like that, a ghost roaming the rivers, moaning in pain. Felice's joyous yell causes great surprise to Cleófilas: 'Who would've thought? Who would've? Pain or rage, perhaps, but not a hoot like the one Felice had just let go. Makes you want to holler like Tarzan, Felice had said' (56). Felice – Happy – takes one symbol of the oppression of women and cuts right into it, exposing the potential for strength and inspiration, drawing from the symbol what it can have as an empowering force. La Llorona was, after all, a mother like Cleófilas, and a woman like both Cleófilas and Felice.

This transformation of a negative symbol into a positive one is also reflected in the recuperation of the figure of La Malinche. Indeed, it is possible to say that the model for Mexicana and Chicana femininity is based on a triptych composed by La Malinche, La Llorona, and the Virgen de Guadalupe. What they all have in common is that they are all mothers. But only la Virgen has been an uncontestedly positive symbol. Both La Malinche and La Llorona evoke women who have made mistakes: La Malinche was the polyglot Mayan woman taken as a lover by Cortés, and later given to a soldier.[2]

> Her role in the conquest of Mexico has undergone varying interpretations in different periods of Mexican history, but it is only in modern Mexico that she has been completely maligned. In contemporary Mexico, the term 'malinchista' is popularly used to refer to someone who is perceived as being

---

[2] See Shirlene Soto, 'Tres modelos culturales: La Virgen de Guadalupe, la Malinche and la Llorona', *Fem*, 10:48 (October–November 1986), 13–16.

disloyal to his or her people; hence, 'malinchista' connotes a traitor. When this popular image of Malinche merges with the legend of La Llorona her weeping becomes a continuous lament for her supposed responsibility for the fall of the Aztec empire. (Roberta Fernández, 82)

But Felice, at the moment she incorporates the strength of the arroyo as part of her voice, at once embodies the positive sides of the two symbolic figures of La Malinche and La Llorona. She is, after all, in a sense a betrayer of her people, since she refuses to marry and is a free woman not subjected to any man, and therefore a literal thorn in the side of the patriarchal ideology that dictates that women be obedient to their men. La Llorona, in her turn, also disobeyed her husband. Even though there are several versions of the myth, all of them emphasize the fact that La Llorona committed the highest possible crime when she abandoned the house of her husband, and later on, in an act of madness, killed her children. But 'Woman Hollering Creek' refuses the negative weight of the myth and transforms it into positive energy, when, after crossing the arroyo, she 'began laughing again, but it wasn't Felice laughing. It was gurgling out of her own throat, a long ribbon of laughter, like water' (56).

In her discussion of the feminine archetypes in *Woman Hollering Creek*, Alexandra Fitts argues that the characters in the short stories are engaged 'in a continual process of cultural mediation, as they struggle to reconcile their Mexican past with the American present' (11). 'Part of the negotiation', Fitts continues, 'is the incorporation of key feminine archetypes from the Mexican tradition and the reconciliation of these figures in a way that reflects the realities of the modern Chicana experience' (12). Another way to see this negotiation is reflected in the story 'Never Marry a Mexican'. Here, the narrator is called Clemencia – an ironic name considering she has no clemency for her lover's wife even at the moment when a woman needs most respect: Clemencia has sex with Drew on his wife's bed as she is in the hospital giving birth. Later, Clemencia even contemplates taking Drew and his wife's child for herself.

In 'Never Marry a Mexican' Clemencia is portrayed in a double bind: she at once claims her ethnic heritage and despises it. She establishes her gender at the same time as she splits it alongside ethnic lines. This can be seen clearly seen in how she refers to her lover's wife: 'If she was a brown woman like me, I might've had a harder time living with myself, but since she's not, I don't care . . . She's not *my* sister' (76) (emphasis in original). And later, she imagines herself taking from the other woman her white son, and seducing him. Clemencia's situation illustrates the drama of her mother, a Mexican-American woman who first marries a middle-class Mexican man and suffers discrimination from his middle-class Mexican family. But Clemencia's mother is also a traitor to the ideal of 'Mexicanness' because later she marries a white man, which leads to her own 'brown' daughters leaving her house and looking for residence in the Mexican part of town, in a fruitless attempt to recover a 'home'. This move, instead of enabling them finally to find a place where they belong, just leaves both confused and afraid of the nightly violence on the streets. This is the moment when Clemencia takes a white lover, Drew. Not just any white man, but a white man married to a white woman she loves to despise because, in spite of being cheated on by her own husband, she politely answers the phone call Clemencia makes to the house in the middle of the night: 'No Mexican woman would react like that' (77).

Even though Clemencia feels the hurt of discrimination against a woman like her mother, 'a Mexican girl who couldn't even speak Spanish, who didn't know enough to set a separate plate for each course at dinner, nor how to fold cloth napkins, nor how to set the silverware' (69), she ignores the class dimension of this discrimination and concentrates on the ethnic discrimination only, thus ignoring the possible gender allegiance she could have had with other women, even Drew's white wife. As Alexandra Fitts argues in her critical study of the book's feminine archetypes:

> Though Clemencia struggles with the allegiance she feels, or is forced into, with others of her race, her lack of loyalty to other women is much clearer. Where La Malinche is considered primarily a traitor to her race, we see in Clemencia the impact of a woman's betrayal of the 'sisterhood' of other women. The problem is that Clemencia feels no such sisterhood with white women – already excluded from their society, she is well aware of the power differential between a white woman and a dark-skinned woman, and for her, this difference negates any kind of kinship they might share. (15–16)

Clemencia's lack of clemency is directed not just to the wife, but also to her son. In a text that does not clarify whether the scene is real or imagined, she says:

> I can tell from the way he looks at me, I have him in my power. Come, sparrow. I have the patience of eternity. Come to *mamita*. My stupid little bird. I don't move. I don't startle him. I let him nibble. All, all of you. Rub his belly. Stroke him. Before I snap my teeth. (82)

From her envy of the other woman, she evolves into a serpent hypnotizing the innocent bird. She is both the serpent woman Coatlicue and a *vagina dentada* who will unman the child of the man she once loved and who refused to abandon his wife and child. The episode in which Clemencia goes to Drew's house and leaves gummy bears in places where the wife will find them emphasizes this desire to hurt the wife, humiliate her in her most intimate space, represented by the smallest of the Russian Babushka dolls, which she substitutes for a gummy bear.[3]

In her analysis of this story, Jean Wyatt writes in *Tulsa Studies in Women's Literature* that Clemencia's 'spiritual isolation' – from Drew, from white society, and from Mexican-American society – 'suggests that she glimpses the contrasts

---

[3] See Ana María Carbonell's discussion on the presence of Coatlicue in Viramontes and Cisneros, *Melus*, 24:2 (Summer 1999), 53–74.

between the concrete reality of the maternal body – warm, alive, smelling, radiating heat – and the insubstantiality of her own position in an abstract space' (253).

How to resolve this 'insubstantiality'? If this question is posed to Cisneros, the writer, she will answer with another work of fiction, which delves into the 'substance' of what it means to be, at the same time, Mexican and American, a duality that has its share of pain, as well as its fountain of what can only be described as 'connectedness'. Thus, the next fictional text, published in 2002, *Caramelo, or Puro Cuento*, tries to come to terms with – or at least provide the beginnings of – the complexities Cisneros raises in the previous works.

## A shawl, a language, a history

In a lecture delivered in 1986, Cisneros said, 'If I were asked what it is I write about . . . I would have to say I write about those ghosts inside that haunt me, that will not let me sleep, of that which even memory does not like to mention' ('Ghosts and Voices', 73). If we take these words literally, it is possible to say that in both *The House on Mango Street* and *Woman Hollering Creek*, the great majority of the voices that Cisneros hears come from women. Indeed, she dedicates *House* to 'A Las Mujeres – To The Women'. However, in *Women Hollering Creek* the dedication in Spanish and English, reads:

> For my mamá,
> Elvira Cordero Anguiano,
> Who gave me the fierce language.
> *Y para mi papá,*
> Alfredo Cisneros Del Moral,
> quién me dió el lenguaje de la ternura.
> Estos cuentitos se los dedico
> con todo mi corazón.

*Caramelo, or Puro Cuento*, is dedicated, simply, and only in Spanish, 'Para tí, Papá'. If we take for a moment the narrative line these dedications suggest, and align them with Cisneros's biography, we can see that the first novel reflects a more gender-specific alliance, whereas the next ones begin to demonstrate a movement towards an ethnic – Mexican – allegiance. It is possible to say too that her dedication in *House* expresses her inspiration obtained with a group of women writing at that moment about issues related to Chicana life and experience, especially Cherríe Moraga and Gloria Anzaldúa, whose groundbreaking *This Bridge Called My Back: Writings by Radical Women of Color* was published in 1981. When she published *Women Hollering Creek*, Cisneros dedicated it to both her parents, acknowledging her debt to both languages that each represents – the 'fierce language' of the Mexican-American mother, and the 'lenguage de la ternura' of the Mexican father. Now, with *Caramelo*, Cisneros acknowledges the singular influence her father has had in her life. The father, in this case, is both the person of the father and what the father represents, Mexico, or a 'Mexico principle'. But still, even in this case, the gender factor is a fundamental one. It is no wonder, therefore, that the central part of the novel consists of a 'conversation' between Celaya and her dead grandmother – the Awful Grandmother – feared and disliked by the grandchildren, but a figure with whom Celaya must make peace if she is ever to understand who she is and where she comes from.

In an interview with Gayle Eliott in 2002, Cisneros said that the only reason she writes, 'is so that I can find out something about myself. Writers have this narcissistic obsession about how we got to be who we are. I have to understand my ancestors – my father, his mother and her mother – to understand who I am' (Eliott 2002). After the publication of *The House on Mango Street*, *Women Hollering Creek*, and her volumes of poetry, Cisneros took time to produce her next work, published only after years of research and writing. Carol Cujec writes in *World and I* that Cisneros said, in a phone interview, that she felt the pressure: 'In the past, when I wrote other books, most of the time people had no idea what I was doing, nor did they care. What I felt this time was the pressure of the public waiting for this book. Even my family, this time they were waiting for this book as well' (228). And so, with the publication of *Caramelo*, both the public and the Cisneros family obtained what they were waiting for.

The 'caramelo' of the story is the unfinished shawl that Celaya's grandmother had, the only memento she has of her own mother, who died when she was a child. For Soledad, later called 'the Awful Grandmother', this object is her connection with a life left unfinished, unlived, when her father remarried and sent the young girl to live with a relative. For Celaya, who 'inherits' this shawl, the burden to tell Soledad's story leads her to a 'conversation' with her dead grandmother, who complains of the 'liberties' Celaya takes in writing her story.

But before Celaya learns of the existence of the shawl, the novel introduces the extended Reyes family on both sides of the border: Celaya's family, her two uncles and their families go to Mexico by car, all the way from Chicago. In Mexico, they stay at the house of the grandparents, the Awful Grandmother and the Little Grandfather, who live in the same compound as their only daughter, aunt White Skin and her own daughter. In this domestic space the children play, fight, make and break alliances, while the parents relive old stories and revive old likes and dislikes. This first section ends with a standout between Celaya's mother and the Awful Grandmother. Cisneros leaves the reader hanging and starts the new section providing a flashback into the Awful Grandmother's past with the help of Celaya, now the storyteller who wants to recuperate a sense of who the grandmother, Soledad, is.

The novel starts with a motto, 'Tell me a story, even if it is a lie', followed on the next page with a disclaimer:

> The truth, these stories are nothing but story, bits of string, odds and ends found here and there, embroidered together to make something new. I have invented what I do not know and exaggerated what I do to continue the family

tradition of telling healthy lies. If, in the course of my inventing, I have inadvertently stumbled on the truth, *perdónenme*. (*Caramelo*, 1)

What are, exactly, these 'bits of string', or 'kernels of truth' (Cujec, 233), but the story of Cisneros's own family? Indeed, *Caramelo* feels like a fictionalized autobiography, or, better, the 'family-graphy' in which Cisneros herself recuperates her sense of who she is and where she comes from. In an interview given to Ed Morales in October of 2002, Cisneros says that this book is her way to 'to pay homage to what she feels is a discarded past':

> I really wanted to write about my father because I felt as if his life didn't count ... He served in World War II, but people don't think about men like my father when they think about American history. That hurt me very deeply, to have someone I cared about so much erased and forgotten once he died, as if he meant nothing.

In her attempt to pay homage to her father, Cisneros ends up digging deeper into her whole family history, weaving a story that spans four generations. *Caramelo* dramatizes, in a sense, how the private lives of Mexican immigrants and their descendants find their way within the fabric of American society, one foot in each culture. In his study of Chicano autobiography (1990), Ramón Saldívar discusses the autobiography of another Chicano, Richard Rodríguez, and makes the following point:

> This privileging of the private viewpoint is significant, but not, I would stress, because autobiography has to be either public or private in purview. Autobiography is demonstrably capable of embracing both perspectives and putting them into dialogue ... (159)

Indeed, as we see in *Caramelo*, Cisneros not only tells the stories of her family, but anchors those stories firmly in the public history of Mexico through the footnotes, which she uses to give information about the history of Mexico, about figures of Mexican popular culture (songs, fotonovelas, telenovelas). In one case, she acknowledges that the song that one of the characters sings was written by '*the author's great-grandfather, Enrique Cisneros Vásquez*' (123, italics in original).[4]

---

[4] Cisneros's use of footnotes has not been well received by all reviewers. Carol Cujec says that they 'can be overwhelming at times, as we are introduced to numerous minor characters in footnotes and even footnotes to footnotes. This gives a sense of the vastness of experience connected to one family.' Quoted from 'Caramel-Coated Truths and Telenovela Lives: Sandra Cisneros Returns with an Ambitious Novel about the Latino Community', *World and I*, 18:3 (March 2003), 233. The reviewer of Desijournal refers to the footnotes as 'one too many' (25 May 2005). Xelena Gonzalez, of the *San Antonio Current*, comments that San Antonians 'who have never seen Mexico or walked the streets of Chicago can simply judge (Sandra Cisneros's) description of our city and easily trust in her ability to capture and recreate a strong sense of place'. In spite of all of this positive evaluation, Gonzalez also says that the

The understanding of the trajectory of Sandra Cisneros's work requires an understanding of the development of the work of other artists from immigrant Latin American backgrounds in the US. Marc Zimmerman traces this development in three phases: an initial romantic one in which the literature is attempting to replicate the home base; a second phase marked by hopes, but also by problems and conflicts, racism, and an affirmation of roots; and a third phase of settlement and reaching out to other minorities and to those in the mainstream (Zimmerman, 20–1).

What makes Zimmerman's distinctions particularly pertinent in Cisneros's case is what he expands on the third phase, which, he writes, comes about when 'the culture itself becomes self-critical and de-centered from earlier male discourse; feminist and post-nationalist issues become crucial, as do a wide range of alternative cultural models and directions' (21). What we see in Cisneros's artistic trajectory is that, actually, she was able to look inside her own culture and write about it from a feminine perspective. In *Caramelo*, even though her stated aim was to pay homage to her father, the narrative structure leads her to revisit her paternal grandmother's life, to try to finish the *rebozo* – here functioning as a metaphor for her family's history – her grandmother's only material trace of her own mother. Celaya does not finish the *rebozo*, the same way the novel does not tie all the loose ends. It is possible to say that one thread, at least, was followed to its origin: she understands her grandmother and, in some way, becomes one with her. Such understanding is very well represented, not just in the 'dialogue' the two of them conduct in the second part of the book, but more in the chapter 'Becoming Invisible', when the narrator traces Soledad's life to the moment of her death:

> Now that she was ill, with her breathing heavy, and her consciousness rising and falling, she became aware of that familiar feeling of shedding her body once again. It both delighted and frightened her. She was turning invisible. She was turning invisible . . . The body led her, a wide rowboat without oars or a rudder, drifting . . . That's what she felt now as she was dying and her life was letting her go. A saltwater of well-being . . . Wise, delicate, simple, obscure. And it was good and joyous and blessed. (347–8)

The grandmother does return, as we see in the novel, as the one who dialogues with Celaya, corrects her when she is taking too many liberties with her story. She becomes Celaya's alter ego, even as she realizes the past will never return, and she is homesick for a country 'that doesn't exist anymore. That never existed. A country I invented. Like all emigrants caught between here and there' (434).

---

storyteller 'can be annoyingly long-winded' and, even though she acknowledges the 'considerable amount of research it must have required', *Caramelo* is a ' "Bible-weight size" book'. 'An unfinished *rebozo*; Sandra Cisneros' second novel, "Caramelo", is released in paperback', *Current*, 703, San Antonio, Texas (5 November 2003), 20.

As people in constant flux through the borders – political, linguistic, cultural – Cisneros's characters bring to the forefront of the literature of the United States this necessary awareness of borders. She has done this with a feminine voice that is at once witty, precise, and poetic. Like the *rebozo* belonging to Celaya's grandmother Soledad, the story of the Chicanas and Chicanos in the US is not complete. It is being woven day to day, through the work of every person of Mexican descent, with their struggles, their dreams, their hopes, their suffering, and their accomplishments.

## Works Cited

Bloom, Harold (ed.). *Sandra Cisneros's 'The House on Mango Street'. Bloom's Guides. Comprehensive Research and Study Guides*. Philadelphia: Chelsea House Publishers, 2004.

Busch, Juan Daniel. 'Self-Baptizing the Wicked Esperanza: Chicana Feminism and Cultural Contact in *The House on Mango Street*', *Mester*, 22–23:1–2 (Fall–Spring 1993–94), 123–34.

Carbonell, Ana María. 'From Llorona to Gritona: Coatlicue in Feminist Tales by Viramontes and Cisneros', *Melus*, 24:2 (Summer 1999), 53–74.

Cisneros, Sandra. *Caramelo, or Puro Cuento*. New York: Alfred A. Knopf, 2002.

—— 'Ghosts and Voices: Writing from Obsession', in 'From a Writer's Notebook', *The Americas Review*, 15:1 (Spring 1987), 73.

—— *The House on Mango Street*. Houston: Arte Público Press, 1984. New York: Vintage Books, 1991.

—— *Woman Hollering Creek and Other Stories*. New York: Random House, 1991.

Cujec, Carol. 'Caramel-Coated Truths and Telenovela Lives: Sandra Cisneros Returns with an Ambitious Novel about the Latino Community', *World and I*, 18:3 (March 2003), 228–35.

Eliott, Gayle. 'An Interview with Sandra Cisneros' *The Missouri Review*, XXV:1, 2002. Online at http://www.missourireview.org/index.php?genre=Interviews&title=An+Interview+with+Sandra+Cisneros

Fernández, Roberta. ' "The Cariboo Café": Helena Maria Viramontes Discourses with Her Social and Cultural Contexts', *Women's Studies*, 17 (1989), 71–85.

Fitts, Alexandra. 'Sandra Cisneros's Modern Malinche: A Reconsideration of Feminine Archetypes in *Women Hollering Creek*', *International Fiction Review*, 29 (January 2002), 11–12.

González, Myrna-Yamil. 'Female Voices in Sandra Cisneros' *The House on Mango Street*', in Harold Augenbraum and Margarite Ferneandez Olmos (eds.). *US Latino Literature; A Critical Guide for Students and Teachers*. Westport, Connecticut: Greenwood Press, 2000, 101–12.

Gonzales, Xelena. 'An unfinished *rebozo*; Sandra Cisneros' second novel, "Caramelo", is released in paperback', *Current*, 703, San Antonio, Texas (5 November 2003), 20.

Guajardo, Paul. *Chicano Controversy; Oscar Acosta and Richard Rodriguez*. New York: Peter Lang, 2002.

McCracken, Ellen. 'Sandra Cisneros' *The House on Mango Street*: Community Oriented Introspection and the Demystification of Patriarchal Violence', in

Asunción Horno-Delgado et al. (eds.), *Breaking Boundaries; Latina Writings and Critical Readings*. Amherst: University of Massachusetts Press, 1989, 62–71.

Moraga, Cherríe, and Gloria Anzaldúa (eds.). *This Bridge Called My Back: Writings by Radical Women of Color* (1981). Revised and expanded edition, New York: Kitchen Table/Women of Color Press, 1983.

Morales, Ed. 'Imaginary Homeland', *The Library Journal* (1 October 2002). Online at http://www.libraryjournal.com/index.asp?layout=articlePrint&articleid=CA24463

Olivares, Julián. 'Julián Olivares on the Poetics of Space', in Harold Bloom (ed.), *Sandra Cisneros's 'The House on Mango Street'. Bloom's Guides. Comprehensive Research and Study Guides*. Philadelphia: Chelsea House Publishers, 2004, 77–80.

Rodriguez, Richard. *Hunger of Memory: The Education of Richard Rodriguez*. New York: Godine, 1982.

Saldívar, Ramón. *Chicano Narrative: The Dialectics of Difference*. Madison: University of Wisconsin Press, 1990.

Soto, Shirlene. 'Tres modelos culturales: La Virgen de Guadalupe, la Malinche and la Llorona', *Fem*, 10:48 (October–November 1986), 13–16.

Wyatt, Jean. 'On Not Being La Malinche: Border Negotiations of Gender in Sandra Cisneros's "Never Marry a Mexican" and "Woman Hollering Creek"', *Tulsa Studies in Women's Literature*, 14:2 (Fall 1995), 243–72.

Zimmerman, Marc. *US Latino Literature: An Essay and Annotated Bibliography*. Chicago: March/Abrazo Press, 1992.

# 3

# The Island as Mainland and the Revolving Door Motif: Contemporary Puerto Rican Literature of the United States

PATRICIA M. MONTILLA

The literature of Puerto Ricans in the United States spans well over a hundred years, dating as far back as the nineteenth century, prior to the Treaty of Paris of 1898, by which Puerto Rico became a territory of the US following the Spanish American War. Many scholars have traced its origins and evolution, delineating its various stages of development within literary genres. The purpose of this chapter, therefore, is not to provide another historical account of Puerto Rican literature in the US, but to highlight two prominent characteristics in recent US Puerto Rican literary production: the depiction of the island as the mainland, or rather its presence as a primary geographic and literary space, and the *leitmotif* of the Revolving Door.[1] While this review is somewhat panoramic in scope, it is not an all-encompassing analysis of contemporary Puerto Rican literature in the US. Its intent is to examine these concepts in the poetry, autobiographical writings, and fiction by US Puerto Rican authors during the last twenty-five years, with a particular emphasis on the works of Puerto Rican women in the US in response to their rapidly growing number since the 1980s.[2] In identifying both the island of Puerto Rico and the Revolving Door as prominent motifs in

---

[1] The 'Revolving Door' is a term utilized by historians and sociologists to describe the back-and-forth pattern of migration of people between the island of Puerto Rico and the mainland United States, whereby Puerto Ricans migrate both to and from the two places owing to family ties, economic hardships and/or opportunities, and health reasons, among others. In *Puerto Ricans in the United States* (Westport, Connecticut: Greenwood Press, 2000), María E. Pérez y González uses the term to describe the most current stage of Puerto Rican (im)migration to the mainland, beginning in 1965 and continuing today. See 36–8.

[2] Frances Aparicio likens this phenomenon to the rise in Chicana and Latina feminist studies and fiction writing. She notes that Puerto Rican women writers of the United States 'have been nurtured by the Anglo Feminist movement as well as by the differentiating discourses of other women of color'. For further discussion on the recent surge of Puerto Rican women's writings, see also Carmen S. Rivera's *Kissing the Mango Tree: Puerto Rican Women Rewriting American Literature* (Houston: Arte Público Press, 2002).

contemporary Puerto Rican literature of the US, I will also discuss how these recurring literary trends vary between authors and texts and how they reflect the diverse realities and experiences of Puerto Ricans living in the US.

The island of Puerto Rico has been a constant trope in US Puerto Rican literature since its emergence. In his essay entitled '"De lejos en sueños verla . . .": visión mítica de Puerto Rico en la poesía neorrican' ('Seeing her from Afar in Dreams . . .': The Mythical Vision of Puerto Rico in Neorican Poetry),[3] Efraín Barradas notes that a utopian image of the island can be traced back to the early chronicles written by the monks recording life in the Spanish colony, and that this idealized vision has a long tradition in the history of Puerto Rican letters (60–1). It is, therefore, not surprising that a quixotic portrayal of the island continues to be present in the texts written by US Puerto Rican or Neorican writers on the mainland.[4] But as Barradas states in his discussion of Piri Thomas's *Down These Mean Streets* (1967), the idyllic image of the island in Puerto Rican literature of the US is often one of nostalgia; transmitted from the position of exile, the island is depicted as a paradise lost by those who for one reason or another were forced to leave it behind and migrate to the mainland (62–3). In *Down These Mean Streets*, which many scholars consider to be the inaugural autobiographical testimony of the Puerto Rican experience in the US (though previous testimonial writings do exist),[5] the image of a bygone utopia is communicated by Thomas's mother and sharply contrasts with the hostile, urban landscape of New York that the author depicts throughout his work.

Initial readings of contemporary Puerto Rican literature of the US suggest that such a dichotomous view of Puerto Rico and the mainland still prevails.[6] In the last quarter-century, the island has indeed continued to occupy the principal geographic and literary space created by US Puerto Rican authors who often contrast life in Puerto Rico to life in the mainland US. But closer readings of these texts reveal that the vision of the island, while still an essential element, is

---

[3] This and all subsequent translations are mine.

[4] As Frances Aparicio, Efraín Barradas, and other scholars have noted, the polemical terms *Nuyorican* and Neorican have held multiple connotations throughout the years. The term *Nuyorican* is generally used to identify the literary movements created by Puerto Ricans living and writing poetry in New York during the 1960s and 1970s, while the term *Neorican* more clearly refers to the corpus of Puerto Rican literature in the US following this specific movement (Aparicio 26). Barradas, however, uses the two terms interchangeably (Barradas, 63). Throughout this chapter, I shall use the terms as distinguished by Aparicio.

[5] For an overview of autobiographical writings written by members of the Puerto Rican community in New York before World War II, see Eugene V. Mohr's chapter, 'Proto-Nuyoricans' in *The Nuyorican Experience: Literature of the Puerto Rican Minority* (Westport, Connecticut: Greenwood Press, 1982), 3–43.

[6] The juxtaposition of the sunny, tropical landscape of Puerto Rico and the gray, concrete, and often cold and inhospitable environment of North American cities such as New York, Patterson, New Jersey, and Chicago can be found in the writings of Edward Rivera, Judith Ortiz Cofer, Rosario Morales and Aurora Levins Morales, and Esmeralda Santiago, among others.

a lot more complex, ambiguous, and at times even subversive. The notion of the island as the mainland suggested in the title of this chapter, therefore, is meant figuratively to underscore the notable presence of Puerto Rico in the poetry, autobiographies, and fiction of Puerto Rican writers of the mainland.

In some cases, US Puerto Rican writers recreate the island in their works, blending memory with fiction to produce their own personal and artistic visions.[7] This internalization of the island first emerged during the Nuyorican movement of the 1960s and 1970s, as Puerto Rico became a symbol of ethnic pride and political resistance against the racism, economic and political oppression, and marginalization that many Puerto Ricans living in New York endured.[8] As Barradas states in the above mentioned essay, for the Nuyorican poets, Puerto Rico is not simply 'an external myth – an edenic island – but an internal attitude that serves (the Neorican) to combat all of the difficulties and problems presented by the antagonistic world in which he lives' (73).

In Post-Nuyorican literature, the representation of Puerto Rico takes on multiple guises that go far beyond the mythical image of an island paradise. In the spirit of the Nuyorican movement, US Puerto Rican writers continue to reinvent the island in their works. Its geography and culture serve as material for creating experimental and abstract art, as is often the case in the poetry of Hernández Cruz, or are fused together with aspects and images of life on the mainland to become an emblem of biculturalism, as in Tato Laviera's poems and the numerous memoirs that have appeared in recent years. But perhaps the most innovative use and representation of the island is found in the texts by US Puerto Rican women writers, for whom the island is not only the setting for many of their narratives, but also a literary strategy through which to critique patriarchal society in Puerto Rico as well as on the mainland, and question conventional notions of gender and sexuality.

Closely tied to the representation of Puerto Rico is the Revolving Door pattern of migration that is so unique to Puerto Rican Americans because of the island's status as a Commonwealth of the United States and its geographic proximity. Also labeled 'return migration', this back-and-forth movement of Puerto Ricans alternating residence between the mainland and the island, and the challenges it presents for families, is characteristic of contemporary US Puerto Rican literature.[9] Poets, memoirists, and novelists alike transcribe childhood and adult accounts of leaving and later returning to the island from places

---

[7] The recent poetry of Victor Hernández Cruz, published in *Maraca: New and Selected Poems* (2001), and Judith Ortiz Cofer's memoir *Silent Dancing: A Partial Remembrance of a Puerto Rican Childhood* (1990) are excellent examples of this artistic fusion of the imaginary and the real in representing the island of Puerto Rico.

[8] For an overview of the Nuyorican poetic movement, see the studies by Aparicio, Barradas, and Sánchez González.

[9] Joseph P. Fitzpatrick discusses this 'cultural uprooting in reverse', and the difficulties that many return migrants experience, in *Puerto Rican Americans: The Meaning of Migration to the Mainland* (Englewood Cliffs, New Jersey: Prentice-Hall, Inc., 1971), 21–4.

like Georgia, New York, New Jersey, Massachusetts, Illinois and California. The Revolving Door phenomenon has also become a literary paradigm.

The notion of the island as the mainland and the reverse pattern of migration that characterizes the US Puerto Rican experience are mirrored in the life and work of Victor Hernández Cruz. Born in the mountain town of Aguas Buenas, the poet moved to New York with his family at the age of five and resided there for thirty-four years until 1989, when he returned to his hometown in Puerto Rico to live. Although scholars do not typically include Hernández Cruz among the Nuyorican poets of the late 1960s and early 1970s, they have noted similarities between his works and theirs, particularly in his early collections of poetry: *Papo Got his Gun* (1966), *Snaps* (1968), *Mainland* (1973), and *Tropicalization* (1976).[10] By the 1980s, however, the poet's writings became less direct in tone and urban in theme. Also by Hernández Cruz, *By Lingual Wholes* (1982), *Rhythm, Content and Flavor* (1989), *Red Beans* (1991), and *Panoramas* (1997) are much more experimental with regard to word play and imagery. Selections from these collections, as well as new compositions, appear in the anthology *Maraca* (2001), and are distinguishable from earlier writings by the poet's manipulation of images, words, sounds, space, and time. Though leaning toward the hermetic, the recent poetry of Hernández Cruz continues to explore the island and the theme of migration. For example, 'Snaps of Immigration' from *Red Beans* (1991) is a poem divided into nine stanzas that recalls the journey from Puerto Rico to New York by juxtaposing the island and city landscapes. But instead of the conventional representation of a tropical paradise contrasted to a cold, Northern city, the poem communicates the migratory experience as it is perceived through the senses:

> 1
> I remember the fragrance of
> the Caribbean
> A scent that anchors into the
> ports of technology.
>
> 2
> I dream with suitcases
> full of illegal fruits
> Interned between white
> guayaberas that dissolved
> into snowflaked polyester.
>
> 3
> When we saw the tenements
> our eyes turned backwards

---

[10] According to Aparicio, the poetic works of Hernández Cruz 'also address a series of themes related to the Nuyorican movement: growing up in New York City, drugs, music, political opposition, and social denouncement' (30).

> to the miracle of scenery
> At the supermarket
> my mother caressed the
> parsley. (138)

Each stanza or 'snap' in the poem communicates a particular fragrance, visual image, texture, or sound, as sensed and recorded from memory by the poetic voice. This method of presenting Puerto Rico through various stimuli also appears in a series of poems published in *Maraca* (2001) for the first time and entitled *Letters from the Island* (1995–2000).

The texts that constitute *Letters from the Island* were written after the poet's return to Puerto Rico. Although composed in English, each of the poems renders a particular aspect of Puerto Rico. In an interview with Carmen Dolores Hernández, Hernández Cruz identifies himself as a US Puerto Rican writer, despite the fact that he now lives on the island, and notes the importance that Puerto Rico has in his poetry:

> I consider myself an American writer because I write in English and not Spanish. It must sound like a wild contradiction, but my poetry is in English and thus part of the North American literary landscape. I am not saying that I, the person, is a North American. I live in Puerto Rico and lead a total personal and cultural life in Puerto Rican Spanish. I write in Spanish also, so that I am a Latin American writer as well . . . (65)

Hernández Cruz's assertion regarding the role that the mind and perception have in his poems reveals an essential aspect of his work. In *Letters from the Island*, the Puerto Rican landscape, past and present, materializes through a free association of ideas that is reminiscent of vanguard art, specifically Cubist and Surrealist poetry, in its juxtaposition and simultaneous representation of thoughts and visual images. In 'Rain', the poet captures the sight and sensation of rain in the tropical climate of the island: 'Rain/Blue sky/Heat rises/Moving white clouds/ To a corner/Wind Blows them/Back gray, Afternoon/Rain/The sound of thick/ Drops/A distant mountain/Still blue sky (. . .)' (168). The poem consists of short, disjointed phrases that together describe the weather pattern as viewed and felt by the poetic voice. In 'from capital F? White Table', Hernández Cruz utilizes the flora and fauna of Puerto Rico in rendering the island:

> How a lizard hears
> the flies and bees as a concert
> of dance and music
> Before they look
> making the actual sight
> Just a verification
> of their imaginations.
> The odor of papaya
> guanabana and green

> Plaintains such olfato
> eaten through flesh (. . .) (173)

Like a collage, the poem incorporates various objects, images, and sensations, as well as the thoughts that these elements of nature conjure in the mind of the poetic voice. Recorded and communicated to the reader in this unique way, the geography and culture of Puerto Rico serve as artistic material to create new, highly sensorial poetry.

Also emerging in the wake of the Nuyorican poets, Tato Laviera, like Hernández Cruz, echoes the voices of his precursors while at the same time paving a new direction in the Puerto Rican literature of the US. Born in Santurce, Puerto Rico, Laviera moved to New York City with his mother in 1960 at the age of nine. He has published four collections of poetry: *La Carreta Made a U-Turn* (1979); *Enclave* (1981); *AmeRícan* (1985); and *Mainstream Ethics* (1989). *La Carreta Made a U-Turn*, Laviera's highly acclaimed first book, resembles the poetry of the Nuyorican movement in its critique and dismantling of the American Dream and its depiction of the harsh living and working conditions endured by many Puerto Ricans in New York. The book is also innovative in its exploration of biculturalism and for questioning of the role and treatment of women in Puerto Rican society.[11] Many of the poems in *La Carreta Made a U-Turn* are marked by the use of code-switching between English and Spanish. The island of Puerto Rico appears throughout the book, as both a place of origin and a symbol of the complex nature of Puerto Rican identity owing to the island's relationship with the US. In 'Graduation Speech', the poetic voice employs both languages to express its desire to return to the island as well as to reflect upon its biculturalism: 'i think in spanish/ i write in english/ i want to go back to puerto rico,/but i wonder if my kink could live/in ponce, mayagüez and carolina/tengo las venas aculturadas/escribo en espanglish' (17). Laviera's representations of Puerto Rico and of acculturation, communicated in English and Spanish, reveal reluctance and self-doubt at belonging to two worlds and speaking two languages. This duality is also depicted in the poem 'Haiku': 'shanghai streets of san juan/split between two realities/and one people' (69). Here, however, the people of Puerto Rico are represented as one society, while the actual island remains divided in two. But not all depictions of Puerto Rico present diverging realities. In the third section of the book the poet pays homage to Puerto Rico by employing elements of Puerto Rican folkloric music known for idealizing life in the countryside. In 'la música jíbara', a poem written entirely in Spanish, Laviera transcribes the song of the *jíbaro*, the rural Puerto Rican peasant, and praises the mountains, the sun, and the coffee of his beloved island.

Although Laviera's second book, *Enclave* (1981), focuses on life in the Puerto Rican community of New York, the island of Puerto Rico appears as an

---

[11] See the eleven poems that appear in *La Carreta Made a U-Turn* under the title 'Loisaida Streets: Latinas Sing'. For an analysis of these compositions, see Aparicio, 28–9.

emblem of cultural pride and throughout the book is tied to the theme of migration. The poem entitled 'sky people (la gente del cielo)' is a tribute to the many individuals who partake in the island's airborne migration. The Puerto Ricans who leave the island for the mainland are portrayed as the guardians of Puerto Rican culture: 'la gente del cielo,/ fingering on clouds,/climbing further and further/to preserve taíno folklore' (39). The poem unites all Puerto Ricans, regardless of their place of residence: 'as God gleefully conceded,/ what we had perceived all along,/ that Puerto Rico is 100 by 35 by 1000/ mountains multiplied by the square root/ of many cultures breathing: ONE' (39). The island is much more than a geographical space; it is a diverse yet unified community that is perpetually growing and expanding as *la gente del cielo* disperse throughout the continent.

The Puerto Rican migrant's role as the preserver of culture is also prevalent in *AmeRícan* (1985). In the poem 'nuyorican', the poetic voice addresses the island directly as though he were its protector: 'yo peleo por ti, Puerto Rico, ¿sabes?/yo me defiendo por tu nombre, ¿sabes?' (I fight for you, Puerto Rico, you know? I defend myself for you, you know?) (53). Upon returning to the island, however, the Nuyorican speaker is treated with disrespect and disdain by the Puerto Ricans who still reside there: 'now I return, with a *boricua* heart, and you spurn me, you look down on me, you attack my speech while you eat mcdonalds in american discos' (53). Migration to the mainland, as well as the use of English, are regarded as acts of treason, even when, ironically, Puerto Ricans on the island consume North American culture. The poem's closing lines tie together the concept of the island as the mainland as well as the Revolving Door motif as the poetic voice discusses going back to the mainland: 'if you don't want me, well I have an exquisite puerto rico where I can find refuge in New York and in many other streets that honor your presence, preserving all of your values' (53). As in 'sky people', the speaker alludes to the transfer and conservation of the island and its culture to New York by the Puerto Ricans living on the mainland. Reminiscent of the Nuyorican movement, the poem also portrays Puerto Rico as a state of mind and a strong cultural marker of identity much greater than a mere geographic space.

The island and revolving pattern of migration are intrinsically linked to the bicultural identity that the collective poetic voice affirms and celebrates throughout *AmeRícan*. The combination of the words 'American' and 'Puerto Rican' creates a clever neologism that when enunciated sounds like the statement 'I'm a Rican', thus marking the biculturalism of the subject. The Revolving Door motif is captured in the following lines from the poem whose title shares the same name as the book:

> AmeRícan across forth and across back
> back across and forth back
> forth across and back and forth
> our trips are walking bridges! (94)

The back-and-forth travel of Puerto Ricans between the island and the mainland is presented as a positive force. Their journeys, like bridges, link peoples and cultures together, promoting empathy, tolerance, and diversity.

In *Mainstream Ethics* (1989), the theme of migration is portrayed as a spiritual journey in 'migración'. The poem is written primarily in Spanish and integrates the lyrics of Noel Estrada's famous ballad, 'En mi Viejo San Juan', and the sad narrative of an elderly Puerto Rican man who is sitting on the steps of an abandoned building in the midst of winter. Referred to throughout the text as 'calavera' or skull, the disheartened, old man contemplates his decision to migrate to the US while singing and wishing he could return to Puerto Rico. But just as in Estrada's song, the dream never materializes: 'venimos para regresar,/ solamente nos quedamos/sentados en los stoops/porque el sueño se pudrió,/en la ilusión de los huecos/de un edificio abandonado' (we come to return/only we stay/sitting on the stoops/because the dream rotted/in the illusion of the holes of an abandoned building) (38). Only by singing Estrada's song can the old man go back to his birthplace to rest, for 'nadie quería morirse en américa' (nobody wanted to die in America) (38). This desire to return to Puerto Rico before dying is also tied to the Revolving Door motif and can be found in numerous memoirs published by US Puerto Rican writers since the 1980s.

Edward Rivera's *Family Installments: Memories of Growing Up Hispanic* (1982) opens and closes in the small, mountain village of Puerto Rico where the author was born. The narrative recounts the Rivera family's history in Bautabarro and their eventual trek to New York City. Unlike many immigrant memoirs, however, Rivera's story is in large part one of return migration. Toward the end of the book, the narrator's older brother moves back to the island upon obtaining a lucrative position as a croupier at one of San Juan's most exclusive hotel casinos, and his parents soon follow. When Rivera's father can no longer work owing to a debilitating disease, he and his wife leave New York for Puerto Rico so that he may die in his place of birth. Thus, a great portion of the book focuses on the island. The vision of Puerto Rico that Rivera presents varies from beginning to end. At first, Bautabarro is rendered as a poor, illiterate town, a 'tangle of weeds' and *barro* or mud where there is little hope for social and economic advancement, while New York is idealized as the land of wealth. But this latter vision of the mainland dissolves quickly after the protagonist's father moves to East Harlem and cannot earn enough money to send for his wife and children for over a year. The family's neighbors and acquaintances experience similar hardships: 'Then there were the rumors spread by people who had friends and relatives living in Nueva York. These friends and relatives wrote back dismal descriptions of the places where they lived and worked. Apparently the devil himself had moved to Nueva York and was working overtime there' (67). Yet while the American dream eludes his parents, it does not escape from the author, for New York is the place where the protagonist obtains both a college education and a graduate degree, feats that may not have been possible to achieve had he stayed in Bautabarro. When he eventually goes back to the island for his father's funeral, Rivera also returns to his village. The topography of Bautabarro, which at the start of the story is portrayed as inhospitable, is somewhat romanticized in the end, even though Rivera finds it only vaguely familiar and soon returns to New York. The island, with its geography and memories, then becomes the primary source of material for the book. The depiction of both the island and the mainland, however, is one of ambiguity.

In their collection of autobiographical essays and poems entitled, *Getting Home Alive* (1986), Aurora Levins Morales and her mother Rosario Morales also present Puerto Rico, as well as the Revolving Door pattern of migration, with ambivalence. Although a longing for the island and its culture is prevalent throughout the text, there is also a yearning to be on the mainland, for its diversity and for the freedom and autonomy women have in the United States. For example, in 'Immigrants', Aurora Levins Morales pays homage to her Puerto Rican and Russian-Jewish heritage and traces her family's journeys from Puerto Rico and the Ukraine to New York. The story of her Puerto Rican grandparents is one of return-migration; they left for New York in 1929, but retired in Puerto Rico, fulfilling her grandfather's dream. The narrator's grandmother, however, 'longs for New York or some other US city where a woman can go out and about on her own, live among many voices speaking different languages, out of the stifling air of that house, that community, that family' (23). In contrast to the open and independent lifestyle of the mainland, Puerto Rican society is portrayed as a suffocating environment that confines women to their husbands and homes. Though Rosario Morales provides in 'Hace tiempo' a nostalgic and rather idealized account of leaving her native New York with her husband to live temporarily in Puerto Rico, she expresses a strong desire to return to the mainland in 'Puerto Rico Journal', a diary that records her thoughts during a trip back to Puerto Rico and in which she reflects upon whether the island or the mainland is home. Similar to Rivera's experience upon returning to his hometown of Bautabarro, Rosario Morales finds that her house no longer exists, except in her imagination. What has not changed on the island, however, are women's roles:

> I come here and say this is too much like home for comfort, too many people nagging, harping, pushing you into line, into feminine behavior, into caution and fear, provocativeness and manipulativeness, full of predatory males who punish you for being female. Little freedom of thought and action, freedom to expand, grow, dare to do something different, to change. Not for my parents' daughter. (80)

Rosario Morales's observations of the narrow and stifling female gender roles and behaviors imposed upon women in Puerto Rico lead her to identify more with New York, her place of birth, despite her strong allegiance to the island. But mother and daughter do not choose one place over the other to call home; instead, they invent a new Puerto Rico for themselves. In 'Puertoricanness', Aurora Levins Morales recreates the island in Northern California. The author describes an awakening and hunger to reconnect with Puerto Rico; she does so by transforming her home in Oakland into a Puerto Rican household, surrounding herself with sounds, scents, and images that remind her of the island: the crow of a rooster, the aromas of Puerto Rican food, and the green foliage of tropical plants. The longing for Puerto Rico and the need for independence are reconciled by transforming the island, as a physical and a literary space. This transformation is a key element in the writings of Puerto Rican women in the US, as also seen in the autobiographical and fictional works of Carmen de Monteflores, Nicholasa Mohr, Judith Ortiz Cofer, and Esmeralda Santiago, all of whom were born on the island and moved to the mainland, where they write mainly in English about Puerto Rico.

Carmen de Monteflores's novel *Singing Softly: Cantando bajito* (1989) is set entirely in Puerto Rico and narrated in the form of flashbacks. The protagonist, Meli, explores her memories of the island in an effort to understand her decision to migrate: 'I imagine myself here because I need to understand why I left the island. And why I didn't return' (4). Meli recalls life in her family's village of Bocarío and recounts the stories she learned as a child about her great grandmother, grandmother, and mother. The literary voyage is one of self-discovery: 'When I take Meli's hand, I walk into a world made real by longing. With her I recreate my closeness to abuelita. My veined hand becomes hers; Meli's small one is my own, reaching across time to hold, recognize, find home' (15). To comprehend why she left the island, the protagonist recreates the voices of three generations of women. At the end of the novel, Meli returns to the island for her grandmother's funeral and realizes the motive behind her voluntary exile: to escape the cycle of oppression, poverty, racism, and violence that the women in her family endured. Throughout the novel, the beauty of the Puerto Rican landscape is sharply contrasted to the harsh realities of the women in her life, who suffered grave injustices because of their gender, skin color, and class position. The mainland US only appears occasionally in the text in reference to Meli's departure from the island to attend art school in New York, but it is rendered, nonetheless, as a place of hope and an opportunity for change.

In contrast, Nicholasa Mohr's novels and short fiction relate the experiences of Puerto Ricans growing up and living in New York. In her much-cited essay entitled 'Puerto Rican Writers in the United States, Puerto Rican Writers in Puerto Rico: A Separation Beyond Language', Mohr distinguishes herself from writers on the island in the following manner: 'My birth makes me a native New Yorker. I write here in the United States about my personal experiences and those of a particular group of migrants that number in the millions' (87). Her first novel, *Nilda* (1973), is a *Bildungsroman* about a young adolescent girl growing up in New York City during World War II and captures the hardships and achievements of the members of her community. Mohr's short stories from *In Nueva York* (1977) are also set in New York's Puerto Rican *barrio*, though the characters often express a common yearning for Puerto Rico. In 'Old Mary' and 'Lali', Old Mary and her son Chiquitín wish to retire on the island, affirming that they do not want to die in New York. But in Mohr's *Rituals of Survival: A Woman's Portfolio* (1985), the island of Puerto Rico emerges as a complex and subversive literary trope. The book is a collection of six brief narratives of resistance, each dedicated to a particular woman. The book opens with 'Aunt Rosana's Rocker (Zoraida)', the provocative story of Zoraida, a woman living in the *barrio* as a housewife to a brutish husband and the mother of three children, who also gives birth to a stillborn child and suffers multiple miscarriages. A rocking chair in the couple's bedroom, which belonged to her aunt Rosana in Puerto Rico, is Zoraida's only escape from her insolent husband and dire home life:

> She had always had it, ever since she could remember. When she was a little girl, her parents told her it was a part of their history. Part of Puerto Rico and her great Aunt Rosana who was very beautiful and had countless suitors. The chair was made of oak with intricate carving and delicate caning. As a little girl, Zoraida used to rub her hands against the caning and woodwork admiringly, while she rocked, dreamed and pretended to her heart's content. Lately it had become the one place where she felt she could be herself, where she could really be free. (29)

The rocking chair symbolizes Puerto Rico and Zoraida's cultural heritage, but it also functions as an instrument through which the protagonist can acquire a sense of autonomy, feel peace, and obtain self-gratification. While sitting in the rocker, Zoraida experiences the joy of sex that she does not share with her husband. As Ellen McCracken has noted, the story 'pits patriarchal authority against a young woman's desire to control her sexuality; the protagonist Zoraida has transgressed dominant power relations by finding sexual pleasure alone, apart from her husband' (202). The only memory and object that Zoraida has left of Puerto Rico, the rocking chair, serves as a vehicle for freedom.

The island also provides the protagonist in Mohr's 'Happy Birthday (Lucia)' with a means of liberation. Lucia is a young, though sick woman who lives in a poorly run hospital outside of Manhattan with other terminally ill patients and compassionless and abusive nurses. As she lies in her deathbed waiting for her absent lover to visit on her birthday, she reflects upon her childhood in Sierra de Luquillo, the mountain village of Puerto Rico that she left behind after taking a job as a maid for a wealthy Puerto Rican family who then moved to New York. Lucia remembers her distant relatives and first love and summons images of the riverbed in her hometown:

> Lucia stepped into the river and felt the water envelop her. She turned and swam toward the deeper part. Slowly, and without any resistance, Lucia let the current take her downstream and she drifted with the river into a journey of quiet bliss. (102)

As in 'Aunt Rosana's Rocker', Puerto Rico sets the protagonist free. By slipping deeper into the remembrance of the river, a metaphor for death, Lucia is able to alleviate her pain and leave the desolate and degrading environment of the hospital. The story also brings to mind Tato Laviera's poem 'migración'. Just as the old man sitting in front of the abandoned building is able to go back to Puerto Rico to die by singing a ballad, Lucia is able to end her life where it began, when she relives her memory of bathing in an island river.

While many of Mohr's characters seek freedom through highly imaginative renderings of Puerto Rico, the protagonists in the works of Judith Ortiz Cofer and Esmeralda Santiago do so by distancing themselves from the island. In her poetry, autobiographical writings, and novels, Ortiz Cofer explores both the gains and the losses that leaving and returning to the island offers Puerto Rican Americans, including her own self as a woman and a writer. In her poem 'Exile' from *Terms of Survival* (1987), she identifies Puerto Rico as an essential component of her work: 'I left my home behind me/but my past clings to my fingers/so that every word I write bears/the mark like a cancelled postage stamp/of my birthplace' (46). Also expressed in the poem's title and opening line, the theme of migration is another key element of her writing and appears in a variety of forms. Ortiz Cofer's first novel, *In the Line of the Sun* (1989), begins and ends in Puerto Rico, like Rivera's *Family Installments*. It is the return-migration story of the restless Guzmán, a precocious adolescent who leaves his hometown of Salud for New York and New Jersey in order to escape the strict moral codes of behavior that foil his love affair with La Cabra, a much older woman prostitute. Guzmán goes to the mainland in search of a better life only to encounter numerous misfortunes: he escapes a labor camp where he is kept as a prisoner, lives homeless in New York, and receives a nearly fatal stab wound, causing his body to permanently lean to one side. Never fulfilling his dream of returning to Puerto Rico a rich man, the jaded Guzmán does eventually go back to his village and marries Salud's most overly pious moralizer who ironically happens to be La Cabra's daughter.

Throughout *In the Line of the Sun*, Puerto Rico and New Jersey are both depicted as poor yet lively settings, replete with activity and people. Ortiz Cofer places many of her characters in *El Building*, a densely populated housing project in Patterson, New Jersey that resurfaces in her memoir, *Silent Dancing: A Partial Remembrance of a Puerto Rican Childhood* (1990). In both texts, *El Building* is a microcosm of the island, transported and recreated by the Puerto Ricans who live there through their music, food, language, and customs. Those who dwell there, such as Guzmán's sister, Ramona, and the author's mother, resist leaving the building, despite its dismal appearance and state, because of its cultural semblance to Puerto Rico. Even in Patterson, the island is at the center of the protagonists' worlds.

Ortiz Cofer's own memories of Puerto Rico shape her experiences in New Jersey in *Silent Dancing*, a memoir that masterfully captures the Revolving Door pattern of migration. The poems and vignettes that comprise the book trace her family's perpetual, back-and-forth travel between the island and New Jersey following her father's tours of duty with the Navy. Blending together recollections of her childhood, island myths and legends, her grandmother's stories, and the voices of many individuals whose lives touched hers, Ortiz Cofer reflects upon her development as a woman and a writer. The memoir concentrates on women's lives in Puerto Rico and in New Jersey, highlighting their trials and triumphs as well as their role in helping the author forge a new identity as a bicultural, Puerto Rican American woman.

Ortiz Cofer's more recent writings present migration as an opportunity for change and renewal. In the poem 'Arrival', from *Reaching for the Mainland* (1995), coming to the United States is likened to birth:

> When we arrived, we were expelled
> like fetuses
> from the warm belly of an airplane.
> Shocked by the cold,
> we held hands as we skidded
> like new colts on the unfamiliar ice. (26)

The mainland represents a place of new beginnings, rebirth, and reinvention. This view of migration is also at the center of Ortiz Cofer's 2003 novel, *The Meaning of Consuelo*, where moving to New York provides the characters the means to escape familial constraints and rigid societal norms regarding gender and sexuality. A concrete subdivision of San Juan called El Camino Terrace is the setting for much of the novel's action. Its endless rows of identical cement block houses reflect the imposing conformity of the Puerto Rican bourgeoisie of the 1950s. The narrator, a clever and independent teenage girl named Consuelo, recounts aspects of her life that threaten the norms and values dictated by Puerto Rican bourgeois society and lead to her becoming an outsider of her community. Consuelo's assertiveness during her first sexual encounter, her unshakable loyalty and friendship to her gay cousin, Patricio, and her sister Mili's mental illness and tragic disappearance place the protagonist in the role of social pariah. In the end, migration to the more diverse and tolerant environment of New York offers both Consuelo and Patricio a nurturing space to be themselves.

The move to the mainland is also rendered as a quest for change in the autobiographical writings and fiction of Esmeralda Santiago, whose female protagonists leave Puerto Rico in search of refuge and independence. Her coming-of-age memoir, *When I was Puerto Rican* (1994), documents her long journey from Macún, a small, rural village in Puerto Rico to New York City, where she earns a scholarship to the School of Performing Arts and later, entrance to Harvard University. The majority of the book takes place in Puerto Rico; Santiago, or Negi, as she is referred to throughout the text, remembers moving back and forth between Macún and the slums of San Juan following the turbulent pattern of her parents' tumultuous relationship, until migrating to the mainland with her mother and siblings. Initially, Santiago's mother goes to New York temporarily seeking treatment for her son's injured foot, which no one on the island is able to cure. There, she experiences an awakening that ultimately inspires her to leave her children's father, a non-committal and often absent mate. Negi describes her mother's metamorphosis in the following passage:

> (. . .) there was something new about her, a feeling I got from the way she talked, the way she moved. She had always carried herself tall, but now there was pride, determination, and confidence in her posture. Even her voice assumed a higher pitch that demanded to be heard. I was puzzled and frightened by this transformation but at the same time enthralled by it. (189)

Negi observes the assertiveness that her mother acquired during her stay in New York with trepidation, for although she sees her mother as more beautiful than ever before, the narrator also intuits that it will result in a more permanent life change. Negi remembers with bitterness the day she boarded an airplane for New York with her mother and siblings: 'For me, the person I was becoming when we left was erased, and another one was created. The Puerto Rican *jíbara*, who longed for the green quiet of a tropical afternoon, was to become a hybrid who would never forgive the uprooting' (209). At the same time, however, she recognizes that this hybridization also allowed her to break out of poverty and away from the subjugating female gender role that her mother fought so hard to escape by leaving Puerto Rico.

Conflicting views surrounding migration also appear in Santiago's two autobiographical sequels. In *Almost a Woman* (1998), readers learn that following ten difficult years in Brooklyn, the author's mother returns to Macún with her younger children while Negi remains in the US. The third book to form what is for the moment an autobiographical triptych, *The Turkish Lover* (2004) describes Santiago's own return to the island after thirteen years, 'having exceeded even the most optimistic expectations for a poor girl from a huge family raised by a single mother under the most challenging conditions in a hostile culture and environment' (337). But the author notes that the years spent in the US and her education have transformed her. Like Rivera in *Family Installments*, Santiago finds that many aspects of her hometown, as etched in her memory, either do not exist or are no longer familiar. Yet the island, real or imagined, remains the primary source of her artistic production.

Set initially in Vieques, a small islet located off the east coast of Puerto Rico, Santiago's 1996 novel, *América's Dream*, presents a harsh though triumphant story of migration to the mainland. The main protagonist is a woman who, like the author's mother, dreams of a better life for herself and her child. A hotel housekeeper, América González, resides in a small house with her alcoholic mother, her abusive lover, Correa, and their teenage daughter, Rosalinda. At the beginning of the novel, América's mother Ester announces that the 14-year-old Rosalinda has run away with a boy, and América fears that her daughter is destined to repeat her mother and grandmother's same mistakes. Then América's life changes drastically. Following years of emotional and physical abuse, the protagonist is presented with the opportunity to leave Correa upon receiving a job offer to work as a nanny for an American couple from Westchester, New York. Despite the warnings that América receives from return migrants living in Vieques who tell her of cockroach-infested slums, incessant crime, and endless poverty in New York, she flees Puerto Rico out of fear for her life, as her lover's beatings have become increasingly more violent.

In Westchester, the protagonist of *América's Dream* leads a relatively peaceful and luxurious lifestyle, taking care of two children and visiting the Bronx by train during her time off, where she discovers the Puerto Rican community, a replica of the island she left behind. But América's tranquil existence in the suburbs of New York City is short lived. Her estranged lover tracks her down and nearly ends her life; América survives only by killing Correa first. After the attack, the protagonist moves to the Bronx, obtains a job as a hotel housekeeper in Manhattan, and sends for her daughter whom she was forced to leave behind in Puerto Rico. The cycle of teenage pregnancy, abandonment, alcoholism, and violence that América feared would claim Rosalinda is broken as mother and daughter create a new life for themselves in New York. In the end, the protagonist's American dream, alluded to in the novel's title, is fulfilled, therefore presenting a positive view of migration to the mainland.

Representing an array of viewpoints, genres, and styles, US Puerto Rican literature continues to flourish in the twenty-first century. Amid this diversity, however, these texts are united in their embodiment of Puerto Rico, as writers continue to find inspiration in the island. Whether its serves as a medium to create a fictionalized or lost paradise, to produce experimental art, to manifest a state of being, or depict an economically or socially stifling locus, Puerto Rico, and its topography and culture, continue to nourish this growing corpus of American literature. At the same time, Puerto Rican writers of the US pay homage to the millions of individuals who travel through the Revolving Door, recording their histories, their struggles and their triumphs all over the mainland. This phenomenon of back-and-forth migration continues today, at the same time that a greater US Latino identity is being forged by people of diverse ethnicities and backgrounds, suggesting that a more kaleidoscopic, expansive literature will evolve, though it is likely that the island will remain a constant presence.

## Works Cited

Acosta-Belén, Edna. 'The Literature of the Puerto Rican Migration in the United States: An Annotated Bibliography', *ADE Bulletin*, 91 (1988), 56–62.
—— 'The Literature of the Puerto Rican Minority in the United States', *The Bilingual Review/La Revista Bilingüe*, 5:1–2 (1978), 107–16.
Aparicio, Frances. 'From Ethnicity to Multiculturalism: An Historical Overview of Puerto Rican Literature in the United States', in Francisco Lomelí, Nicolás Kanellos, and Claudio Esteva-Fabregat (eds.). *Handbook of Hispanic Cultures in the United States: Literature and Art*. Houston: Arte Público Press, 1993.
Barradas, Efraín. *Partes de un todo: Ensayos y notas sobre literatura puertorriqueña en los Estados Unidos*. San Juan: Editorial de la Universidad de Puerto Rico, 1998.
Fitzpatrick, Joseph P. *Puerto Rican Americans: The Meaning of Migration to the Mainland*. Englewood Cliffs, New Jersey: Prentice-Hall, Inc., 1971.

Hernández, Carmen Dolores. *Puerto Rican Voices in English: Interviews with Writers*. Westport, Connecticut: Praeger Publishers, 1997.
Hernández Cruz, Victor. *Maraca: New and Selected Poems, 1966–2000*. Minneapolis: Coffee House Press, 2001.
Laviera, Tato. *AmeRícan*. Houston: Arte Público Press, 1985.
—— *Enclave*. 1981. Houston: Arte Público Press, 1985.
—— *La Carreta Made a U-Turn*. 1979. Houston: Arte Público Press, 1992.
—— *Mainstream Ethics (ética corriente)*. Houston: Arte Público Press, 1989.
McCracken, Ellen. 'Latina Narrative and Politics of Signification: Articulation, Antagonism, and Populist Rupture', *Crítica: A Journal of Critical Essays*, 2:2 (1990), 202–7.
Mohr, Eugene V. *The Nuyorican Experience: Literature of the Puerto Rican Minority*. Westport, Connecticut: Greenwood Press, 1982.
Mohr, Nicholasa. *In Nueva York*. New York: Dial Press, 1977.
—— *Nilda*. New York: Harper & Row, 1973
—— 'Puerto Rican Writers in the United States, Puerto Rican Writers in Puerto Rico: A Separation Beyond Language', *The Americas Review*, 15:2 (1987), 87–92.
—— *Rituals of Survival: A Woman's Portfolio*. Houston: Arte Público Press, 1985.
Monteflores, Carmen de. *Singing Softly: Cantando bajito*. San Francisco: Spinsters/Aunt Lute Book Co., 1989.
Morales, Rosario, and Aurora Levins Morales. *Getting Home Alive*. Ithaca, New York: Firebrand Books, 1986.
Ortiz Cofer, Judith. *In the Line of the Sun*. Athens: University of Georgia Press, 1989.
—— *Reaching for the Mainland & Selected New Poems*. Tempe, Arizona: Bilingual Press/Editorial Bilingüe, 1995.
—— *Silent Dancing: A Partial Remembrance of a Puerto Rican Childhood*. Houston: Arte Público Press, 1990.
—— *Terms of Survival*. Houston: Arte Público Press, 1987.
—— *The Meaning of Consuelo*. New York: Farrar, Straus, and Giroux, 2003.
Pérez y González, María E. *Puerto Ricans in the United States*. Westport, Connecticut: Greenwood Press, 2000.
Rivera, Carmen S. *Kissing the Mango Tree: Puerto Rican Women Rewriting American Literature*. Houston: Arte Público Press, 2002.
Rivera, Edward. *Family Installments: Memories of Growing Up Hispanic*. New York: Morrow, 1982.
Sánchez González, Lisa. *Boricua Literature: A Literary History of the Puerto Rican Diáspora*. New York: New York University Press, 2001.
Santiago, Esmeralda. *Almost a Woman*. Reading, Massachusetts: Perseus Books, 1998.
—— *América's Dream*. New York: HarperCollins, 1996.
—— *The Turkish Lover*. Cambridge, Massachusetts: Da Capo Press, 2004.
—— *When I was Puerto Rican*. New York: Vintage Books, 1994.
Thomas, Piri. *Down These Mean Streets*. New York: Alfred A. Knopf, 1967.

## 4

## Am I Who I Am?: Identity Games in US Cuban Literature

### JORGE FEBLES

During the past two decades, scholars from diverse disciplines have published a remarkable amount of academic research on the Cuban diasporic subject and, by extension, on the sidebar issue of *Cubanía*, particularly as it impacts Cuban-American identity. When perusing even superficially the many articles, collections of essays and books centering on transnationalism, diasporic commonalities, and transculturation,[1] I am invariably struck by the frequency with which authors explore their own *Weltanschauung* and life experiences in order to generalize about *The Cuban Condition*, to employ Gustavo Pérez Firmat's oft-quoted title. Since its appearance in 1989, this perceptive incursion into national idiosyncracies as well as the transcultural and translational nature of Cuban culture has become required reading for scholars who broach the topic of *Cubanía* as immanent identity marker. Despite the academic rigor evident in Pérez Firmat's monograph, like many other probers into the question, he posits premises in his introduction that underscore a subjective approach to the issue. He explains, for instance:

> It pleases me to think that *The Cuban Condition*, with its concentration on things Cuban and its indulgence in oral metaphors, has something of the flavor

---

[1] I refer to texts such as Miguel González-Pando's *The Cuban Americans*, Ruth Behar's and Juan León's special issues of the *Michigan Quarterly Review* titled *Bridges to Cuba / Puentes a Cuba*, María de los Ángeles Torres's *By Heart / De memoria: Cuban Women's Journeys In and Out of Exile*, Román de la Campa's *Cuba on My Mind: Journeys to a Severed Nation*, Damián J. Fernández's and Madeline Cámara Betancourt's *Cuba, the Elusive Nation: Interpretations of National Identity*, María Cristina García's *Havana USA: Cuban Exiles and Cuban Americans in South Florida, 1959–1994*, Juan Pablo Ballester's, María Elena Escalona's and Iván de la Nuez's, *Cuba: la isla posible*, Andrea O'Reilly Herrera's *Re-Membering Cuba: Legacy of a Diaspora*, Rafael Rojas's *Isla sin fin*, Ambrosio Fornet's *Memorias recobradas* and, of course, Gustavo Pérez Firmat's seminal works, *Life on the Hyphen: The Cuban-American Way* and *Next Year in Cuba: A Cubano's Coming of Age in America*. These are but a few of the books written on the subject during the period 1990–2005. Of course, countless essays focusing on the theme have appeared in academic journals, newspapers, and magazines.

of an *ajiaco criollo* (Cuban stew). But then as now, my fundamental interest lies in the complicated intercourse between New World and Old World culture, and more particularly, in how Cuban texts rewrite some of the masterworks of the Spanish and European literary tradition. Thus, I hope that my discussion will be of use not only to students of Cuban literature but also to those interested in the broader issues of national and continental identity (14).

Delving into the works of Fernando Ortiz, Nicolás Guillén, Eugenio Florit, Carlos Loveira, Luis Felipe Rodríguez and Alejo Carpentier, Pérez Firmat initiates a quest to inscribe Cubans – and by extension himself as an individual born in Cuba though raised in the US – within more or less fixed, if quite peculiar, cultural paradigms. The fact that he dedicates the book to an all-embracing 'us' (v) that transcends borders further highlights his personal quest, which is dynamically complemented by the following lamentation: 'As a "native" Cuban who has spent all of his adult life away from the island, the notion of "Cuban" voice is for me as alluring as it is problematic. A Cuban voice is what I wish I had, and what I may never have' (14). Given the aura of probability that it adds to the dictum, this emphasis on the 'may' problematizes authorial self-doubts. Pérez Firmat writes about Cuba to endure, to justify himself as critic and as cultural entity. He asserts with regard to the persistent analytical motif of his work:

> My desire to demonstrate the centrality of translation in Cuban criollist literature cannot but reflect an attempt to legitimize and place my own work. By trying to define the tone and timbre of a certain Cuban voice, I am trying also to define my own voice, to explore my own means and possibilities of survival as a writer, and even as a Cuban writer (15).

Hence, Pérez Firmat implies that at the core of his inquiry into *the Cuban condition* lies an exploration of his private *Cuban condition* or lack thereof. This propensity to look outwards and inwards at once underlies not only a substantial portion of recent investigations into the matter of the deterritorialized subject as relevant other within discourse pertaining to the nation or transnation, but also a sizable amount of creative work produced by US Cuban authors.

Numerous meditations on transnational *Cubanía* wax vehemently on how the concept of displaced nationhood develops into a feeling, an attitude that manifests itself in literature, in the visual arts, in daily deportment and social interaction, in life itself and quite concretely in the lives of individuals of Cuban ancestry who came of age in the US or indeed were born in it. To a substantial degree, they affirm both critically and experientially what James Clifford has termed 'the main features of diaspora: a history of dispersal, myths/memories of the homeland, alienations in the host (bad host?) country, desire for eventual return, ongoing support of the homeland, and a collective identity importantly defined by this relationship' (305). In fact, Clifford's hypotheses, developed upon those espoused earlier by William Safran, inform at least partly appraisals of diasporic identity conducted by many cultural critics including Ruth Behar,

Andrea O'Reilly Herrera, Isabel Álvarez Borland, Adriana Méndez Rodenas, Antonio Vera León, and Eliana Rivero.

In 2001, O'Reilly Herrera edited *ReMembering Cuba: Legacy of a Diaspora*, an indispensable book in order to decipher what I have called in a slightly irreverent manner the 'Am I Who I Am?' syndrome. As the dueling capitals imply, this heterogeneous gathering of memories means to constitute a coherent (or better yet, a purposely incoherent) portrait of transnational subjects in order to authenticate their voices, recollections, and struggles, thereby inscribing them at least as *others* in the historiographic discourse pertaining to the Caribbean island in question. Such an endeavor supposes an arbitrary postmodern leap, since deterritorialized Cubans have assiduously been described as *voiced* entities whose *devoicing* would appear necessary so as to facilitate the country's harmonious evolution within the family of nations. O'Reilly Herrera refutes such a radical appraisal by providing informants representative of different ages, stages of assimilation, educational background, political inclinations and so forth, a place to expound on their life experiences. The ruling principle behind the book resides solely in a willingness by collaborators to discuss their peculiar sense of *Cubanía* as well as their perceptions of the island they forsook or were forced to abandon as adults or children, or to which they envision themselves innately linked because of heritage. This collection expands on Pérez Firmat's imagined need to examine *self* as the starting point to define *ourselves* within the confines of unnatural spaces, and quite specifically in this instance, of the US.

*ReMembering Cuba*'s testimonial nature, indicative of ideological inclinations and sentimental peculiarities vividly shared or ardently rejected by the ideal readers for whom the text seems intended (that is to say, either members of the described collectivity or anthropologically inclined voyeurs), leads to the question that will guide my critical approach in this chapter. 'To what extent are these testimonies . . . the unavoidable byproduct of an externally induced play spirit whereby individuals surrender to a self-induced *ilinx* or temporary "state of dizziness and disorder"?' (Caillois, 12). Johan Huizinga comments when applying to poetry his theories on games:

> (Play) is an activity which proceeds within certain limits of time and space, in a visible order, according to rules freely accepted, and outside the sphere of necessity or material utility. The play-mood is one of rapture and enthusiasm, and is sacred or festive in accordance with the occasion. A feeling of exaltation and tension accompanies the action, mirth and relaxation follow. (132)

I intuit a similar bent on a collection in which commentators must partake of a self-exploratory game in accordance with pre-established conditions while sharing an identical playing field. In every instance, individuals are required to describe themselves as selves framed within or outside a community that shares one commonality: Cuban ancestry. They must do so also in relationship to place, to the dual or even multiple arenas that they have chosen or been forced to inhabit, and against place: the forsaken land mass and cultural environment where, at least imaginedly, play may have been exercised differently. Rather than a multi-voiced carnivalesque narrative, what emerges from such a restrictive recipe is a somewhat monologic[2] artifact in which the repetitive discourse resembles on occasion the act of bearing witness at an evangelical church. Yet, this stratagem proves fruitful not only within the scope of *ReMembering Cuba* but also in the more complex identity games played within the US by writers of Cuban descent.

Given the nature of this chapter, I will not strive to supplement the plethora of thoroughly documented interpretations of *Cubanness* or *Cuban-Americanness* produced by Rivero, Pérez Firmat, Behar, Rojas, O'Reilly Herrera, Damián Fernández, Duany, Méndez Rodenas, Fowler Calzada, Fornet, and de la Nuez, to name but a few of the scholars who have explored the topic. Instead, I propose to dialogue succinctly with the personalistic discourse on which some of them found their approximations to the identity question. While doing so, my objective is to complicate further what, to me, have become schemes emanating from postmodern critical paradigms. At times it may appear that I assume the cynical outlook toward national or for that matter transnational identity that Rojas has ascribed to Julián del Casal, Virgilio Piñera, and Reinaldo Arenas, master builders of a nihilistic counter-discourse that refutes the paradigmatic 'metarrelato identificatorio' ('La diferencia', 39), or metanarration that espouses the motif of a coherent Cuban identity. This nation-building construct is crafted on the basis of unifying images detailed by Martí in texts such as 'La cuestión racial' (The Race Question), 'Mi raza' (My Race) and 'Nuestra América' (Our America), often epigrammatized lyrically by him also in lines such as the following, from a rhymed letter to Néstor Ponce de León (dated 21 October 1889): 'En la patria de mi amor/quisiera yo ver nacer/el pueblo que puede ser,/sin odios y sin color' (I would like to see born/in my beloved homeland/an ideal nation/devoid of hatred and racial differences (*Gran enciclopedia*, 12, 173)). Nonetheless, rather than subverting in parodic fashion extremely valid inquisitions into nationality and the manner in which the individual Cuban-American perceives himself or herself within the US both as member of a collectivity and as sentient persona, I intend to define this identity quest as a fertile trope that has produced a vast literary corpus, described in detailed fashion by Álvarez Borland in her seminal study, *Cuban-American Literature of Exile: From Person to Persona* as well as by Carlos Espinosa Domínguez in his more recent *El peregrino en comarca ajena* (The Pilgrim in Alien Lands).

While pursuing my objective, I will focus somewhat arbitrarily on selected authors and texts that evince discovery *games* founded on the 'Am I Who I Am?' theme. Throughout I will argue that the identity metanarrative formulated or augmented by specific writers of Cuban descent, who view themselves explicitly or implicitly as part of a transnational continuum, evolves to a substantial

---

[2] Mikhail Bakhtin, *Problems of Dostoevsky's Poetics*, ed. and trans. Caryl Emerson (Minneapolis: University of Minnesota Press, 1984), 82.

degree from their ludic instinct, that is to say, from a desire to play in a most sacred sphere: the realm of ego-centered imagination. As such, when tangling emotionally with the trope authors succumb to the subjacent *gravitas* of the play spirit. As Huizinga attests:

> The consciousness of play being 'only a pretend' does not by any means prevent it from proceeding with the utmost seriousness, with an absorption, a devotion that passes into rapture and, temporarily at least, completely abolishes that troublesome 'only' feeling. Any game can at any time wholly run away with the players. (8)

Scriptural rapture and passionate endeavors to understand one's persona by understanding the collectivity that shaped it, therefore, coalesce in a substantial amount of Cuban-American writing. They lie at the core of romantic or ironic efforts to play *at being*, to regret *not being* and to reposition characters (and by extension authors) in a place – mythic, holy, or crudely *real* – where full realization or complete self-awareness may have been achievable under given circumstances.

When Heredia wrote in exile melancholic lines such as 'Las palmas ¡ay! las palmas deliciosas' (The palm trees, oh!, the delicious palms) (165) or '¡Mi patria! . . . ¡Oh Sol! Mi suspirada Cuba' (My country! . . . Oh Sun! The Cuba I yearn for) (160), he echoed in *Cuban* the Ovidian longing for the homeland also prevalent in other displaced nineteenth-century writers including Mercedes de Santa Cruz y Montalvo (Condesa de Merlín), Gertrudis Gómez de Avellaneda, and, of course, José Martí. The latter perpetuated in national and transnational letters the idea of the self perpetually alienated on a ground never wholly his. Aphorisms akin to 'Fuera de la patria, si piedras negras se reciben de ella, de las piedras negras parece que sale luz de astro!' (When living outside the native land, if one receives black stones sent from there, the black stones seem to emit a starry light!) (*Amistad*, 12, 154) convey the archetypal exilic nostalgia that inspired a number of insightful autobiographical texts. Pablo Medina's *Exiled Memories*, Pérez Firmat's *Next Year in Cuba*, Virgil Suárez's *Spared Angola: Memories of a Cuban Childhood*, Carlos Eire's *Waiting for Snow in Havana: Memories of a Cuban Boy*, and Román de la Campa's *Cuba on My Mind*, for example, reproduce in contrasting manner the Ovidian attachment to place that, according to Pérez Firmat (*Cincuenta lecciones*, 30), is endemic to *the Cuban condition* of a deterritorialized transcultural people.

Yet, for the most part neither these autobiographers nor the other writers to whom I will refer in this chapter concern themselves with a national recovery project similar to the one desired by Martí and other nineteenth-century foundational narrators. Rather, as Pérez Firmat has also asserted, their Ovidian anguish blends with – indeed, may be even superseded by – a Plutarchian volition to find solace under different suns. Most Cuban-American authors achieve this ambiguous state by assimilating, at least, partially quite distinct cultural mores and by replicating always *foreign* sounds and letters so accurately that they truly may appear to be entirely what they speak, and more specifically what they write. After all, writing – particularly at its most dynamic and superficially evocative level – is a controlled enterprise that entwines linguistic and cultural experiences. It is not the byproduct of one's life but of one's lives, whether they transpire exclusively in one particular region (Emily Dickinson), or nation (Lezama Lima), or multiple habitats (Nabokov, Joyce, Arenas, Sarduy). The confessional tone assumed almost inevitably by those who deal with personal and collective identity in fictional, theatrical or poetic ventures more often than not results from the skillful manipulation of words and feelings. Consequently, a spirit of play – of serious play to be sure, but play still – distinguishes Cuban-American creative discussions of identity. By juxtaposing explicitly or implicitly Ovidian suffering and Plutarchan content or perhaps resignation, bicultural writers convey a schizophrenic duality that allows them to probe confessionally into themselves and critically, lovingly or parodically into the collectivity whence they emerged.

Members of the so-called one-and-a-half generation, that is, children born in Cuba but educated and culturally shaped in the US, have deftly exploited the identity riddle. According to Pérez Firmat, their inherent biculturalism suggests an unresolvable dichotomy: 'One-and-a-halfers are no more American than they are Cuban – and vice versa. Their hyphen is a seesaw: it tilts one way, then another' (*Life*, 6). These 'Cubanglos', as the critic also designates them, 'gain in translation. One-and-a-halfers feed on what they lack. Their position as equilibrists gives them the freedom to mix and match pieces from each culture: they are "equi-libre" ' (*Life*, 7).[3] Pérez Firmat's somewhat rosy outlook – which he contradicts after a fashion in subsequent texts such as the lyrically bittersweet *Cincuenta lecciones de exilio y desexilio* (Fifty Lessons on Exile and Un-Exile) – confirms an inescapable truism: Cuban-Americans are what they are now, not what they once were nor what they would wish to be. Yet, their felt or contrived duality lends itself to doubts pertaining to issues of territorial and cultural attachment that vary in intensity depending upon the individual. This readily textualized 'Cubangst', as Eliana Rivero so aptly designated it, has inspired most identity games played by Diasporic writers.

Pablo Medina corroborates in light-hearted manner the prior assessment's validity. While questing for (or questioning) his identity, he compares himself to Aeneas, an uprooted wanderer destined to feel permanently out of place. In Medina's case, Cuba – 'the geography of origins' ('Where', 234) – is forever irretrievable. Miami, on the other hand, represents a contaminated ambience that belies true Cubanness, and New York is merely a residential site, a not entirely hospitable abode. Therefore, Medina inserts himself in a much larger and

---

[3] This impression may very well apply to members of a subsequent generation that Pérez Firmat characterizes as CBAs (Cuban-Bred Americans) and Andrea O'Reilly Herrera far more lyrically names 'The Lost Generation'. As the children of exiled Cubans who were born in the US, members of this group generally struggle with identity questions akin to those experienced by the 'one-and-a-halfers'.

welcoming home: 'There is, after all, Western civilization, from which I dangle like a spider suspended over the void, and books to write, and people to love. Aeneas did not have an easy life, but a meaningful one. That is good enough for me. *Ciao'* ('Where', 235). His playful solution to exilic turmoil, which replicates Rushdie's claim in 'Imaginary Homelands' to be recognized as an 'international writer' endowed with the pleasant freedom of the literary migrant to 'choose his parents' (21), comprises another facet of the identity game.

For that reason too, Carlota Caulfield – a writer once removed from Medina because of her Cuban education – can view her image fragmented in a prism that transforms her into a gleefully multi-hyphenated woman ('Even Names', 240), destined to be forever foreign on the island of her birth and in the US. Like Medina, Caulfield finds her identity precisely in her creative gift, which she relates to the forsaken birthplace. 'Live and invent,' she avers. 'Be a Cuban and keep inventing as a way of survival' ('Even Names', 240). To retain this connection, she exercises consciously her *tongue ties*, embracing Spanish to add 'substance to her art' ('Even Names', 241), while clinging to childhood memories and ancestral diversity as mechanisms that guarantee self-recognition. Hers is a wandering intellect able to produce books like *A las puertas de papel con amoroso fuego (At the Paper Gates with Burning Desire)*, in which – a woman finding herself in women – she dialogues poetically not only with the 'tres lindas cubanas' (three beautiful Cubans), the Condesa de Merlín, Gertrudis Gómez de Avellaneda, and Juana Borrero, but also with Lucrezia Borgia, Flora Tristán, an Inca virgin dedicated to the Sun, George Sand, Gabriela Mistral, Frida Kahlo, and Anaïs Nin among others. Aimée G. Bolaños synthetizes cogently Caulfield's project:

> Sus cartas, a la vez que componen artísticamente una diversidad de sujetos femeninos, tienen como hilo de engarce una búsqueda de sí misma en el seno de diferentes culturas, de diversas historias, enunciaciones y modos de creación, una mirada cosmopolita que alimenta el imaginario propio, participando en la construcción de subjetividades culturales de poderosa identidad discursiva. (78–9)
>
> (Her letters, at the same time that they forge a variety of feminine subjects, hold in common a personal quest for self amidst different cultures, histories, patterns of enunciation and creative modes, a cosmopolitan outlook that feeds her own imaginary while partaking in the construction of cultural subjectivities enriched by a powerful discursive identity.)

As Bolaños notes, by pursuing such a heterogeneous self-affirmation, by playing such a complex self-defining game, Caulfield stretches identity to the maximum nationalistic paradigms in ways endemic to Cuban literary history, thus embroiling accepted transcultural hypotheses.

In *Cuban-American Literature of Exile*, Álvarez Borland divides into two groups those authors who labor in the US. A '*first generation* of writers', she states, 'left Cuba as adults and were fully educated on the island' (6). Álvarez

Borland describes this coterie as 'multilayered' because it includes older authors who left during the 1960s or somewhat later, such as Nováa Calvo, Hilda Perera, Benítez Rojo, Montes-Huidobro, and Heberto Padilla, as well as members of the so-called 'Mariel Generation' like Reinaldo Arenas, Carlos Victoria, Reinaldo García Ramos, and Jesús J. Barquet. The second group she subdivides for analytical expediency. Following Pérez Firmat's terminology, Borland refers to the '*one-and-a-half generation*', conventionally defined as 'a subgroup of writers who left Cuba during their early adolescence and thus had Cuban childhoods and US adulthoods' (7). Although many have opted for English as their language of choice, '(t)hey feel that the content and the spirit of their works make them Cuban writers. They are both Cuban and American, or perhaps they are neither' (Álvarez Borland, 8). The ensuing subcategory consists of 'younger writers who came from Cuba as infants or who were born in the United States to parents of the first exile generation' (Álvarez Borland, 8).

Álvarez Borland attests that such

> *Cuban-American ethnic writers* (. . .) have moved further away from Spanish since some of them learned English and Spanish simultaneously as young children. Others (. . .) never really mastered the Spanish language, although they heard it in their homes from their parents and relatives. These authors write simultaneously for an American and Cuban audience (8).

In a sense, she subsumes this inharmonious group in an overarching classification whose axis is Oscar Hijuelos, an older writer of Cuban descent, and whose most representative figure is Cristina García.

For brevity's sake, the second segment of this chapter will focus mainly on the manner in which selected members of the *second generation* confront textually the issue of transnational *Cubanía*, that is to say, on the manner in which certain writers still problematize cultural or national identity as trope in their work despite having resided in the US for decades or, indeed, having been born there. As has already become transparent, my commentary will not pursue a chronological or progressive approach. Rather, I will intersperse allusions to particular authors and works as called for by the issues upon which my impressions evolve.

A number of contemporary critics have postulated that the question of an all-embracing *Cubanía* dwells at the core of the island's intellectual evolution. Rojas, for instance, avers that 'el grueso de la discursividad sobre cultura cubana raras veces se ha desenmarcado del metarrelato de la identidad-sintesis' (rarely has the bulk of Cuban cultural discourse deviated from the identity as synthesis metanarrative) ('La diferencia', 37). Meanwhile, Iván de la Nuez contends that national identity as the great theme conceived by the liberal creole bourgoisie, despite its *unscientific* nature, has prospered in the chauvinistic discourse of post-revolutionary Cuba (26–7). It is this 'ferocious sense of national identity one encounters in Cubans' (de la Campa 10) that, according to Román de la Campa, has transformed Miami for countless Cuban-Americans into 'a nation within a nation, a control tower of resistance against undesired influences – most of the time from Cuba, but occasionally from the United States' (10). Not surprisingly, therefore, with marked frequency, Cuban-American writers have replicated this hyperbolic identity sense or quest, translating it as fundamental creative trope.

Virgil Suárez's poetry exemplifies vividly the strength inherent in such a metaphorical endeavor. Born in 1962, Suárez left Cuba for Spain with his parents in 1970. Four years later, the family settled in Los Angeles, California. A 'one-and-a-halfer' who handles dexterously both his adopted and his native languages, Suárez chooses to write almost exclusively in English. Yet, practically all his books, be they fiction, non-fiction or poetry, echo that preoccupation with *Cubanía* associated with identity games. Two of his poetry anthologies are named *In the Republic of Longing* and *Palm Crows*, while others include poems like 'La tempestad de las palabras blancas' (A Tempest of White Words), 'How the Days Go in the Tropics', 'The Kaleidoscopic Nature of Irascible Palms', '*Carbonero*' (Coalman), 'Prospero in Havana' (all from *Guide to the Blue Tongue*), 'Adolescencia' (Adolescence), '*Gusano* at the Hatuey Brewery', 'Benny Moré in the Heyday of My Father's Youth', 'Poem for Barbarito Diez'[4] and 'Cuban-American Gothic' (all found in *Banyan*).

'River Fable', Suárez's pathetic meditation on his father's death, illustrates the author's recurrent concern with his particular *Cuban condition*. The poem conveys dramatically an identity crisis exaggerated by the loss of a link not so much to an irretrievable past but to a forever inaccessible could-have-been, signaled by another's voice and memory. The disheartening poetic frame clarifies the negativity implied by this manifestation of the trope. 'This is about a Cuban boy who couldn't follow/the breadcrumbs home through a dense forest/to save his own life, or his father's, as both man/and boy stood by the river's edge' (*Banyan*, 3), the poetic voice explains initially, proceeding later to describe his father's demise. The poem concludes with a single line: 'This is about a Cuban boy who can never go home' (3). In a sense, the impossibility of going home transcends geography. Cuba as physical entity has been replaced for the Diasporic subject by the idealized, or created by an individual who lived it in a fashion perennially inaccessible to the poetic voice. Although not a particularly nostalgic writer in the saccharine vein, Suárez does imbue his verses with recollections of the island that associate him as much with the Cuban-American bicultural dilemma as with the ideological spectrum of those who consciously displaced themselves. In 'Urchins', a poem from *Palm Crows*, he compares his

---

[4] Some of the allusions employed by Suárez to ascertain Cubanness merit brief clarification. *Gusano* (Worm), a term often used by Martí with negative implications, is a pejorative appellation to designate counter-revolutionary Cubans within the island. Hatuey is the name of a Cuban beer now manufactured again in the United States by the Bacardi company. Benny Moré and Barbarito Diez were Cuban musical icons who became very popular during the 1940s and 1950s.

present condition with that of trapped echinoderms drying atop a fishing boat captured in a family photograph:

> dragged out, exposed, dying in the sun, much like what would happen to us in our own country, those of us called *gusanos*, the dissidents, those who quickly learned to live with less, in exile, for another forty years, I look at that picture of the urchin slaughter and my eyes burn, burn because I understand what it means to be away from the waters we call home. (*Palm Crows*, 29)

This defining exilic anxiety – deemed impossible by Fowler Calzada owing to the author's logical unawareness of island politics at the time of his departure[5] – is a significant manifestation of the identity games played by Suárez and other writers, both older and younger than he, who perceive displacement as a misfortune imposed by an unforgiving political system.

The 'Am I Who I Am?' syndrome that lies at the core of most Cuban-American identity games, so readily answered in modern Cartesian terms by enlarging the Ortega y Gasset dictum, 'I am I and my circumstances . . . wherever I may happen to reside',[6] promotes quite diverse texts marked by the omnipresence of conflicted egos. This *leit-motif* stems at least partly from the fact that the unresolvable anxiety it produces – the 'Cubangst' classified by Eliana Rivero – injects the Cuban Diasporic phenomenon into a postmodern and postcolonial discourse that characterizes the trans-nation as borders that expand, perpetually marking the individuals destined to inhabit it owing to an accident of birth or to inherited culture. *The Cuban condition* depicted in multiple creative works emanates from a permanent state of personal and even collective quasi-carnivalesque crisis whose precise source not even the Oracle at Delphi could accurately decipher. Rushdie, who shares a creative mindset with many Cuban-American authors, has described it as such:

> It may be that writers in my position, exiles, or emigrants or expatriates, are haunted by some sense of loss, some urge to reclaim, to look back, even at the risk of being mutated into pillars of salt. But if we do look back, we must also do so in the knowledge – which gives rise to profound uncertainties – that our physical alienation from India almost inevitably means that we will not be capable of reclaiming precisely the thing that we lost; that we will, in short,

---

[5] In his 'Miradas a la identidad en la literatura de la diáspora' (Gazing at Identity in the Literature of the Cuban Diaspora), Víctor Fowler Calzada refuses to apply the expression 'literature of exile' to the creative output of 'one-and-a-halfers' and CBAs. He justifies his position by referring to the designation's charged political implications. *La Habana Elegante*/www.habanaelegante.com (Summer 2001).

[6] My assertion coincides with Eliana Rivero's description of her cultural duality: 'I am a hybrid, a *puente,* a being of two places at once, but also of one *place* which is dual and fluid and rich. The anguish is gone; a sense of wholeness now presides over the process. I can recognize the nostalgia that I indulged in some years ago as part of the becoming; I can also see that I am what I am *(soy)* where I am *(estoy) – soy lo que soy donde estoy'* ('Fronterisleña', 673).

create fictions, not actual cities or villages, but invisible ones, imaginary homelands, Indias of the mind. (10)

Devoid of the certainty of place, the artist is torn internally as well when looking for self in space. Pérez Firmat, quintessential master of these identity games, abbreviated the dilemma quite nicely in a poem from *Equivocaciones*. 'Soy yos' (I am I's) he wrote in 1989, elucidating critically and fictionally in five subsequent books (*Life on the Hyphen*, *Next Year in Cuba*, *Cincuenta lecciones de exilio y desexilio*, *Anything but Love* and, it may be argued, in segments of *Tongue Ties*) why his split *I* may be employed as synecdoche for a particular generation, or for *the Cuban condition*, or perhaps even for all those dispersed writers to whom Rushdie refers. As an 'ajiaco of contradicciones' (stew of contradictions), this 'little square from Rubik's Cuba' (*Carolina*, 164) comes to terms with his hybridity, recognizing that – despite the pangs of absence from a site where he will never belong – his *place*, his personal territory, has been defined historically as well as culturally. Thus his admonition to 'one-and-a-halfers':

> What this generation has to come to understand is that, even though we may have been born in Cuba, we came of age in the United States, and that even though Cuba was our first abode, Miami is our permanent home. And that makes us *others*, different from Cubans and different from Americans. (*Para una*, 23–4)

Other writers within and without this particular generation, more susceptible to the crisis generated by separation from the coveted homeland, devise far more dramatic identity games. Pedro Monge Rafuls, who by age should be included among 'one-and-a-halfers' but who by avocation and life experiences may be described better as a *first generational* author, is a case in point. Although he has written plays in English like *Trash* – a dark drama dealing with a *marielito* forced by circumstances into male prostitution and the murder of a Catholic priest – and although since 1997 he has headed in New York City the OLLANTAY Center for the Arts, an organization dedicated primordially to the promotion of Hispanic theater, he perceives himself essentially as a Cuban writer in exile. Monge Rafuls has averred:

> Influenced by my condition as an exile in New York during the second half of the century. What is Cuban in me mixes with Anglo-American art and the art of the Latin American immigrants whom I have come to know well. My works, which are doubtlessly Cuban, emanate from these circumstances. ('Reflexiones', 50)

This volition to imbed his works in a Cuban literary tradition leads him to articulate identity games such as those played in his one-act piece *Recordando a mamá* (Remembering Mother). Alberto and Aurelia, brother and sister, both depicted as 'cincuentones marchitos' (withered fifty year-olds) (*Recordando*,

256), converse in sado-masochistic manner while they keep vigil next to their mother's casket at a Queens' funeral home. Their conversation unfolds around a lack of erotic, emotional, and personal fulfillment related implicity to the trauma of displacement, associated somewhat with the dead matron. Aurelia anathematizes the cadaver by screaming: 'No, you cannot be in Cuba. Your wishes couldn't have been fulfilled. I am absolutely sure that you are really hurting right now' (*Recordando*, 264). By implicitly equating Cuba and heaven, the character stresses the dominant identity motif: Human beings achieve wholeness exclusively in their home country. Any place but the motherland is hell for characters unable to cope with deterritorialization. Other plays by Monge Rafuls, including *Nadie se va del todo* (Nobody Leaves Entirely), perhaps his most important inquiry into *the Cuban condition*, espouse equally dynamic portrayals of the identity issue.

Writers such as Cristina García, emblematic of that generation of Cuban-Americans who migrated to the US as infants or in fact were born in the US, construct different variations of the game in question. Álvarez Borland argues that such authors postulate a more distanced perspective of the exilic trauma, dramatizing instead 'the anxieties felt by an ethnic writer about the issues of voice and identity' (137). In *Dreaming in Cuban*, a fundamental text of such paradigmatic angst, García uses female voices to articulate at once the fragmentation of the family structure after the 1959 revolution and the negative implications of male-dominant societies. Hence, Álvarez Borland states that '(f)rom the perspective of gender issues, García's text is indeed unique because it becomes a pioneering voice in telling the story of the Cuban diaspora from the point of view of Cuban women' (139).

Yet this sociopolitical pursuit blends throughout with schizophrenic turmoils linked to a curious desire of belonging to culture, language, and place, to a nation both invented and real. As Méndez Rodenas ascertains,

> Cristina García draws the island's geography from a very peculiar perspective, enlarging the margins of the nation in order to embrace the extraterritorial and collective displacement experience (. . .) as well as the emotional undertones that define the Cuban diaspora in the United States (395).

Pilar, the novel's identity searcher, confesses at the end of *Dreaming in Cuban*: 'I'm afraid to lose all this, to lose Abuela Celia again. But sooner or later I'd have to return to New York. I know now it's where I belong – not *instead* of here, but *more* than here' (236). Her quest for wholeness, leads to a *realistic* conclusion akin to the one at which Pérez Firmat arrives in his 'Dedication':

> The fact that I
> am writing to you
> in English
> already falsifies what I
> wanted to tell you.
> My subject:

how to explain to you
that I
don't belong to English
though I belong nowhere else,
if not here
in English. (126)

The *Cubanglo* punster and the ethnic Cuban writer share a selfsame conundrum, described uncomfortably in English by the poetic voice that the first concocts, and quite comfortably by the Cuban-Bred American replica conceived by García. Pilar's awkwardness of expression would never have anything to do, logically, with her true mother language, with her *tongue ties*, and everything to do with Spanish, her second language, even if it defines the cultural roots whence she emanated and which she strove to reclaim. For that reason, Pérez Firmat and García play the identity game within a similar arena, seeking to score points with converging moves.

Like García, Andrea O'Reilly Herrera, another *ethnic* writer, 'strives to make up for the absence from the homeland through a family romance' (Méndez Rodenas, 394) in *The Pearl of the Antilles*. This voluminous narrative relates the progressive disintegration of a Cuban family from 1949 through 1986. The novel reads somewhat like a plantation saga complete with a former slave mammy, Tata, gifted with alluring mythical powers. Female protagonists promulgate the ideological essence of a somewhat introspective text based at least partly, I surmise, on family recollections complemented by paradigmatic readings and the author's own fertile imagination, which allows her to partake as implied teller in an often bizarre state of ilinx, of self-induced vertigo. In crafting this text, O'Reilly Herrera manufactures her *own private Cuba*, to paraphrase another Pérez Firmat title, where a few names (La Habana, Cienfuegos, San Miguel de los Baños) suffice to forge an arbitrary geography. Framed between them are awkwardly named environs (Tres Flores plantation, Treinta Sierras, Calle Semilla, La Sagrada Familia school in Havana) peopled at times by individuals who bear remarkably contrived names: Señora Pedro Amargo de Miramar, Padre Rabia, Padre Sinfuente, Señora Marazul, Rudolfo, Faustino Aragona, Vincente, Señor Fieras). In addition, Spanish phrases and words, often misspelled, are interspersed throughout the text haphazardly *à la* Hemingway. In that sense, O'Reilly Herrera confers on Cuba's national language the 'ornamental role' (*Tongue*, 141) that, according to Pérez Firmat, it has acquired in Latino writing. 'Rather than a medium for literary expression', explains the critic, '(Spanish) has become a token of cultural filiation, like wearing dashikis or dousing your children with violet water' (*Tongue*, 141).

Regardless of O'Reilly Herrera's conscious effort to produce a *Cuban* artifact, the entire text insinuates a curious alienness inspired partly by geographic quaintness and historical imprecision. Nonetheless, the novel succeeds in communicating the essence of an identity game to which the implied author clearly relates. By pondering the fate of several 'Pearls of the Antilles' – the moniker ascribed to those female characters who assume protagonist roles – Lilly, the CBA narrator, reclaims her right to be one of them, another 'Pearl of the Antilles', despite the fact that her father is Anglo-American and her mother a refugee from the idyllic Tres Flores. To employ O'Reilly Herrera's own critical terminology, Lilly – like the author – affirms her right to voice the Cuban component of her *Cubandness*.[7] She locates herself in place through saga as indispensable cog of an unfinished *family* story.

In 1977, Iván Acosta's *El súper* – whose film version directed by León Ichaso and Manuel Arce earned several international awards – helped to establish a novel approach to the identity game. The satiric treatment of Cuban anxiety transparent in this play sought at once to justify and to demythologize a collectivity often pigeonholed in a peculiar corner of the sociopolitical spectrum. By depicting comically or in exaggerated fashion the travails of the humble family headed by Roberto Amador Gonzalo, superintendent of a decrepit apartment building on Manhattan's West Side, Acosta – another 'one-and-a-halfer' – succeeds in adding universality to this Cuban émigré experience. Rather than succumbing to the melodramatic treatment of the theme, the playwright externalizes the identity game, distancing himself humorously from his characters, and particularly from his protagonist, in order to create contrapuntal discourses that debunk and enhance each other at once. As a result, a critic like Vincent Camby may conclude that '*El* súper is much less about politics than it is about the disorientation of exiles who become living metaphors for the human condition' (58). Yet Amador Gonzalo's antics convey also a certain pathos. When he opts to abandon New York for Miami with his family at the end of the play, he undertakes a regressive movement, sentencing himself to enervating nostalgia and to the pervasive role of historical victim.

Although the parodic method has been employed successfully by other Cuban-American authors, Roberto G. Fernández has mastered like no other the carnivalesque art of portraying grotesquely a community in a perpetual state of crisis. Thus, he performs dialogically what Acosta accomplishes monologically. Fernández has written several works in Spanish, the most significant of which are *La vida es un special* ~~1.50~~ *.75* (Life is a Special ~~1.50~~ .75), *La montaña rusa* (The Roller Coaster) and *En la Ocho y la Doce* (The Corner of Eighth and Twelfth). He has attained substantial recognition in the US and abroad, however, for two books in English: *Raining Backwards* and *Holy Radishes*. Even though Fernández frequently mocks 'one-and-a-halfers' like himself, he ridicules most frequently that first exilic generation associated with his parents. In so doing, he

---

[7] In her introduction to *ReMembering Cuba*, O'Reilly Herrera appends an arbitrary 'd' to the word Cuban in order to enhance its expressive possibilities. She follows Stuart Hall's hypothesis that rather than hyphenating gentilics or adjectives reflective of skin coloration when discussing ethnic or racial identity, one should avoid binary oppositions by linking the terms in question with the conjunction 'and'. She explains: 'Adding a "d" to "Cuban" allows for the infinite number of "couplings" and identifications that together constitute the Cub*and* "presences" in the United States' (xxx).

questions the persistent myth of 'la Cuba de ayer' (the Cuba of yesteryear), the bizarre political atmosphere fabricated by Miami's Cubans, racial and sexual stereotypes inherent in the collectivity, its socioeconomic value system, etcetera.

Additionally, he indulges in linguistic play that suggests an uncontainable state of flux. Fernández parodies the broken English of his elders, the Spanglish of his peers, the varieties of Spanish employed in his version of Miami, and even the hegemonic language bastardized by Anglo-Americans. The result is an effervescent identity game because, in his texts, Cuba becomes an ever-changing point of reference that differs in accordance to its exiled interpreters. The author forces Cuban-Americans to view themselves in a convex mirror that distorts their self-image and, ergo, their sense of identity. Fernández himself, on the other hand, has declared that his homeland is Miami, that 'three-ringed circus' (Montané, 1-C) where he feels most comfortable. Nonetheless, by allowing contradictory voices to clash euphorically while playing identity games, his own narrative persona – distant though it may seem – participates in the carnivalesque quest for self. Additionally, as I have tried to demonstrate elsewhere[8] the author's Miami, in its function of inhabited space, is implicitly juxtaposed to a minuscule *patria chica* that almost invariably superimposes itself upon the scattered metropolis. In that sense, as Eliana Rivero has argued, both his conception of space and the 'agridulce discurso nostálgico' (bittersweet nostalgic discourse) veil 'penas de ausencia en la burla' (sorrowful longing in his mockery) ('Cubanos', 43). Hence, Fernández's identity games still indulge, albeit in grotesque and debasing manner, in the literary recovery of the imaginary homeland.

Matías Montes-Huidobro, a *first generation* writer beyond the scope of this chapter, has published two novels – *Esa fuente de dolor* (That Source of Pain) and *Concierto para sordos* (Concert for the Deaf) – in which he dissects Cuba as a land made unholy by imperial rape, governmental corruption, personal laxity, and a maddening sequence of fraternal warfare. In conceiving such a violated territory as unsacred, Montes-Huidobro coincides critically with Stuart Hall ('Pensando', 481–2): a land so aggrieved is not an auspicious home, even if it has shaped his first-person narrators' individual imaginary. Montes-Huidobro's dark portrayal of such a *source of pain* and torn identity is counterbalanced by the last *second generation* construct on which I will focus briefly. Fowler Calzada, in discussing Ruth Behar's *Poemas que vuelven a Cuba* (Poems that Return to Cuba), associates the collection with what he terms the 'tragic zone' ('Miradas') of US Cuban literature in the sense that most texts imply 'una identidad que es percibida como fragmentaria y fragmentada' (an identity that is perceived as fragmentary and fragmented) ('Miradas'). Fowler Calzada's appraisal rightly links this book with Montes-Huidobro's scatological pessi-

---

[8] See my essay 'La tríada Belle Glade, Miami, Xawa: tres nombres, tres culturas y un solo espacio novelesco en la narrativa de Roberto G. Fernández', *Hispanic Journal*, 25:1–2 (2004), 225–41.

mism, Suárez's permanent poetic anxiety, and García's formulation of a search for self-definition.

In 'Juban América', a subsequent essay, Behar addresses the identity game in a manner that, despite its specificity, synthesizes the perception of transnational *Cubanía* endemic not only in all the authors and texts cited so far, but also in the countless others certainly deserving of consideration, were one to treat the topic comprehensively. After a lengthy explanation of her Jewish and Cuban roots, as well as of her immigrant condition in a land no longer foreign, where even her parents fit within an odd *Latino* umbrella that signals an arbitrary *otherness*, she concludes by citing Rushdie's aforementioned essay in order to claim for herself the right to concoct a personal locus where she can comfortably locate herself. The site is a collage, a compendium of individual and collective images, of real and dreamt-up experiences, which she idiosyncratically supplements via a physical reconnection with the homeland.[9] 'This essay', she maintains, 'has been a first effort on my part to begin to imagine Juba, a Juba that I want to build, salt pillar by salt pillar, from both family stories and my own struggle to reclaim all the little forgotten villages of my mestiza identity' (165). By doing so, Behar pretends to resolve the issue that led her to study anthropology: 'to solve the puzzle of (her) identity' (165). Thus, the identity *ilinx* that she plays enthusiastically, along with so many other spinners who circle around the same subject to produce a euphoric artistic vertigo notwithstanding the pathos whence it may emanate, has after all a final purpose: inventing a sacred arena where the game may be played perpetually to the satisfaction of the individual actor.

Alfonso Hernández Catá, in his *Mitología de Martí* (Mythology Surrounding Martí), includes an apocryphal anecdote that for some reason bothered me greatly when I read it many years ago as a young *Other* (and I do not employ such nomenclature facetiously, since that was the designation assigned in official documents to Cuban parolees) growing up in America. Since those graduate student days I had thought little about a text that, nonetheless, must have traveled with me as unconscious baggage, and which appears particularly relevant when closing this chapter on Cuban-American identity games. The 'Apólogo de Mary González' (Apologue of Mary González) consists of a dialogue between José Martí and the protagonist, a young lady who, despite being born in Valladolid, has grown up in the United States and attends high school in New Jersey. In addition, her mother was born in Boston of Spanish parents. The *pater familias*, a Spanish liberal, extends a luncheon invitation to Martí during which the patriot plans to approach him about contributing to the cause of Cuban independence. The initial encounter between Mary and the iconic national hero reveals immediately Hernández Catá's pedagogic intention. After the young woman voices her admiration for Martí and indicates that she plans to attend

---

[9] Behar also discusses her experiences in Cuba, and concludes her essay as follows: 'To imagine it all is not enough. This Jubana will have to taste the salt of memory and of loss, but she will have to make a *rinconcito* for herself in the Cuba of the present' (168). See her essay 'Juban América', *Poetics Today*, 16:1 (Spring 1995), 151–70.

Cuban revolutionary gatherings in the future, the patriot-turned-teacher addresses her in admonitory tone:

> También yo la conocía a usted de nombre. Sé que, aun cuando ha nacido en Valladolid, se ufana de ser americana; que tiene el primer puesto en todas las asignaturas de savia inglesa... Y el acento es yanqui puro. Cuando tengamos confianza le diré que su boca puede reprocharle a su nariz el que se entrometa un poco en su conversación: Su inglés es nasal, y su español, suena ya un poquito a falso. (298)

> (I also knew you by name. I know that, even though you were born in Valladolid, you boast about being an American; I know that you have the best grades in your class in any subject pertaining to Anglosaxon culture... And your accent is pure Yankee. When we become better acquainted I will tell you that your mouth should tell your nose that it interferes excessively in your speech. Your English is quite nasal, and your Spanish already sounds a bit foreign.)

Mary, evidently not sufficiently American yet to tell Martí to go take a flying leap, defends herself as best she can: '¡Vine de tan chica! ... El idioma de mi niñez no ha sido el español, y casi tengo que traducir ... ¡Como que cuento y rezo en inglés!' (I was so young when I came to this country! ... Spanish was not the language of my childhood, and I almost have to translate what I say ... I even count and pray in English!) (298). To which Martí replies: 'La corriente nos arrastra, mas hay que nadar contra ella' (The tide may drag us, but we must struggle against it'). Hernández Catá creates an intense situation where the articulator of Cuba's primordial foundational narrative (Rojas, *José Martí*, 130) dialogues with an immature young woman exclusively for the sake of refuting her Spanish-Americanness, the hybridic or hyphenated nature that she claims as identity sign.

Mary, to her credit, initially defends her belief system: 'Ya sé que va a decirme lo que otros me han dicho: Que me he americanizado demasiado, que me siento americana hasta la médula ... No lo niego. Para mí el pueblo más grande y más liberal del mundo, es éste' (I know that you are going to tell me what others have already said: That I've become too Americanized, that I am American to the bones ... I don't deny it. In my opinion, this is the greatest and the freest country in the world) (300). Martí's counter-argument centers on his oft-cited references to 'the good Spaniards', always juxtaposed to the 'bad ones' who insist on retaining colonial control over Cuba, as well as on his fear of the 'Monster' whose dollar perturbs him as emblem of economic imperialism. A segment of his very unapostolic speech is especially provocative given its strident xenophobia:

> Con los españoles como su padre y aun con los otros, me entiendo. Con los norteamericanos, no... Y usted fundiéndose en esta raza es algo que se me pierde y me da ganas de llorar... Porque usted se casará con un americano, y sus hijos no mirarán nunca más con ojos puros hacia nuestros países; antes

bien, se servirán de su heredado conocimiento de nuestras flaquezas para mejor perdernos. De un Smith aun puedo fiarme. De un González norteamericano no me fiaré jamás. (302)

(I can communicate with Spaniards like your father and even with the other ones. But with the Americans, never . . . And to think of you becoming one with this race is something that baffles me and makes me want to cry . . . Because you will marry an American, and your children will never look lovingly upon our countries; rather, they will exploit their inherited knowledge of our weaknesses in order to mislead us. I can trust somebody named Smith. I will never trust a North American González.)

Thenceforth, poor Mary González is overwhelmed by Martí's rhetoric, to the point that when he asks her at the end to say her name out loud, the girl responds: 'María González' (306). Another victim has been saved from the awful specter of ethnic hybdrity. A Cuban patriot has convinced a Spanish maiden no less to remain true to her Peninsular roots, to her transnational identity. Therefore, he has saved her from a fate worse than death: marrying an American, procreating bi-ethnic children, becoming indeed a hybrid, a hyphenated denizen of the US.

Hernández Catá's self-serving vivification of Martí underscores the root of the identity games still performed by Cuban-American writers. These manifestations of the play spirit take multitudinous routes not necessarily exclusive of each other.[10] Throughout this chapter, I have attempted to describe the following components of all-consuming *ilinx*: deterritorialized longing for unattainable self-authentication; coming to grips with hybridity; underscoring the validity of transnational *Cubanía*; distancing oneself aesthetically from nostalgia and the quest for individual and collective identity through satire or parody; and finally, manufacturing a personal place, an imaginary homeland, which mimics features of the abandoned or perhaps even unknown mother country. By employing such thematic and formal strategies, most US Cuban authors juxtapose collective and individual identity to an absorbing hegemonic culture, as if to substantiate Santí's dictum that 'la Patria . . . está en todas partes' (One's Fatherland is everywhere) (15). Regardless of age or even birthplace, they strive to perpetuate self by transforming it into selves, into the will of a transnational people that, as Richard Blanco affirms in 'América', still try every Thanksgiving to superimpose pork over turkey (5). The imaginary homelands in which they amble,

---

[10] Hernández Catá attempts to inscribe himself entirely into Cuban literature with *Mitología de Martí* and *Un cementerio en las Antillas*, both texts that uphold a liberal political credo with which he was not necessarily identified throughout his life as a member of the Cuban diplomatic corps. Additionally, the author, truly a transnational citizen, was born in Aldeadávila de la Ribera, Spain, and – after migrating to that country as a young man – became a member of the so-called 'Generación de 1905', a group of writers who coupled decadent modernistic tendencies with erotic naturalism and quasi-Freudian analysis. As a result, he was often derided in the island as a Spanish writer who pretended to be Cuban.

internal replicas or parodies, for that matter, of a space that becomes more alien and alienating each passing year, acquires an emphatic poetic viability. This notwithstanding, like Rushdie, I fear that these engaging games, given their contagious nature and often excessively personalistic aura, may be leading to 'the adoption of a ghetto mentality' (19), perhaps suicidal in nature. But then again, if what emanates from such literary endeavors is the predominance of that 'sujeto di-vertido' described by Vera León, who, as malleable borderland inhabiter, 'entra y sale, toma y deja elementos de las culturas que lo constituyen' (enters and departs, takes and leaves elements of the cultures that shape him) ('Escrituras', 77), then the games – these varied ilinxes – may truly be worthwhile . . . at least for the foreseeable future.

## Works Cited

Álvarez Borland, Isabel. *Cuban-American Literature of Exile: From Person to Persona*. Charlottesville/London: University of Virginia Press, 1998.
Bakhtin, Mikhail. *Problems of Dostoevsky's Poetics*, ed. and trans. Caryl Emerson. Minneapolis: University of Minnesota Press, 1984.
Ballester, Juan Pablo, María Elena Escalona, and Iván de la Nuez. *Cuba: la isla posible*. Barcelona: Destino, 1995.
Behar, Ruth. 'Juban América', *Poetics Today*, 16:1 (Spring 1995), 151–70.
—— *Poemas que vuelven a Cuba*. Matanzas, Cuba: Vigía, 1995.
—— and Juan León (eds.). *Bridges to Cuba / Puentes a Cuba*, special edition of *Michigan Quarterly Review*, 33:3 (1994).
Blanco, Richard. *City of a Hundred Fires*. Pittsburgh: University of Pittsburg Press, 1998.
Bolaños, Aimée G. 'Dulce María Loynaz y Carlota Caulfield escriben cartas de amor: hacia una literatura insular de signo infinito', *Caribe*, 6:2 (2003–04), 65–83.
Caillois, Roger. *Man, Play, and Games*, trans. Meyer Barash. New York: Schoken Books, 1979.
Campa, Román de la. *Cuba on My Mind: Journeys to a Severed Nation*. London/New York: Verso, 2001.
Caulfield, Carlota. *At the Paper Gates with Burning Desire. Poems / A las puertas del papel con amoroso fuego*. Bilingual edition, trans. Angela McEwan. Oakland: InteliBooks, 2000.
—— 'Even Names Have Their Exile: Collage of Memories', in Andrea O'Reilly Herrera (ed.). *ReMembering Cuba: Legacy of a Diaspora*. Austin: University of Texas Press, 2001, 236–41.
Clifford, James. 'Diasporas', *Cultural Anthropology*, 9:3 (1994), 302–38.
Eire, Carlos. *Waiting for Snow in Havana: Memoirs of a Cuban Boy*. New York: Free Press, 2003.
Espinosa Domínguez, Carlos. *El peregrino en comarca ajena*. Boulder, Colorado: Society of Spanish-American Studies, 2001.
Febles, Jorge. 'La tríada Belle Glade, Miami, Xawa: tres nombres, tres culturas y un solo espacio novelesco en la narrative de Roberto G. Fernández', *Hispanic Journal*, 25:1–2 (2004), 225–41.

Fernández, Damián J., and Madeline Cámara Betancourt. *Cuba: The Elusive Nation: Interpretations of National Identity*. Gainesville: University Press of Florida, 2000.

Fernández, Roberto G. *En la Ocho y la Doce*. Boston and New York: Houghton Mifflin, 2001.

—— *Holy Radishes*. Houston: Arte Público Press, 1995.

—— *La montaña rusa*. Houston: Arte Público Press, 1985.

—— *La vida es un special 1.50.75*. Miami: Ediciones Universal, 1981,

—— *Raining Backwards*. Houston: Arte Público Press, 1985.

Fornet, Ambrosio. *Memorias recobradas*. Santa Clara, Cuba: Ediciones Capiro, 2000.

Fowler Calzada, Víctor. 'Miradas a la identidad en la literatura de la diáspora'. *La Habana Elegante* (Summer 2001), www.habanaelegante.com

García, Cristina. *Dreaming in Cuban*. New York: Ballantine Books, 1992.

García, María Cristina. *Havana USA: Cuban Exiles and Cuban Americans in South Florida, 1959–1994*. Berkeley: University of California Press, 1996.

González-Pando, Miguel. *The Cuban Americans*. Westport, Connecticut: Greenwood Press, 1998.

Hall, Stuart. 'Pensando en la diáspora: en casa, desde el extranjero', trans. Carlos A. Jáuregui, in Carlos A. Jáuregui, and Juan Pablo Dabove (eds.). *Heterotropías: narratives de identidad y alteridad latinoamericana*. Pittsburgh: Biblioteca de América, 2003, 477–90.

Hernández Catá, Alfonso. *Mitología de Martí*. Buenos Aires: Club del Libro, 1929.

—— *Un cementerio en las Antillas*. Madrid [self-published], 1933.

Huizinga, Johan. *Homo Ludens: A Study of the Play Element in Culture*. German edition: 1944. Boston: Beacon Press, 1955.

Martí, José. *Amistad funesta. La gran enciclopedia martiana*. 12, ed. Ramón Cernuda. Miami: Editorial Martiana, 1978, 132–97.

—— 'A Néstor Ponce de León'. *La gran enciclopedia martiana*. 12, ed. Ramón Cernuda. Miami: Editorial Martiana, 1978, 171–3.

Medina, Pablo. *Exiled Memories*. Austin: University of Texas Press, 1990.

—— 'Where Are You From? A Cuban Dilemma', in Andrea O'Reilly Herrera (ed.). *ReMembering Cuba: Legacy of a Diaspora*. Austin: University of Texas Press, 2001, 233–6.

Méndez Rodenas, Adriana. 'En búsqueda del paraíso perdido: La historia natural como imaginación diaspórica en Cristina García', *Modern Language Notes*, 116:2 (2001), 392–418.

Monge Rafuls, Pedro R. *Nadie se va del todo*, 1991. *Teatro: 5 autores cubanos*, ed. Rine Leal. New York: Ollantay Press, 1995.

—— *Recordando a mamá. El tiempo en un acto: 13 obras de teatro cubano*, ed. José Triana. New York: OLLANTAY, 1999, 248–70.

—— 'Reflexiones de Pedro R. Monge Rafuls', in *Presencia negra: teatro cubano de la diáspora*, ed. Armando González-Pérez. Madrid: Betania, 1999, 49–50.

Montané, Diane. 'Cuban Author Finds Humor in Differences'; 'Upbeat', *The Miami News* (12 August 1988), 1-C; 9-C.

Montes-Huidobro, Matías. *Concierto para sordos*. Tempe, Arizona: Bilingual Press/Editorial Bilingüe, 2001.

—— *Esa fuente de dolor*. Sevilla: Algaida Editores, 1999.

Nuez, Iván de la. 'Un fragmento en las orillas del mundo: Identidad, diferencia y fuga de la cultura cubana', in Juan Pablo Ballester, María Elena Escalona, and Iván de la Nuez (eds.). *Cuba: la isla posible*. Barcelona: Destino, 1995, 25–33.
O'Reilly Herrera, Andrea (ed.). *ReMembering Cuba: Legacy of a Diaspora*. Austin: University of Texas Press, 2001.
—— *The Pearl of the Antilles*. Tempe, Arizona: Bilingual Press, 2001.
Pérez Firmat, Gustavo. *Anything but Love*. Houston: Arte Público Press, 2000.
—— *Carolina Cuban in Triple Crown: Chicano, Puerto Rican and Cuban American Poetry*. Tempe, Arizona: Bilingual Press/Editorial Bilingüe, 1987, 121–67.
—— *Cincuenta lecciones de exilio y desexilio*. Miami: Universal, 2000.
—— *Equivocaciones*. Madrid: Betania, 1989.
—— *Life on the Hyphen: The Cuban-American Way*. Austin: University of Texas Press, 1994.
—— *Next Year in Cuba: A Cubano's Coming of Age in America*. New York: Doubleday, 1995.
—— *The Cuban Condition: Translation and Identity in Modern Cuban Literature*. Cambridge: Cambridge University Press, 1989.
—— *Tongue Ties: Logo-Eroticism in Anglo-Hispanic Literature*. New York: Palgrave MacMillan, 2003.
—— 'Trascender el exilio: la literatura cubano-americana hoy', in Ambrosio Fornet (ed.). *Memorias recobradas*. Santa Clara, Cuba: Ediciones Capiro, 2000, 16–29.
Rivero, Eliana. 'Cubanos y cubanoamericanos: perfil y presencia en los Estados Unidos', in Ambrosio Fornet (ed.). *Memorias recobradas*. Santa Clara, Cuba: Ediciones Capiro, 2000, 30–50.
—— ' "Fronterisleña" Border Islander', in Ruth Behar, and Juan León (eds.). *Bridges to Cuba/Puentes a Cuba*. Part 2. Special issue of the *Michigan Quarterly Review*, 33:4 (1994), 669–74.
Rojas, Rafael. *Isla sin fin*. Miami: Ediciones Universal, 1998.
—— *José Martí: la invención de Cuba*. Madrid: Colibrí, 2000.
—— 'La diferencia cubana', in Juan Pablo Ballester, María Elena Escalona, and Iván de la Nuez (eds.). *Cuba: la isla posible*. Barcelona: Destino, 1995, 34–9.
Rushdie, Salman. 'Imaginary Homelands', in *Imaginary Homelands: Essays and Criticism 1981–1991*. New York: Penguin, 1992, 9–21.
Santí, Enrico Mario. *Bienes del siglo: Sobre cultura cubana*. México, D.F.: Fondo de Cultura Económica, 2002.
Suárez, Virgil. *Banyan*. Baton Rouge, Louisiana: Louisiana State University Press, 2001.
—— *Guide to the Blue Tongue*. Urbana/Chicago: University of Illinois Press, 2002.
—— *In the Republic of Longing*. Tempe, Arizona: Bilingual Press/Editorial Bilingüe, 1999.
—— *Palm Crows*. Tucson: University of Arizona Press, 2001.
—— *Spared Angola: Memories of a Cuban Childhood*. Houston: Arte Público Press, 1997.
Torres, María de los Ángeles. *By Heart / De memoria: Cuban Women's Journeys In and Out of Exile*. Philadelphia: Temple University Press, 2003.
Vera León, Antonio. 'Escrituras bilingües y sujetos biculturales', in Juan Pablo Ballester, María Elena Escalona, and Iván de la Nuez (eds.). *Cuba: la isla posible*. Barcelona: Destino, 1995, 66–77.

# 5

# Afro-Cuban Identity in the Theater of the Diaspora

## ARMANDO GONZÁLEZ-PÉREZ

The black influence in the Caribbean in general and in Cuba specifically permeates all aspects of life. Cuba is ethnically and culturally a product of the mixing of European (Spanish) and African influence. In her seminal book, *El monte* (The Forest) the ethnologist Lydia Cabrera states that: 'The weight of the African influence in the white population that claims to be white is incalculable even though at first glance one cannot determine it. Our people will not be understood without knowing the Black man' (9).[1] Nicolás Guillén's poem *La canción del bongo* (The Song of the Bongo Drum) brilliantly conveys the *mestizo* characteristics of Cuban society:[2]

>   En esta tierra mulata
>   de africano y español
>   (Santa Bárbara de un lado,
>   del otro lado Changó),
>   siempre falta algún abuelo
>   cuando no sobra algún Don,
>   y hay títulos de Castilla
>   con parientes en Bondó . . .
>   (*Sóngoro Cosongo* . . . 12–13)

>   (In this mulatto island
>   of African and Spanish blood
>   (Saint Barbara on one side,
>   on the other, Changó)
>   a grandfather is always missing,
>   when there isn't a Don too many
>   and there are titles from Castile
>   with relatives from Bondó . . .)

---

[1] I am indebted to Jill González-Pérez and Belén S. Castañeda for their insightful readings of this essay and for their invaluable suggestions. The word *monte* can be translated in various ways: forest, woodland, woods, mountain. According to Afro-Cuban beliefs, the *monte* is a sacred place where the human and the divine come together.

[2] The bongo drum is a percussion instrument of a hollow cylinder with a piece of skin stretched tightly over one or both ends. It is played by beating with open hands or sticks.

The religious syncretism alluded to in this poem focuses on *Santería*, a fusion of Catholicism and West African Yoruba religion practiced in Cuba and other Caribbean nations. Other African influences come from the people in the Calabar region and the Bantu-speaking people in the Congo. *Santería* is the belief in one god (Olodumare, Olorun, Olofi), the creator, and a number of deities that represent various forces of nature or ethical principles called *orishas*.[3] The most important *orishas* in Cuba are Elegua, Obatalá, Ochún, Oyá, Yemayá, Changó, Orula, and Babalú-Ayé. All Cubans are familiar with these deities from the Yoruba pantheon, and as a result, they are considered an integral part of the Cuban folklore and beliefs. Rogelio Martínez Furé states in an interview that 'Cuba is among the countries with the greatest diversity of popular religions of African origin; these religions are alive and in an open process of growth, both here and abroad . . .' (28). Isabel Castellanos adds that in the exile community

> . . . this culture, far from drying up, is blossoming, expanding and starting other cultural endeavors in the midst of the US society. The African spirit is invincible. It resists all social, economic and political changes to which it is being subjected. It never dies. It modifies itself but always retains its very essence. (*Cultura Afrocubana*, IV, 33)

The Afro-Cuban influence in the theater goes back to colonial times. In his book *Los bailes y el teatro de los negros en el folklore de Cuba* (The Dances and Theater of the Blacks in the Folklore of Cuba), the Cuban anthropologist Fernando Ortiz describes the intrinsic theatricality of these beliefs brought to Cuban shores by different groups of slaves (431–4). The critic Rine Leal observes in *Teatro bufo*:

> . . . If we accept that Taino Indians' ceremonial dances were a pre-dramatic liturgy, there is no problem in stating that the liturgical chants and religious ceremonies of the Black men for a Black public are also an early form of Cuban theater art. (63)

The playwright and critic Matías Montes Huidobro adds:

> We find a strong magical element which derives from the surviving African religions in Cuba, from a rich literary, religious and magical world that can be traced back to the origin of the Yoruba people, called in Cuba lucumís . . . Magical world, theatrical world and Black world seem to be synonymous. (*Persona*, 43–5)

In Cuba, among the authors who have incorporated the black theme in their works before and after the revolution are Flora Díaz Parrado, *Juana Revolico*

---

[3] Other popular *orishas* or saints of the Yoruba pantheon in Cuba are Ogún, Osaín, Ochosí, Aggallú, Oyá, and Obbá.

(1944); Paco Alfonso, *Yari-Yari, mamá Olúa* (Yari-Yari, Mamma Olúa) (1947) and *La hierba hedionda* (The Smelling Grass) (1951); Dora Alonso, *Caín o La hora de estar ciegos* (Cain and the Hour to be Blind) (1955); Carlos Felipe, *Réquiem por Yarini* (Requiem for Yarini) (1960); Virgilio Piñera, *Electra Garrigó* (1948); José Triana, *Medea en el espejo* (Medea in Front of the Mirror) (1960) and *La muerte del Ñeque* (The Death of the Ñeque) (1963); José Ramón Brene, *Santa Camila de La Habana* (Saint Camila of Havana) (1962); José Millián, *Mamico Omi Omo* (1965); Eugenio Hernández Espinosa, *María Antonia* (1967); León Fulleda, *Plácido* (1982), and *Chago de Guisa* (1987); and Abelardo Estorino, *Parece blanca* (She Appears Almost White) (1994).

## The theater of the Diaspora

In the theater of the Diaspora, playwrights and artists including Matías Montes Huidobro, José Triana, Raúl de Cárdenas, José Corrales, Manuel Pereiras García, Pedro R. Monge-Rafuls, Manuel Martín Jr, Héctor Santiago, Dolores Prida, Caridad Svich, and Leandro Soto have been inspired by the Afro-Cuban religion and folklore. The black presence in their artistic endeavors is very important. All of them utilize, in one way or another, the African influence with its rich repertoire of songs, dances, choral prayers, pantomimes, and dialogues. They represent different generations and their experience in exile ranges from those who left Cuba at the beginning of the revolution to those who left later at a younger age. The older generation prefers to write in Spanish while the younger one often writes in English as well as in Spanish. Such is the case of Manuel Martín Jr, *Rita and Bessie* (1986); Caridad Svich, *Brazo Gitano* (Gypsy's Arm) (1988)[4] and Dolores Prida, *Botánica* (1991).[5] The critics have classified these authors as belonging to the Teatro Cubanoamericano (Cuban-American Theater).[6] On the other hand, an artist like Leandro Soto relies on the visual. His work *Emociones / E-Motions* (1999) can be classified as performance art. Some of these authors use the Yoruba language in their plays, especially in songs, chants, and prayers as in the plays *Las hetairas habaneras* (The Havana Courtesans) (1977), *La navaja de Olofé* (Olofé's Razor) (1982), *Los hijos de Ochún* (Ochún's Sons) (1994), and *Otra historia* (Another Story) (1996). All these plays and performances, written or staged outside Cuba in Spanish or English, are an integral part of the cultural body of the Cuban experience. Little is known of the Afro-Cuban theater in the Diaspora whose writers have had to struggle against misunderstanding, indifference, and prejudice regarding the publication,

---

[4] The play is written in English with a few words in Spanish.

[5] A *Botánica* is a bodega or small shop common in many Hispanic communities which sells medicinal and religious items used in *Santería*.

[6] In his article 'Rasgos comparativos entre la literatura de la isla y del exilio: el tema histórico en el teatro' (published in *Ollantay* (1993), 53–62), José A. Escarpanter classifies the plays written in English as Cuban American Theater and divides the different groups of Cuban playwrights into two generations: the divided generation and the exile generation.

dissemination, and staging of their plays. Manuel Martín Jr vividly expresses this rejection:

> Upon my return from Italy, and disenchanted in interpreting Latin characters in the way that the Americans see us (not like we really are) I met Magali Alabau who had arrived from Cuba. We decided to open a theater in 1969. The Theater Duo with only twenty seven seats was the first seed in all our experiments as authors, producers, and directors . . . In 1976, after a hazardous tour in Central and South America and feeling in my own flesh the rejection of the Cuban exiles in international festivals . . ., I decided to write works in which I could find my own voice. From this search were born *Swallows* (based on interviews with Cubans from the island and the United States), *Union City Thanksgivings*, and *Rita and Bessie*. (González-Pérez, *Presencia negra*, 248)

The rejection and prejudice suffered by Cuban exile writers like Manuel Martin Jr was due partly to the campaigns carried out by the Castro government to discredit anyone who would not accept the new revolutionary discourse and had decided to leave Cuba.

## Plays and performance

The selection of the following works for discussion takes into account the intrinsic artistic value of the plays and performances, the varied theatrical styles of the authors, and the different approaches used to treat the black theme. The first work chosen is *La navaja de Olofé* (Olofé's Razor), a complex play that uses Afro-Cuban mythology extensively.[7]

Matías Montes Huidobro wrote *La navaja de Olofé* in 1982. This is a difficult play in which the author freely interprets some Yoruba *patakíes* related to the *orishas* Changó, Ochún, and Yemayá.[8] The plot is simple. It revolves around the love and sexual relationship of the protagonists. They are a young mulatto and his mistress during carnival time in Santiago de Cuba. However, the plot becomes more complex when the author, through the use of the magical element of *Santería,* introduces the theme of incest. Each character assumes a double identity by taking on the characteristics of a Yoruba deity. As a result, there are different levels of interpretation of the play. The young mulatto protagonist acquires the attributes identified with the deities Changó and Olofé, and his mistress can be identified with the sensual Yoruba goddess Ochún and her sister Yemayá. The razor, alluded to in the play, is symbolic. It is the instrument used for shaving by the male protagonist in the play or the weapon used by the woman at the end of the play in carrying out a symbolic castration. The razor also represents the phallic symbol of strength and sexual power identified with Olofé, the

---

[7] All of the quotations from the plays and performance discussed in this chapter come from the critical anthology compiled by Armando González-Pérez, *Presencia negra: teatro cubano de la diáspora* (Madrid: Betania, 1999).

[8] A *pataki* is an oral legend from Nigeria.

supreme deity in the Yoruba pantheon, and Changó, the personification of virility, the macho-man.

Matías Montes Huidobro states the following concerning the origin of *La navaja de Olofé*:

> The origin of this play is found in a play that I wrote in the 1950s entitled *The Mask* (it is fortunately lost today). In that play the role of the male/female relationship was treated briefly and the Afro-Cuban element was rather folkloric. At the end of 1970 and the beginning of 1980, I reworked that text completely and created a play that has a more solid Afro-Cuban context. (*Presencia negra*, 35–6)

The elements of *Santería*, in conjunction with the Freudian aspect of the work, play a pivotal role in the plot development. However, it is important to point out that the author incorporates the Afro-Cuban elements in the play according to his own peculiar interpretation and artistic purpose. It is obvious that he did not intend to reproduce the Afro-Cuban folklore and beliefs faithfully, but rather to portray their essence. For example, the god's name Olofi is changed to Olofé. However, there is no doubt that in *La navaja de Olofé* the use of Yoruba magic and myth contributes to plot development and enriches the stage presentation, opening the play to different interpretations. The incest theme relates to the Freudian theory of the Oedipus complex, as well as to the Yoruba legend of the possible love between Changó and his mother, the goddess Yemayá.

*La navaja de Olofé* is a dramatic and powerful play that ends with the triumph of the woman (Ochún/Yemayá) in the battle of the sexes. She symbolically castrates her young mulatto lover Changó/Olofé and becomes Olofé, the all-powerful creator. Montes Huidobro's theatrical technique of a play within a play is brilliant, and his use of *Santería* allows him to underscore the multiple roles of his characters. *La navaja de Olofé* is an intriguing Afro-Cuban play that displays the artistic creativity of one of the leading Cuban playwrights of today.

*Rita and Bessie* was written in 1986 and revised in 1992 by Manuel Martín Jr.[9] The main protagonists are two famous black singers, one Cuban and the other American. Bessie Smith, the legendary blues singer, lived from 1894 to 1937. The famous Cuban Rita Montaner lived from 1900 to 1958, and sang light opera as well as popular music. Although far apart age-wise and culturally, the two women magically meet. As they compete against each other, each recounts her life story. Themes of racism, gender discrimination, and politics unfold. These two women vie for a role in the locked office of an agent in the Chrysler Building in New York City. From the very beginning, the play focuses on the

---

[9] Rita Montaner was one of the most beloved singers of popular music and light opera in Cuba. She was born on 20 August 1900 and died of throat cancer on 17 April 1958. Bessie Smith is known as the Empress of the Blues. She was born in Chattanooga, Tennessee, but her date of birth is uncertain, variously given as 1894, 1898, and 1900. Bessie died in Clarksdale, Mississippi on 26 September 1937.

theme of racism. Bessie refers to the discrimination that barred her from a good education: 'BESSIE – I know nothing about your high class Havana schools but, baby, in America you were lucky if they let you go through the public school door (*Laughs bitterly*). No siree, no high class school for a "nigguh" (*Presencia negra*, 253). Bessie also speaks of being a child in a car accident and being taken to a hospital where she was denied water because she was black:

> BESSIE – (*As a young girl*.) Can anyone gimme a glass of water? Nurse, I'm dying of thirst.
> NURSE'S VOICE – What are you whimpering about nigger?
> BESSIE – (*As a young girl*.) Water, please. I wanna some water . . .
> NURSE'S VOICE – You are not allowed to have any.
> BESSIE – (*As a young girl*.) An ice cube. Please! I'm dying of thirst!
> NURSE'S VOICE – No way!
> BESSIE – (*As a young girl*.) Please, please. Oh, Lord! My leg hurts so!
> NURSE'S VOICE – Nigger, you are lucky that someone got you out of the crash. (*Pause*.) Bitch, who asked you to go riding in a stolen car?
> BESSIE (*As a young girl*.) Water, I wanna some water . . . (273)

As the plot advances, Rita also discusses her life. Despite Rita's remembrance of an idyllic life in Cuba where she was groomed to be an opera singer, we begin to realize how much discrimination she suffered. We flash back to a conversation she had with the composer with whom she worked:

> COMPOSER'S VOICE – How would you like me to accompany you in your first recital?
> RITA – But, Maestro, I could not possibly accept this honor.
> COMPOSER'S VOICE – Yes, you could, Rita. (*Whispers to an imaginary character standing next to him*.) How do you think we can make her skin look lighter? (*To Rita*.) Wouldn't you like to be an operetta star?
> RITA – Of course Maestro.
> COMPOSER'S VOICE – If you cooperate I'll make you a star. (*Whispers to an imaginary character standing next to him*.) We must change the color of that dress. It makes her look too dark. (256)

Later we hear two women in the audience expressing their intense prejudice:

> VOICE OF WOMAN # 1 – You saw it. He touched her.
> VOICE OF WOMAN # 2 – He had to. He was supposed to be in love with her.
> VOICE OF WOMAN # 1 – But she is a Negress . . .
> VOICE OF WOMAN # 2 – She's almost white.
> VOICE OF WOMAN # 1 – There's no such thing as almost . . . You are either Black or White. (257–8)

We also realize that Rita was persecuted during the Batista dictatorship:

> RADIO ANNOUNCER'S VOICE – It is with deep regret that we announce that due to Rita's illness, her program will be replaced by . . .

> RITA – (*Grabs an imaginary microphone.*) Liars! You fascist censors. You want to silence my voice. But no one, do you hear me, no one, is going to silence my voice. My voice is the voice of my people. Do you hear me? The voice of my people! (*Struggles with two imaginary policemen who are trying to take her way*). (264)

Finally, the agent appears and the women compete for the role. Both of them are willing to conform to what is wanted of an actress/singer/dancer. Despite their desperate audition, the agent rejects both of them. Bessie is too dark and heavy, and the blues are dead. In Rita's case, she is too ethnic. According to him, these two great artists are not marketable any more because of their skin color.

This rejection results in the two women facing the reality of their lives. Rita remembers her fight for acceptance:

> I have witnessed many things. Of course, I knew they pretended to accept me. Hell! I made them accept me. Me, with the cinnamon skin, too light for a negro, too dark to pass.
>
> But I made them accept me! Me, with an overwhelming talent that two hundred whites couldn't match. Me, touring around the world with a basket of fruit on my head and yards of muslin ruffles hanging from my waist. Here comes the rumba dancer! Hang on to her train!!! Impersonator! I became an impersonator. A Latin woman impersonating the Latin image that was demanded and expected (. . .) (270)

She again recalls her persecution and the deplorable political situation of her country:

> They silenced my radio show but they couldn't cut my tongue out. My whip! How could I shut up? How could I witness the procession of presidents, dictators and politicians fucking up my country as if she were a whore and not speak up. You see, truth is ugly and they didn't want changes made, and I exposed the truth and truth exposed lies and liars. They wouldn't let me speak so changes could be made, but others will speak for me. (271)

Bessie also remembers the ugliness of her life:

> BESSIE – What do you wanna hear? That I grew up in the red light district in Philadelphia. Or better yet, that I had to fight rats in a single room in New York's Hell's Kitchen. Wait, that I toured the Southern states with an all-White band and wasn't allowed to use the public dining room or the bathrooms . . . (272)

Just as Rita is one of many Cubans who fought for political justice and equality, Bessie is one of many black entertainers who endured prejudice and racism. She emphatically states that all black women singers past, present, and future share with her the determination to accomplish their dreams despite their suffering and the horrors of racial discrimination:

BESSIE: Talk about impersonations! What else you wanna hear? That my name is not Bessie, and the real story that I'm a bastard, my name is Ethel. No, no, my name is Billie, no, no, my name is Josephine, and I was born in Saint Louis, perhaps my real name is Ma, and I'm the only one, Mother of the blues ... No, no, my name ... I've got so many names that they have swollen my fat body. Fat accumulated for one hundred years. One hundred years draggin' my fat body through the American wasteland. Oh, baby, they wanted to kill my dreams, but no sonafabitch was goin' to do that because others like me will stand up and will dream them with me ... (*The magnified sound of a gun shot is heard over a loudspeaker*). No one, ya' hear me? No one will be able to stop the dreamers. (272)

The play ends with the realization that both women are dead. They are liberated from the oppression and cruelty of their lives. In *Rita and Bessie*, these two popular singers represent all the ethnic minorities and political dissidents who have suffered throughout time. The locked room in which they await their audition symbolizes their restricted lives. The author uses his knowledge and sensitivity to portray the miserable human condition of these two women. Manuel Martín Jr leads us through their lives and shocks the reader/spectator at the end with the realization that they are dead. Now they are united and free. The play ends with the following declaration made by Rita: 'Together we will find a way out. Hold on sister. We are bursting the gates of heaven!' (276). Both Bessie and Rita are free at last. Free at last!

José Corrales and Manuel Pereiras García's *Las hetairas habaneras* and Raúl de Cárdenas's *Los hijos de Ochún* are plays that focus on the political theme in an Afro-Hellenic context. The intertextuality of these two dramatic pieces is evident. As a point of departure, *Las hetairas habaneras* focuses on Euripides' play *The Trojan Women*, while *Los hijos de Ochún* is inspired by Aeschylus' tragedy *The Persians*. In the play written by Raúl de Cárdenas, the war between the Greeks and the Persians is presented from the viewpoint of the conquered. Even though neither play follows closely the characteristics of Greek tragedy, they do adhere to the development of one theme and the use of the chorus. José Corrales and Manuel Pereiras García ably employ parody in their ethnic/ erotic/political play in order to subvert the Cuban revolutionary discourse. The parody revolves around the character of Menelao Garrigó, who personifies Fidel Castro. Religious syncretism permeates the play and is seen especially in the second act, when the prostitutes hum songs praising the child Nicomedes, who ironically represents the 'new man' under the revolution. The songs incorporate elements of Christian liturgy and African beliefs:

CHORUS: – Bless him Elegua/ deities of the forest bless him/ all the deities,/ From the royal palm and the silk-cotton tree/ I bring strength,/ haughtiness, bravery and charm./ And also with tobacco and coffee/ I bring to this child/ his grace and virtue.' Diosdada wants her daughter, a favorite of the god of prophecy Orula, to consult the Oracle of Ifá (*diloggún*) (*Presencia negra*, 104) in order to find out her grandson's future.[10] Yemayá and San Roque, who are identified in *Santería* with the dark Virgin of Regla[11] and the capricious orisha Elegua, prepare to punish the grandmother and the prostitutes for their irresponsible behavior toward the revolution:

> YEMAYÁ: That is nothing. For Diosdada, for all of them, I want the worst punishment. I want her grandson, Nicomedes, be left crippled, blind in one eye, blind forever . . . Let's go San Roque. Come with me. Diosdada will pay with her grandson for all her misdeeds. (*Presencia negra*, 104)

Corrales and Pereiras García are familiar with Afro-Cuban folklore and approach the black theme in their play with artistic sensibility and without prejudice. Corrales clarified his intensions when he explained that he and Pereiras García 'wished to place *Las hetairas habaneras* at the level of the common people. We had to, consciously and unconsciously, place ourselves artistically in a way of thinking and being that would fit comfortably within the racially mixed culture of Cuba' (*Presencia negra*, 94). This racially mixed culture referred to by both authors is indeed one of the characteristics of Cuba's multicultural society. But it is not the Afro-Cuban culture that foreigners often wrongly interpret in a stereotypical way. Corrales again indicates his feeling regarding the multicultural aspect of Cuban society:

> No one has to tell me that 'Black is beautiful'. For a long time, Cubans have taken it for granted and there are hundreds of examples that show that within negritude there is as much beauty as in other races. As an example we have Rita Montaner, Olga Guillot, La Lupe, Kid Chocolate, Kid Gavilán, Eusebia Cosme, and Wifredo Lam, who represent a great variety of beauty. Black beauty has been captured in the narratives of Lydia Cabrera, in the poems of Emilio Ballagas and Alina Galliano, and in the paintings of Lam. (*Presencia negra*, 93)

In *Los hijos de Ochún*, Raúl de Cárdenas uses Afro-Cuban mythology to evoke the tragic conflict of the Bay of Pigs, the war between brothers.[12] For example, the Persian queen Atossa becomes Ochún, who is identified in *Santería* with the Virgin del Cobre (Our Lady of Charity), patron saint of Cuba. Her son Xerxes becomes the Ibeyes, the Yoruba twin deities. They are Taebo and Kainde, twin sons of the African Aphrodite Ochún and Changó, the god of thunder, lightning and drums. In the play, however, Changó is a minor character

---

[10] The Yoruba priests and priestesses use the Oracle of Ifá (*diloggún*) to foretell the future. Orula, the wise one, is the *orisha* of divination.

[11] The patron saint of the fishing village of Regla, near Havana, is a dark Virgin who is identified in *Santería* with the *orisha* Yemayá.

[12] On 15 April 1961, about 1,500 Cubans in exile landed on the southern coast of Cuba at the Bay of Pigs (Playa Girón) in an attempt to overthrow the government of Fidel Castro. The invasion failed and many were taken prisoner.

who is identified with the ex-dictator Fulgencio Batista. On the other hand, Ogún, with his hatred and paranoid fears, is the incarnation of Fidel Castro. *Los hijos de Ochún*, rather than simply dealing with the outward results of armed conflict, delves into the causes of the conflict from the perspective of the conquered. The rivalry between the brothers Changó and Ogún reflects the present Cuban dilemma when Ogún accuses Changó's sons of provoking the conflict:

> OGÚN: I am Ogún, the god of iron and war/ who has come to devour them,/ so that Changó will pay all he owes me/ with the lives of his sons . . . / I have come to fulfill my eternal destiny/ with your blood/ because of my eternal hatred for Changó./ The account will be settled./ The cursed worms have returned. They have returned silently,/ to violate the sacred principles/ of our revolution. (*Presencia negra*, 157–8)

Ogún declares that history is on his side and that he is only fulfilling the wishes of the gods. Yet, Taebo and Kainde accuse him of being the true culprit of such tragedy by lying and selling out the country, with hate and rancor, to a foreign power. They have returned to Cuba out of duty to the homeland (*Presencia negra*, 157–8).

The tragedy ends with the capture and execution of Kainde by Ogún's order and the miraculous escape of his brother Taebo. The *itutu*, or Yoruba drumbeats, accompanied by the Miami chorus and an *akpuón*, or soloist, bring the play to an end. The majestic entrance of the goddess Ochún to receive the funeral procession of her dead son, wrapped in a Cuban flag, is cathartic. Ochún symbolizes the Cuban mothers whose sons have died in the power struggle. Taebo praises the courage of his brother and that of those who died for their country. The final verses of the play express the hope that someday there will be freedom for all Cubans:

> We are the furies, the tears of the mother that cries./ We are the wrath of the just patriot / who fought against Spain./ We are the bronze-skin of Maceo./ We are the poetry of Martí./ We are Cuba, we are one,/ and one in all who offered / their lives for liberty . . . / We are Cuba and Cuba shall be reborn again.
> (*Presencia negra*, 201)

The play *Los hijos de Ochún* aptly combines an elegant prose with great lyricism by using the chorus of Miami and the chorus of Havana as counterpoints with the constant interaction of the Afro-Cuban deities. In this play, the author uses various modern techniques of American drama and incorporates general characteristics of Aeschylus' tragedy *The Persians* in order to put the Cuban conflict in an Afro-Hellenic context underlining the eternal rivalry of the Yoruba gods Changó and Ogún. According to the author, the purpose in writing this play

> . . . no era solamente de llevar a la escena un capítulo de nuestra lucha por el renacimiento de la democracia en Cuba, sino a la vez hacerla visualmente rica

y espectacular. La incorporación de los elementos yorubas, parte esencial de nuestra cultura, con sus orishas y leyendas, eran exactamente lo que esta pieza necesitaba.

(... was not only to bring to the stage a chapter of our fight for the rebirth of democracy in Cuba, but at the same time to make this drama visually rich and moving. The incorporation of the Yoruba elements, an essential part of our culture, with its *orishas* and legends, was exactly what this dramatic piece needed.) (*Presencia negra*, 142)

To conclude, the Perfomance *E-Mociones* (*E-Motions*) by the artist Leandro Soto also shows the tapestry of Cuban society through its visual images. This is a society that by its very nature is multicultural where Blacks, Whites and Asians, especially Chinese, have contributed greatly. *E-Mociones* reflects this fact not only as an attitude, but also as a conscious aesthetic value where all cultures can be integrated from a spiritual and human context. This performance is a brilliant exercise of the universal language of images because, as the author states: 'It is an exercise of the universal language of images that speaks to the psyche, to the metaphor of the theater "because words at times are misunderstood"' (*Presencia negra*, 289).

The part of *E-Mociones* entitled 'The Spirits are Calling' presents a priestess of the Yoruba religion who wants to be alone. In a relaxed and meditative state, she is possessed by the spirits of the *orishas* or Yoruba deities that make her dance against her will. She hears and relates to the 'batá' drumming.[13] Her culture is an essential part of her being. Her African influence is not mere nostalgia, but real and takes hold of her. Visually the character shows feelings and carries out contradictory moves that go from stretching to relaxing, and from possession to consciousness of the trance. The stage directions of this Performance are extremely important. A light illuminates her throne, and the colors used on the stage are the emblematic colors identified with the Yoruba *orishas* Changó, Obatalá, and Yemayá. The dance she performs is associated with the dances attributed to Changó and Yemayá. At the end of her dance, a figure jumps on her back, symbolizing the *orisha* that has taken possession of her spirit on a tropical evening.

## Conclusion

The works discussed here represent an example of the variety of experiences and styles of the Afro-Cuban theater in the Diaspora. They portray a rich literary, religious, and magical world emanating from the African religions and folklore brought to Cuba by the different groups of slaves in the colonial time. The

---

[13] The *batá* drums are named *iyá*, *Itótele*, and *Okónkolo*. These drums, a big one, a medium-size one, and a small one, have been used for centuries to invoke the gods of Africa. They speak to the *orishas*, call them, and are played by master drummers.

characters in these dramatic pieces are no longer the stereotypical black buffoons or the mulatto women of the vernacular theater, nor are they the colonial carriage drivers or plantation servants that appeared in the past.[14] They are now real people who laugh, cry, feel, and suffer like any other human being. The ability of the playwrights discussed above to portray a person in all their complexity continues to be the focus of those who live in exile but carry Cuba in their hearts. As Matías Montes Huidobro argues,

> Afro-Cuban theater did not end in Cuba with *María Antonia*, who is the Carmen of Eugenio Hernández, nor with the marginalized dissidents in Abrahán Rodríguez's play *Andoba*. Like the characters in Rodriguez's play everyone came as they could, in rafts from far away, to this shore. (lecture given at the Miami Pen Club in 2000).

It is clear that Cuban playwrights and artists in exile continue to scrutinize the African influence in all aspects of Cuban culture and life. Through their works, they express their most intimate feelings as they rediscover their roots and search for their national identity in a foreign land. Indeed, the rich tapestry of Afro-Cuban folklore is alive in Cuba and in the Diaspora, and continues to be a main focus of inspiration for writers and artists from both shores.

## Works Cited

Alfonso, Paco. *La hierba hedionda*. La Habana: Editorial Letras Cubanas, 1981.
—— *Yara-Yari, mama Olúa*. La Habana: Editorial Letras Cubanas, 1981.
Alonso, Dora. *Caín o La hora de estar ciegos*. 1955.
Brene, José Ramón. *Santa Camila de La Habana*. La Habana: Ediciones El Puente, 1963.
Cabrera, Lydia. *El monte*. Miami: Ediciones Universal, 1975.
Cárdenas, Raúl de. *Los hijos de Ochún. Presencia negra: teatro cubano de la diáspora*. Madrid: Betania, 1999.
Castellanos, Isabel, and Jorge Castellanos. *Cultura Afrocubana*, vol. IV. Miami: Ediciones Universal, 1994.
Corrales, José, and Manuel Pereiras García. *Las hetairas habaneras*. Honolulu: Editorial Persona, 1988.
Díaz Parrado, Flora. *Juana Revolico*. Teatro. La Habana: Editorial Lex, 1944.
Dworkin y Méndez, Kenya C. 'De bufos y otros patriotas: En torno al teatro cubano de los tabaqueros tampeños', *Gestos: Teoría Práctica del Teatro Hispano*, 14:27 (1999), 85–100.

---

[14] For this popular type of theater in nineteenth-century Cuba and the Tampa Bay area, see Kenya C. Dworkin y Méndez, 'From Factory to Footlights: Original Spanish-language Cigar Workers' Theater in Ybor City and West Tampa, Florida', in *Recovering the US Hispanic Literary Heritage*, III (2000), 332–50; 'De bufos y otros patriotas: En torno al teatro cubano de los tabaqueros tampeños', *Gestos: Teoría Práctica del TeatroHispano*, 14:27 (1999), 85–100. Also see Matías Montes Huidobro's introduction to his critical edition of *Los negros catedráticos* (Honolulu: Editorial Persona, 1987).

―― 'From Factory to Footlights: Original Spanish-language Cigar Workers' Theater in Ybor City and West Tampa, Florida', in *Recovering the US Hispanic Literary Heritage*, III (2000), 332–50.
Escarpanter, José A. 'Rasgos comparativos entre la literature de la isla y del exilio: el tema histórica en el teatro', *Ollantay* (1993), 53–62.
Estorino, Abelardo. *Parece blanca*. Teatro. La Habana: Editorial Letras Cubanas, 1994.
Felipe, Carlos. *Réquiem por Yarini. Teatro cubano contemporáneo: antologia*, ed. Carlos Espinosa Domínguez. Madrid: Sociedad Estatal Centenario, Fondo de Cultura Económica, 1992.
Fulleda, León. *Chago de Guisa*. La Habana: Casa de la América, 1989.
―― *Plácido*. 1982.
González-Pérez, Armando. *Presencia negra: teatro cubano de la diáspora*. Madrid: Betania, 1999.
Guillén, Nicolás. *Sóngoro Cosongo. Motivos de Son. West Indies LTD. España: poema en cuatro angustias y una esperanza*. Buenos Aires: Editorial Losada, S.A., 1952.
Hernández Espínosa, Eugenio. *María Antonia*. Teatro. La Habana: Editorial Letras Cubanas, 1994.
Leal, Rine. *Teatro bufo: Siglo XIX: Antología*. 2 tomos. La Habana: Editorial Arte y Literature, 1975.
Martín Jr, Manuel. *Rita and Bessie. Presencia negra: teatro cubano de la diáspora*. Madrid: Betania, 1999.
Martínez Furé, Rogelio. 'Black Culture, Cuban Culture', in *Cuban Update*, XXVI (1991), 27–38.
Millián, José. *Mamico Omi Omo*. La Habana: Ediciones El Puente, 1965.
Montes Huidobro, Matías. *La navaja de Olofé*. Honolulu: Editorial Persona, 1991.
―― (ed.) *Los negros catedráticos de Francisco Fernández*. Honolulu: Editorial Persona, 1987.
―― *Persona, vida y máscara en el teatro cubano*. Miami: Ediciones Universal, 1973.
Ortiz, Fernando. *Los bailes y el teatro de los negros en el folklore de Cuba*. La Habana: Letras Cubanas, 1987.
Piñera, Virgilio. *Electra Garrigó. Teatro cubano contemporáneo: antologia*, ed. Carlos Espinosa Domínguez. Madrid: Sociedad Estatal Centenario, Fondo de Cultura Económica, 1992.
Prida, Dolores. *Botánica. Beautiful Señorita and Other Plays*. Houston: Arte Público, 1991.
Soto, Leandro. *Emociones/E-Motions*. 1999. *Presencia negra: teatro cubano de la diáspora*. Madrid: Betania, 1999.
Svich, Caridad. *Brazo Gitano*. Ollantay: *Theater Magazine*, vol. VI, No. 11, 1999.
Triana, José. *La muerte del Ñeque*. La Habana: Ediciones R, 1964.
―― *Medea en el espejo*. Madrid: Verbum, 1998.

# 6

# Between the Island and the Tenements: New Directions in Dominican-American Literature

## ELIZABETH COONROD MARTÍNEZ

While Dominican-American literature has not figured as prominently as the other groups in US Latino classifications, Dominicans have recently soared to comprise the fourth-largest Latino population in the United States. In fact, the US Dominican population represents one of the most rapidly growing of all Latino groups. The 2000 Census reported 764,495 Dominicans living in the US, but other studies have shown that the count was not adequately defined and that the population is much higher. By using federal Current Population Survey (CPS) statistics, a count conducted by the Mumford Center at the University of Albany and the North-South Center at the University of Miami identified more than a million Dominican-Americans.

One of the earliest critical overviews of literature in the US published by Latin American-derived peoples was Marc Zimmerman's *US Latino Literature* (1992). It did not, however, include an entry for Dominican-American literature. Five years later, though, William Luis's *Dance Between Two Cultures: Latino Caribbean Literature Written in the United States* found space for two chapters on Dominican-American writers, as well as two chapters each on Puerto Rican and Cuban-American writers. In 2000, the Caribbean-focused literary journal *Callaloo* published a special issue on Dominican-American literature, edited by Lizabeth Paravisini-Gebert and Consuelo López-Springfield, which included forty-two contributors. Thus, the diversification of US Latino literary contributions has coincided with the arrival of greater numbers of Dominicans.

In the early 1990s, the only well-known author of Dominican heritage writing in English was Julia Alvarez. As the twenty-first century was ushered in, however, a new generation of Dominican-American novelists burst onto the pages of US Latino literature. This new generation includes Junot Díaz with *Drown* (1996), Loida Maritza Pérez with *Geographies of Home* (1999), Nelly Rosario with *Song of the Water Saints* (2002), and Angie Cruz with *Soledad* (2001) and *Let it Rain Coffee* (2005). Nearly all of these novels have also been published in Spanish translation.

Meanwhile, major poets on the island are being discovered in English translation in journals and bilingual anthologies. These poems help to broaden pan-

Caribbean cultural understanding. It is an apt moment to devote attention to Dominican-American literature, as this immigrant population becomes more and more visible on the East Coast. Contemporary eminent literary critic José Alcántara Almánzar has noted that the Dominican Republic falls behind its neighboring islands, Cuba and Puerto Rico, in terms of exporting its literature in translation to other nations. Alcántara himself was co-editor of a 1979 *Encyclopedia of Caribbean Writers*, while his considerable literary criticism has been published only in Spanish. He spent 1987–88 on an academic exchange at Stillman College in Alabama, but otherwise resides on the island. He is an excellent short story writer and has received the Dominican national prize for short story twice, in 1983 and again in 1989. Born in 1948, Alcántara is a member of the new generation of Dominican writers.

A principal poetic voice of the nineteenth century in the Dominican Republic is a woman, Salomé Ureña Henríquez (1850–1897), who created several patriotic verses in homage to her nation (her life has been depicted in a recent novel by Julia Alvarez). Since girls were not permitted to study beyond grade-school, she received further instruction from her parents, and began writing poems as a teenager. Once she was a nationally recognized poet, she further contributed to her nation by founding the first high school for girls.

Two prominent Dominican writers who have had an impact on Dominican-Americans are Juan Bosch (1909–2001) and Pedro Mir (1913–2000). The first is the son of a Puerto Rican mother and Dominican father. He fled his homeland in 1937, residing in Puerto Rico and then Latin America until he could return to the Dominican Republic in the waning days of dictator Rafael Leonidas Trujillo's regime. Bosch, who became president in 1963, published a novel in 1936, but it is his stories that are noted for revealing the essence of the Dominican people, especially the *campesinos* or country folk who were essential in the heyday of plantations but who now try to survive on their own off the land.

Like Bosch, Pedro Mir also had North American connections by way of Puerto Rico: he was born in Santo Domingo of a Puerto Rican mother and a Cuban father. Mir is best-known outside the Caribbean for his short stories and for three celebrated poems: 'Hay un país en el mundo' (There is a Nation in the World) (1949), on the need for the oppressed of the world to have a space where they can gestate their own liberty; 'Contracanto a Walt Whitman' (Countersong to Walt Whitman) (1952), a tribute to the US poet; and 'Amén de mariposas' (Amen by Butterflies) (1969), a tribute to the Mirabal sisters whose assassination was ordered by Trujillo. The final stanza of the first, an epic poem, surges – following dramatic descriptions of the movements of mountains and new placement of aspects of nature – to declare:

> Afterwards
> I want only peace
> A nest
> Of contructive peace in each palm
> And perhaps with relation to the soul

A swarm of kisses
And forgetfulness

A member of Bosch and Mir's generation was Aída Cartagena Portalatín (1918–94), a forerunner in evoking Afro-Caribbean heritage in her poetry, writing, and speeches. She traveled extensively to Europe, Africa, and Latin America during the mid-twentieth century, in representation of the Dominican nation. Julia Alvarez pays tribute to her in an essay titled 'Doña Aída', in her book *Something to Declare* (1998). Hilma Contreras, born in 1913, is well-known for her existentialist short stories, describing life in the countryside and the underlying impact of patriarchal rules on girls' lives. Several male writers in a subsequent generation have followed in her footsteps to create an Afro-Dominican context. They include Juan Sánchez Lamouth, Antonio Viau Renaud, and Norberto James Rawlings. Each is third-generation Dominican, of West Indian, Haitian and African-American descent respectively, and writes in Spanish.

The contemporary literary generation has in common with earlier writers a life frequently lived in exile or transition, and the desire to reveal the hybrid nature of Caribbean culture. Those who reside in the US have the additional trademark of writing in a combination of Spanish with English, although mostly in English. Dominicans who live and publish in the US are more keenly aware of the denial of their African heritage, and represent society's erroneous definitions while collecting the strands of their hybrid past and present. Born in the Dominican Republic but educated in the US, critic/professor and director of the CUNY Dominican Studies Institute Daisy Cocco de Filippis has compiled a book spanning two centuries of short writings by Dominican women writers. The themes of these writings include the need for women's rights and for recognition of the true roots of the Dominican people.

Born in the Bronx in 1948, poet and visual artist Sandra María Esteves is one of the earliest voices of the dual experience of suffering discrimination on the island and in the US. Her mother is Puerto Rican and her father Dominican. She writes in English and Spanish, and first became involved in literary collaborations in 1972. She is now a principal member of the literary generation espousing a Nuyorican identity. Esteves has stated that, upon having been struck by her teachers for speaking Spanish, she was aware she genuinely did not know which of her words were one or another language. She therefore became afraid to speak at all and withdrew, expressing herself only in artistic drawings. Her entry into poetry occurred after she translated for others at the Nuyorican Poet's Café, and then sought the opportunity to share her own verses on stage. Her oft-anthologized poem, 'Here', begins:

I am two parts/a person
boricua/spic
past and present
alive and oppressed

given a cultural beauty
and robbed of a cultural identity

Although a founding poet of the Nuyorican poetry movement, Esteves has not been remembered as prominently as male poets, such as Miguel Piñero. Her book *Yerba Buena* earned her a citation from *Library Journal* as the best of the small press offerings for 1980, but she often laments the difficulty in getting access to publishing opportunities. She describes the need for a restoration of the roots of Caribbean heritage in the following stanza from 'It is Raining Today':

> La lluvia contains our history
> In the space of each tear Cacique valleys and hills
> Taíno, Arawak, Carib, Ife, Congo, Anglola, Mesa
> Mandinko, Dahome, Amer, African priests tribes
> Of the past
> Murdered ancestors
> Today, voices in the mist
> Where is our history? (Santiago, 19)

A poet popular on the island and in the US is Soledad Alvarez, of the same generation as Esteves. She resides in Santo Domingo, where she was born in 1950. She completed a degree in literature at the University of Havana, and writes in Spanish, but her poetry is now being translated into English and included in various anthologies. Her themes include the perspective of the female as well as the underdogs of society, whose voices often go unheard and unheeded.

Women writers often pay tribute to their female predecessors, and strive to help others on to the literary path. Sherezada 'Chiqui' Vicioso was born in Santo Domingo in 1948, but she completed her education in the US with a BA at the City University of New York (CUNY) in Brooklyn and an MA at Columbia University. She worked for the United Nations in Latin America for many years, but she resides primarily in Santo Domingo. In 1980 she founded a circle of women poets in New York to help fledgling poets achieve publication. A significant member of the circle was Julia Alvarez, who was assisted by Vicioso in getting her first book of poems published. Vicioso did an academic study on Salomé Ureña Henríquez (as well as on her son, literary figure Pedro Henríquez), which attracted Alvarez's attention. Vicioso's poetry published in the 1980s has been collected in translation in recent anthologies, such as Cocco de Filippis's books. By the 1990s, Vicioso was working primarily on drama, and in 1998 she received a national drama award in the Dominican Republic. In a non-fiction essay published in the special *Callaloo* issue, Vicioso explained the ambiguous nature of color identification in the Dominican Republic, and the flight from blackness as one of the characters explains the preference for the terms such as 'india clara' (light Indian) over 'black' as a marker of identity (1014).

Vicioso's narrative describes a long-standing attempt by the Dominican hegemony to eradicate blackness by redefining the term in Spanish, 'negro' (*moreno* or 'dark' is used in contemporary society), as Indian. The result of this racist campaign, initiated in the nineteenth century, is the basis of contemporary Dominican culture, which separates its citizens into groups of *blancos* and *indios*, leaving black completely out of its society. The nation is based on the Hispanic colonial romanticized notion of the Spaniard as the father conquering or subduing the native Indian woman, who becomes the mother of a *mestizo* race.[1] This fallacy continues to be espoused by the elite, which refuses to include in a census – thus denying state benefits – those who are black (hence the bribe to be classified as lighter), instead identifying them as Haitians or 'temporary' despite their being born in the Dominican Republic. Recent literature seeks to rebalance Dominican sense of identity and correct this erasure.

Novelists, who by writing in English help broaden modern discourse on culture, depict the lives of Dominicans who come to the US for the fabled American dream and economic betterment but instead must raise their children in tenements and unsafe urban areas. They are often relating the story of their parents, who trade increasing poverty and lack of jobs on the island for New York's supposed opportunities. Representing the generation ahead of them, the first voice in Dominican-American writing is Julia Altagracia Alvarez. Born in New York City in 1950, Alvarez was nearly immediately transplanted to the island where she grew up until she was ten years old. Her family then fled Trujillo's dictatorship and settled in Brooklyn, where her father established a medical practice. She attended college in Connecticut and Vermont, and earned a master's degree at Syracuse University in 1975. Alvarez's work continually explores her own *hyphen* identity, that of being neither entirely Dominican nor American. She often refers to herself as a Dominican *gringa*, or the hybrid offspring of Dominicans. In her essay, 'La Gringuita: On Losing a Native Language' (published in *Something to Declare*, 61–73), she describes her US classmates and teacher's condescending treatment when they heard her speak Spanish, as well as the reaction to her as a *gringa* during summers spent in Santo Domingo.

Alvarez has published five novels, five books of poetry, several children's and young adult books, and a collection of essays, *Something to Declare* (1998), which has been celebrated for its insightful analysis of the problematics of living in two cultures and seemingly belonging to neither. Alvarez's many literary awards and fellowships came early in her career; poetry awards in 1980, 1982, and 1984–85; a prize in narrative from Third Woman Press in 1986, the same year she received a fellowship to participate in the Bread Loaf Writers Conference, and a PEN Oakland Award. The following year she was awarded a National Endowment for the Arts grant, and began crafting novels. Alvarez is currently writer-in-residence at Middlebury College in Vermont.

Her first book of poetry, *The Housekeeping Book*, appeared in 1984, when she was well into her thirties. A collaboration with Chiqui Vicioso, it was

---

[1] This was exemplified in the 1882 novel *Enriquillo* by Manuel Jesús Galván.

supplemented by new poems – with themes often celebrating nature – under an edition titled *Homecoming*, published in 1991. In 1996, Alvarez issued *Homecoming: New and Collected Poems*, which includes both previous and various new sections, with prevalent themes of domestic duties, celebrating daily life, and finding ritual in the mundane. Her poems often explore family stories from the perspective of the female, a search for identity, and her views on patriarchal tradition in her culture. The 'homecoming' is also a return to the home of language, necessary for those living in exile. Another collection of poems, *The Other Side* (*El otro lado*) (1995), takes its exploration to the countryside of the Dominican Republic (where Alvarez lived as a writer-in-residence). Her poems continue to reveal an intimate style, and the plight of workers on the island, such as maids, as well as their transition from the island to New York, struggling with trying to quickly acquire a new language. The immigrant voice is strongly represented.[2] Alvarez's most recent book of poetry, *The Woman I Kept to Myself* (2004), continues themes of cultural identity interwoven with images from nature, and the perspective of a female who chooses the path of writing in place of traditional roles including becoming a mother.

In her first novel, *How the García Girls Lost Their Accents* (1991), Alvarez innovatively portrayed the need to assimilate and discard cultural and linguistic differences once one is *American*, through the experiences of four sisters. But the novel also depicts irreconcilable gender messages for girls raised in the US. Upon spending summers on the island, they discover that if they are not chaperoned, they can lose their honor, that boyfriends monitor their activities and discourage reading, and that male babies – especially light-skinned – are considered a greater treasure for a family than female babies. Racial distinctions are noted using the terms prevalent in Dominican society, *café-con-leche* and a 'caramel color body' for the Dominicans, while those of darker complexion are called Haitians. Although not as overt as the US literary generation that follows her, Alvarez's novel begins to open discussion on caste or class systems that has not occurred in recent Dominican literature in Spanish.

Her second novel, *In the Time of the Butterflies* (1994), depicted life under the Trujillo dictatorship during the 1940s and 1950s, while the third, *¡Yo!* (1997), continued the story of one of the characters of her first novel who has become a writer, fomenting discussion of family and cultural conflicts. A fourth novel, *In Search of Salomé* (2000), takes place both in the US and on the island, portraying the career of the poet Salomé Ureña Henríquez – a young woman who finds a way to enter the literary world when women had little access – and of her daughter who lived in the US. Alvarez's characters are always female, and take positions contrary to the dictates of their society and culture.

*In the Time of the Butterflies* is an excellent historical portrayal of life on the

---

[2] For an interesting assessment of poetry by Alvarez and other Dominican-Americans, see William Luis's *Dance Between Two Cultures*, Chapter 6. An excellent text on various Dominican-American poets is Daisy Cocco de Filippis's *Poemas del exilio y de otras inquietudes / Poems of Exile and Other Concerns* (New York: Ediciones Alcance, 1988).

Caribbean island in the early twentieth century. In the novel the principal character, Minerva, meditates on both the decorations and the origins of the island, erased by European invasion. She states that it always rains at this time of year because the god of thunder Huracán always acts up on the 'holiday of the conquistador'[3] who killed off the native Tainos.[4] During Trujillo's festivities, the Spanish ambassador 'presents this illustrious descendant (Trujillo) of the great Conquistador (Columbus) with yet another medal' (95).

Alvarez's novel demonstrates this attitude on the part of Trujillo, but does not discuss Haiti. For other recent writers, Haiti is part and parcel of the Dominican story. While Alvarez's novel signals Trujillo's need to identify with a white, European race, it does not specifically depict Afro-Caribbean heritage.[5] The Showtime film based on *In the Time of the Butterflies* and bearing the same name deals with the issue of race more directly. The film shows that the targeting of black Haitians was central to Trujillo's political agenda. In fact, one of his principal atrocities of his regime was the massacre of thousands of Haitians in 1937.[6]

Haiti was an important symbol of autonomy and independence in the Caribbean and Latin America for having achieved freedom from European colonialism in 1804. But its strength (a twelve-year struggle with France, independence, and nineteenth-century preeminence) was greatly diminished by 1915 (Dash, 52). Cuba and Puerto Rico, which ceased to be colonies of Spain in the twentieth century, took on greater importance in the Caribbean as the US forged and shaped their economies and politics. The Dominican Republic's personality has rested in the shadows behind these two. Alvarez's novel alludes to this early history, while the film immediately relates not only the terror of Trujillo's reign, but also what Dominicans look like, substantiating a sense of the Afro-Caribbean. The Showtime film is more forceful by having the subversive character Lío Morales state that Trujillo has 'a secret campaign to murder thousands

---

[3] Alvarez's *In the Time of the Butterflies*, 93 (other references to this novel follow in parenthesis).

[4] The Tainos were friendly to Christopher Columbus when he first arrived, helping the Spaniards build a fort and other structures, but they were soon forced into more and more brutal labor extracting gold inland. They attempted to rebel and went to battle in 1495, suffering a disastrous defeat. From then on, they were for all practical purposes enslaved. In 1519, two-thirds of the remaining Taino population succumbed to a smallpox epidemic, leaving fewer than three thousand (Bell, 16) on Hispaniola. As a comparison, the Taino population on the island now known as Puerto Rico – called *Borikén* by the Taino – was estimated at 30,000 when the Spaniards first arrived (Wagenheim, 39). They also were forced into hard labor, rebelled and were crushed, and also succumbed to European diseases.

[5] From 1822 to 1844 the entire island was occupied and ruled by the Haitian government. Two recent novels that passionately reveal the Haitian-Dominican story are Edwidge Danticat's *The Farming of Bones* (she was born in Haiti and moved to the US when she was 12), and Cuban-Puerto Rican Mayra Montero's *The Red of His Shadow*.

[6] Trujillo benefited from the fact that the Haitian government was weak and not as favored by the US as his own. He provided a cash settlement for the victims' families and the affair was officially closed (Bell, 68). Danticat's novel specifically engages the Haitian massacre.

of Haitians because they are contaminating the Dominican race'. The declared general belief in the Dominican Republic has been that Dominicans are white and Haitians black.[7] While fewer Africans arrived on the Spanish side of the island during the colonial era, several generations since independence disavow the idea that Dominicans are only white.

*In the Time of the Butterflies* also demonstrates a strong authoritarian and patriarchal culture inherited from Spain. While Minerva adores her father, she is heavily disappointed to discover he has a second family – a common-law wife and three children – living in a nearby village. The shortened film version missed including this important facet, instead imparting a sense of men in charge. In Alvarez's novel, Minerva teaches her younger sister, Mate, about the great poet and Cuban revolutionary hero José Martí, and quotes from his poetry on several occasions. Martí is a super-hero to all Latin Americans for his writing as well as his desire for Latin American nations' autonomy and independence. The film, however, has Lío giving Minerva a copy of a book by José Martí. She tells him she knows who Martí is, but takes the book nonetheless, also accepting his coquettish advances. The film thus makes it seem as if Minerva learned about José Martí from Lío, whereas, according to the novel, she learns about clandestine activities from him. The novel shows that as early as 1948 Lío Morales is seeking asylum outside the country, and wants to take Minerva with him to work with outside forces. But her father intercepts the letters from Lío, and hides them.

Minerva does not require guidance from Lío. She is already revolutionary in mind and spirit. In the novel, she is the one who has instructed Mate about the great poet Martí. Also, on Mate's birthday, she presents her sister with a book of poems by Chilean Gabriela Mistral, reinforcing the providing of a woman model by a woman (and another incident not included in the film). Mistral was the first Latin American to win the Nobel Prize for literature, in 1945, when Minerva is a college student. Minerva wants justice and a better life in her nation. She reads voraciously, studies, and prepares to become an attorney. Her sisters are also intelligent women. In fact, Alvarez demonstrates – with the thoughts of Minerva's older sister, Dedé – that women would approach leadership differently. Dedé reacts to Lío's comments:

> . . . a long lecture about the rights of the *campesinos*, the nationalization of sugar, and the driving away of the Yanqui imperialists. She had wanted something practical, something she could use to stave off her growing fears. First, we need to depose the dictator in this and this way. Second, we have arranged for a provisional government. Third, we mean to set up a committee of private citizens to oversee free elections. She would have understood talk like that. (77)

---

[7] Currently when visitors to the Dominican Republic point out people of African heritage to those who state that Dominicans are white, the response is simply that they are Haitian.

Alvarez's characters desire education, careers, administering their own businesses, and having the freedom to walk the streets. None of these things are possible (without Trujillo's permission) in the Dominican Republic of the 1940s and 1950s. The national struggle, for Alvarez, is one of memory against the erasing of island history and origins, origins that pre-date Columbus as well as Trujillo. Alvarez's novel *remembers* those who have been overlooked or ignored in mainstream depictions. The Dominican story cannot be told without an understanding of the Spanish conquest and a Hispanic class system inherited from colonial Spain (where Whites reigned supreme); nor without the story of the Taínos, whose cultural stories continue despite their extinction. The film restores African heritage to the Dominican story. Equality and understanding of all aspects – race, gender, and class – of community and nation is needed to achieve balance in a society.

Alvarez broaches the fact that Trujillo has US support (US involvement in the Dominican Republic is also cited by subsequent novelists): after a failed coup attempt in the late 1950s, Minerva asks why US officials withdrew. 'They got cold feet,' she is told. 'They say they don't want another Fidel. They would rather have a dozen Trujillos' (273). Trujillo is not only associated with the Spaniards who conquered and subdued the island just as he, 450 years later, kills at will and keeps his subjects subdued, he is also honored by Spain and supported by other imperialist nations, including the US. Towards the end of the film, Trujillo impassively evokes a chilling statement, following Minerva's plea to free her and her sisters' husbands from prison: 'I will do everything I can to end your troubles.' He then orders the massacre of the three sisters. Thus, Alvarez's writing and the complement of this film show that the process of 'ending' Latin American problems by the hegemony has consistently resulted in their deaths.

## The new generation

The sense of US intervention and the experience of immigration to the US for reasons of drastic economic need permeate the writings of the next generation. Their works inaugurate a generation that is neither Dominican nor American, forging a sort of Dominican-New York identity, akin to the Nuyorican. The majority of Dominican immigrants are working-class people; they cluster in the lowest tiers of the labor market and rank among the lowest-paid groups of workers in the US. Vibrant portraits of their lives are evident in five recent novels by four writers: Loida Maritza Pérez, Junot Díaz, Angie Cruz, and Nelly Rosario. All but Cruz were born on the island and soon transplanted. Their stories portray the problematics of inner-city life, dead-end jobs and the dream of making dollars and returning home to the island.

### *Loida Maritza Pérez*

Loida Martiza Pérez was born in 1963; her family moved to Brooklyn when she was three years old. Her novel is somewhat similar to those of Cruz and Pérez –

a female protagonist escapes her family circumstances by leaving to pursue an education – but this strong novel also demonstrates a cycle of abuse, physical, mental, and sexual. As Julia Alvarez has put it, Pérez addresses the heart of darkness at the center of the American Dream. Her protagonist, one of the youngest in a brood of fourteen, returns home after only eighteen months away at college to try to help repair a crisis in her family (a sister has disappeared). As with the other novels, the family home, with a central mother figure, serves as a metaphor of the cultural identity being sought, both personal and national. Therefore, the protagonist must return in order to understand herself.

*Geographies of Home* (1999) is a substantial novel with complex characters but, unlike a traditional novel, the ending is left open. The main character, Iliana, is resolved to unite her search for personal identity with that of her family and culture. She is painfully aware of the negative aspects of a patriarchal culture, learned in her own family and exacerbated by living conditions in the inner city. This lesson transfers to the greater environment around her. As she walks down the street and hears catcalls,

> She told herself that if ignored the man would go away. Yet she could not help but recall her brothers' notion that a woman's walk conveyed her sexual status and availability. If she had been penetrated, and recently at that, her hips would thrust forward and sway as if unhinged. If she remained intact, she would walk as if protecting what she foolishly deemed a treasure . . . Surely her walk had convinced him that she was loose. (307)

In her family however, one of her brothers is having an affair with another's wife, her youngest brother appears to have sexually molested one of the sisters, who is mentally unstable because of a brutal rape she could not tell her family about. Another sister continues to live with a man who beats her. This family – residing in its own dilapidated 'home' in Brooklyn – could represent a microcosm of American society, or the effects of living under the dire abuses of the Trujillo regime. Iliana's painful memory of her father beating her when she was three years old is recalled by her own father towards the end of the novel, when he states that she needed to learn 'to be afraid'.

Issues of racism arise both outside and in the home. Her community is one in which she is a double or triple minority. Iliana remembered how she yearned to look like the Puerto Rican or black American girls so that she could identify as belonging to either group. She used to hate the question, 'Where you from?' because few of her classmates knew of the Dominican Republic and several of her black friends assumed that she 'claimed to be Hispanic in order to put on airs' (190).

At college, Iliana encounters epithets on paper, pinned to the door of her dorm room. She doesn't date and her closest friend is a gay male. As a strong and independent type, she is often accused of acting like a man. At home, her sister teases that she leaves in order to be with a man: 'A big, black stud. That's what you want.' When Iliana retorts 'what could be wrong with that', her sister states she could do better.

'Better? What the hell is that supposed to mean?'
'You know how black men are.'
'No, Marina. Tell me.'
'They're lazy and undependable.'
'You've been watching too much TV,' Iliana snapped.
'TV, my ass. Look at all your brothers.'

When Iliana asks her if she thinks blacks are inferior, including herself, Marina responds: 'I'm Hispanic, not black.' Iliana retorts, 'What color is your skin?' and her sister continues to insist she is Hispanic (38).

Iliana's mother contemplates returning to the island, but she and her husband had remained in order 'to be near their married children and because their youngest children, remembering little of their birth land, considered it a backward, poverty-ridden place. Now she wondered if by emigrating they had unwittingly caused their children to yearn for a wealth generally portrayed as easily accessible to anyone in the States' (21–2). She eventually betrays the western religion they have adopted and returns to *Santería*, which adds a mystical quality to the novel. In fact, the elements outside a physical reality (also found in Cruz's and Rosario's novels) lift the narrative from the insanity of the characters' lives to another level where they can find redemption and resilience in family.

The novel includes occasional phrases in Spanish and has a riveting tempo, leaving the reader both aghast at and sympathetic to the characters' plights. In an interview with the journal *Meridians*, Pérez discusses the immigrant experience and says she considers borders 'imaginary', stating that 'home' becomes even harder to define when one is also taken as an 'outsider in one's native country for having lived abroad'. She adds that those who leave are more prone to question myths about history, culture, class, and race, for example, 'the myth that Dominicans are *Indios*, or Spanish. These myths negate the African and purposefully warp history.' Pérez completed her degree at Cornell in 1987, the place where fellow Dominican-American writer Junot Díaz would pursue graduate work.

## *Junot Díaz*

Junot Díaz was born in 1968, and arrived in the US aged seven. He grew up in northern New Jersey and completed his degree at Rutgers University before going on to Cornell. His collection of ten interrelated stories, also considered a novel, *Drown*, was published to great acclaim in 1996. A Spanish translation of this text was released the following year, under the title of a different story in the collection, *Negocios*. As an urban youth, Díaz worked in furniture delivery and at a steel mill during college. He considers himself 'lucky' to have been offered scholarships, and for the opportunity in his youth to attend a good high school. As he stated in an interview, one could 'accidentally end up, by freak accident of geography, being bused into a school which has more money than the school you would have gone to if you had lived two blocks away'. In commenting on his plans before college, Díaz observed that 'immigrants have a terrifying work ethic, I knew I could never be adequate to my parents. I saw what they did and knew I could never duplicate it.'[8] Instead, Díaz planned to prepare for a career as a teacher, and discovered his writing talent on the side. His work has been greatly celebrated – more so than that of his female counterparts – for his crisp, spare writing style, and his stories of startling and at times disturbing violence poetically relate Dominican-American life.

The setting for many of the stories in *Drown* is the US East Coast, as immigrants arrive, seek work, and experience being robbed or cheated by employers or by acquaintances. 'Negocios', a considerable story of forty-five pages, depicts a man in his twenties who leaves his wife and children behind and heads for the US to make a better life for them. He arrives in Miami and finds a job washing dishes in what was 'once a gringo diner of the hamburger-and-soda variety, the (Cuban sandwich) shop was now filled with *óyeme*'s and the aroma of *lechón*'. He works two long shifts per day with four-hour breaks in between, on one break napping in the storeroom, the other sleeping on the floor of the living room in an apartment he shares with three Guatemalans. He avoids thinking of his family, only of 'today and tomorrow', and when he has learned a little English leaves on a bus for New York (which gets him halfway, he hitch-hikes the rest of the way). He had not been able to save any money, and discovered that one of the Guatemalans was not paying rent, deceiving the others by having them pay it all.

During his first year the character lives in Washington Heights, in a roach-infested flat above a restaurant. He has two jobs and saves a good amount of money in order to pay someone to arrange a marriage for him and thus his legal residence. But he is cheated out of his money. As he learns more English, he finds better jobs, and eventually meets a Dominican woman with a daughter and an apartment in Queens. He marries and moves in with her, and with a close friend finds a high-paying job at Reynolds Aluminum where he is subjected to heavy work and the least preferable shifts. He makes the acquaintance of a friend who has a cluster of hot dog carts, and dreams of creating his own *negocio*. Another friend takes him to a housing construction site in New Jersey, which will need superintendents, he tells him, who will receive salary and free rent. The main character begins to dream about bringing his first family over from the island to live at this site, and secretly stashes money. But after a severe back injury at the Reynolds plant and three weeks' medical leave, he is demoted, and eventually loses his job. The story ends with his thoughts of returning to the island.

'Aguantando' serves as a contrast to the above story, focusing on the experience of a mother of two young boys, left behind to survive and cope alone (as the title suggests) once her husband leaves for New York. It is told from the perspective of the younger son, Rafa, who is left at an aunt's house for several months when his mother loses a job at the Embajador chocolate factory, where

---

[8] Diógenes Céspedes and Silvio Torres-Saillant, 'Fiction is the Poor Man's Cinema. An Interview with Junot Díaz', *Callaloo*, 23:3 (2000), 892–907.

'she pulls twelve-hour shifts for almost no money at all'. When his mother returns to collect him, she is wearing a bright red dress and her nails are painted, seeming to indicate another type of work she has had to take on. Abuelo talks to the child 'about the good old days, when a man could still make a living from his *finca*, when the United States wasn't something folks planned on'. His mother receives a letter that *papi* is returning, and nervously prepares for the day, but when he never arrives, she is despondent. The child climbs his tree and dreams of seeing his father; he is taller because 'Northamerican food makes people that way'. He'll be driving a car, wearing a silk shirt and good leather shoes; the child's words echo the dreams of his village.

Other stories depict the same narrator searching for his father; reunited with him; a character working a job delivering furniture in New Jersey; an adolescent drug dealer reacting to the knowledge that his best friend is gay. The first story in the collection, 'Ysrael', takes place on the island and features two brothers, Rafa and Yunior, who are living in the countryside (for reasons of economic hardship, their mother is unable to care for them). They are obsessed with a boy in a nearby town who wears a mask because his face was eaten off by pigs, but when they meet him, they are jealous of the boy's close relationship with his father; Rafa reacts by giving Ysrael a serious beating. The boys are dealing with their lack of a father and the sustenance he might provide, as well as the lack of a sense of nation and its sustenance. The Dominican's invisibility, as pointed out by Anne Connor (2002), is represented in each of the young, defenseless characters, Yunior and Ysrael (the latter's perspective featured in the story 'No face'). The grasping for an identity or something solid on which to base an identity permeates the stories, further complicated by the sexual fondling of Yunior without his consent by a man who sits beside him on a bus. This occurrence serves as prelude to the same character's first homosexual encounter later in the story 'Drown'.

Díaz acknowledges the influences of Nuyorican poets as well as of African-American poets and novelists. He recognizes that the 'generation right before me grew up in the US at a time when they were invisible. They didn't talk about being Puerto Rican or Dominican' (Céspedes, 896). His generation is 'a nation asserting their Latino roots', which includes people of diverse ethnic/racial heritage. These sentiments are echoed by young novelists such as Angie Cruz and Nelly Rosario, albeit from a female perspective.

*Angie Cruz*
Angie Cruz, born in 1972 (like Nelly Rosario) in New York City, poignantly renders sexual awakening and the female perspective in her first novel, *Soledad* (2001). The title character is a 20-year-old art student who is proud of her tiny apartment shared with a roommate in Manhattan, and ashamed of the ghetto where she was raised. When her mother falls ill, she is forced to return home and face the cultural element of her *barrio*, as well as the family skeletons in the closet. The novel offers the following tantalizing description of Washington Heights:

> As soon as I arrive at 164th Street I'm attacked. I trip on the uneven sidewalk. The air-conditioners spit at me. The smell of onion and cilantro sting my eyes. I start to sneeze, the humidity is thick, sweat beads drip on the small of my back. Hydrants erupt . . . *Merengue* blares out of car speakers, the Dominican flag drapes in place of curtains on apartment windows, sneakers hang from lampposts, Presidente (beer) bottles, pizza boxes and old issues of *El Diario* burst out of the trash cans on the corner. (13)

Soledad – an apt name for a person who prefers to live apart from her family despite traditional convention – is a protagonist who aspires to a life different from that of her mother, aunt and female cousin. Once she lives under their roof again, however, she begins to evaluate memories and stories from the past, which include her mother's origins as a prostitute who was purchased (by the man Soledad assumes to be her father) and brought to New York. He is a drunk and wife-beater who seems to have accidentally fallen to his death from a window in their fifth-floor apartment when she was a teenager. As Soledad descends into remembrances of childhood, she recalls the sexual abuse perpetrated by him.

While Soledad is the principal chronicler, other characters tell their stories in the first or third person, demonstrating the personality of a particular character, such as: 'Flaca tries to send her mother a telepathic message. Go to sleep messages' (161). Since Soledad's mother is sick and unable to speak, her perspective is revealed as thoughts and reflections in italics. The multiple shifts of perspective create an analysis of the Washington Heights experience, to which the main character returns, and by the end of the novel also to the Dominican ancestral home of the island. Magical qualities are connected to this past. One day when Soledad opens a photo album she finds in a closet, spirits fly loose and then haunt the apartment. Her aunt tries to help her get rid of them, but when all remedies fail, they decide to take a trip 'back home'. In the final scene, she is lying with her head in her mother's lap, and her mother

> tells me about the day I was born, how when she first looked down at me, so tiny and vulnerable, she named me Soledad. My name means loneliness in Spanish, the language my mother speaks and dreams in. She said this name would open people's hearts to me and make them listen. (237)

Cruz's second novel, *Let It Rain Coffee* (2005), relates the story of a family that immigrates to New York, prompted by Esperanza's daring escape to Puerto Rico on a flimsy boat with other refugees. She is pregnant, and has left a two-year-old son behind with her husband Santo (whose name denotes saintliness but also the first word of the capital). While she works in Puerto Rico, Santo arranges the papers for their move. In New York, he works long hours as a taxi driver and Esperanza takes on a double-shift at a nursing home. She has named her daughter Dallas and son Bobby, because of her dream to live the lives she sees portrayed by characters in the US soap opera *Dallas*. The novel describes her arrival:

She walked into a neighborhood in the early eighties celebrating the grand openings of freshly painted *bodegas*, travel agencies, *botánicas*, liquor and discount stores. Back then she didn't see the buildings as gray, or the city as grimy, or mind the crowds of people sitting on the front stoops . . . The police might have called it loitering, but Esperanza called it community. (9)

They each must work long hours to provide for the family, but Esperanza falls into the lure of consumerism, ordering items from TV advertisements to decorate their cramped apartment, and charging to the maximum on her first credit card, which she doesn't realize needs to be paid. Contrasts are made between life in New York and life on the island through characters' thoughts and memories, especially through Santo's father, Don Chan, who comes to live with them shortly after Santo's mother's death, in 1991. He is of Chinese ethnicity; he washed ashore as a child, and another child – his future wife – found him and took him home to her parents, who adopted him. On one occasion when little Chan goes to the city with his adoptive father, a character is persistent in trying to buy the child, stating that he knows he can get a lot of hours of work out of the Chinese. Once Chan is older and married, the changes in political leaders following Trujillo's death and the US military invasion in 1965 affect their lives as much as the censorship and restrictions of the dictatorship. Don Chan has little faith in US society, and does not take well to living in New York. He continues to recall his earlier life as he fades into old age in Washington Heights. The principal story takes place between Don Chan's arrival in New York in 1991, and 1999, when Esperanza and her children make a visit home to fulfill Don Chan's wish to die there.

The saying 'Let it rain coffee' is stated early in the novel, to express strong desire for a miracle, for something to occur that might give Dominicans on the island something to sell, to improve their livelihood. When Santo is murdered in his taxi the next year after Don Chan's arrival, the family struggles to find a way to survive financially and emotionally. Esperanza expects her 15-year-old son to help out, and asks him to get a job at McDonald's. He is shy and has trouble talking to the manager once he gets there. Don Chan wants to help, but 'he couldn't work at his age. At least in Los Llanos he spent his days in his garden and watched over the goats. How could he grow anything in all this concrete?' (102). Esperanza asks him to watch her teenagers once she begins taking overnight jobs doing in-home care, but he is oblivious to their activities.

Like Díaz, Cruz makes an issue of Dominican characteristics, originating from various mixtures including Chinese and African. In the hospital morgue, Santo's daughter looks at her 'beautiful father who was dark like her grandmother, with thick hair, whose lips were full' (59). Soledad's mother has 'skin the color of caramelized sugar, and full lips'. In *Drown*, Rafa taunts his younger brother about his complexion, his hair and the size of his lips, calling him Haitian. In each case, anti-Haitian sentiment and pervasive racism is consistently demonstrated; younger characters see all Latinos as representatives of African heritage. Santo's daughter, Dallas, for example, assumes a boy she is interested in is White, but he says he is Puerto Rican, which surprises her.

Positive memories invoke the taste and smell of the island. When Díaz's characters attend Dominican parties in New York, they are awed by the smell and array of typical dishes, such as *chicharrones*, fried chicken, *tostones*, *sancocho*, rice, fried cheese, and yucca. Shortly before he dies, Santo is transformed idyllically by the smell of pineapple and coconut from a woman's drink in a bar. Yet, the vocabulary and colloquial language used by characters in the new Dominican-American novels is typical of New York neighborhoods. Cruz has stated that her first novel 'was created by a community of people, not just me, and also all of my mother's sacrifices and my grandmother's stories and all their love' (Torres-Saillant, 116). Cruz cites as major influences the writing of Sandra Cisneros, Toni Morrison (for her sense of the magical in everyday lives), and Cristina García (for her shifts of point of view). Cruz has been the recipient of several writing fellowships, and is co-founder of an organization, Women in Literature and Arts (WILL), which helped bring about Nelly Rosario's first novel.

*Nelly Rosario*
Rosario's *Song of the Water Saints* (2002) launches its story in 1916, during the American occupation of the Dominican Republic, and continues through four generations of women. The first character is a young woman who is lured, with her boyfriend, to engage in sex before the lens of an American pornographer. This sets the stage for her own life as well as that of the Dominican people. Graciela is a street-smart girl in Santo Domingo, where the escalating economic crisis makes it difficult to survive. Her sailor boyfriend will eventually disappear at sea, and she struggles to raise their daughter, Mercedes, whom she will abandon when she is thirteen. Graciela eventually contracts a disease from a new partner, which will cause her death. Her often brutal experiences (as well as her dreams and her imagination) are depicted with great sensitivity and cultural revelation. Rosario's distinctive use of English captures the rhythm of Dominican Spanish.

Mercedes is a more self-confident character; she becomes involved in religion, gets married, and efficiently runs a shop during the Trujillo dictatorship. Facing the instability after 1960 and a new US occupation, Mercedes and her husband immigrate to New York, taking with them the daughter her own child has abandoned. Leila shares Graciela's passion and restlessness, and turns to the streets once they live in high-rise, rat-infested buildings. This is a strong first novel, with touches of magical elements (the title's enigmatic Water Saints), and yet effectively rooted in the reality of the immigrant experience. Rosario has stated that she wanted to explore characters in the two countries 'that raised me'.

Her own family arrived in Brooklyn the same year she was born, 1972, and Rosario was educated in the American educational system with occasional trips to the island. As a result, her writing reflects:

> . . . a black consciousness . . . Maybe if I were on the island, I probably wouldn't. I'm not saying that there are not people who do have that consciousness and who are working within that, but just from how I grew up, my family,

my origins, I don't think I could've made that big leap. Because again, it's the shame around color, the shame around race, and the shame around sexuality that keep literature in Spanish from discussing this.[9]

Rosario feels her novel, which was awarded the 2002 PEN Open Book, demonstrates 'the intersection' between Domincan colonial views and the contemporary US, a sentiment shared in various degrees by all the Dominican-American writers.

The next literary generation will likely further explore the new phenomenon of Dominican immigration broached in Cruz's second novel: that of the boat people who risk their lives to cross the channel to the island of Puerto Rico – so that they can merge into a population that looks and sounds like them – in order to find work and the possibility of access to the US. The Dominican *borderland* or the cultural expectations and experience of a new generation is well represented by contemporary Dominican-American authors writing in English. Alvarez initiated representation of the Dominican Republic and its history through the experiences of mothers, sisters, and daughters. The next generation of women writers has created female characters who defy tradition and use their own experiences to represent cultural identity. Their novels demonstrate that the Dominican experience is one of a double-Diaspora, that its African heritage needs to be discussed together with its island and Spanish history. With a surge in immigration and the impact of the US on Dominican society, the nation's post-Trujillo history is now interwoven with life in New York. Dominican-American literature constitutes a provocation against the official history of either the Spanish-Dominican or the US political context that separates Latino from African-American. It therefore occupies a significant place in US Latino literature.

## Works Cited

Alcántara Almánzar, José (ed.). *Caribbean Writers: A Bio-bibliographical-Critical Encyclopedia*. Washington, DC: Three Continental Press, 1979.
Alvarez, Julia. *Homecoming: New and Collected Poems*. New York: Plume, 1996.
—— *How the García Girls Lost Their Accent*. Chapel Hill: Algonquin Books, 1991.
—— *In Search of Salomé*. New York: Plume, 2001.
—— *In the Time of the Butterflies*. Chapel Hill: Algonquin Books, 1994.
—— *Saving the World*. New York: Algonquin Books, 2006.
—— *Something to Declare*. Chapel Hill: Algonguin Books, 1998.
—— *The Other Side / El otro lado*. New York: Dutton, 1995.
—— *The Woman I Kept to Myself*. New York: Algonquin Books, 2004.
—— *¡Yo!* Chapel Hill: Algonquin Books, 1997.
Alvarez, Soledad. *Vuelo Posible*. Santa Domingo, no publisher. 1994.

---

[9] An interview with four writers, including Pérez and Rosario, titled 'Voices from Hispaniola', was published in the journal *Meridians*, 5:1 (2004), 69–91.

Andrews, George Reid. *Afro-Latin America, 1800–2000*. Oxford: Oxford University Press, 2004.
Bell, Ian. *The Dominican Republic*. Boulder, Colorado: Westview Press, 1981.
Bosch, Juan. *Cuentos escritos en el exilio*. Santo Domingo: Julio D. Postigo e Hijos, 1968.
Candelario, Ginetta E. B. 'Voices from Hispaniola: A *Meridians* Roundtable with Edwidge Danticat, Loida Maritza Pérez, Myriam J. A. Chancy, and Nelly Rosario', *Meridians: feminism, race, transnationalism*, 5:1 (2004), 69–91.
Cartagena Portalatín, Aída. *Yania Tierra, poema documenta*, 1981. Translated as *Yania Tierra, document poem*, by M.J. Fenwick and Rosabelle White. Washington, DC: Azul Editions, 1995.
Castro, Max J., and Thomas D. Boswell. 'The Dominican Diaspora Revisited: Dominicans and Dominican-Americans in a New Century', *The North–South Agenda*, 53 (January 2002), 1–25. Coral Gables: North–South Center, University of Miami.
Céspedes, Diógenes, and Silvio Torres-Saillant. 'Fiction is the Poor Man's Cinema. An Interview with Junot Díaz', *Callaloo*, 23:3 (2000), 892–907.
Cocco de Filippis, Daisy. *Documents of Dissidence, Selected Writings by Dominican Women*. New York: CUNY Dominican Studies Institute, 2000.
—— and Emma Jane Robinett (eds.). *Poemas del exilio y de otras inquietudes / Poems of Exile and Other Concerns: A Bilingual Selection of the Poetry Written by Dominicans in the United States*. New York: Ediciones Alcance, 1988.
Connor, Anne María. 'Desenmascarando a Ysrael: The Disfigured Face as Symbol of Identity in Three Latino Texts', *Cincinnati Romance Review*, 21 (2002).
Contreras, Hilma. *Cuatro cuentos*. Cuidad Trujillo: Editora Stella, 1953.
Cruz, Angie. *Let It Rain Coffee*. New York: Simon & Schuster, 2005.
—— *Soledad*. New York: Simon & Schuster, 2001.
Danticat, Edwidge. *The Farming of Bones*. New York: Penguin, 1999.
Dash, Michael J. *The Other America: Caribbean Literature in a New World Context*. Charlottesville: University Press of Virginia, 1998.
Díaz, Junot. (ed.). *The Beacon Best of 2001: Great Writings by Women and Men of All Colors and Cultures*. Boston: Beacon Books, 2001.
—— *Drown*. New York: Riverhead Books, 1996.
—— 'Language, Violence, and Resistance', in Daniel Balderston and Marcy Schwartz (eds.), *Voiceovers: Translation and Latin American Literature*. Albany: State University of New York Press, 2002.
—— *Negocios* [stories from *Drown*, in Spanish]. New York: Vintage Books, 1997.
Esteves, Sandra María. *Yerba Buena*. Greenfield, New York: Greenfield Press, 1981.
Galván, Manuel de Jesús. *Enriquillo*. 1882. Translated as *Cross and the Sword* by Robert Graves. Bloomington: Indiana University Press, 1954.
Henríquez, Salomé Ureña. *Poesías completas*. 5th edn. Santo Domingo: SEEBAC, 1975.
hooks, bell. *Outlaw Culture, Resisting Representations*. New York: Routledge, 1994.
Luis, William. *Dance Between Two Cultures: Latino Caribbean Literature Written in the United States*. Nashville: Vanderbilt University Press, 1997.
Mann, Charles C. '1491' (cover story). *Atlantic Monthly*, 289:3 (March 2002), 41–53.

Martínez, Elizabeth Coonrod. 'Recovering a Space for a History Between Imperialism and Patriarchy: Julia Alvarez *In the Time of the Butterflies*'. *Thamyris* (Amsterdam) 5:2 (Autumn 1998), 263–79.
Mir, Pedro. *Poesías completas*. México, D.F.: Siglo Veintiuno, 1994.
Montero, Mayra. *The Red of His Shadow*, trans. Edith Grossman. New York: Ecco Press, 2001.
Paravisini-Gebert, Lizabeth, and Consuelo López-Springfield (eds.). *Callaloo*, 23:3, Dominican Republic: Literature and Culture (Summer 2000).
Pérez, Loida Maritza. *Geographies of Home*. New York: Penguin Putnam, 1999.
Pescatello, Ann M. *The African in Latin America*. New York: Knopf, 1975.
Rawlings, Norberto James. *Obras 1969–2000*. Santo Domingo: Consejo Presidencial de Cultura, 2000.
Rosario, Nelly. *Song of the Water Saints*. New York: Pantheon, 2002.
Sagás, Ernesto, and Orlando Inoa. *The Dominican People, A Documentary History*. Princeton: Marcus Wiener Publishers, 2003.
—— and Sintia E. Molina. *Dominican Migration, Transnational Perspectives*. Gainsville: University Press of Florida, 2004.
Saldívar, José David. *Border Matters: Remapping American Cultural Studies*. Berkeley: University of California Press, 1997.
Sánchez Lamouth, Juan. *Antología de Juan Sánchez*, ed. Diógenes Céspedes et al. Santo Domingo: Ediciones Ferilibro, 2001.
Santiago, Robert (ed.). *Boricuas: Influential Puerto Rican Writings – An Anthology*. New York: One World/Ballantine, 1995.
Stinchcomb, Dawn F. *The Development of Literary Blackness in the Dominican Republic*. Gainesville: University Press of Florida, 2004.
Torres-Saillant, Silvio. 'Writing has to be Generous: An Interview with Angie Cruz', *Calabash: A Journal of Caribbean Arts and Letters*, 2:2 (Summer/Fall 2003), 108–27. http://library.nyu.edu/calabash/vol2iss2/0202108.pdf
Vicioso, Sherezada. *Salomé Ureña de Henríquez (1850–1897): A cien años de magisterio*. Santo Domingo: Comisón Permanente de la Feria del Libro, 1997.
Wagenheim, Kal. *Puerto Rico, A Profile*. New York: Praeger, 1975.
Winn, Peter. Americas, The Changing Face of Latin America and the Caribbean. New York: Pantheon Books, 1992.
Zimmerman, Marc. *US Latino Literature: An Essay and Annotated Bibliography*. Chicago: Abruzo Press, 1992.

# 7

# Three Central American Writers: Alone Between Two Cultures

## VINCENT SPINA

Conny Palacios, Rima de Vallbona, and Omar Castañeda represent three different Central American genres (poetry, novel, and short story, respectively). They also come from three different moments in the process of adaptation or the lack of adaptation to life abroad in the United States. Palacios is the most recent arrival (1981) and her poetry, written in Spanish, is still richly textured by the poetic traditions of her native Nicaragua. Her prose-poem 'Lo que Homero no contó' (What Homer Didn't Say) focuses on the need to migrate to the US but is clearly embedded in Nicaraguan poetic traditions.[1] The novelist provides a different window on Central American literature in the US. Although most of her short stories and novels are in Spanish, Rima de Vallbona's novel, *Mundo, demonio y mujer*[2] (The World, the Devil, and the Flesh) is constructed so that the influence of American culture, particularly North American feminism, clearly plays a role in the mental and spiritual development of the main character Renata. Unlike Palacios and Vallbona, Guatemalan writer Omar Castañeda, who died from an overdose of drugs in 1997,[3] wrote in English. Although born in Guatemala, he was raised in the Midwest and became an American citizen at 11 years of age. His work depicts characters who seem more intimately involved in Anglo culture. His short story 'On the Way Out'[4] reveals the struggle of the main character, a Guatemalan male, to define himself both as an American and a Latino, and to find some sense of dignity and meaning in his life. Despite the differences, no matter how long these writers have lived in the US, their prior cultures play essential roles in their adaptation to North American society. The interplay between what came before and what exists now is laden with

---

[1] *Percepción Fractal* (Fractal Perception) (Managua, Nicaragua: PAVSA, 1999), 26–7.
[2] Rima de Vallbona, *Mundo, demonio y mujer* (Coral Gables, Florida: Editorial Ponce de León, 2002).
[3] For information on the circumstances surrounding his death, see *The Chronicle of Higher Education*, 27 June 1997.
[4] Omar S. Castañeda, 'On the Way Out', in *Remembering to Say 'Mouth' or 'Face'* (Boulder: Fiction Collective 2, 1993).

ambiguity and ambivalence, setting up the possibility of the emergence of truly human situations.

Two challenges immediately arise when analyzing 'Central American' writers. The first is that, in contrast to Mexico, Puerto Rico, and Cuba, the countries with the oldest and largest Latino communities within the US, Central America is not a single country, much less a culturally homogeneous geographical area. Seven countries make up its extension: Belize, Guatemala, El Salvador, Honduras, Nicaragua, Costa Rica, and Panama. Hundreds of distinct indigenous groups inhabit the isthmus and continue to speak their Pre-Colombian languages. From the early sixteenth century, the Spaniards relied on the labor of African slaves, and their descendants are present in all the modern nations. In the last two centuries immigrants from Asia, Europe, the West Indies, and the Middle East have transformed many towns and cities throughout the isthmus. For example, there are significant populations of English speakers, in a majority African ancestry, on the eastern coasts of Honduras, Nicaragua, Costa Rica, and Panama, many of whom arrived in the nineteenth century from the West Indies to work on the railroads and other industrial projects including the Panama Canal. Many have preserved a good deal of the English heritage derived from the West Indies, including the Anglican religion. Moreover, the official language of Belize is English, and the country's history is more closely related to the English colonization of the Americas.

The second challenge is that the countries of Central America do not have long-established communities within the US. It has only been since the 1980s – after the bloody civil wars unleashed against brutal and corrupt military dictatorships – that significant numbers of Nicaraguans, Salvadorans, and Guatemalans have established communities in Florida and California, respectively. Most of what is now the western US *was* Mexico in the first place. The Puerto Ricans of New York and of the smaller cities of New Jersey and Connecticut now represent a third and fourth generation for this community, while the Cubans had been establishing communities in Florida well before the Cuban Revolution of the 1960s. The writers who have sprung up from these communities normally express their commitment to them with forms of expression demonstrating or implying a call for social justice vis-à-vis the surrounding Anglo-American society. At the same time, they enjoy a kind of insulation from the surrounding community and a refuge from the discrimination often expressed in their writings.[5] Lacking these community ties, Central American writers (or the voices and characters expressed in their writing), must deal directly with the surrounding culture with no recourse to the kind of buffer an ethnic community may offer. Because of this, the writer him or herself must find the context from which the work will develop. Ultimately, this is a problem for all artists, but it

---

[5] I am thinking of such writers as the Mexican-American Rudolfo Anaya and the Cuban-American Oscar Hijuelos. As for Puerto Rican writers, one should consult Pedro López-Adorno's anthology, *Papiros de Babel/Antología de la poesía puertorriqueña en Nueva York* (Río Piedras, Puerto Rico: Editorial de la Universidad de Puerto Rico, 1991).

becomes acute when the writer has no base in an established community to which to relate his or her own writing. With respect then to the Central American writers, this base must be created from scratch.

In view of these factors of diversity and the lack of a long standing tradition of writing by Central American writers within this country, this chapter focuses on Conny Palacios, Rima de Vallbona, and Omar Castañeda not only because they represent three different genres but also because they are manifestations of three different stages of cultural adaptation to living in the US. The most important factor in focusing on them, however, is the excellence of their work.

## Conny Palacios: the poetry of duality

The influence of the Latin American literary tradition, and especially that of Nicaragua on Conny Palacios's work is obvious.[6] The poet Pablo Antonio Cuadra has had a particular significance with respect to the essential duality of the Nicaraguan character, a theme enunciated and elaborated upon in many of Palacios's poems and also in her short novel *En carne viva*. According to Cuadra, the sense of duality, found even in the Pre-Columbian cultures of Nicaragua, informs almost every aspect of life and culture in that country, including the poetry of Rubén Darío.[7] Indeed, the works of Palacios reflect this same sense of duality. Of her novel, the critic María Luisa Negrín states:

> The protagonist's alienated being is repeated (*se desdobla*) in this vagabond who returns in order to deliver the manuscript (the body of the novel itself) to the son of her friend (the protagonist), but immediately the duality between the vagabond and the sick woman (the protagonist), who has disappeared, is established.[8]

The text of the novel plays on the idea of the character who disappears and the one who remains, and, more literally, between the one who emigrates from Nicaragua and the one who stays behind. This dynamic of departure and remaining becomes essential in the understanding of the poem, 'Lo que Homero no contó'. The poem returns to the theme of Ulysses abandoning Calypso in order to return to Ithaca and Penelope. Given this context we may assume that Ulysses, of course, is the one who departs, and Calypso the one who remains. This observation is true enough from a historical point of view, but Palacios gives the theme a twist by sending Calypso in search of Ulysses. Palacios writes:

---

[6] Anthony J. Robb, *La poética de Conny Palacios* (Managua, Nicaragua: PAVSA, 2004), 12.

[7] 'La dualidad en *Poema del momento extranjero en la selva, La mitología del jaguar* y *El nacimiento de Cifar* por Pablo Antonio Cuadra', *Simposio Internacional de Poesía Nicaragüence del Siglo XX/Homenaje a Pablo Antonio Cuadra* (Managua, Nicaragua: Asociación Pablo Antonio Cuadra, 2003), 2. This and all subsequent translations are mine.

[8] María Luisa Negrín, 'La dimensión de la locura, el exilio y la agonía en la novela *En carne Viva*', *Revista de la Academia Nicaragüense de la Lengua*, 27 (Septiembre 2003), 191.

Y ya obsesa por tanta angustia decidí buscarlo en las islas cercanas para ofrecerle la inmortalidad si se quedaba conmigo. Así pues un día arribé a su playa empujada por los vientos, con los pies descalsos, con mi canasta rebosante de poesía.

(And already obsessed with so much suffering I decided to search for him on the nearby islands so as to offer him immortality if he would stay with me. Thus one day blown by winds, barefoot, dressed in my robes of algae, and with my basket overflowing with poetry, I arrived at his shore.) (26)

In this way, while retaining her role of the abandoned woman, Palacios's Calypso doubles her role by assuming Ulysses' also, the role of the wanderer or searcher. When she finds her Ulysses she endeavors to explain to him her reasons for searching him out in the first place. She states that she wrote in circles in the sand about the interrupted sequences of their parallel lives, but she could hardly understand them herself. She had forged them in the highest tree-tops, in the trembling beat of a dove's wing . . ., because what she wished to explain was 'the moment' (*lo fugaz*) attempting to be 'the eternal' (*lo eterno*) (26). This last image is one of profound duality: On the one hand, at the poetic level we understand what it means for 'the moment' to become 'eternal', especially in the context of romantic and sexual love, and also in the context of the poem itself, which, through its very writing, turns the moment into the immortal. On the other hand, at the level of rational thought, the 'moment' remains just that – momentary. What is seen as one – the momentary and the eternal – ultimately remains two. In the same way, we may say that the one who remains and one who travels, though united in one person, also remain two aspects of the individual, ultimately at odds with each other.

Two other short poems concentrate on one aspect of this same duality, while opening the scope of dualities to other possibilities. In 'Le pido a la brisa' (I Petition the Wind) the poet writes:

> Tendida
> sobre el césped,
> y demarcada
> por el rítmico laberinto
> de tu respiración . . .
>
> Abro la transparencia
> de mis estancias,
> y le pido a la brisa
> el perfume
> de todas las semillas
> para poblar mis extensiones,
> para amordazar mi soledad. (29)
>
> (Lying
> in the grass
> and contained

> within the rhythmic labyrinth
> of your breathing . . .
>
> I open the transparency
> of my dwelling places,
> and I petition from the wind
> the perfume
> of every seed
> to populate my space,
> to silence my solitude.)

In the next poem, 'Para poder hablarte' (To Speak to You), Palacios writes:

> Para poder hablarte
> en el vacío
> y decirte cosas de
> mucho secreto . . .
> Cruzo
> el alto emparrado del espacio
> que nos separa,
> con mi cántaro al hombro,
> derramando
> el agua celeste de mis versos. (28)
>
> (To speak to you
> in the emptiness
> and tell you the most
> secret things . . .
> I must cross
> the arbors of space
> that separate us,
> on my shoulder a pitcher
> spilling out
> the sky blue water of my poems.)

If in the first poem we encounter the Calypso who waits passively for her lover, in the second she actively seeks for him. At the same time, while in the first poem she waits for the lover to fill her emptiness and her silence, again it is she who goes to him with the fullness of her poetry in the second. Thus, Palacios presents us with the double image of the one who remains behind and the one who travels on. Now, as stated before, Pablo Antonio Cuadra, though he also expresses some apprehension with regard to this kind of duality and its consequences to the soul or psyche of the individual, is somewhat optimistic about this state of affairs. He writes that Nicaragua is a land of dualities in terms of the gamut of realities within its borders, from its cultures (Indian and European) to its geography (a tropical and volcanic landscape surrounded by cool and placid lakes and seas). But for him, while reflecting on the ideas of Rubén Darío himself, Nicaragua is also a land of fusion.[9] In the poetry of Palacios, however,

---

[9] Pablo Antonio Cuadra, 'Los hijos de septiembre', *El Nicaragüense* (1997), 18.

the case seems to be otherwise. In this respect the critic Omar García-Obregón, commenting on *En carne viva* (In the Flesh), writes this about the novel:

> In contrast to the modern narrator who often exploits ambiguity from a position of bipolarity, the postmodernist will make use of 'fractal' resources which allow for an infinite dissemination, at least with regard to theory as seen from the point of view of quantum theories within a narrative that avoids ultimate classification by setting up a kind of Derridean sense of 'différance'.[10]

Applying these ideas to 'Lo que Homero no contó' (What Homer Didn't Say), we arrive at a similar conclusion: it is the trauma of being abandoned by Ulysses that causes the splitting of Calypso's psyche into the one who waits behind and the one who seeks. But neither as the abider nor as the seeker does she attain her goal of union with Ulysses. Furthermore, as she narrates in the poem, she is not even able to express her entire gamut of feelings with regard to her lover. The poems ends: 'Entonces abrí los pétalos de mis manos y lo dejé ir y se me fue como agua entre los dedos . . . El resto ya lo saben . . .' (Then I opened the petals of my hands and I let him go and he left me like water through my fingers . . . The rest is known . . .) (27). A fractal situation emerges in this way then: the consequences of Ulysses' decision to abandon Calypso are not entirely predictable. A doubling of psyche takes place but will there ever be a fusion, a synthesis of character? Calypso states ironically that we know the rest, but the depth of character and suffering of Calypso herself remain veiled to us. As in the case of a fractal, we have an approximation to the meaning of her loss, but 'the rest' is obscured in the pendulum swing between the two 'individuals' who are the result of the split: the one who abides and the one who actively seeks, the empty vessel waiting for fulfillment and the 'pitcher', spilling out the water of its poetry.

The absence of details is striking in the three poems cited, and in the novel itself. We do not know where the wanderer (the migrant) eventually voyages. It is as though another unexpected consequence of travel emerges. The traveler is unable to give names to what is now before her. Thus the narrators of these poems, and those of the novel also, do not express in any way their sense of loneliness or abandonment through images that would establish what is their new reality. On the contrary, Palacios, in a constant play of intertextuality, creates a poetic fabric richly nuanced by the poetic tradition of Nicaragua, to the extent that even her references to the Homeric tradition find roots in the works of Pablo Antonio Cuadra.[11] At the same time she adds a rather disconcerting facet of her own to this tradition: is synthesis possible or does the seeker or the

---

[10] Omar García-Obregón, 'Discurso social y fantasmagórico en la narrative nicaragüense de los 90: *En carne viva* de Conny Palacios', *El Pez y la Serpiente* (November–December 1999), 99.

[11] Cuadra's own references are numerous, and in *El Nicaragüense*, already mentioned, one of his articles is entitled 'Homero y el gran lago'.

traveler remain divided within herself, at odds with herself? In this way, Palacios's works question the concept of 'adaptation' to the new circumstances surrounding the traveler. She suggests a retreat to interiority, a rethinking of past experience, to deal with the solitude of the present situation.

## Rima de Vallbona: coming to terms with the 'Anglo world'

In contrast to what we have seen in the poetry and prose of Conny Palacios, the Costa Rican writer Rima de Vallbona freely accepts the concepts and modes of living that invade the characters of her novel *Mundo, demonio y mujer*. Indeed, many of the epigraphs that begin the chapters of the novel are quotations taken from American feminist magazines, while others reflect ideas about feminism developed in the US. Yet, to conclude that this was a novel concerning the 'discovery' of feminism by the main character, Renata, who is Hispanic, would amount to a gross misreading. If anything, what comes to the surface is that concepts developed in the epigraphs represent a reality distinct from the one the main character lives. In addition, while at times Renata understands the possibilities that the new culture offers with respect to her own development as an individual, her spiritual, psychic, and intellectual commitment to her own Hispanic culture are too deeply felt and experienced to allow her merely to cast them off and accept an entirely new system of living and feeling. It may also be added that at other times the values expressed in these two modes of living are so disparate that they seem to bear no relationship whatsoever to each other. Each exists within its own history and set of circumstances and can only derive meaning for itself within its own parameters. Furthermore, as in the case of the voices and narrators whom we sense in the works of Palacios, 'Hispanic culture' for Renata ultimately refers to the culture of *her* country[12] and not to the Latino cultures that have developed within the Mexican, Puerto Rican, and Cuban communities that have taken root within the US.[13]

Finally, *Mundo, demonio y mujer* is a highly complex novel, an interweaving of multiple voices that center on Renata, a writer and intellectual. The chapters tend to be divided into conversations the main character has with a group of women friends from various Hispanic countries, some of whom are also intellectuals and professors and all of whom are middle class. Though the novel deals in the main with Renata's journey to intellectual freedom from her domineering and intellectually abusive husband, Antonio, it touches on many more

[12] Though Vallbona doesn't mention Costa Rica within the novel, the descriptions of Renata's country plus Renata's own Spanish dialect point directly to this country. See also Cida S. Chase, 'Elemenentos estructurales y pluralidad del lenguaje en *Mundo, demonio y mujer*', in Jorge Chen Sham (ed.), *Nuevos acercamientos a la obra de Rima de Vallbona* (San José, Costa Rica: Editorial de la Universidad de Costa Rica, 2000), 33–48.

[13] This sentiment of isolation is clearly expressed in the novel when the main character realizes that having a language in common with Mexicans does not make her a part of what they experience in their country. She is an upper-class Hispanic white woman, and the Mexicans are as distrustful of her as they are of the Americans who are all around them.

themes than can be mentioned here. For this reason the focus becomes the meeting of the Hispanic and the Anglo cultures as experienced by the main character, though for the sake of clarity some of the narrative techniques the author uses should be mentioned. The novel is divided into twenty-four chapters each beginning with an epigraph. The chapters themselves are further divided into weekly conversations Renata maintains with several other Hispanic women of diverse national origins, interior monologues, letters to her husband, and other first- and third-person narrations.

With regard to what is meant here by the Hispanic culture within which Renata is rooted, it is necessary to consult two of the most significant critics of Vallbona's narrative, Jorge Chen Sham and María Amoretti. Both critics acknowledge the influence that the Spanish philosopher and novelist Miguel de Unamuno has had on Vallbona's thinking and writing, and how this influence has affected her work. Amoretti, for instance, notes that although *Mundo, demonio y mujer* reveals all the superficial qualities of a feminist novel (i.e. a novel dealing with the liberation of a female character from a male-dominated social situation), 'the Unamunian pathos appears once again and this time explicitly, since the protagonist herself cites him as a character of one of her dreams'. She goes on to add that the '... Unamunian pathos ... reappears then, saturating the work and many of Vallbona's works with a feeling of unrequited emptiness in spite of the processes of self-awakening of her female characters'.[14]

In commenting on Vallbonian narration, Chen elaborates further about pathos within the philosophy of Miguel de Unamuno:

> For Unamuno, man's conflict is developed beneath the form of a tension, a scission of the subject confronted with a reality that overcomes him. This perspective of a suffering ego surrounds the philosophic thinking and the literary production of the Basque writer (Unamuno), producing an interior splitting (*desdoblamiento*) of the subject. Confronted with this agonizing ego, condemned to suffer in search of self-realization and the assumption of his own being, Unamuno creates, within a system of compensations, the contemplative ego, seeking salvation through faith (a belief in human transcendence) and through a quietism into which man thrusts himself towards his own intimate refuge.[15]

In addition to the elements contained in this synthesis of Unamuno's thinking, we may add that the pathos mentioned here is also conditioned upon humanity's intimate knowledge of its own demise, which, in turn, causes a response: a search for some kind of immortality, either through giving birth to a new generation or through writing. Obviously, Renata, as a mother (she is the

---

[14] 'La morada interior y sus espectros', Introduction to *Mundo, demonio y mujer*, 9.
[15] Jorge Chen Sham, *Radiografías del sujeto agónico: culpa y transcendencia en la novelística de Rima de Vallbona* (San José, Costa Rica: Ediciones Perro Azul, 2001), 114.

mother of three) and as a writer, is affected by this facet of Unamunian philosophy.

The narration also makes it clear that Renata is an extremely spiritual person deeply affected by her Catholic upbringing, which manifests itself throughout the novel in terms of her awareness of sin and her own feelings of guilt. Her Catholic background is revealed in an interior monologue that appears early in the work. Renata reflects on how much of what she has learned about God still weighs on her. She acknowledges that the Christian God has broken away from the vengeful God of the Old Testament. Nevertheless, she states that God is still there in the depths of her being, making her tremble with fear (77). At the same time her obsession with guilt and with sin becomes apparent in a conversation she has with one of her friends, Faustina, at one of the periodic meetings Renata attends.

> 'Yesterday I didn't feel like paying for the photocopies that came out badly. The business itself where I made them should have been responsible for that. But no sooner did I get behind the wheel when I felt the need to go back and tell them the truth: "Listen, I lied; I made more copies, but I paid for fewer because it was up to you to tell me how to run the copier. Do you all understand? Owning to five copies I didn't pay for, I am being devoured by guilt."' (78).

Renata's obsession with guilt is also reflected in her intellectual and creative endeavors. Within the context of the novel, she is compiling a study of the life of an eighteenth-century nun and mystic, Sor María Marcela. At the same meeting with her friends Renata mentions that, from her childhood, the nun was convinced that she was to blame for everything that happened around her (80). The nun, of course, was referring to everything bad that happened to her. In her autobiography, which Renata is studying, she recounts that God caused her younger sister to die because she, Sor María, would not dedicate her life to Him. She goes on to relate that a few months later, He also caused her mother's death.

Within the text this character finds a relatively simple cause for guilt, but for Renata the case is more complex. Amoretti explains: 'Christian Genesis, more than the history of the beginning of the world and of man, is the history of the birth of sin' (15). With regard specifically to Vallbona's literary output, she adds that we are dealing with the sin of sexual desire. And 'because of this Eva becomes an isotopic figure in many of her writings and also in this one (*Mundo, demonio y mujer*). The title is evidently a deconstruction of what Catholic catechism defines as the three enemies of the soul: the world, the devil and the flesh' (16).

Vallbona implies that the mere fact of being woman is sin; her essence is sin. In the case of Sor María Marcela, there is a solution: complete devotion to God through mysticism, the traditional Catholic way of renouncing the life of the body in favor of the life of the soul. With respect to Unamuno, once more, the philosopher was confronted with a similar problem: on the one hand, his writings from his most famous philosophical work, *Del sentimiento trágico de la vida* to his novels represent a search for transcendence, but such transcendence, by its very nature, hinges upon a complete acceptance of religious doctrine and a complete belief in a God expressed in this doctrine: conditions impossible for a rational being to fulfill, since by their very nature they exclude rationality.

For Renata the situation is even more exacerbated. She is relatively isolated within a society not her own whose customs she sometimes finds appalling.[16] She is mentally abused by her career-focused husband who constantly reminds her that her literature and classes are worthless: 'Who cares about your literature, your classes and your scribbling out stories, novels, poems? What you do is a waste of time, and you know that very well. My work is what really counts' (281). Thus, in addition to an ontological sense that life itself is a sin – at least the life of the body – she must deal with her isolation from the surrounding society and with spousal abuse.

If we return now to the epigraphs that begin each chapter, we may agree with the critic Cida S. Chase who, quoting Jorge Chen Sham, notes that they tend to globalize the situation of the main character and that of her friends in the conversation group: The 'I' becomes a 'we'.[17] We may add that they are wide-ranging in their sources, from the *Journal of Marriage and Family* to *Ms Magazine*, from poets to philosophers. The themes are mostly related to the feminist movement but are also broader, from the inequality of salaries between men and women to the place of lesbians within the feminist movement. And though the novel makes many references to Renata's living in Houston, Texas, and to the effects this has on her life as a Hispanic woman, it is the epigraphs that clearly demarcate the differences between her Hispanic culture and the Anglo culture with which she is now confronted and to which she is reacting. This is most clearly seen in the lifestyle she chooses for herself and her decision to divorce her husband.

Though she has suffered her husband's verbal and mental abuse for years, she finally does decide to divorce him, and she continues with her career as a scholar, teacher, and writer. Additionally, she falls in love and for a time enjoys the romantic relationship that her husband has denied her. In this sense, she not only overcomes the taboos placed on women by the patriarchal society that surrounds them, but also the admonitions and humiliations of her mother who throughout the novel, expressed through the memories of Renata herself, acts as an enforcer of these very same taboos. Her message to her daughter is that she is a woman and as such dependent on a man for her livelihood, while, at the same time, her own efforts to succeed as an individual are worthless because of her sex.

While it may be that her acceptance of the new thinking available to her

---

[16] Despite the many criticisms Renata has regarding her own culture, she is repelled by what she considers the lack of care for the individual in American society. On pages 137 to 139 of the novel she and her friend Faustina discuss how the elderly are treated in the US, in spite of the wealth. The implication is, of course, that all things being equal, such a situation would not occur in their own countries.

[17] Chase, 'Elementos estructurales', 35.

through the woman's movement liberates Renata from an oppressive social situation, such acceptance can do nothing to change the concept she has of herself on the ontological level. If her very flesh is the problem, if her mere essence of being a woman is a sin, and if the former modes of religious mysticism no longer provide a solution, what peace and what sense of freedom are left to her? For Amoretti, Renata's existential situation at the end of the novel is rather bleak, '. . . saturated with an overwhelming melancholy for a world which is definitively renounced without ever being less desired. This is because the separation between the self and the world, as Büber mentions, makes of the self an empty self . . .' (30).

Chen agrees with much of this criticism (172) and he elaborates on what he calls 'creative guilt'. For Chen the feeling of guilt – within the Catholic world, at least – leads to the need to confess. The confession in turn is the revelation of the individual's interior, his/her soul. In the case of the writer or the artist, in general, 'confession' takes the form of the writing itself. By confessing, the writer becomes more conscious of him or herself. And this consciousness of self is revealed in the artistic work, the creation. This is certainly Renata's predicament, but Chen also realizes that with respect to this protagonist: 'instead of liberating her, (her creation) makes her more aware of her personal and generic alienation' (172). The novel thus ends when, one morning as Renata awakes, she hears a neighbor whistling 'It's a wonderful world'. And her response is: 'If it only were' (394).

The novel also offers two resolutions that are less pessimistic. In the first place, as we have mentioned, Renata is a resident of Houston. By the end of the novel, she has already lived there for many years. She remembers her first flight into the city and her feelings of profound disappointment:

> As the plane descended, Renata had the strange feeling that she had taken the wrong flight, one whose final destination was not the one she had planned. Maybe the pilot who had announced the final descent was mistaken. How could this city, whose geography was the same as any in the third world, form a part of the titanic continent of the north, the one that filled her adolescent dreams? (370)

Years later, after she has met a friend of her husband's at the airport, her daughter Gabriela chides her: 'Mom, I can't believe what I heard you say to Marielos? . . . Haven't you always complained about Houston . . . Selfishly, you never even considered the fact that your children were born here, that we grew up here and our friends and classmates live here' (379). Her daughter's comments cause her to realize how much the city has grown over the decades that she has lived there, in terms not only of size but of culture too. She thinks of its music halls and of the fact that the city now has an internationally recognized symphony orchestra. She remarks finally:

> Do you know, Gaby, it took me a long time, but I believe that Houston has helped me to understand that every Promised Land is a land in the process of

becoming, of taking form and becoming itself. Just like Israel today and this city. And me too. After so many years I'm finally beginning to understand what until now was only potentially in me. (381)

What we have here is the main character's acceptance and affirmation of the self. Renata, as she herself affirms, has grown and is growing, thanks to the feminist thinking she discovers in the US. On the ontological level, however, matters are quite different. Though she is not what we would call a practicing Catholic, Catholic cosmology as experienced within the Hispanic world is still in force; indeed, it is what informs her thinking and her acts from the very center of her being. To change it would be to become another being. Her understanding of the Catholic concept of sin has become more intellectualized and she can objectively criticize or in other ways comment on it. But her perception of self at the metaphysical level as essentially sinful has not been deconstructed, to the same extent that the Catholic understanding of transcendence remains fully operative within her. On the one hand, this perception of self will always be the cause of her alienation (indeed, this is true no matter in what society or culture she lives), but, as Chen points out, it is the source of her creation. We may add that this perception of an essentially sinful self plus the need for and the drive toward transcendence provide the dynamic tension from which her art is born.

Although the focus has been on Renata and the effects that living in the US have on her, it is necessary to speak of her daughter Gabriela or Gaby. Unlike her mother, Gaby was born in the US and is much more at home with American pragmatism than with her mother's Catholic teleology and eschatology. In contrast to Renata's and, indeed, her husband Antonio's understanding of the relationship between marital partners, Gabriela enters into a trial period of living together with her boyfriend David. She points out that instead of losing respect for her for having lost her virginity, as Antonio has warned, the relationship has grown. She is fully confident that Renata will understand this, though Renata herself, without revealing it to her daughter, is distraught over her daughter's decision and cannot overcome her old belief that in women chastity is all that matters (140).

Gaby goes on to add that she cannot understand how Renata and Antonio have managed to live so many years in a loveless relationship that has even proved to be abusive for Renata. She tells her mother that the most important thing about life is to live it in all its intensity regardless of others' criticisms (141). Thus through this character we see other possibilities of life. Returning to Unamunian thinking for a moment: we have mentioned that one of the ways he considers to transcend death (and perhaps the self) is through our heirs. By extension, therefore, Gaby becomes a metonymy for a kind of transcendence for Renata herself. As her literal daughter she is the promise that old metaphysical structures can or will become deconstructed and a life, fully lived and free from guilt, is possible.

### Omar Castañeda: on being American

If Renata's daughter Gabriela holds out a promise of future integration into American society, the case is highly more problematic when not frustratingly tragic for the protagonist, Hermanegildo Hernández, in Castañeda's short story 'On the Way Out', the first narration in his book of short stories *Remembering to Say 'Mouth' or 'Face'*. In the first place, though both characters represent a generation of Central Americans born in the US, Gabriela is the daughter of professional parents, is a university graduate and is a professional herself. Hermanegildo is an enlisted man in the US Air Force; from what the reader can gather from the story itself, his mother is a poorly educated immigrant from Guatemala. There are racial differences also. Though not directly germane to the above discussion of *Mundo, demonio y mujer*, Renata is white, as is her daughter who intends to marry an Anglo-American. Hermanegildo is *ladino*, a mixture of white European and Mayan Indian; and this becomes an important factor to consider within the narration.

'On the Way Out' may be divided into two parts. In the first, the reader learns of the events that lead to the protagonist's overdosing on heroin. The second part shows him paralyzed, in a hospital, slowly recovering under his mother's care. In addition to the obvious linkage of the two parts through chronology, Castañeda creates a subtext in the first part based on the *Popol-Vuh*. This subtext becomes the main text of the second part when the protagonist's mother begins to make statues she believes will help exorcise her son's devils. The statues are based on the mythology depicted in this Quiché Mayan text.

The story begins with this line: 'Long before I am supposed to die, I learn all there is to learn about swearing from my mother' (13). From there, the first-person narration paints a rather humorous, if not stereotypical image of this mother,[18] a woman given to emotional outbursts, frantic and overly burdened as she attempts to raise her eight children, of whom he, the narrator, is the 'black sheep'. The stereotyping, however, tells us as much about the protagonist's own ambivalence with regard to his race and cultural heritage while it adds humor to the rather tragic events of the narration itself. The protagonist has joined the Air Force in order to support a young woman, Violet, he has made pregnant. They have a baby daughter, but soon, according to his account, she is cheating on him.

The desire to have an 'American' family counterpoints his attitude toward his mother's English and serves as an indicator of his desire to be more American. He further states that he, against his wife's wishes, named the first child 'Ann' because he did not want her to suffer what he did as a child growing up among Anglo children who mocked his own name with nicknames such as 'Hernia', 'Her-nuts'; or they simply called him a 'Wet-back' and mockingly told him to speak 'Spickish' (14).

He goes on to narrate the following: how he began to use heroin, an incident

---

[18] He achieves this most often by deliberately satirizing her pronunciation of English words; i.e., 'Gahd-dahm eat' for 'God damn it'; 'Ju-knighted Estates' for 'United States', etc.

in which he beat his wife, was knocked into unconsciousness (apparently by one of her lovers hidden in the house or perhaps the MPs – the narration doesn't indicate), ended up discharged from the service, was sent to a drug rehabilitation program, met a young woman in a clothes store, bought more drugs with her, and overdosed at her home. Prior to this overdose, the narrator mentions his stay within the rehabilitation program. They call him 'Herman'. He confesses how bad he feels about having used drugs, and how he actually comes to be considered a model rehabilitated addict. But in the narration of this part, Castañeda's use of irony becomes evident, to the extent that these scenes become auguries of the fact that the narrator will soon become addicted once more. This ends the first section of the story, which nonetheless offers one of the most extraordinary accounts of the actual effects of drugs I have read in fiction. In a review of the book I wrote:

> First, I do not believe that writing thus far has produced a more powerful rendering of the drug experience and the ritual involved. For the main character, we are not merely dealing with escape here or with disease or with what the modern hype on drug addiction would have us believe. What we have is a total rejection of this world for the one of drugs, a world of just *as total* pleasure.[19]

The second section concerns the protagonist's recovery. He is paralyzed from the neck down and has been in a coma for two months. Upon his waking, his mother has begun a type of cure based in the mythology of the *Popol-Vuh*, and it is at this point that we realize that certain images contained in the first section anticipate what is to follow in the second. The first of these images is the narrator's reference to the calabash within his wife's stomach and to the fact that she is pregnant with twins. While these references seem to function merely as idiosyncrasies related to the narrator's style of communication, they become quite relevant in reference to the Mayan understanding of creation as an essentially dual process. According to the *Popol-Vuh*, the first gods themselves are a husband and wife, Xpiyacoc and Xmucane, also called 'Grandfather' and 'Grandmother'. Their children are twins One Hunahpu and Seven Hunahpu, who in turn are the co-fathers of the twins Hunahpu and Xbalanque, whose mother is Xquic.[20]

In the introduction to his translation Dennis Tedlock strongly emphasizes that:

> To this day the Quiché Maya think of dualities in general as complementary rather than opposed, interpenetrating rather than mutually exclusive. Instead

---

[19] Vincent Spina, 'Old Heroes, Gods and Demons', *Collages and Bricolages: The Journal of International Writing*, VIII (1994), 88. In place of 'a world', the original text read 'of world'. This is a misprint.

[20] Dennis Tedlock (trans.), *Popol-Vuh: The Mayan Book on the Dawn of Life* (New York: Touchstone Books, 1996), 33, mainly taken from this translation and study, and those of Delia Goetz and Sylvanus G. Morley (Norman: University of Oklahoma Press, 1983).

of being in logical opposition to one another, the realms of divine and human action are joined by a mutual attraction. If we had an English word that fully expressed the Mayan sense of narrative time, it would have to embrace the duality of the divine and the human in the same way the Quiché term *kajulew* or 'sky-earth' preserves the duality of what we call the 'world'. (59)

In this light it is necessary to return to the protagonist's wife Violet. On the one hand she has certainly betrayed the marital bond, but as the future mother of twins, she relates back to Xquic, the mother of One Hunahpu and Xbalanque, who are embodiments of phases of the sun and moon, respectively, and who prepare the earth for the coming of the first humans. The reference to Xquic is confirmed when we consider that while in the underworld, her homeland, she is impregnated by the head of One Hunahpu, which has taken the form of a calabash and hangs from a tree she has come to investigate (98–9).

The presence of the *Popol-Vuh* as a subtext within the first section of 'On the Way Out', throws further light on the author's powerful account of the drug experience. Throughout the *Popol-Vuh* itself and, indeed, in much of Mayan pictorial and plastic representations of Mayan religion, the importance of blood cannot be more underlined. The Mayan gods need human blood to survive. Creation, like so much of Mayan thought, is also a dual process: while the gods create humans, they are weak; humans must feed the gods so that they will not die. The food they need is blood. This blood comes from the captives taken in wars against other nations; it also comes from the nobles themselves who, according to what is depicted on murals from Mayan ruins, mutilated themselves offering their blood to the gods. Hermanegildo, just before overdosing himself, contemplates while he injects the young woman he has met:

> I pull the plunger to the top, then shoot it all back. She's out of her mind. That rush is purely psychological. It's the true thrill of shooting. Playing with blood, jacking, on the edge, watching the blood swirl into the barrel. This is what really makes the addict. This is what makes every shooter in the world shoot ice water, alcohol, aspirin, anything soluble. This is what finally makes junkies the demons they become. It is not the drug, it is the blood game, the venal tearing, that makes vampires of addicts. (24)

What, then, was a ritual that connected the individual to the gods through a bloodletting that established a reciprocity of creation between the human and the divine becomes, at the level of the addict, an attempt to establish the same relationship. Without the belief system, however, and without the infrastructure of a believing culture, the ritual becomes addiction; connection to the gods becomes connection to the demonic. Nonetheless, at least in relation to the protagonist, his addiction is not merely escape but a quest for a kind of transcendence he cannot reach within the parameters of the Anglo culture in which he lives.

Returning to the peculiar opening of the short story itself – 'Long before I am supposed to die' – two interpretations become possible: the first is somewhat evident; the narrator is foreshadowing his near fatal-drug overdose. Nonetheless, his use of the present tense, while not exactly undermining or effacing this interpretation, opens textual time to another possibility: to declare 'long before I am supposed to die' may also suggest that the narrator is cognizant of his demise in a time in a more distant future.

Tedlock explains that the first humans of the *Popol-Vuh* had perfect vision, and could see when death would come. Subsequently, the gods, jealous of their own creation, limit this power. They compensate humanity for this limitation by giving them the *Popol-Vuh* itself, which is a book of complete knowledge. In the narration, then, when Hermanegildo implies that he knows the time of his death, he is placing himself on par with the first humans. But since, as the narration also makes clear, he has no knowledge of this sacred text, he must have attained this knowledge in another way. This 'other way' can only be his mother, who, as we shortly learn, is profoundly aware of the book. The identification of his mother with the sacred book of the Mayas and his satirizing of her as the one who taught him all there was to know about swearing – thus partially deconstructing her as a credible witness to the truth she wishes to impart to him – become the text of the second part of the short story.

On his third day awake after being in the coma, the protagonist narrates how his mother covers him with a sheet, straddles his face and hangs a poster of the oil painting *Xquic* by the Guatemalan painter Roberto González Goyri on the hospital ceiling. The painting depicts the demigoddess Xquic holding out her hand to the skull-calabash head of One Hunahpu. He, in turn, is spitting into her hand; the saliva, according to the *Popol-Vuh*, is what impregnates her with the hero twins Hunahpu and Xbalanque, demigods of death and resurrection.[21]

Curiously, the protagonist interprets the painting as an image of himself represented by the skull and of his mother depicted as Xquic. He thus becomes the father and she becomes his wife. The interpretation is valid if we consider that, at this point, Hermanegildo is paralyzed from the neck down, and thus, like One Hunahpu, he is only a head. The idea, however, is scandalous in view of the fact that she is his mother, and her straddling his head to hang the poster only emphasizes this relationship since, traditionally, Mayan women, though they knelt down, maintained a similar position when giving birth.

In Western tradition and literature such transformations and simultaneity of identities are relatively impossible outside the realms of surrealism and the magic real. But a brief perusal of Mayan murals and the plastic arts reveals quite a different understanding of reality. Here things are in a constant state of transformation. Serpents may have two heads, one on each end of the body; they may be plumed; gods may be half animal. The implication here is that the essence of these beings is in a state of flux. Rosemary A. Joyce affirms this with regard to gender, but in view of Mayan art itself and especially with respect to Castañeda's short story, this state of flux is true for many aspects of this culture.

---

[21] On several occasions these twins feign death and are dismembered only to return. They are also associated with the sowing and harvesting of corn.

According to Joyce, 'Postclassic Yucatecan Maya society treated gender as emerging through performance, marked by the provision of distinctive costumes, and given substance through a series of rituals of transition over the life of a person.'[22]

Viewed this way, the simultaneity of identities from the hospital scene illustrates a similar state of flux. The mother/son, husband/wife relationship is still an open issue. As the narration proceeds, his mother takes the protagonist home where she has been working on a series of statues. The first one is rectangular and consists of legs and arms, and other body parts that seem to be emerging from a vagina that overpowers all the other images (28). He then describes a series of statues she has made:

> And one work is really a series of works, starting with an amorphous lump of clay spotted with flecks of light, swatches of cloth, and bric-a-brac . . . The last is partly hominid – the chest and up – but the bottom part looks at first like randomly scratched clay. It isn't until I look closer that I see that the legs and part of the the belly are composed of various figures blending into one another. I can distinguish parrots, alligators, monsters, crowds of boys, storm clouds, the Guatemalan flag, a calabash like a soccer ball among ghastly players, two boys with heads like the sun and moon. (29)

The figures almost all originate in myths related in the *Popol-Vuh* (the flag, as an element of humor reflects on his mother's peculiar personality). The two boys are Hunahpu and Xbalanque. In the same way that, according to Joyce, ritual creates identity from flux, the statues are intended to recreate the protagonist, transporting him from the chaos of his former life to the promise of a future. He states at the end that he believes his mother really believes in magic, implying that he doesn't. Nevertheless, he affirms that she saved his life (29). His last hope is that his daughter will grow to love him. He wonders if he really had twin sons – 'from my little and inconsequential spitting' – (30), and what will become of them. Thus to find himself, the protagonist is taken back to his origins identified by his mother as her 'Espanish', which in reality is the mestizo culture, the mixture of the Mayan and Spanish traditions that essentially identifies Guatemala.

## Conclusion

When we consider the selected works of these three authors, despite their different nationalities, the difference in the amount of time they have lived in the US, the diversity of their experience and of the genres in which they write, it is surprising to realize how much they have in common. On reading these works the sense of alienation in the protagonists and narrators becomes clear. With

---

[22] Rosemary A. Joyce, *Gender and Power in Prehispanic Mesoamerica* (Austin: University of Texas Press, 2000), 132.

regard to Palacios's poems, as well as in the novel, the sense of alienation derives from the narrator's having lost a lover. Her search leads her away from her homeland but is of no avail. On the contrary, she finds herself alone. But as importantly, she finds herself frustrated, for, while she is filled with poetry (the very mysteries that Calypso wishes to convey to Ulysses), there is no one to whom she can give her gift. At the same time, the absence of her beloved amounts to an emptying of her soul. We are thus left with a kind of duality that cannot be resolved in any way. On the one hand, she has so much to offer; on the other, the loss of the beloved leaves her with nothing.

With respect to the places to which she must go to find the beloved – the foreign lands to which she will travel – their presence in terms of imagery and in terms of their effects on the narrator hardly enters into the picture. On the contrary, she retreats within herself; her images are derived from her literary and cultural heritage, and these images become the sole expression of her sensibility and sense of alienation.

With Vallbona's Renata, the presence of her literary and cultural past also plays a vital role. But within the narration, the surrounding Anglo culture is not only present to her but offers an alternative with respect to her dilemma as an individual held in a state of inferiority solely because of her gender. This alternative, however, does not result in a solution to her deeper ontological need. At this level, she clings to her own philosophical and religious heritage. As with the philosopher most influential in her intellectual and psychic formation, Unamuno, she searches for transcendence. Full transcendence, however, is only found within the religious and mystical life, which she can no longer fully accept. Her own literary creativity stems from this *a priori* frustrated search, and, while indeed she may produce a body of literary work of lasting beauty and meaning, her need for transcendence remains necessarily frustrated. The result is that while she enjoys her friendships with other intellectuals (both men and women) and has much hope for the future of her daughter, she remains essentially alienated and trapped within her own sense of mortality.

Castañeda's protagonist poses a more curious dilemma: his desire is to be 'American'. But, on the one hand, he is confronted with the bigotry of the Anglo culture in which he lives, and on the other, he is aware of something essentially inauthentic – at least for him – within the culture, hence the irony in the scenes dealing with his rehabilitation. In the end, owing to his mother's intervention, he finds consolation in his 'cultural roots' of which, just as ironically, he is hardly aware. Nevertheless, whatever optimism or hope there is in the narrative, it is to be found in his *ladino* heritage, the mixture of Mayan and Hispanic heritages and traditions.

These literary creations also share the fact that they exist in isolation. In none of the three authors is there a sense of community. And though this will most likely change for Nicaraguans and Guatemalans in the future (both of these nationalities, in contrast to Costa Rica, now have growing communities within the US), it seems to be a trait that identifies writers from Central America. The literary work is there and growing. It is rich in human expression and in the expression of diverse heritages, but the creators are alone and without the 'buffer' possessed by writers who belong to the traditional Hispanic communities.

## Works Cited

Amoretti, María. 'La morada interior y sus espectros', introduction to *Mundo, demonio y mujer*. Coral Gables, Florida: Editorial Ponce de León, 2002.
Castañeda, Omar S. 'On the Way Out', in *Remembering to Say 'Mouth' or 'Face'*. Boulder: Fiction Collective 2, 1993.
Chase, Cida S. 'Elementos estructurales y pluralidad del lenguaje en *Mundo, demonio y mujer*', in Jorge Chen Sham (ed.), *Nuevos acercamientos a la obra de Rima de Vallbona*. San José, Costa Rica: Editorial de la Universidad de Costa Rica, 2000, 33–48.
Chen Sham, Jorge. *Radiografías del sujeto agónico: culpa y transcendencia en la novelística de Rima de Vallbona*. San José, Costa Rica: Ediciones Perro Azul, 2001.
Cuadra, Pablo Antonio. 'Los hijos de septiembre', '¿Cúal es nuestro Ulises? ¿Cúal es nuestra aventura?', *El Nicaragüense*. Managua, Nicaragua, 1997, 18.
García-Obregón, Omar. 'Discurso social y fantasmagórico en la narrativa nicaragüense de los 90: *En carne viva* de Conny Palacios', *El Pez y la Serpiente* (November–December 1999), 99.
Goetz, Delia, and Sylvanus G. Morley (trans.), *Popol Vuh*. Norman: University of Oklahoma Press, 1983.
Joyce, Rosemary A. *Gender and Power in Prehispanic Mesoamerica*. Austin: University of Texas Press, 2000.
López-Adorno, Pedro. *Papiros de Babel/Antología de la poesía puertorriqueña en Nueva York*. Rio Piedras, Puerto Rico: Editorial de la Universidad de Puerto Rico, 1991.
Negrín, María Luisa. 'La dimensión de la locura, el exilio y la agonía en la novella *En carne viva*', *Revista de la Academia Nicaragüense de la Lengua*, 27 (September, 2003).
Palacios, Conny. *En carne viva*. Coral Gables, Florida: La Torre de Papel, 1994.
—— *Exorcismo del absurdo; Percepción fractal*. Managua. Nicaragua: PAVSA, 1999.
Robb, Anthony J. *La poética de Conny Palacios*. Managua, Nicaragua: PAVSA, 2004.
Spina, Vincent. 'La dualidad en "Poema del momento extranjero en la selva", "La mitología del jaguar" y "El Nacimiento de Cifar" por Pablo Antonio Cuadra', in Jorge Chen Sham (ed.), *Simposio Internacional de Poesía Nicaragüense del Siglo XX/Homenaje a Pablo Antonio Cuadra*. Managua, Nicaragua: Asociación Pablo Antonio Cuadra, 2005, 99–115.
—— 'Old Heroes, Gods and Demons' (review). *Collages and Bricolages: Journal of International Writing*, VIII (1994), 88.
Tedlock, Dennis (trans.). *Popul-Vuh: The Mayan Book on the Dawn of Life*. New York: Touchstone Books, 1996.

Unamuno, Miguel de. *Del sentimiento trágico de la vida en los hombres y en los pueblos*. Madrid: Alianza Editorial, 2003.
Vallbona, Rima de. *Mundo, demonio y mujer.* Coral Gables, Florida: Editorial Ponce de León, 2000.

# 8

# American Dream, *Jeitinho Brasileiro*: On the Crossroads of Cultural Identities in Brazilian-American Literature

## ANTONIO LUCIANO DE ANDRADE TOSTA

The Brazilian cartoonist Henfil lived in the United States between 1973 and 1975. In 1983 he published *Diário De Um Cucaracha* (Diary of a Cucaracha), which was a collection of some of the letters that he had written to his friends during these years. While telling his personal experiences in his *Diário*, Henfil reveals his impressions of his host society, and often uses them to establish a comparison with his native Brazil. His reflections, filled with political and economic commentary, range from simple factual descriptions to serious cultural analysis. In both cases, the US becomes a mirror from which Brazil is either praised or criticized, and Brazil provides the perspective for his examination of North American culture. In *A Travessia Americana* (The American Crossing), Carlos Eduardo Novaes says that 'Our country is always the reference. Whether we want it or not, we all travel with Brazil in our suitcases' (17). Henfil's letters are evidence that Novaes is right. He traveled throughout the US and Canada with his friend Paulo Perdigão for thirty-eight days in 1983. *A Travessia Americana* is a report of their experiences during that trip.[1] Novaes's book, therefore, is a travel narrative. Like Henfil's *Diário*, Novaes's *crônicas* analyze US society with a lot of humor and a pinch of irony. Every now and then Novaes also turns his gaze to Brazil, although not as emphatically as Henfil does. Both works are registers of an intercultural encounter that would be intensified after the 1980s, when Brazilian immigration to the US would take on much larger proportions.

According to Christopher Mitchell, Brazilian immigration to the US started 'almost abruptly in the mid-1980s' and Teresa Sales agrees. New York City, for example, home to many Brazilians nowadays, had few Brazilians at that time. As Henfil reports in his *Diário*, at the end of 1973:

> There are few Brazilians. There must be many on 46th Street, where there are some stores where they speak Brazilian Portuguese that are meant only to assist

---

[1] Perdigão is represented by the character Luís Paulo in *A Travessia Americana*.

Brazilians. But the Brazilians that come here leave after they go shopping. There are few (Brazilians) residing here. And they don't form a ghetto. (120)

Bernadete Beserra points out that until the end of the 1980s, when the Brazilian press started exploring the topic, 'Brazilian emigration was an unusual and almost unthinkable occurrence'.[2]

Citing Darién Davis, Beserra mentions sporadic Brazilian immigration to the US before then, and also emphasizes the sudden increase after the mid-1980s.[3] Henfil's *Diário* shows some of these pioneering Brazilians that both Beserra and Davis talk about, ranging 'from broke students who had fellowships, to high-level bankers and diplomats' (35). But his letters already give indications of a Brazilian community in New York, for instance, when he refers to 'a colônia verde-amarela' (green and yellow colony, the colors of the Brazilian flag) in describing his first Thanksgiving among 'besieged and disintegrated Brazilians' (Henfil, 35). He also says that he hired a Brazilian cleaner and comments: 'Assim, estamos só de brasileiros em volta da gente' (Therefore, we are surrounded only by Brazilians) (15). Moreover, Henfil talks about Brazilians' feeling of homesickness in the US and the new arrivals; he mentions that there were already Brazilian restaurants and stores that specialized in Brazilian products on 46th Street, and stresses in his letters Brazilians' 'segregation' and common fear of deportation (35).

The Palácio do Itamarati, the organization responsible for Brazil's foreign relations, claims that in 2004 there were some 800,000 Brazilian immigrants in the US.[4] However, José Carlos Sebe Bom Meihy suggests a more realistic number would be around 1,500,000.[5] More recently, *Revista Veja*, a traditional and popular Brazilian magazine, cites research carried out by the Getúlio Vargas Foundation of Rio de Janeiro that places the number of Brazilians living in the US at one million. The study compares the Brazilian immigrants to the US with the American immigrants in Brazil, who are said to number only 14,000. Other differences are interesting to look at. For example, most Brazilians in the US are women, about thirty years old, married, and working as house cleaners, cooks, waitresses, and shop assistants, whereas most Americans in Brazil are men,

---

[2] Teresa Sales, 'Identidade Étnica Entre Imigrantes Brasileiros na Região de Boston, EUA', *Cenas do Brasil Migrante*, eds. Rossana Rocha Reis, and Teresa Sales (São Paulo: Boitempo, 1999), 18. Christopher Mitchell, 'As Recentes Políticas de Imigração dos Estados Unidos e seu Provável Impacto nos Imigrantes Brasileiros'. *Políticas Migratórias: América Latina, Brasil e Brasileiros no Exterior* (São Carlos: EDUFSCar, 2002), 177–98. Bernadete Beserra, *Brazilian Immigrants in the United States: Cultural Imperialism and Social Class* (New York: LFB Scholarly Publishing, 2003), 6.

[3] Darién J. Davis, 'To Be or Not to Be Brazilian: Carmen Miranda's Quest for Fame and "Authenticity" in the United States'. Paper presented at the IV Meeting of the Brazilian Studies Association, Washington, DC, 1997.

[4] Quoted in José Carlos Sebe Bom Meihy, *Brasil Fora de Si: Experiências de Brasileiros em Nova York* (São Paulo: Parábola Editorial, 2004), 40.

[5] Meihy, *Brasil Fora de Si*, 41. For official and unofficial estimates of the number of Brazilians living abroad, see Meihy, 40 and 41.

about sixty years old, single, and are mainly missionaries, university professors, or high school teachers. Because of these and other discrepancies, the Brazilian magazine calls it 'an uneven exchange'.[6]

Although distinct in writing styles, letters and *crônicas* share features that would characterize the majority of existing Brazilian-American texts. The first obvious attribute is their autobiographical nature. Whether fictionalized or not, most Brazilian-American texts remain highly based on personal experience. There are more strictly autobiographical works, such as Carlos Stozek Filho's *Um Brasileiro nas Tropas do Tio Sam* (A Brazilian in Uncle Sam's Army). Stozek was an immigrant who was forced to serve as a recruit in the US Army in 1963 and 1965 owing to the immigration laws at the time. Later he decided to publish his memories as a book. There are other works that are fictional, but still rely heavily on personal experience. A good example is Sergio Vilas Boas's *Os Estrangeiros do Trem N* (The N Train Foreigners). In an interview with the ethnic newspaper *The Brazilians* in 1999, the author confessed that 'any similarity between fiction and reality (in his work) is not mere coincidence'.[7] Vilas Boas explains that the material for his book came from the over one hundred interviews that he conducted in New York, as well as from newspapers, books, photographs, internet websites, magazines, and TV shows.[8] For that reason, he claims that 'Everything that is written (in *Os Estrangeiros do Trem N*) is verisimilar – reality either felt or experienced.'[9]

These two kinds of literary texts, fictional and non-fictional, provide us with one of the possible ways to categorize Brazilian-American literature. This way of grouping, however, will not conceal their similarities. After all, both categories are also examples of 'documentary' literature. Juan Duchesne Winter explains that this kind of literary tradition, which includes the *crônicas*, memories, diaries, epistolary collections, and travel books, among others, has marked the Latin American literature since the 'discovery'.[10] The documentary quality of *crônicas*, such as those in Novaes's *A Travessia Americana* is evident, but *crônicas* are more than documentary texts. As Massaud Moisés points out, 'The *crônica* oscillates between the journalistic text and literature, between the report (. . .) of a trivial event, and the recreation of the everyday life through fantasy.'[11] This fluctuation is seen in Novaes's *A Travessia Americana*, since it 'is neither a travel diary, nor a touristic guide, or a sociological, paisagistic, existential, or political panel. It is a bit of all of this and much more.'[12] The same applies to

[6] Meihy, *Brasil Fora de Si*, 45.
[7] *The Brazilians*, 297, 18.
[8] Sergio Vilas Boas, *Os Estrangeiros do Trem N* (Rio de Janeiro: Rocco, 1997).
[9] *Os Estrangeiros do Trem N*, 9.
[10] Juan Duchesne Winter, *Narraciones de testimonio en América Latina: Cinco Estudios* (Río Piedras: Editorial de la Universidad de Puerto Rico, 1992), 4.
[11] *A Criação Literária: Prosa* (São Paulo: Cultrix, 1979), 247, and Sonia Nolasco, *Moreno Como Vocês* (São Paulo: Francis, 2003).
[12] Paulo Perdigão, Introduction', in Carlos Eduardo Novaes, *A Travessia Americana* (São Paulo: Editora Ática, 1985), 7.

other compilations of *crônicas*, such as Lucas Mendes's *Crônicas da Big Apple* (Big Apple *Crônicas*), in which the Brazilian journalist tells his experiences in his more than twenty-eight years of life in the US, and Edney Silvestre's *Dias de Cachorro Louco: Trinta Histórias de Nova York* (Mad Dog Days: Thirty New York Stories).

Brazilian-American fictional works are just as complex texts, since 'The *Brazuca* novels (also) draw upon the report, the autobiography and biography, the testimony and journalistic texts.'[13] Brazilians who live and work – often illegally – abroad often call themselves *Brazucas*. As it is used here, the term in fact refers to fictional works that describe the experiences of Brazilians and their descendants, not only in the US, but also in countries such as Paraguay, Japan, Portugal, Spain, and Switzerland. Antônio Candido argues that

> since the beginning Brazilian fiction tended to the documentary form, and during the nineteenth century it promoted a sort of a major exploration of life in the city and the countryside in all areas, in all classes, revealing the country to its inhabitants, as if the intention were to shape its meaningful and complete picture.[14]

*Brazuca* fiction is part of this tradition. These narratives are 'almost always written in colloquial language with modest constructions', and 'focus on descriptive fidelity and verisimilitude; in other words, the direct and objective representation of reality'.[15] Like *crônicas*, they 'elaborate a language that speaks to us in a manner that is close to our most natural way of being'.[16]

These *crônica*-like characteristics, along with others such as the emphasis on everyday life, the common essayistic tone, and the use of humor and irony, allow us to confer upon most *Brazuca* texts published to this date the status of 'minor literature'. This is how Candido puts it:

> The *crônica* is not a 'major genre'. We cannot conceive of a literature made by great *cronistas* that can be given the universal brightness of the great novelists, dramaturges, and poets. We would not even consider giving the Nobel Prize to a *cronista*, no matter how good he may be. Therefore, it seems that the *crônica* really is a minor genre. (13)

Designating them as 'minor', however, as in the case of the *crônicas*, does not conceal their magnitude. Candido has discussed how the *crônicas*' style, which is also found in *Brazuca* novels, 'breaks with the monumental and the emphatic' (14). According to him, these characteristics that we admire and so often

---

[13] Antonio Luciano de Andrade Tosta, 'Latino, *Eu?* The Paradoxical Interplay of Identity in *Brazuca* Literature', *Hispania,* 87:3 (2004), 576–85.

[14] Antônio Candido, 'Literatura e subdesenvolvimento', *A Educação pela Noite e Outros Ensaios* (São Paulo: Editora Ática, 2000), 172.

[15] Tosta, 577.

[16] Antônio Candido, 'A Vida ao Rés-do-Chão', A *Crônica: O Gênero, Sua Fixação e Suas Transformações no Brasil* (Campinas: Editora da Unicamp, 1992), 13.

impress us in literature can act to 'fake reality and even the truth', whereas the *crônica* always helps us to 'establish or reestablish the dimension of things and people. Instead of providing a sublime scenery, in a multitude of adjectives and flaming periods, it focuses on the minuteness and shows its unsuspected grandeur, beauty, or singularity' (14). Hence, the same characteristics that permit us to classify *Brazuca* novels as 'minor' are the ones that make them important documents, as they provide us with a clear and updated picture of Brazilian immigration in the US, and of Brazilians' perceptions of themselves, of Americans, and of the US and Brazil. Most *Brazuca* texts were published in Brazil, and are written in Portuguese by first-generation immigrants or individuals who either lived for a short period, or just visited the foreign country. *Brazuca* literature includes not only novels and *crônicas*, but also poetry, short stories, songs, a film, and a play. *Brava Gente Brasileira em Terras Estrangeiras* (Brave Brazilian People in Foreign Lands), an anthology edited by *Brazuca* author Angela Bretas in 2004, brings poems, *crônicas*, and short stories written by *Brazucas* in the US, Japan, Germany, and Switzerland. The 2002 movie *A Fronteira*, by Roberto Carminatti and Zeca Barros, Fernando Holz's 2002 song 'Diáspora Brasileira' and Édel Holz's 2004 play 'Meu Brasil é Aqui!' are examples of Brazilians' diverse cultural production in the United States.[17]

Although most *Brazucas* in the US cannot yet be called Brazilian-Americans *per se*, given the temporary nature of their immigration, *Brazuca* texts do mark the starting point of a Brazilian-American literature. After all, the same configuration has marked other Latino and ethnic literatures in the US. In his study of Hispanic and Latino Caribbean literature written in the US William Luis, for example, separates these narratives into two major categories: 'The first consists of works by writers who were raised and educated in their native countries and later emigrated or were forced to flee to the United States. While in the United States, they continued to write in the vernacular, mostly about themes pertaining to their island of provenance.'[18] The second category includes 'Latino writers who were born or raised in the United States and who for the most part write in English . . . They compose a literature that searches for their own identity and origins in the United States.'[19] According to Luis's model, Brazilian-American literature would be restricted to the first group. Those born in the US of Brazilian origins, or who emigrated at a very young age, are still to make use of literature to express the complexities of their intercultural experiences. But it will not take long for them to begin to do so, and the contemporary *Brazuca* texts will provide a valuable and essential background so that they can be interpreted and studied.

---

[17] It is important to mention that there are also Brazilian scholars such as Cristina Ferreira Pinto and Dário Borim, who live and work in the US, who are still better known for their academic work, but who have also written fiction both in English and Portuguese. Pinto seems to prefer poetry, whereas Borim has written many *crônicas* and short stories.

[18] William Luis, *Dance Between Two Cultures: Latino Caribbean Literature Written in the United States* (Nashville: Vanderbilt University Press, 1997), xi.

[19] Luis, xi.

Valéria Barbosa de Magalhães divides the works of fiction 'about Brazilians in the USA' between those published in the 1980s and the 1990s. She argues it is important to do so, as the 1980s were considered the 'lost decade' for immigration scholars, whereas the 1990s showed a more consolidated immigration.[20] Magalhães mentions texts by authors José Victor Bicalho, Henfil, Reinaldo Moraes, Sonia Nolasco, Carlos E. Novaes, and Silviano Santiago as belonging to the 1980s generation, and Tereza Albues, Roberto Athayde, Júlio Bráz, Silvana Batista, Norma Guimarães, Thales de Leon, Regina Rheda, Luis Alberto Scotto, and Sérgio Vilas Boas to the 1990s (2). It is necessary to expand her list so as to include Belchior Neto, Carlos Stozek Filho, Lucas Mendes, Edney Silvestre, and Angela Bretas in the 1990s, and João Santana in the early 2000s. The complexity of this genre even allows us to add the testimonies in Heloisa Maria Galvão's *As Viajantes do Século Vinte* (The Travelers of the Twentieth Century) to the list of non-fictional works of the present decade. Galvão interviewed eleven Brazilian immigrant women in the Boston area, and their stories narrated in Galvão's book oftentimes cover the same themes and show some of the characteristics of most *Brazuca* works of prose.

Magalhães suggests that there are thematic similarities between the works in each decade:

> The period in which each book was published shows themes that translate the preoccupations of the time to which they refer. The novels of the 1980s emphasize the amazement with the consumerism and with the vanguard of the 1980s in the US and stress the Brazilians' involvement with drugs, which was common in the period. The ones that depict the 1970s also treat the theme of exile. But the books of the 1990s are more about the job market, the fear of deportation, the dilemma of whether returning or not, and the relationship between Brazilians abroad. (2)

In addition, Magalhães distinguishes four frequent myths in the novels she analyzes. The first is the myth of passage, which describes the change to a new life. There is the myth of paradise, which can be seen in the immigrant's feeling of awe and experience of success in the new land. Magalhães also cites the myth of Phoenix, which is in the immigrant's heroic search for a rebirth, and last but not least, the myth of the eternal return, which is present in the constant indecision whether to go back to Brazil or not. It is important to note, as Magalhães reminds us, that these works set the pace in the discussion of Brazilian immigration to the United States, since a good number of them were published in Brazil well before the first academic work about the Brazilian immigration appeared in the South American nation.[21]

---

[20] Valéria Barbosa de Magalhães, 'História Oral e Imigração: A Identidade dos Brasileiros nos EUA a Partir de Obras de Ficção Escrita'. Unpublished manuscript, 2.

[21] Magalhães, 5–6. The work Magalhães is referring to is the 1994 Portuguese translation of Maxine Margolis's *Little Brasil*.

## The American dream and the Brazilian jeitinho

*Brazuca* works discuss Brazil and the US, and what it means to be Brazilian and North American. This discussion of national identity and cultural traits often happens by way of a comparison (implicit or explicit) between the Brazilian 'jeito de ser' (way of being) – the so-called *jeitinho brasileiro*,[22] which is a mark of national identity that emphasizes a happy, cordial, relaxed, and sensual attitude – and the American lifestyle, revealing how Brazilian-ness fits within the North American standard of living. Whereas this cultural encounter on occasion points to Brazilians' admiration of a number of American values, such as organization, practicality, and independence, these very same features – and numerous others – are equally shown as incompatible with Brazilian culture. As Ana Cristina Braga Martes's research shows, 'Americans are, invariably, identified . . . as "cold", "tough", "very serious", "distant", "excessively formal", "greedy", etc. To these "adjectives", (they) juxtapose "happiness", "warmth", "friendship", "informality" and not unusually the Brazilians' "jeitinho".'[23]

The US is generally characterized as a more rigid place in *Brazuca* works, where the law is tougher. This is suggested, for instance, in a scene in Edel Holz's play *O Meu Brasil é Aqui!* (My Brazil is Here!) in which Geraldinho, a 16-year-old *Brazuca* tells Cacilda that he is going to have a date with an 18-year-old girl, and his father reacts saying that, 'Os dois são de menor. Aqui essas coisas dão cadeia, viu? Olha lá . . .' (They are both under-age. One may go to jail for that here, OK? Be careful . . .).[24] The same sense of inflexibility appears in a scene in Bretas's novel *Sonho Americano*, when four friends go camping and complain about the area's many rules:

> Lotado, naquela época do ano, o *camping*, repleto de barracas, possuía regras e mais regras: – Não pescar com isca tal. / Não usar isqueiros. Atente ao fogo. / Proibido caçar aves silvestres. / Barulho após as 22 horas é proibido. / . . . Não perturbar seu vizinho de barraca. / Bebidas alcoólicas são proibidas.
>
> (The camping area was crowded and full of stands at that time of the year. There were rules and more rules: Do not fish with such and such bait. / Do not use lighters. Attention to fires. / It is prohibited to hunt wild birds. / It is prohibited to make noise after 10 pm. / . . . Do not disturb those in your neighboring tent. / Alcoholic beverages are prohibited).[25]

The enumeration of rules – and prohibitions – in this scene is clearly a commentary on the Brazilian perception of American society as a whole. They list a

---

[22] Lívia Neves de H. Barbosa, 'The Brazilian Jeitinho: An Exercise in National Identity', in *The Brazilian Puzzle*, eds. David J. Hess, and Roberto DaMatta (New York: Columbia University Press, 1995), 46.

[23] Ana Cristina Braga Martes, *Brasileiros nos Estados Unidos: Um Estudo Sobre Imigrantes em Massachusetts* (São Paulo: Paz e Terra, 1999), 158.

[24] Edel Holz, *O Meu Brasil é Aqui!*, 328.

[25] Angela Bretas, *Sonho Americano* (São Paulo: Scortecci, 1997), 79.

number of characteristics that are typically regarded as American, such as organization, concern with nature, cleanliness, respect for the others and their rights, as well as discipline. All of these restrictions lead the *Brazucas* to pose the question, 'Isso é camping ou campo de concentração?' (Is this a camping area or a concentration camp?) (*Sonho Americano*, 79). Their dissatisfaction suggests, not surprisingly, that Brazilians see themselves as more relaxed and flexible than North Americans.

In the first *crônica* in Novaes's book, rigidity and excessive control even give American culture a military quality:

> Seen from a distance, from Rio de Janeiro, North American society may seem like a big and relaxed happening, where each person does whatever he wants. Seen from within, in the individuality of their anonymous citizens, it reveals the organization of a military establishment. There is a permanent exaltation of freedom. The spaces of individuals' interior freedom, however, are filled with massive doses of words of order: Stop! Walk! Buy! Sell! Save! The big sergeant is hidden behind the plaques, the publicity, the official discourses. The people enjoy an envious freedom and behave like mechanical dolls. (12)

One of the general points that the passage makes is that a person's 'contact' with a foreign culture allows him to destroy stereotypes and uncover unfamiliar aspects of that society. Specifically speaking, a more serious criticism is made. Novaes suggests that Brazilian perceptions of American culture can easily shift from appreciative to disapproving because its essence is actually different from what it exhibits. In fact, two of the major pillars of American identity – the notions of freedom and individuality – are questioned, being rendered as under the thumb of American capitalist and dominant ruling discourse. Again, this criticism automatically implies a contrast with Brazil, insinuating that it is in the South American nation where one can really find freedom and democracy.

Having feelings of disillusionment and dissatisfaction towards one's host nation, however, is not an unforeseen attitude, since, after all, immigration creates a 'contact zone', which, as Mary Louise Pratt explains, is a social space 'where cultures meet, clash, and grapple with each other, often in contexts of highly asymmetrical relations of power, such as colonialism, slavery, or their aftermath as they are lived out in many parts of the world today'.[26] No matter how natural and expected such friction and tension may be, its regularity challenges the validity of the migratory act itself in *Brazuca* works, since, as the passage from Novaes's *crônica* shows, it defies the so-called 'American dream', which is the main reason for the immigration. Like the 'jeitinho brasileiro', the 'American Dream' is a mark of national identity and a major one. As Jim Cullen points out, 'The term seems like the most lofty as well as the most immediate

---

[26] Mary Louise Pratt, 'Arts of the Contact Zone', *Professing in the Contact Zone: Bringing Theory and Practice Together*, ed. Janice M. Wolff (Urbana, Illinois: National Council of Teachers of English, 2002), 4.

component of an American identity, a birthright far more meaningful and compelling than terms like "democracy", "Constitution", or even "the United States".'[27]

In his introduction to *A Travessia Americana*, Paulo Perdigão asks,

> Have you heard of the 'American dream'? . . . It has to do with ideas of freedom, dignity, audacity, pioneers – the still unconquered America, not polluted by the machines and the capital, with its solemn majestic meadows, at the time of the conquerors and their caravans of covered wagons. It has also to do with the Hollywood myths that enticed the children and adolescents in the 40s: the America of the grand green mansions of Beverly Hills and Malibu, of great war heroes, of the West, of charm and gallantry, of the enchanted world of James Dean and Marilyn Monroe. (5)

The 'American dream' that places most Brazilians on the journey to the US, however, is typically different from what led Novaes and Perdigão to make their own trips. Their tour of North America in search of charming, enchanted, 'Hollywoodian' sites was not motivated by the economic and other personal reasons that have driven thousands of Brazilians to the US, although the imperial effect of the US media might have, in some cases, influenced their decision to immigrate. The American dream is a major theme in most *Brazuca* novels, as is its failure. The character Caio in Julio Emílio Braz and Silvana Pimentel Batista's *Rua 46* (46th Street), for instance, states the nature of his American dream: 'Quando o avião decolou, subiram comigo todos os meus sonhos de um sucesso rápido e definitivo' (When the plane took off, all my dreams of a fast and definitive success went up with me).[28] Caio says that his flight companions were also seeking out their dreams: 'Todos nós – Laura, Silva, Gustavo e eu – estávamos decepcionados com o Brasil. Preferimos voar ao encontro de nossos sonhos em outro lugar' (All of us – Laura, Silva, Gustavo and I – were disappointed with Brazil. We preferred to fly in the direction of our dreams elsewhere) (13). But in the prologue to *Rua 46* there is already an indication that the dream will not be easy to achieve, since one of the characters is caught by Immigration: 'That was death. The end of everything . . . Dreams being destroyed in the hot asphalt . . . In that same instant someone shouted in his ears: – Immigration!' (8) In fact, Caio and Laura do live happily ever after later in the novel, but Antonio's deportation indicates that the American dream is not exactly for everyone.

The minority part of *Brazuca* authors are very critical of their American experience. Their writings show, as Davis has pointed out, that 'Brazilians who leave their country seeking a better life have learned that the so-called "Amer-

---

[27] Jim Cullen, *The American Dream: A Short History of an Idea that Shaped a Nation* (Oxford: Oxford University Press, 2003), 5.

[28] Júlio Emílio Braz and Silvana Pimentel Batista, *Rua 46* (São Paulo: Saraiva, 1995; reprint 2002), 12.

ican Dream" might always remain elusive'.[29] A *Brazuca* poet in Japan, Maria Alice Hanashiro, says that 'temos a liberdade de sonhar, temos a liberdade de imaginar lindos sonhos, temos a liberdade de buscar o nosso compromisso' (we have the freedom to dream, to imagine beautiful dreams, to search for our commitment) (3–5). But, as Ricardo Moura Ferreira suggests, the trajectories told in these stories are presented 'sometimes . . . as dreams, others as nightmares' (14). The confrontation of the utopian search for the American dream with the harsh reality of the immigrant is also one of the themes of the soap opera *America*, which aired on *Globo* network in 2005. In the opening episode of this Brazilian soap, a character who had immigrated to the US returns to the *favela* 'slum area' in Rio de Janeiro after six years of life in the US. She wants to bring her niece with her to the US, and it is by emphasizing the American dream that she manages to convince her sister to allow her daughter to travel with her. The *Brazuca* émigré contrasts her old life in Brazil with her present life in the US:

> America is another world, Madá. Everyone progresses there . . . See my own case. What did I have when I was here? Nothing. I lived in worse conditions than you do, didn't I? I didn't make even enough to buy food . . . I had the guts to go there, my sister . . . In six years I have put my life together.

She brings lots of gifts to her niece and stresses the wonderful opportunity that she is giving her: 'A Drica cai ter outra vida (Drica can have another life) . . . You are safeguarding her future. Hers and yours. Because when she grows, you will grow too.' The character also shows her sister and niece photos of her house as proof of her accomplishments, and highlights the symbols of her success: 'Take a look at how big the swimming pool is! / Wow, how lavish! / This is my car, which I change every year.'

The visit of this character to the *favela* actually transforms not only her niece's life, but also 'Sol's', who is actually the soap opera's protagonist. She was a child then and friends with the émigré's niece. The *Brazuca* gives a memento, a miniature city, to Sol, and says,

> Do you know what this is? It's America. It's exactly like you see it here. Pretty, clean. Everybody is happy. And there are no beggars in the middle of the streets. Can you believe it? It is full of waiters who have become millionaires and house cleaners who have become movie stars. Everyone has the right to everything there. To own their houses, good food, education, free health, everything. It's America.

These words echo in Sol's mind and her quest for the American dream takes up a large part of the soap opera. As an adult, Sol is denied a visa to enter the US

---

[29] Darién J. Davis, 'The Brazilian-Americans: Demography and Identity of an Emerging Latino Minority', *The Latino Review of Books*, 3:1/2 (1997), 11.

and ends up crossing the border from Mexico. She tries to 'buy' a marriage so she can stay legally in the US, but at some point another character warns her of the limitations of the American dream: 'A gente vende este sonho pro mundo inteiro . . . Algumas pessoas conseguem o que vieram buscar, mas a maioria não' (We sell this dream to the whole world . . . Some people manage to get what they came for, but the majority does not).

Bretas emphasizes that 'A realidade do dia a dia na nova terra é repleta de obstáculos e muitos desistem do sonho inicial' (The everyday reality in the new land is full of obstacles and many people give up their initial dream) (*Sonho Americano*, 9). In *Brazuca* texts reality constantly defies the dream, subverting, sabotaging, and turning it upside down, which is why the protagonist Maria in Bretas's novel feels 'a sensação de estar despertando de um pesadelo permanente' (the sensation of being awakened from a permanent nightmare) (*Sonho Americano*, 9 and 29).

The stories in *Sonho Americano* present several examples of the impediments that resist the fulfillment of the 'American Dream'. Characters' problems begin during their attempt to cross the border, when the group starves and a child witnesses the death of her father. They end up being caught by immigration officers while they are still in Canada. When the protagonist arrives in the US, she learns that her boyfriend Lucas had been deported, which also happens to her friend Hugo later (27). Maria is almost raped twice (27). Moreover, she is a victim of prejudice, and to top it off, has a miscarriage: 'A dor de não ter realizado o sonho de ser mãe a sufoca' (the pain of not having had her dream to become a mother suffocates her) (52, 61, 65). In fact, in this passage having a child symbolizes the beginning of a new life in a new land, and the loss of her baby suggests the impossibility of her 'American dream' coming true.

Another comparable symbolic moment is when Maria is unable to buy 'coco ralado' (shredded coconut) to make pudding because she cannot tell the employee what she wants in English. As a result, 'Maria finalmente decide ir embora, desistindo de fazer seu sonhado pudim de coco' (Maria finally decides to leave, giving up the idea to make her dreamed of coconut pudding). (*Sonho Americano*, 60). This interpretation makes sense especially if we remember that Bretas uses 'food' as a metaphor for the 'American dream' in her poem 'Imigrantes' (Immigrants): 'Cruzam fronteiras/ Em fileiras/ Formigas buscando comida' (They cross frontiers/ In lines/ Ants in search of food) (17). But the failure to make 'coconut pudding' in this scene can also be read as an allusion to one's inability to reproduce Brazilian life in the US, which is one aspect of the *Brazuca* experience that can be claimed to be harmful for the realization of the 'American dream'.

Similar situations are depicted in the soap opera *America*, as well as in other *Brazuca* novels. Thales de Leon's *Clandestinos: Aventuras Verídicas de Um Guia de Imigrantes Ilegais nas Fronteiras Americanas* (Clandestines: True Adventures of an Illegal Immigrants' Guide on the American Frontiers), for instance, shows the obstacles and difficulties of those who cross the border illegally. A quick look at the themes of some of the poems, short stories, and *crônicas* in Bretas's 2004 anthology *Brava Gente Brasileira em Terras Estrangeiras* (Brave Brazilian People in Foreign Lands) reveals some of the reasons why the American experience turns out to be a nightmare for some Brazilians. Besides topics such as 'dreams' and the Brazilian 'jeitinho', common examples are 'absence', 'saudade', 'loneliness', 'separation', and 'homecoming'. Brazilians are by and large very attached to their home country and especially to their families, and this is clear in *Brazuca* writings. 'A falta de entes queridos transforma o sonho americano em pesadelo' (not being near loved ones transforms the American Dream into nightmare), explains Maria in *Sonho Americano* (118). Martes's research shows that Brazilians in the US remain attached to several aspects of their lives in Brazil (183). This powerful bond of affection, as Davis has also suggested, makes Brazilians maintain strong ties and intense communication with their native land, which helps to foster a better sense of community. After all, 'Intimate contact with relatives and friends in the home country is (. . .) also indicative of the immigrants' desire to retain a piece of their homeland' (Davis, 'Brazilian-Americans', 10–11). Keeping Brazil in memory is, in fact, considered a way to preserve national identity: 'Sou mesmo brasileira. Daquelas que mesmo estando distante não se esquecem' (I am a real Brazilian. One of those who even distant do not forget), writes *Brazuca* author Valeria Trauer in her *crônica* 'Orgulho de Ser Brasileira' (Proud of Being Brazilian) (Martes, 183).

Such intense connection makes the effort to replicate Brazilian life in the host country an essential and natural part of the in-betweeness of *Brazucas'* experience: 'São clandestinos do destino; que se sujeitam a vida dividida. . . entre o aqui e o lá' (116). (They are clandestine beings of destiny; that agree to a life divided . . . between here and there), writes Bretas. All in all, as Kátia Mota and others have suggested, many *Brazucas* are working in the US to build their lives in Brazil.[30] An example in Bretas's novel is the character Hugo, who 'manda dinheiro para a família dele mensalmente e quer ganhar o bastante para construir uma casa lá' (sends money to his family (in Brazil) monthly and wants to make enough money to build a house there) (*Sonho Americano*, 108). Furthermore, as Martes comments, 'It is looking at Brazil that they evaluate American society. Not unexpectedly, various aspects that are considered positive in the United States are exactly those that are considered negative in Brazil, and vice-versa' (Martes, 153). This is shown in a scene in *Sonho Americano*, when, in the first hours of 1988, a group of Brazilians who are working at a New Year's party imagines what would be happening in Brazil at that very same time: 'There must be a great party in Brazil right now – one of them says. / I keep imagining the wonderful Carnaval that is going on there now! – comments another one. / – I myself felt very sorry to be here and not there' (89).

The growth of the Brazilian community, added to this constant link with

---

[30] Kátia Santos Mota, 'Aula de Português fora da Escola: Famílias Imigrantes Brasileiras, Esforços de Preservação da Língua Materna', *Cadernos CEDES*, 63:24 (2004), 151.

Brazil, has helped *Brazucas* to create a sense of a 'little Brazil' in their communities. Teresa Sales explains that this feeling of 'it even seems that we are in Brazil' is a result not only of the space that American society has opened for the ethnic group, in which Portuguese can be used in the education at schools, for business, and for basic services, but also of the new social networks that Brazilians have created.[31] One can notice this when the character Dorival in Holz's play says,

> Eu esqueço que nos Estados Unidos as veiz. . . Só falo português o tempo todo, meus amigos são tudos brasileiros, bebo minha lourinha geladinha, faço feijão, costelinha de porco, couve, feijoada. Tem de tudo no supermercado brasileiro . . . Tem jeito não, gente . . . O meu Brasil é aqui!
>
> (I sometimes forget that I am in the United States . . . I only speak Portuguese all the time, all my friends are Brazilians; I drink my cold beer, cook beans, pork ribs, cabbage, *feijoada*. There is everything in the Brazilian supermarket . . . There is no way out, everyone . . . My Brazil is here!) (Holtz, 461–6)

The same sensation is observed in *Sonho Americano*. During a concert by Brazilian singer Milton Nascimento in Downtown Boston, 'There was a nostalgic mixture of spontaneous smiles in faces that were strange until then in the air . . . It was as if a little piece of Brazil had dislocated to that space' (102).

Although this 'transplanted' Brazil is beneficial for the community in many ways, it may also foster a sense of rejection of American culture in some *Brazucas*. Many *Brazucas* do not learn English and avoid interactions with Americans, since they are able to survive that way by living and working within their ethnic communities. 'Para mim, *too much* é tomate mesmo' (For me, 'too much' is really *tomate* (tomatoes)), says a character in *Sonho Americano* (134). But sometimes it is important to adapt to American ways so that the dream can be achieved. It is necessary to know that 'too much' is indeed different from 'tomate'. One component of the *jeitinho brasileiro* that is problematic in American culture, for instance – and certainly in Brazilian culture as well – is the act of *dar um jeitinho*, which is, broadly speaking, the ability to solve a problem.[32] This is clear in a scene in *A Travessia Americana*, when Novaes is driving over the speed limit and tries not to get a ticket:

> Ainda tentei me desvencilhar. Joguei uma 'cascata'. Disse que me confundira, porque no Brasil nos orientávamos por quilometros. O guarda já deve ter ouvido esta história outras vezes. Preenchendo um interminável formulário, nem se dignou a levantar os olhos.
>
> (I did try to get away with it. I told a lie. I said that I had confused myself,

---

[31] Teresa Sales, *Brasileiros Longe da Casa* (São Paulo: Cortez, 1998), 140.
[32] See Barbosa, 38, and DaMatta, 99. Also see Virginia Leite's article 'Mau Jeito Nacional'.

because in Brazil we use kilometers. The policeman must have heard this story before. He filled out an endless form and did not even bother to raise his eyes) (13).

This scene shows a negative side of the *jeitinho*, when it is a mixture of 'malandragem' (trickery), malice, and 'safadeza' (knavishness) geared to one's selfish and not unusually illicit personal interests. This skill is bound to create problems in a well-structured society like the American. As Novaes's scene shows, the *'jeitinho'* as a rule will not allow one to dodge American culture, values, and rules easily, demanding Brazilians to adjust to the new cultural rules.

But the *jeitinho* might also function as an instrument that will enable one to safeguard the prospect of the American dream, as in Regina von Arx's poem 'Sonhador': 'De calar a dor contida no peito/ com *jeito*,/ defeito de um sonhador' (Of shutting up the pain in the chest/ comfortably,/ defect of a dreamer).[33] Cullen explains that 'beyond an abstract belief in possibility, there is no *one* American Dream' (7, emphasis in original). Moreover, he comments that the American Dream fails, as when focusing on the quest for equality, which, according to him is 'the most noteworthy – and unsuccessful – of all American Dreams' (Cullen, 8). *Brazuca* narratives often present a persistent threat of failure. Immigrants in *Sonho Americano* are pictured as being forced to 'se desdobrar para manter viva a simples esperança de um sonho' (do lots of extra work in order to keep the simple hope of a dream alive) (134). One of the *jeitinhos* that they make use of is exactly keeping strong ties with Brazil, since it lessens their feeling of 'saudade', isolation, and not-belonging.

In *Sonho Americano* '*jeitinhos*' towards the American dream are put into practice from the beginning of their adventure. Indeed, since entering the US through Mexican or Canadian borders successfully, for instance, is a good example of this Brazilian trait. For some, it is an attribute to be proud of, and for others to be ashamed of. Although nowadays Brazilians are regarded as the group of nationals that crosses the Mexican borders to emigrate to the United States in the highest numbers, they were not, naturally, the first ones to implement this *jeitinho*, nor are they the only ones to do so at the moment. A number of those who manage to arrive in the US legally holding tourist visas have also put a kind of *jeitinho* into effect through the forging of documents such as work contracts, pay checks with higher salaries, and proof of college attendance, which are expected to ease Brazilians' access to the so-desired tourist visa.

In Angela Bretas's novel, the protagonist Maria is unable to obtain a visa to the United States, but she manages to get one to Canada, which becomes her entrance door to the US. Maria and her fellow travelers are arrested while still in Canada. Although the narrative indicates that the dream would then be over, 'algemas em punhos, olhos chorosos, preces não ditas, sonhos desfeitos' (handcuffs on her wrists, teary eyes, unsaid prayers, failed dreams) (*Sonho*

---

[33] Regina von Arx, 'Sonhador', in *Brava Gente Brasileira em Terras Estrangeiras*, ed. Angela Bretas (São Paulo: Scortecci, 2004), lines 5–7. Emphasis is mine.

*Americano*, 19), we soon learn that 'no desespero de ver seu sonho destruído, decidira pela segunda vez tentar atravessar a fronteira' (desperate for seeing her dream fall through, she had decided to try to cross the border for a second time) (21). Maria is released from jail in Canada after paying a small fine and promising to return to Brazil, but she works things out with two other Brazilians and '*dá um jeitinho*' (work things out) to make a second attempt to cross the US–Canada border. Although in this case it is an illegal act, the *jeitinho* here also functions towards the fulfillment of the dream. It is a skill that operates as the means to an accomplishment, an instrument of personal attainment that enables the carrying out of a task. It is, therefore, not incompatible with the dream. On the contrary, it is an accessory to it.

According to Lívia Neves de H. Barbosa, one of the facets of the *jeitinho*, as shown in Novaes's attempt to get away with not paying the ticket, is that it transforms a situation of the individual into a situation of the person (Bretas, *Sonho Americano*, 41). This works well in a personalist society like the Brazilian, where, as Roberto DaMatta explains, there is a constant mediation between the person and the law, of which the *jeitinho* is regularly a vehicle.[34] But it does not match societies like the North American, where laws and rules, unlike in Brazil, are generally regarded as fair and of public interest (DaMatta, 9). 'O "jeito" é um modo de realizar' (the *jeito* is a way to accomplish things), says DaMatta (97). Therefore, in many instances it is a tool that guarantees what the law apparently does not. As Barbosa explains, the laws in Brazil promise fairness and impartiality, but do not secure them (Barbosa, 44). Hence 'the jeitinho transforms one form of equality into another' (Barbosa, 44), which would not make sense in societies where the laws already assure equality, or are more commonly believed to do so, as in the US.

The *jeitinho brasileiro*, whether representing Brazilianness, or simply expressing the subverting and employing the practical act of *dar um jeito* is an important national cultural construction for the study of *Brazucas*' interaction with American society and their struggle towards the American dream. As it has been shown, these Brazilian traits are sometimes helpful and useful for the Brazilian community, but others must be modified so that the Brazilian immigrant may truly adapt to his new reality. Integration to the American society is a step in the direction of the American dream and should not conflict with the preservation of one's cultural heritage. Bretas's protagonist Maria seems to have the solution:

> A única maneira de não viver entre os dois polos era fundir as duas personalidades, e para isso não teria que fazer nada mais do que seguir adiante em seu destino.

[34] DaMatta, 97. According to Sérgio Buarque de Holanda, the originality of Brazilian culture – of which the *jeitinho* is an example – is, in part, owing to its Iberian heritage. He suggests that the Portuguese and the Spanish peoples attributed a great deal of importance to the person as an individual. For Holanda, self-sufficiency was a central characteristic to these cultures, as it allowed the person to survive without depending on others (32–3).

(The only way of not living between the two poles was to fuse the two personalities, and for that I would not have to do anything besides moving ahead in destiny). (Bretas, Sonho Americano, 163)

\* I would like to acknowledge that Kathleen de Azevedo's novel *Samba Dreamers*, which is the first Brazilian-American novel published in English in the US, was published after the completion of this essay and therefore is not included in my analysis here. See below.

## Works Cited

*A Fronteira*. Dir. Roberto Carminatti. Motion Factory, 2002.
Albues, Tereza. *O Berro do Cordeiro em Nova York*. Rio de Janeiro: Civilização Brasileira, 1995.
Athayde, Roberto. *Brasileiros em Manhattan*. Rio de Janeiro: Topbooks, 1996.
Azevedo, Kathleen de. *Samba Dreamers*. Tucson: The University of Arizona Press, 2006.
Barbosa, Lívia Neves de H. 'The Brazilian Jeitinho: An Exercise in National Identity'. *The Brazilian Puzzle*, eds. David J. Hess, and Roberto DaMatta, New York: Columbia University Press, 1995, 35–48.
Beserra, Bernadete. *Brazilian Immigrants in the United States: Cultural Imperialism and Social Class*. New York: LFB Scholarly Publishing, 2003.
Bicalho, José Victor. *Yes, Eu Sou Brazuca ou A Vida do Imigrante Brasileiro nos Estados Unidos da América*. Governador Valadares: Fundação Serviços de Educação e Cultura, 1989.
Boas, Sergio Vilas. *Os Estrangeiros do Trem N*. Rio de Janeiro: Rocco, 1997.
Borim, Dário. *Paisagens Humanas*. Paraguaçu, Minas Gerais: Editora Papiro, 2002.
Braz, Júlio Emílio, and Silvana Pimentel Batista. *Rua 46*. São Paulo: Saraiva, 2002.
Bretas, Angela. *Sonho Americano*. São Paulo: Scortecci, 1997.
—— (ed.). *Brava Gente Brasileira em Terras Estrangeiras*. São Paulo: Scortecci, 2004.
Candido, Antônio. 'A Vida ao Rés-do-Chão', *A Crônica: O Gênero, Sua Fixação e Suas Transformações no Brasil*, Campinas: Editora da Unicamp, 1992, 13–22.
—— 'Literatura e subdesenvolvimento', *A Educação pela Noite e Outros Ensaios*, São Paulo: Editora Ática, 2000, 140–62.
Cullen, Jim. *The American Dream: A Short History of an Idea that Shaped a Nation*. Oxford: Oxford University Press, 2003.
Davis, Darién J. 'The Brazilian-Americans: Demography and Identity of an Emerging Latino Minority'. *The Latino Review of Books* (Spring/Fall 1997), 8–15.
—— 'To Be or Not to Be Brazilian: Carmen Miranda's Quest for Fame and "Authenticity" in the United States'. Paper presented at the IV Meeting of the Brazilian Studies Association, Washington, DC, 1997.
Ferreira, Ricardo Moura. 'Introdução'. *O Sonho Americano* [1997]. Angela Bretas. São Paulo: Scortecci, 2003, 13–14.
Ferreira-Pinto, Cristina. *Poemas da Vida Meia*. Rio de Janeiro: 7 Letras, 2002.
Filho, Carlos Stozek. *Um Brasileiro nas Tropas do Tio Sam*. Rio de Janeiro: Razão Cultural Editora, 1998.

Galvão, Heloísa Maria. *As Viajantes do Século Vinte: Uma História Oral de Mulheres Brasileiras Imigrantes na Área de Boston*. Rio de Janeiro: H.P. Comunicacões Associados, 2005.
Guimarães, Norma. *Febre Brasil em Nova Iorque*. Belo Horizonte: Record, 1993.
Hanashiro, Maria Alice. 'A Ânsia pela Liberdade'. *Brava Gente Brasileira em Terras Estrangeiras*, ed. Angela Bretas, São Paulo: Scortecci, 2004, 257.
Henfil. *Diário De Um Cucaracha*. Rio de Janeiro: Record, 1983.
Holanda, Sérgio Buarque de. *Raízes do Brasil* [1936]. São Paulo: Companhia das Letras, 1995.
Holz, Fernando. 'Diáspora Brasileira', in Fernando Holz, *Minh'Alma Nua (My Nude Soul)*. Mix One Studios and Zippah Recording, 2002.
Leite, Virgínia. 'Mau Jeito Nacional', *Veja*, 29 April 1992.
Leon, Thales de. *Clandesinos: Aventuras Verídicas de um Guia de Imigrantes Ilegais nas Fronteiras Americanas*. Rio de Janeiro: Domínio Público, 1996.
Magalhães, Valéria Barbosa de. 'História Oral e Imigração: A Identidade dos Brasileiros nos EUA a Partir de Obras de Ficção Escrita'. Unpublished essay, 2001.
Margolis, Maxine. *Little Brasil: Imigrantes Brasileiros em Nova York*. Campinas: Papirus, 1994.
Martes, Ana Cristina Braga. *Brasileiros nos Estados Unidos: Um Estudo Sobre Imigrantes em Massachusetts*. São Paulo: Paz e Terra, 1999.
Meihy, José Carlos Sebe Bom. *Brasil Fora de Si: Experiências de Brasileiros em Nova York*. São Paulo: Parábola Editorial, 2004.
Mendes, Lucas. *Conexão Manhattan: Crônicas da Big Apple*. Rio de Janeiro: Campus, 1997.
Mitchell, Christopher. 'As Recentes Políticas de Imigração dos Estados Unidos e seu Provável Impacto nos Imigrantes Brasileiros', *Políticas Migratórias: América Latina, Brasil e Brasileiros no Exterior*, São Carlos: EDUFSCar, 2002, 177–98.
Moisés, Massaud. *A Criação Literária: Prosa*. São Paulo: Cultrix, 1979.
Mota, Kátia Santos. 'Aulas de Português fora da Escola: Famílias Imigrantes Brasileiras, Esforços de Preservação da Língua Materna', *Cadernos CEDES*, 63:24 (2004), 149–63.
Neto, Belchior. *Aventureiros do Dólar: Romance de Amor entre os Emigrantes para os Estados Unidos*. Belo Horizonte: Imprensa Oficial, 1990.
Nolasco, Sonia. *Moreno Como Vocês*. São Paulo: Francis, 2003.
Novaes, Carlos Eduardo. *A Travessia Americana*. São Paulo: Editora Ática, 1985.
*O Meu Brasil é Aqui!* By Édel Holz. Dir. Édel Holz. Perf. Giovannini Silva, Arieli Portela, Adolfo Paes, Marcelo Pinheiro, Hatem Halabi Jr, André Luís Ferreira, Alberto Sanches, Juliand Harten, Mary Caufield, and Gilcéia Paes. Actors' Workshop, South Boston, 19 September 2004.
Perdigão, Paulo. 'Introduction', in Carlos Eduardo Novaes, *A Travessia Americana*, São Paulo: Editora Ática, 1985, 5–7.
Pratt, Mary Louise. 'Arts of the Contact Zone', in *Professing in the Contact Zone: Bringing Theory and Practice Together*, ed. Janice M. Wolff, NCTE, 2002, 1–18. Also in *Revista Veja*, 29 (June 2005), 45.
Rozen, Beti. 'Conjecturando o jeito', in *Brava Gente Brasileira em Terras Estrangeiras*, ed. Angela Bretas, São Paulo: Scortecci, 2004, 87.
Sales, Teresa. *Brasileiros Longe de Casa*. São Paulo: Cortez, 1998.
—— 'Identidade Étnica Entre Imigrantes Brasileiros na Região de Boston, EUA',

*Cenas do Brasil Migrante*, eds. Rossana Rocha Reis, and Teresa Sales, São Paulo: Boitempo, 1999, 17–44.
Santana, João. *Aquele Sol Negro Azulado*. Rio de Janeiro: Versal Editores, 2002.
Scotto, Luiz Alberto. *46th Street: O Caminho Americano*. São Paulo: Brasiliense, 1993.
Silvestre, Edney. *Dias de Cachorro Louco: Trinta Histórias de Nova York*. Rio de Janeiro: Record, 1995.
Tosta, Antonio Luciano de Andrade, 'Latino, *Eu?* The Paradoxical Interplay of Identity in *Brazuca* Literature', *Hispania*, 87:3 (2004), 576–85.
Trauer, Valeria. 'Orgulho de ser brasileira', in *Brava Gente Brasileira em Terras Estrangeiras*, ed. Angela Bretas, São Paulo: Scortecci, 2004, 376–7.
Von Arx, Regina. 'Sonhador', in *Brava Gente Brasileira em Terras Estrangeiras*, ed. Angela Bretas, São Paulo: Scortecci, 2004, 315.
Winter, Juan Duchesne. *Narraciones de testimonio en América Latina: cinco estudios*. Río Piedras: Editorial de la Universidad de Puerto Rico, 1992.

# 9

# Argentine Writers in the US: Writing South, Living North

## SERGIO WAISMAN

I begin this chapter by admitting a certain amount of skepticism, for it is not at all clear to me that the handful of Argentine writers whom I will be discussing here – Argentine writers who have spent significant portions of their careers living and writing, primarily in Spanish, in the United States – belong in a volume on US Latino literature. If US Latino literary identity includes a movement towards writing mostly in English from a Latin American heritage, then the Argentine writers discussed here will seem out of place. But issues of identity and language in US Latino literature are considerably more complex than this, while the category of the US Latino itself can still be said to be in a process of formation.[1] In addition, I strongly believe that there is much to be gained by expanding the dialogue between the fields of US Latino and Latin American literary and critical studies, and that such a dialogue could offer important contributions to both fields.[2] The presence of a number of South American writers in the US presents us with an unexpected 'contact zone', to borrow Mary Louise Pratt's term,[3] which raises important issues related to the relationships between language, nation, tradition, exile, and identity.

---

[1] Several recent anthologies have expanded the realm of Hispanic literature of the US to include Spanish-American writers, in English translation, who can be considered precursors of US Latino literature. See, for example, Nicolás Kanellos (ed.), *Herencia: The Anthology of Hispanic Literature of the United States* (New York and Oxford: Oxford University Press, 2002); Roberta Fernández (ed.), *In Other Words: Literature by Latinas of the United States* (Houston: Arte Público Press, 1994); or Harold Augenbraum and Margarite Fernández Olmos (eds.), *The Latino Reader: An American Literary Tradition from 1542 to the Present* (Boston and New York: Houghton Mifflin Company, 1997).

[2] Despite a handful of recent attempts to articulate what might be called a 'literature of the Americas' – see especially the essays in Juan Poblete (ed.), *Critical Latin American and Latino Studies* (Minneapolis and London: University of Minnesota Press, 2003); and Gustavo Pérez Firmat (ed.), *Do the Americas Have a Common Literature?* (Durham and London: Duke University Press, 1990) – there is still much work to do in this area.

[3] As opposed to the contact zones that Pratt discusses in *Imperial Eyes* (London and New York: Routledge, 1992), involving European and North American writers and travelers in Latin America, in this chapter I will consider a handful of South American writers in the US.

Two seemingly disparate but actually quite related questions arise immediately. First, how does writing from abroad, from the US in this case, affect the place of a Latin American writer in Latin America? And second, what place does a Latin American writer living and writing in the US occupy in the US? Both questions involve a North–South flow, of writers and texts alike. Both questions involve traveling and translation, they both involve a displacement, a recontextualization, spatial and temporal, physical and literary, imaginary and real. As we will see, when texts and writers travel, their movement affects the cartographies and traditions of both source and target languages and cultures. A nation's literary tradition is usually associated with language. Tradition is said to exist in the language spoken in that particular nation, while the concept of the nation itself tends to be defined in terms of the nation's language and tradition.[4] But the map of a country's literary tradition seldom corresponds directly to the map of that country's political and geographic borders. What happens when a writer travels in or out of that nation, or when a text travels in or out of that language and tradition? Similarly, what happens when texts and styles and ideas are introduced in and out of traditions through translation?[5] Are Latin American writers working in the US still writing within the context of their own national traditions, or are those very traditions somehow altered by these contributions from abroad?

The Argentine writers whom I will discuss here are a heterogeneous group: they do not all belong to the same literary generation, they are not all from Buenos Aires, they write in different genres and styles, with different degrees of success and, without a doubt, with different objectives and skills.[6] They are

Their gaze, if anything, is peripheral, minor, upon both Latin America and the empire of the North.

[4] As Roberto Ignacio Díaz has said, 'In the discourse about literature in this part of the world (Spanish-America], like almost everywhere, language and nation are tightly intertwined. The Romantic alliance of *Volksgeist* and native tongue still informs much thinking about nationhood and cultural community . . .' (13). See his *Unhomely Rooms: Foreign Tongues and Spanish American Literature* (Lewisburg, Pennsylvania: Bucknell University Press, 2002).

[5] For a discussion of the role of translation in shaping Argentine literature, see Patricia Willson, *La constelación del sur: traductores y traducciones en la literatura argentina del siglo XX* (Buenos Aires: Siglo Veintiuno Editores, 2004); and Sergio Waisman's *Borges and Translation* (Lewisburg, Pennsylvania: Bucknell University Press, 2005).

[6] The specific focus of this *Companion* has led me to discuss primarily those Argentine writers who have gone to the US. If the focus were different, one would want to consider Argentine writers who have left Argentina and gone to other countries as well, such as Juan José Saer, who lived in France from 1967 until his death in 2005, although the vast majority of his work continued to be set in his home province of Santa Fe; or Julio Cortázar before him. For a discussion of what can be called a Latin American Diaspora, see Amy K. Kaminsky, *After Exile: Writing the Latin American Diaspora* (Minneapolis and London: University of Minnesota Press, 1999); for a discussion of the appeal that Paris has held for Latin American writers, see Mary Schwartz, *Writing Paris. Urban Topographies of Desire in Contemporary Latin American Fiction* (Albany: State University of New York Press, 1999); for a discussion of Latin American and Spanish exile and writing, see Sophia A. McClennen, *The Dialectics*

grouped here because of geography and happenstance, personal as well as historical; their grouping should not be mistaken for an equating of quality or even of thematic or stylistic interests, unless where specifically stated below. Still, despite their disparity, it is important for anyone interested in Latin American and US Latino literatures to know that these Argentine writers are in the US. Furthermore, as we will see, a number of issues central to both Latin American and US Latino literatures arise by discussing these writers in relation to issues of language, translation, exile, tradition, and identity. The writers are Sylvia Molloy (b. 1938), Ricardo Piglia (b. 1941), Tomás Eloy Martínez (b. 1934), Mario Szichman (b. 1945), Luisa Valenzuela (b. 1938), Alicia Borinsky (b. 1946), Nora Glickman (b. 1944), Alicia Kozameh (b. 1953), Alicia Partnoy (b. 1955), Nora Strejilevich (b. 1951), María Negroni (b. 1951), Gladys Ilarregui (b. 1958), Zulema Moret (b. 1950) and recent arrival Sergio Chejfec (b. 1956). With utmost modesty I also include myself in this list. And it will be useful to recall, for very different reasons, two deceased Argentine writers who briefly lived and wrote in the US: Manuel Puig (1932–90) and Jacobo Timerman (1923–99). The grouping is arbitrary; and yet, in almost every case, distance from Argentina enters into these writers' work, as does the US – certain aspects of its culture, society, and literature – itself.

For almost all of these writers, Argentina's recent history – namely the military coups of 1966 and 1976, the political upheavals of the early 1970s, the Dirty War period of 1976–83 which left 30,000 disappeared and thousands more exiled, and the neoliberal market reforms of the 1980s and 1990s – explains at least part of the reason for their presence in the US. Not only does recent history enter, directly or indirectly, into the work of many of these writers, but a number of these writers also played an important part in disseminating information in the US, during or shortly after the dictatorship, about the human rights violations taking place back home. Luisa Valenzuela had a significant role in the US during the dictatorship, as did Tomás Eloy Martínez immediately afterwards; and the writings of Jacobo Timerman, Alicia Partnoy, Nora Strejilevich, and Alicia Kozameh – themselves survivors of torture in Argentina during the dictatorship – have gone a long way towards informing readers, particularly in the US, of the horrific experiences of thousands during the state terrorism of the Dirty War.

The list, however, is decidedly heterogeneous. At least four from this group write extremely sophisticated, literary prose, both fiction and criticism (Puig, Piglia, Molloy, and the younger Chejfec), one of which stands as one of the most important Argentine writers of the twentieth century (Puig) and the other as one of the most important living Argentine writers (Piglia); one writes in the tradition of literary journalism and has become an international bestseller (Eloy Martínez); one works with Jewish humor and family sagas in Argentina (Szichman); another, a playwright and short story writer, has worked actively to define and advance the emerging field of Latin American Jewish Studies (Nora

*of Exile: Nation, Time, Language, and Space in Hispanic Literatures* (West Lafayette, Indiana: Purdue University Press, 2004).

Glickman); a couple work primarily with women's literature and themes (Valenzuela and Borinsky); four are (or were) survivors of the Dirty War and have worked with the *testimonio* genre (Jacobo Timerman, Alicia Kozameh, Alicia Partnoy, and Nora Strejilevich); and three are very different and interesting poets (Negroni, Ilarregui, and Moret).

One striking commonality between these writers is that the majority have been working in US universities, in departments of Spanish or Latin American Studies, or both. US universities thus play a key role in housing writers from abroad, allowing them to make a living, continue writing and, perhaps most interestingly, shape how Latin American literatures and cultures are taught in the US. In analogous fashion to the role of exiled Spanish Civil War intellectuals and writers in the formation of Hispanism in the US earlier in the twentieth century, a number of South American writers have been central to the formation of Latin American Studies in the US in the last thirty years or so. This role has been played actively and quite prominently by writers such as Tomás Eloy Martínez (first in the University of Maryland, from 1984 to 1987, and more recently at Rutgers University), Alicia Borinsky (at Boston University), Ricardo Piglia (as a visiting professor in a number of universities and more recently as Walter S. Carpenter Professor of Language, Literature and Civilization at Princeton University), and saliently for many years by Sylvia Molloy, including her service as MLA president from 2000 to 2001, and since 1990 as Schweitzer Professor of the Humanities at New York University. Interestingly, a discourse on Latin American literatures and cultures is thus articulated prominently in and from the North, a discourse that helps shape how Latin America is studied and perceived in the North. The space for the articulation of such a discourse is afforded precisely by distance from these writers' home country.

Questions of language, tradition, and nation can of course be asked of writers who do not leave their home countries; but the physical displacement of the writers themselves creates an opportunity to analyze these issues under a different light, under what Edward Said has called the 'double or exile perspective' (47–64). This occurs not necessarily because these writers are exiles *per se* – although a number were exiled during the latest dictatorship – but specifically because of how exile surfaces as a theme in many of their works. Though not herself an exile, Luisa Valenzuela, for example – who has lived in Paris, Barcelona, Mexico, and New York – treats the subject of exile explicitly in her novel *Novela negra con argentinos* (1990; published as *Black Novel With Argentines* in 1992). The protagonists of this novel, Agustín and Roberta, are both Argentine writers living in New York, in a crime novel in which Agustín, in particular, struggles desperately with the ghosts of the recent Argentine past. The characters cannot help but bring their cultural, psychological, and political baggage with them to New York, leading to conflict and disassociation. In the process, the novel explores issues of violence, displacement, gender, and sexuality, while New York functions as the stage where identity is placed in constant motion.[7]

---

[7] For further discussion of Luisa Valenzuela's work, including *Black Novel With Argentines*,

Exile enters as a theme in a more complex fashion in the work of Ricardo Piglia.[8] In *Respiración artificial* (1980; published as *Artificial Respiration* in 1994), arguably the most important novel to come out of the latest dictatorship period, Piglia explores exile through a series of historical references that take us back to Argentina's first dictatorship, that of Manuel Rosas in the first half of the nineteenth century. This historical aspect of *Artificial Respiration* serves as a coded parallel for the situation in which Argentines were living in the late 1970s. By establishing a number of historical and literary connections, including with Sarmiento's *Facundo* of 1845 – itself written from exile in Chile during Rosas's reign – Piglia was able to offer insight about the situation at that time, and to do so through and from literature, by underscoring the importance of language and literature during times of repression and censorship.[9]

In 1992, when *La ciudad ausente* appeared (published in English as *The Absent City* in 2000), now in the transition to democracy, Argentines found themselves in an entirely different situation. The main issues of the day were related to the inheritance of violence and attempts to reconstruct memory. This explains, in part, why *The Absent City* is so concerned with the possibilities of form and representation in the face of an expanding neoliberal market that masked the individual's isolation and sense of loss.[10] The characters of *The Absent City* find themselves disconnected from their own language, facing a kind of internal exile, as they are constantly forced to try to translate a system of signs that is theirs and yet seems entirely foreign.[11] The characters in *The Absent City* are literally marginalized, living an experience of deterritorialization from their own language.

In addition, a number of Argentine writers – like thousands of their compa-

---

see Nora Glickman's 'La New York de Luisa Valenzuela', in Gwendolyn Díaz (ed.), *Luisa Valenzuela sin máscaras* (Buenos Aires: Feminaria Editora, 2002), 141–53; Laura R. Loustau, *Cuerpos errantes: literatura latina y latinoamericana en Estados Unidos* (Buenos Aires: Beatriz Viterbo Editora, 2002), 75–116; Marcela Walter Salas, 'Novelistas argentinos en los Estados Unidos: Todas las muertes de Eva', Diss. University of Houston, 2003, 65–135; and the essays in Gwendolyn Díaz and María Inés Lagos (eds.), *La palabra en vilo: narrativa de Luisa Valenzuela* (Santiago: Editorial Cuarto Propio, 1996). It is interesting to note that Luisa Valenzuela's mother, Luisa Mercedes Levinson – herself an interesting writer and figure in Argentine letters in the middle of the twentieth century – also lived and wrote in New York.

[8] There is a wide body of existing criticism on Piglia's work. An excellent place to start is the collection of essays edited by Adriana Rodríguez Pérsico, *Ricardo Piglia: una poética sin límites* (Pittsburgh: University of Pittsburgh Press, 2004).

[9] As I argue elsewhere, in *Respiración artificial*, in 1980, in the middle of the dictatorship, Piglia proposes a kind of cross between Sarmiento and Kafka: a possible *Facundo* of the future conceived through the distorted visions of the allegorical nightmares of Kafka. See my 'Piglia entre Joyce y Macedonio: Una revalorización estética y política', *Revista de Estudios Hispánicos*, 38:2 (2004), 277–91.

[10] See Francine Masiello, *The Art of Transition: Latin American Culture and Neoliberal Crisis* (Durhan: Duke University Press, 2001), 163–8.

[11] For an analysis of the role of translation in this and other works by Piglia, see Waisman's *Borges and Translation*, 207–18.

triots – were actually exiled during the dictatorship, an experience that played a significant role in the subject matter of subsequent works, or in the ability to publish during exile, or both. Mario Szichman, for example, lived outside Argentina during both dictatorships: 1967–71 and 1976–81 in Caracas, Venezuela, and from 1981 onwards, in the US. Szichman composed portions of his 1981 novel *A las 20:25, la señora entró en la inmortalidad* (the third novel of a trilogy that follows the life of a Jewish family in Argentina through much of the twentieth century), and was able to publish it in both Spanish and English in the US (both editions by Ediciones del Norte; the English translation being published in 1983 as *At 8:25 Evita Became Immortal*).[12]

Tomás Eloy Martínez also lived as an exile in Caracas from 1975 to 1983, and moved to the US in 1984, where he still resides. Eloy Martínez is the author of numerous novels, including two international bestsellers: *The Perón Novel* (1985 in Spanish; 1988 in English translation; translated into twelve other languages) and *Santa Evita* (1995 in Spanish; 1996 in English translation; translated into over thirty languages), both historical, journalistic novels that combine fiction with history, blurring the lines between them.[13]

The internationally best-known work published during exile is journalist Jacobo Timerman's revealing *testimonio* of his experiences of torture during the dictatorship, *Preso sin nombre, celda sin número* (*Prisoner Without a Name, Cell Without a Number*; publication both in Spanish and English translation in 1981). Timerman's *testimonio* is startling not only in the description of the torture that he endured, but also because of the systematic anti-Semitism that he reports as part of the state terrorism of the period. In addition to Timerman, three more writers – Alicia Kozameh, Alicia Partnoy, and Nora Strejilevich – stand out because they were captured and tortured during the dictatorship (or even prior to dictatorship, in the case of Kozameh), and fled Argentina after their release. All three, after different moves in each case, have since settled in the US. And in all three cases, being in the US has permitted, in some way, the publication of their work – which revolves around their experiences – in Spanish and in English translation as well. In one case, Partnoy's *testimonio The Little School: Tales of Disappearance and Survival in Argentina* (1986), the book has appeared in English only, although it is a translation from the Spanish by the author, and remains virtually unknown in Argentina beyond human rights circles. Alicia Kozameh was a political prisoner from 1975 to 1978, and left Argentina in 1980 after continued persecution. Her novel *Pasos bajo el agua* (1987) is a fictionalized account of her traumatic experience and her subsequent exile in California and Mexico; it was published in English as *Steps Under Water* in 1996. Alicia Kozameh has lived in Los Angeles since 1988.

---

[12] For analysis of Szichman's work, see Saúl Sosnowski, *La orilla inminente: escritores judíos argentinos* (Buenos Aires: Editorial Legasa, 1987); and Naomi Lindstrom, *Jewish Issues in Argentine Literature: From Gerchunoff to Szichman* (Columbia: University of Missouri Press, 1989).

[13] For a discussion of the role of exile in *Santa Evita*, see Salas, 210–300.

Nora Strejilevich, also a survivor of the Dirty War, first found political asylum in Canada, and then moved to the US in 1994.[14] Her testimonial novel *Una sola muerte numerosa* (1997) was published in the US in Spanish and in English translation (as *A Single, Numberless Death*, 2002).[15] *A Single, Numberless Death* works with *testimonio*, but goes beyond the genre by combining autobiography, documentary journalism, fiction, and poetry to convey a multiplicity of voices, even as it reworks memory in the context of military repression and state-sanctioned anti-Semitism.

Leaving Argentina also allowed some of these writers to distance themselves and think in a different way. As Nora Strejilevich says, 'Living outside Argentina allowed me to write'[16] (e-mail interview, 4 September 2005). And when asked about the importance of this distance, of having left Argentina, for the writing of *A Single, Numberless Death*, Strejilevich adds:

> Leaving forever implies a break that makes one lose precisely that imaginary unity of which one was constituted, the 'I'. By definition one is multiple, but such chameleonic nature becomes evident in all its intensity in different geographies and languages. Everything I have written is related to that; in other words, with the genocide but above all else with the post-genocide, with the marks, with the dispersion, with the space between the before and the after, with the loss of a way of being in the world, and hence of meaning. In writing one is engaged in a search, in my case amid the wondering. (e-mail interview, 4 September 2005)

Distance and displacement thus appear as both potential themes and – if one is fortunate – vitalizing forces in a writer's work. The cartographies of displacement include geography, the physical space left behind, but also history, a distance from the past and an opportunity to explore new relationships with what has been left behind. Leaving creates a distance, a space, a state of being in-between – nations, cultures, languages – that may open the way for that perspective Said has called 'intellectual exile'. As Francine Masiello has said: 'Distance is always a condition of thinking, it is the space between languages in flux' (154).

When asked about the effect upon his writing of leaving Argentina, Sergio Chejfec – who moved voluntarily to Caracas, Venezuela in 1990, and in 2005 to the US – says:

> Living in another country is an experience of unfolding. . . . Sometimes being abroad is the space that allows one to preserve and delineate one's individual belonging. . . . Leaving Argentina helped me to isolate myself; and isolating

---

[14] Since 2000, Nora Strejilevich has worked as a professor at San Diego State University.

[15] *Una sola muerte numerosa* was finally published in Argentina in 2005 by Catálogos SRL.

[16] I present this and all other quotations in the article in my English translation of the original.

myself helped me to write. . . . Being outside Argentina is not a restriction for me, but an emphasis; it is a different way of being, articulated by distance and a certain estrangement. . . . Argentina for me is a literary ideal: an ambiguous nucleus to which I do not owe referential obedience, but which attracts me because of its diffused force of irradiation. (e-mail interview, 20 July 2005)

Chejfec published his first novel *Lenta biografía* (Slow Biography) in 1990, and has published five more novels since, including *Los planetas* (The Planets) (1999) and *Los incompletos* (The Incomplete Ones) (2004); his work has not yet been translated into English.

Sylvia Molloy, author of two very different, fascinating novels – *En breve cárcel* (1981; translated by Daniel Balderston with the author in 1989 and published as *Certificate of Absence*), and the recent *El común olvido* (2002), which is again being translated by Balderston with the author – elegantly articulates the questions relevant to issues of distance and displacement when she asks:

What does it mean to write in (from) *another* place? How are the subtle relationships between author, language, writing, and nation interwoven? When does the foreignness of a text begin? In its geographic displacement, in the use of another language, in the strangeness of the anecdote, in the effect of translation? I could not imagine myself writing fiction in another language – I still cannot imagine it – but perhaps, somehow, I was already doing it. ('En breve cárcel', 30)

Writing 'in (from) *another* place', as Molloy puts it, creates the possibility – and perhaps the need – to explore the interactions with that 'other' place, including the 'other's' culture and language. Prior to Piglia and Molloy, major literary dialogues between Argentine and US traditions can be found in Borges, but also, in a very different way, in the brilliant novels of Manuel Puig. In fact, arguably the most salient literary dialogue between Argentine and US literatures and cultures may just be Puig's 1980 novel *Maldición eterna a quien lee estas páginas* (*Eternal Curse on the Reader of These Pages* (1982)). Puig lived twice in New York: first in the 1960s, and then as an exile from 1976 to 1979.[17] *Maldición eterna* is written mainly in the form of a conversation between two characters: Señor Ramírez, an old Argentine union lawyer and ex-political prisoner, who is suffering from amnesia and has been sent to recuperate in an asylum in New York; and Larry, a young American history professor who is working as his assistant, pushing him around in his wheelchair. The genre of the

---

[17] Puig moved to New York after living in Mexico, where he finished *Kiss of the Spider Woman* in 1975, and before moving to Brazil, where he would live the last ten years of his life. It can be said that Puig suffered two kinds of exile: first an internal one, deriving primarily from his homosexuality as well as that of some of his characters, and then an external one, from 1975 onward, after his life was threatened by an extreme right-wing paramilitary Peronista group in Argentina. See Salas, 136–43.

novel is in every way a dialogue: between the two characters, but also between their respective cultures, histories, and languages. In and through their conversations, Ramírez seeks to decode the 'other' culture of the North (i.e. Larry's); while Larry, who is very interested in Southern Cone history, tries to decode Ramírez's many references to French novels as a way to help Ramírez recuperate his past and his memory. Decoding secret, 'other' languages is key here, as the entire novel underscores the (im)possibility of reading/interpreting/translating the language, history and culture of the 'other'.

The genesis and (re)writing of *Maldición eterna* itself actually brings these issues to the forefront. Puig wrote the notes and most of the manuscript for the novel originally in English, as the story is based on a series of conversations that Puig had with a neighbor in New York in the late 1970s. Puig then translated the text 'back' to Spanish, so to speak, (re)writing the manuscript into novel form, playing with and expanding the potential relationship between English and Spanish, exploiting the productive potential of translation, and complicating notions of originality and North–South relationships.[18]

These examples illustrate some of the effects of traveling and translation upon Argentine literature in Spanish, including its relation to English and the US. But we must also consider the other side of the coin: what happens to texts when they travel North, with or without their authors, and when they are translated into English? By coming to the US, the writer – the texts – become exposed to a new audience, at first in Spanish and then, if a translator is procured, in English. Although obviously not necessary, being in the US can contribute to interest in translating a certain writer. As critics have been saying for a number of years, canons and even archives are constructed; what is less commonly discussed is how they are constructed differently in different places. A quick survey of the authors studied in this chapter makes evident that North and South have different archives and canons. Crossing geographic and political borders seemingly brings changes in the criteria utilized to evaluate writers; markets open for some, close for others; values rise and fall; the canon turns out to be as volatile as reception.

Translation here plays a determining role in questions of reception and canon-formation. For better or for worse, the reality is that one must be translated into English – one must exist in English, even if in translation – in order to appear somewhere on the US literary and cultural map. Though some of these writers were translated into English before coming to the US and certainly would have been regardless of their time in the US (i.e. Puig, Piglia, etc.), having

---

[18] As Jorge Panesi has said: 'Puig adds a new paradox here to the idea of the original and its expansion: which language is expanded? English? Spanish? Be that as it may, the place of the writer in *Maldición eterna* is a territory of linguistic borders and cultural exchanges. It is related to a movement of expansion and Puig's attempt to internationalize his literature and his novelistic world: everything that he seeks to expand must pass through translation'. 'Memoria, cuerpo y olvido: *Maldición eternal a quien lea estas páginas*', in José Amicola and Graciela Speranza (eds.), *Encuentro internacional Manuel Puig* (Rosario: Beatrix Viterbo Editora, 1998), 155.

a physical presence in the US can serve to draw attention to their work, including that of potential translators and publishers. On the other hand, achieving publishing or even academic success in the US – in English translation, but also in Spanish in US universities – does not necessarily translate into success back home in Argentina, as the stories of Luisa Valenzuela and Alicia Borinsky reveal.[19]

Slightly different is the case of several Argentine poets who have lived and written in the US and who incorporate, in different ways, distance itself as they explore issues of language, representation, gender, and identity. One such poet is María Negroni, who has lived for many years in New York and currently teaches at Sarah Lawrence College. Negroni is a translator from French and English and the author of two books of essays, a novel and six collections of poetry, including two that have also appeared in bilingual Spanish–English translations: *Islandia* and *Night Journey*. As Francine Masiello has said about Negroni's *Islandia*: 'Principal to the texture of her poetry is the interrogation of doubleness; how to speak from the position of exile, how to speak through language belonging to others; how to collect minor experiences under the banner of epic poetry. For Negroni, writing is an act of impostorship tied to translation and exile from power' (154).[20]

Gladys Ilarregui is the author of six books of poetry, including two that have appeared in bilingual Spanish–English translations: *The Cumaean Sibyl* and *Poems at Midnight*. The majority of Ilarregui's literary production has come in the US, where she has lived since 1983 and is currently a professor at the University of Delaware. When asked recently about her experiences as an Argentine poet writing in the US, Ilarregui said: 'When I write I do not think about Argentina or the US (both places already very much incorporated within me, as I have lived almost the same amount of time in the two countries). (Rather), I think obsessively about language. My place of production is language, as a bridge between two experiences' (e-mail interview, 5 July 2005).

Zulema Moret, author of two books of poetry, is currently a professor at Grand Valley State University in Michigan. She has recently edited *Mujeres mirando al Sur* (2004) (Women Looking South), a critical anthology of poetry by South American women poets living and writing in the US. This collection effectively introduces seventeen different writers, some relatively unknown, and their multifaceted perspectives of the South from the North, and of the relationships and flows between North and South, in Spanish.

Another poet who should be mentioned in this context is Diana Bellessi (b. 1946), who spent five years in the US in the early 1970s, and whose poetry includes sophisticated considerations of North–South relationships. Bellessi,

---

[19] A discussion of the different critical and popular criteria in North and South, in different cultures and languages, falls outside the scope of this study, as does the relationship between reception, the market and translation, on the one hand, and quality and literary value, on the other.

[20] See also Masiello, 258–61.

one of Argentina's most interesting living poets, is the author of thirteen books of poetry, including *The Twins, the Dream* (1996), a collaboration with Ursula K. LeGuin in which the writer from the South translates the poetry of the writer from the North, and vice versa. Exploring a series of 'transnational exchanges', as Francine Masiello calls it (161), Bellessi's work seeks connections between different 'others'. Referring to Bellessi's 1998 collection *Sur*, Masiello says: '(Bellessi) deliberately confuses the boundaries of North and South: 'Es sur / el continente entero' (South is / the entire continent) (122), (Bellessi) writes in *Sur*, a book that covers the length of the cordillera from Argentina to Arizona in search of common landscape and language' (239).

It is also important to consider that a number of the writers discussed here had already begun looking and traveling North in their work before arriving in the US. In other words, some of these writers' interest in and dialogue with US, as well as European, literatures and cultures precedes their physical move away from Argentina. Such is the case of Mario Szichman, the prominent Latin American inheritor of the tradition of self-denigrating Jewish humor, who was an avid reader of Saul Bellow, Philip Roth, and Isaac Bashevis Singer, among others, long before moving to the US. This is also the case of Tomás Eloy Martínez, whose brand of literary journalism draws from an American as well as an Argentine tradition; of Luisa Valenzuela's interest in the noir novel; of Piglia's and Sylvia Molloy's ongoing dialogue with Modernism;[21] and of Manuel Puig's work with and inclusion of popular cultures, including Hollywood and music, into his heteroglossic novels (well before his exile in New York in the late 1970s).

This prior relationship with US literatures and cultures is an aspect of the fact that Argentine literature is not – and never was – homogeneous. These writers come from a tradition that already contains a multicultural legacy, as does that of most Latin American literatures. It is crucial to note that Spanish American literature is by no means only in Spanish. As Rolena Adorno and others have insisted, it is impossible even to begin to articulate a full literary history of Spanish America unless native languages are considered.[22] In addition, as Roberto Ignacio Díaz convincingly argues in *Unhomely Rooms*, there are also a number of Latin American writers who have written in European languages other than Spanish (or Portuguese, in the case of Brazil), consideration of which expands our notions of the 'house' of Latin American literature, as Díaz calls it.

The topic of tradition and identity in Latin America is arguably as old as Latin American literature itself. In the case of Argentina, writers and intellec-

---

[21] Piglia himself has fictionalized his relationship to the US – to US literature and culture – in his 1988 novella *Prisión perpetua* (Perpetual Prison), in which Emilio Renzi, a recurrent character in Piglia's work who oftentimes seems to express Piglia's own views, tells the story of his initiation into US literature through his interactions with Steve Ratliff in Mar del Plata.

[22] See, for example, Rolena Adorno, 'Cultures in Contact: Mesoamerica, the Andes, and the European Written Tradition', in Roberto González-Echevarría and Enrique Pupo Walker (eds.), *The Cambridge History of Latin America Literature*, vol. I (Cambridge: Cambridge University Press, 1996), 33–57.

tuals have always sought, in one way or another, to identify what it means to be 'Argentine', even as the issue has remained a mark of the nation's literature. What topics and themes are allowed of Argentine writers? What forms and styles are available to them? Should themes and dictions be limited to the 'local', or can they also include the 'universal'? Some of the most astute answers ever provided to these questions are found in Jorge Luis Borges's seminal 1951 lecture, 'The Argentine Writer and Tradition'. In many ways, this text functions as a road map for writers from Argentina – as well as those from Latin America, and perhaps from the periphery at large – to position themselves with respect to Occidental canons without being defined and restricted by them. The key, according to Borges, is to take a stance of irreverence toward the traditions of the center, a stance which, Borges maintains, Latin American writers are in a position to assume precisely because of their distance and difference from the center. Asserting that 'our tradition is the entirety of Western culture' (*Obras Completas* I, 272), Borges claims marginality itself as a privileged site for innovation, thus setting the stage for a reconsideration of center–periphery dichotomies and preconceptions of influence, value, and canon formation.[23]

To formulate his argument, Borges draws an unexpected analogy between Latin American and Jewish and Irish writers, which suggests an alliance of peripheral traditions whose connections reside precisely in their marginality and in their history of colonization. Borges astutely perceives that it is their simultaneous status as insiders *and* outsiders that has allowed Jews and Irish to act – and innovate – within the cultures of the center without feeling bound by any special devotion to them. Partial difference, feeling themselves different from ('it was enough for them to feel . . . *different*') (*Obras Completas* I, 273) and not entirely a part of the center, is precisely what frees Jewish, Irish, and Latin American writers – and perhaps all writers from the periphery – from the weight of the traditions of the center. Any writer from the periphery, because they are both *a part of* Occidental culture, yet *apart from* it, can draw from any and all literatures with irreverence and thus make all of Western culture theirs, in their own language.[24]

Furthermore, Argentina, like other Spanish American countries, has also had heterolingual writers, to use Roberto Igancio Díaz's term, who are not entirely contained by a definition of tradition that is solely tied to Spanish. There have been Argentine writers (Argentines by birth) who have gone on to write in other languages, such as Eduarda Mansilla de García (1832–92), who wrote *Pablo ou la vie dans les pampas* (1869) in French; Victoria Ocampo, who authored her first book in French (*De Francesca à Beatrice,* 1924); Juan Rodolfo Wilcock

---

[23] On the importance of Borges's demands and full justification of such marginality, see Sylvia Molloy, *Signs of Borges* (Durham and London: Duke University Press, 1994), 32–3.

[24] For an analysis of how Borges undertakes such irreverent taking of Western culture, displacing pre-texts towards an Argentine context in River Plate Spanish through processes of translation, see Waisman's *Borges and Translation*.

(1919–78), who emigrated to Italy in the 1950s and moved from Spanish to Italian in his writings; and Héctor Bianciotti (b. 1930), who moved to France in 1961 and from Spanish to French in his writings (much like the Peruvian avant-garde poet César Moro, or the Chilean Vicente Huidobro in his early years).

Argentina has also received a series of foreigners, travelers, immigrants, and exiles whose work has gone on to enter, in diverse and complex fashions, the Argentine tradition. Most prominent among this group are the Anglo-Argentine W. H. Hudson (1841–1922) and the Modernist Polish writer Witold Gombrowicz (1904–69), who was exiled in Argentina from 1939 to 1963.[25] A naturalist, traveler, and writer born in Argentina to Anglo-American parents, Hudson can and has been claimed by both the English and the Argentine traditions. Hudson is considered one of the greatest English travel writers of all time – Virginia Woolf praises his work in *The Common Reader*, for example – but he is also read widely (in Spanish translation) in Argentina, while Borges has said that: 'It is possible that there is no work of gauchesque literature better than *The Purple Land*. . . . *The Purple Land* is essentially *criolla* (Argentine)' (*Obras Completas* II, 112). In fact, as Díaz argues, *The Purple Land* (1885) actually calls for a hybrid reader: a reader familiar with both the English and the Argentine traditions (Díaz, 124–42).

Continuing to expand the possibilities of Argentine literary tradition – much like Borges before them – Ricardo Piglia and Juan José Saer have both ironically – but perhaps only half ironically – said that Gombrowicz may just be Argentina's best writer of the twentieth century. With such comments, Piglia and Saer take Borges's irreverent stance of a claimed marginality and expand it to introduce an even more complicated network of dialogic foreignness into any definition of the Argentine. In '¿Existe la novela argentina?' (Does the Argentine Novel Exist?), for example, Piglia describes the national culture of Argentina as dispersed and fractured from its inception, and in a constant state of tension with the dominant cultures of the center. And Piglia deliberately inserts Gombrowicz into an Argentine literary genealogy that includes Borges, Roberto Arlt, and Macedonio Fernández, among others, raising all manner of questions about how a national tradition is conceived and constituted. Saer then continues the argument and further explodes the notion of what Argentine literature is in 'La perspectiva exterior' (The External Perspective) by reminding us that Argentine

---

[25] The collaborative translation of *Ferdydurke* from Polish into Spanish through French, coordinated by the Cuban poet Virgilio Piñera has become legendary among certain literary circles in Argentina. On the translation of *Ferdydurke* in Buenos Aires, see Rafael Cippolini, '*Ferdydurke* forrado de niño: Biografía de una versión', *Otra Parte*, 4 (Spring/Summer 2004), 22–7. I also want to mention a recent arrival to Argentina, and a quite interesting writer particularly in this context: Anna Kazumi Stahl (b. 1962), a US writer of Asian descent, author of a book of stories (*Catástrofes naturales*, 1997) and a novel (*Flores de un solo día*, 2003), both in Spanish. See Masiello, 154–6.

literature was founded not only in Spanish, but that it is polyglot and hybrid from its inception.[26]

Like Borges, Cortázar, and Puig before him, and like Saer contemporaneously, Piglia delineates a version of Argentine tradition that can go far beyond the political and geographic borders of the country. In this sense, Piglia helps to take Argentine literature out of Argentina, so to speak – as does Valenzuela's *Black Novel With Argentines*, or Negroni's and Bellessi's poetry set partially in the US – distorting traditions and challenging borders, in expanded River Plate Spanish, via real and imaginary travels across literary and historical maps.

Reimagined cartographies brings us to Sylvia Molloy, whose *El común olvido* proposes a possible return to Argentina – now from the US, from the cultural fulcrum of New York. A leading literary critic, the trilingual (Spanish, English, French) Sylvia Molloy has published widely on Latin American literature and culture. But Molloy's formidable work as a literary critic and decisive presence in American academia has somewhat – and certainly unfortunately – overshadowed her work as a novelist. Any doubts about Molloy's importance as a novelist, however, should be dispelled by the publication of *El común olvido* (*All But Forgotten*)[27] in 2002 and the recent republication of *En breve cárcel* (*Certificate of Absence*)[28] in Argentina.

Though well received by a handful of critics, *Certificate of Absence*, Molloy's first novel, garnered relatively little attention in Argentina. The initial low-key reception for *Certificate of Absence* in Argentina may have been related to the lesbian themes and the complex points of view presented in the novel. The novel, as Molloy herself points out (in the essay 'En breve cárcel'), was not only written in another place (Molloy lived in New York at the time), and set in another place (the setting and the characters are quite ambiguous: an apartment, three women, their desire, their bodies and the narrator's writing), but actually written *from* as well as *in* another place.

The displacement to which Molloy refers is not only geographic – although it is also geographic. It is a movement towards a certain margin, towards an 'other' space, from which her texts can then speak. The connection between two seemingly unrelated kinds of displacements and 'otherness' – geographic/linguistic and gender/sexuality – lies at the core of Molloy's literary project: both her fiction and her critical work. This connection, implicit in *Certificate of Absence* because of the ambiguous nature of the novel and its style, becomes explicit as the driving force of a narrative that explores issues of identity, language, and representation, and their relationship to difference and dislocation, in Molloy's second novel, *El común olvido*.

---

[26] The idea of a Spanish-only tradition prior to the waves of immigration in the nineteenth and early twentieth centuries, it turns out, is a nationalistic myth meant to silence Argentina's history of multiculturalism.

[27] Molloy has indicated that the title of *El común olvido* in English would be *All But Forgotten* ('Bilingualism', 69–70).

[28] The decision to use such a very different title in English than in Spanish was reached by Molloy herself.

*El común olvido* is in many ways an imagined return to Argentina from – but also to – this 'other' space that Molloy creates in her work. The protagonist/narrator Daniel, significantly a librarian and a translator who was born in Argentina but has lived most of his adult life in the US, travels back to Argentina to lay to rest his deceased mother. The narrator's search for a burial place for his mother's ashes soon gives way to the narrator's attempts to decipher a series of mysteries associated with his parents, and eventually to a search for identity itself. The narrator, anxious at being considered a 'foreigner', feels neither entirely American nor Argentine, and oftentimes tries to 'pass' as an Argentine. But the narrator is doubly different; he is doubly hybrid: he is a cultural/linguistic 'other', and his sexuality is 'other'. In fact, in *El común olvido*, cultural, national, and linguistic difference becomes a way to explore sexual and gender difference – and vice versa.

If Molloy imagines a possible return in *El común olvido*, then my novel *Leaving* (2004) contemplates such a return in the form of a young narrator now writing primarily in English, and concludes that it is not possible. This impossibility of returning to an imagined South in *Leaving* is related to a search for a new beginning, in English, in the US. The narrator of *Leaving* undergoes a linguistic and cultural struggle as he seeks to resolve his mixed identity – the contradictions of being Jewish, Argentine, and American; of trying to tell stories and memories to his American interlocutor, in English, when those stories and memories are in Spanish or French or Yiddish – but finds that just as return is not really an option, there is also no resolution to the internal conflict: there is no synthesis.

Consideration of how texts and writers travel helps elucidate North–South relationships, including issues of power, language, and tradition. When a tradition is stretched – by the movements of the writers or of their texts – the concept of the nation stretches out too. When the South expands, when a Latin American text travels North – either in its setting and style, or through translation, or physically by the writer writing and living North – the cartography of the nation is redrawn, as the map of the nation's traditions is stretched and challenged and reconfigured. Translation, in this sense, serves as a perfect model for thinking of these issues, as it focuses our attention on the relationship between individuals, texts, languages, cultures, religions, and nations – and perhaps more importantly on the difference between these and on difference itself: the difference between and the difference already present in the original, as it is in the self. Translation, as Diana Bellessi has said, 'is above all an attempt at alterity' (Balderston and Schwartz, 26). As such, it may just be the best way not only to cross national, cultural, and linguistic borders, but also those of the subject. For, as Molloy suggests, translation holds a certain 'power for the bilingual subject as a permanent reminder of that 'being in between' that marks the bilingual subject's speech, her writing, her tenuous life' ('Bilingual Scenes', 296).

Near the beginning of this chapter I said that I very much believe in the need for an expanded dialogue between the fields of Latin American and US Latino literary and critical studies. I conclude with the idea that one way to conceive of and undertake such a dialogue – though of course not the only one – is through a focus on translation.[29] Translation allows for an immediate dialogue between these fields, as it brings issues of bilingualism, identity, originality, representation and North–South and other transnational relationships to the forefront.

I also conclude with a more personal observation. My interest in translation is not objective. I have done work as a literary translator and I have delved into translation theory; but more than that, I feel that I have lived most of my life in translation – a feeling the implications of which I try to understand in my novel *Leaving*. I, the narrator seems to conclude in *Leaving*, will be a hybrid in the US, a part of me always looking back at Argentina and Spanish (perhaps as my grandparents always seemed to look in two separate directions as they ate *facturas* and sipped hot *mate* while talking in Yiddish), even as I speak myself in both Spanish and English, seeking to make a new home full of incongruous rooms. I, the child of Argentines who, when they left in 1976, did not want to leave Argentina, seek in my own way to return – and in so doing pay constant homage to my parents. Yearning to return, paradoxically, becomes a way of being in English, in the US: the threshold that I am always seeking to cross. I always felt that I was writing mainly an Argentine novel when I was writing *Leaving*. Of course, I now realize that it is also a Jewish novel and I certainly believe it is an American novel. Perhaps I too – perhaps the Argentine writers discussed here, and certainly the US Latino writers discussed by others throughout this *Companion* – can sing (all of) America. Of course we can, and will.

## Works Cited

Adorno, Rolena. 'Cultures in Contact: Mesoamerica, the Andes, and the European Written Tradition', in Roberto González Echevarría, and Enrique Pupo-Walker (eds.), *The Cambridge History of Latin American Literature*, vol. 1. Cambridge: Cambridge University Press, 1996, 33–57.

Augenbraum, Harold, and Margarite Fernández Olmos (eds.). *The Latino Reader: An American Literary Tradition from 1542 to the Present*. Boston and New York: Houghton Mifflin Company, 1997.

Balderston, Daniel, and Marcy E. Schwartz (eds.). *Voice-Overs: Translation and Latin American Literature*. Albany: State University of New York Press, 2002.

Bellessi, Diana. *Sur*. Buenos Aires: Tierra Firme, 1998.

—— and Ursula K. LeGuin. *The Twins, the Dream: Two Voices Las gemelas, el sueño: dos voces*. Houston: Arte Público Press, 1996.

Borges, Jorge Luis. 'El escritor argentino y la tradición'. *Obras Completas* I. Barcelona: Emecé Editores España, 1996, 267–74.

---

[29] An example of the kind of dialogue through translation that I envision here can be found in the anthology edited by Daniel Balderston and Mary E. Schwartz, *Voice-Overs: Translation and Latin American Literature* (Albany: State University of New York Press, 2002).

—— 'Sobre *The Purple Land*'. *Obras Completas II*. Barcelona: Emecé Editores España, 1996, 111–14.
Chejfec, Sergio. e-mail interview. 20 July 2005.
—— *Lenta biografía*. Buenos Aires: Puntosur Editores, 1990.
—— *Los incompletos*. Buenos Aires: Alfaguara, 2004.
—— *Los planetas*. Buenos Aires: Alfaguara, 1999.
Cippolini, Rafael. '*Ferdydurke* forrado de niño: Biografía de una versión', *Otra Parte*, 4 (Spring/Summer 2004), 22–7.
Díaz, Gwendolyn, and María Inés Lagos (eds.). *La palabra en vilo: narrativa de Luisa Valenzuela*. Santiago: Editorial Cuarto Propio, 1996.
Díaz, Roberto Ignacio. *Unhomely Rooms: Foreign Tongues and Spanish American Literature*. Lewisburg, Pennsylvania: Bucknell University Press, 2002.
Fernández, Roberta (ed.). *In Other Words: Literature by Latinas of the United States*. Houston: Arte Público Press, 1994.
Glickman, Nora. 'La New York de Luisa Valenzuela, contrastada', in Gwendolyn Díaz (ed.), *Luisa Valenzuela sin máscaras*. Buenos Aires: Feminaria Editora, 2002, 141–53.
Gombrowicz, Witold. *Ferdydurke*, trans. Virgilio Piñera, Humberto Rodríguez Tomeu, and translation committee with the author. Buenos Aires: Argos, 1947.
Hudson, W. H. *The Purple Land That England Lost: Travels and Adventures in the Banda Oriental, South America*. London: S. Low, Marston, Searle, and Rivington, 1885.
Ilarregui, Gladys. *The Cumaean Sibyl: Selected Poetry*. Bilingual edition, trans. Judy B. McInnis. New Orleans: University Press of the South, 1999.
—— e-mail interview. 5 July 2005.
—— *Poemas a medianoche / Poems at Midnight*. Bilingual edition, trans. Judy B. McInnis. Buenos Aires: Libros de Tierra Firme, 2003.
Kaminsky, Amy K. *After Exile: Writing the Latin American Diaspora*. Minneapolis and London: University of Minnesota Press, 1999.
Kanellos, Nicolás (ed.). *Herencia: The Anthology of Hispanic Literature of the United States*. New York and Oxford: Oxford University Press, 2002.
Kazumi Stahl, Anna. *Catástrofes naturales*. Santiago de Chile: Editorial Sudamericana, 1997.
—— *Flores de un solo día*. Buenos Aires: Seix Barral, 2003.
Kozameh, Alicia. *Pasos bajo el agua*. Buenos Aires: Editorial Contrapunto, 1987.
—— *Steps Under Water: A Novel*, trans. David E. Davis. Berkeley, Los Angeles and London: University of California Press, 1996.
Lindstrom, Naomi. *Jewish Issues in Argentine Literature: From Gerchunoff to Szichman*. Columbia: University of Missouri Press, 1989.
Loustau, Laura R. *Cuerpos errantes: literatura latina y latinoamericana en Estados Unidos*. Buenos Aires: Beatriz Viterbo Editora, 2002.
Martínez, Tomás Eloy. *La novela de Perón*. Buenos Aires: Legasa Literaria, 1985.
—— *The Perón Novel*, trans. Asa Zatz. New York: Pantheon Books, 1988.
—— *Santa Evita*. Buenos Aires, Argentina: Planeta, 1995.
—— *Santa Evita*, trans. Helen Lane. New York: Knopf, 1996.
Masiello, Francine. *The Art of Transition: Latin American Culture and Neoliberal Crisis*. Durham: Duke University Press, 2001.
McClennen, Sophia A. *The Dialectics of Exile: Nation, Time, Language, and Space in Hispanic Literatures*. West Lafayette, Indiana: Purdue University Press, 2004.

Molloy, Sylvia. 'Bilingual Scenes', in Doris Sommer (ed.), *Bilingual Games: Some Literary Investigations*. New York: Palgrave Macmillan, 2003, 289–96.
—— 'Bilingualism, Writing, and the Feeling of Not Quite Being There'. *Lives in Translation: Bilingual Writers on Identity and Creativity*. New York: Palgrave Macmillan, 2003, 69–77.
—— *Certificate of Absence*, trans. Daniel Balderston with the author. Austin: University of Texas Press, 1989.
—— *El común olvido*. Buenos Aires: Grupo Editorial Norma, 2002.
—— ' "En breve cárcel": pensar otra novela', *Punto de Vista*, 21:62 (December 1998), 29–32.
—— *En breve cárcel*. Barcelona: Seix Barral, 1981.
—— *Signs of Borges*, trans. and adapted by Oscar Montero with the author. Durham and London: Duke University Press, 1994.
Moret, Zulema (ed.). *Mujeres mirando al Sur: Antología de poetas sudamericanas en USA*. Madrid: Editorial Torremozas, 2004.
Negroni, María. 'Cultura latinoamericana en Nueva York: un castigo del cielo'. *Ciudad gótica*. Buenos Aires: Bajo la luna nueva, 1994, 27–32.
—— *Islandia: A Poem*. Bilingual edition, trans. Anne Twitty. Barrytown, NY: Station Hill Press, 2001.
—— *Night Journey / El viaje de la noche*. Bilingual edition, trans. Anne Twitty. Princeton: Princeton University Press, 2002.
Panesi, Jorge. 'Memoria, cuerpo y olvido: *Maldición eterna a quien lea estas páginas*', in José Amícola, and Graciela Speranza (eds.), *Encuentro internacional Manuel Puig*. Rosario: Beatriz Viterbo Editora, 1998.
Partnoy, Alicia. *The Little School: Tales of Disappearance and Survival in Argentina*, trans. Alicia Partnoy with Lois Athey and Sandra Braunstein. Pittsburgh: Cleis Press, 1986.
—— (ed.). *You Can't Drown the Fire: Latin American Women Writing in Exile*. Pittsburgh: Cleis Press, 1988.
Pérez Firmat, Gustavo (ed.). *Do the Americas Have a Common Literature?* Durham and London: Duke University Press, 1990.
Piglia, Ricardo. *Artificial Respiration*, trans. Daniel Balderston. Durham: Duke University Press, 1994.
—— '¿Existe la novela argentina?' *Espacios de crítica y producción*, 6 (1987), 13–15.
—— *La ciudad ausente*. Buenos Aires: Editorial Sudamericana, 1992.
—— *Prisión perpetua*. Buenos Aires: Seix Barral, 1988.
—— *Respiración artificial*. Buenos Aires: Editorial Pomair, 1980.
—— *The Absent City*, trans. Sergio Waisman. Durham: Duke University Press, 2000.
Poblete, Juan (ed.). *Critical Latin American and Latino Studies*. Minneapolis and London: University of Minnesota Press, 2003.
Pratt, Mary Louise. *Imperial Eyes: Travel Writing and Transculturation*. London and New York: Routledge, 1992.
Puig, Manuel. *Eternal Curse on the Reader of These Pages*. New York: Random House, 1982.
—— *Maldición eternal a quien lea estas páginas*. Barcelona: Seix Barral, 1980.
Rodríguez Pérsico, Adriana (ed.). *Ricardo Piglia: una poética sin límites*. Pittsburgh: University of Pittsburgh Press, 2004.

Saer, Juan José. 'La perspectiva exterior', *Punto de vista*, 35 (1989), 14–19.
Said, Edward W. 'Intellectual Exile: Expatriates and Marginals'. *Representations of the Intellectual: The 1993 Reith Lectures*. New York: Random House, 1993, 47–64.
Salas, Marcela Walter. 'Novelistas argentinos en los Estados Unidos: Todas las muertes de Eva'. Diss. University of Houston, 2003.
Schwartz, Marcy E. *Writing Paris: Urban Topographies of Desire in Contemporary Latin American Fiction*. Albany: State University of New York Press, 1999.
Sosnowski, Saúl. *La orilla inminente: escritores judíos argentinos*. Buenos Aires: Editorial Legasa, 1987.
Strejilevich, Nora. *A Single, Numberless Death*, trans. Cristina de la Torre with the author. Charlottesville and London: University of Virginia Press, 2002.
—— e-mail interview. 4 September 2005.
—— *Una sola muerte numerosa*. Miami: North–South Center Press, 1997.
—— *Una sola muerte numerosa*, 2nd edn. Buenos Aires: Catálogos SRL, 2005.
Szichman, Mario. *A las 20:25, la señora entró en la inmortalidad*. Hanover, New Hampshire: Ediciones del Norte, 1981.
—— *At 8:25 Evita Became Immortal*, trans. Roberto Picciotto. Hanover, New Hampshire.: Ediciones del Norte, 1983.
—— *Crónica falsa*. Buenos Aires: Editorial J. Álvarez, 1969.
—— *Los judíos del mar dulce*. Buenos Aires: Galerna, 1971.
Timerman, Jacobo. *Preso sin nombre, celda sin número*. New York: Random House, 1981.
—— *Prisoner Without a Name, Cell Without a Number*, trans. Toby Talbot. New York: Knopf: 1981.
Valenzuela, Luisa. *Black Novel With Argentines*, trans. Toby Talbot. New York: Simon & Schuster, 1992.
—— *Novela negra con argentinos*. Buenos Aires: Editiorial Sudamericana, 1990.
Waisman, Sergio. *Borges and Translation: The Irreverence of the Periphery*. Lewisburg, Pennsylvania: Bucknell University Press, 2005.
—— *Leaving*. Oakland: InteliBooks, 2004.
—— 'Piglia entre Joyce y Macedonio: Una revalorización estética y política', *Revista de Estudios Hispánicos*, 38:2 (2004), 277–91.
Willson, Patricia. *La constelación del sur: traductores y traducciones en la literatura argentina del siglo XX*. Buenos Aires: Siglo Veintiuno Editores, 2004.

# 10

## A Balancing Act:
## Latin American Jewish Literature in the United States
## (or Towards a Jewish-Latino Literature)

### LYDIA M. GIL

The study of Latin American Jewish writing as a subdivision of Latin American literature is a relatively new field, with a vast amount of scholarship dedicated to defining, cataloguing, and interpreting texts that, for the most part, have been written from the margins of national and hemispheric literatures. The debate over what precisely constitutes a Jewish literature is still very much alive,[1] even as Jewish-American literature has passed its centennial mark and, in Latin America, it is fast approaching.[2] Although informed by a series of ontological questionings and theoretical interpretive strategies, such a debate continues to focus on the writer's self-definition as a Jew, either ethnically or religiously, and on the persistence of certain themes, folkloric elements, and concerns that have, historically, pertained specifically to the Jewish experience.

A major difficulty arises from attempts at globalizing the 'Jewish experience', which negate the role of national cultures in identity-formation and the impact of assimilation on ethnic self-identification. For example, some critics contend that the question of marginality so prevalent in the golden days of Jewish-American literature has been recently replaced by a preoccupation with the demands of secularism on religious and ethnic identity,[3] a choice that is not yet readily available to the Latin American Jewish writer. As Darrell Lockhart explains, the Jewish Latin American writer operates from a 'double marginalization': geographically and socio-economically, along with the whole of Latin America, as citizens of the Third World, and within their respective societies as outsiders to the dominant Luso- or Hispanic-Catholic tradition (xi).

---

[1] Most recently, Derek Rubin's *Who We Are: On Being (and Not Being) a Jewish American Writer* (New York: Knopf, 2005).

[2] Many critics take as a founding date the publication of Alberto Gerchunoff's *Los gauchos judíos* (The Jewish Gauchos) in 1910, not coincidentally also the year of the first centennial of the Argentine Republic.

[3] Andrew Furman, *Contemporary Jewish American Writers and the Multicultural Dilemma: The Return of the Exiled* (Syracuse, New York: Syracuse University Press, 2000).

However, having been relegated to the periphery of Latin American letters, the Jewish-Latin American writer has been able to draw from both cultural and historical traditions, broadening the scope of both established literatures, and disputing, from the perspective of marginality, the hegemony of dominant segments in society. Therefore, texts by Jewish-Latin American writers can be interpreted as a compelling counter-discourse to their respective official – and, therefore, exportable – national literatures.

Although the obdurate insistence on a homogeneous cultural production and the myth of a common past woven from the confluence of Iberian, Native, and African worlds have certainly helped to relegate Jewish texts to the periphery of Latin American literature, the persistent lens of marginality from where these texts depart may owe even more to the relative youth of the modern Jewish experience in Latin America.[4] As Stephen Sadow points out in his introduction to *King David's Harp*, and leaving aside colonial times, 'in Latin America, the majority of Jews are immigrants of the first or second generation; the third generation is only now being born' (xxi).[5] As a consequence, Jewish writers from Latin America tend to have a closer – living – memory of exile, of Yiddish – and, in some cases, Ladino – the Shoah, official demands for assimilation, and xenophobic clashes than their counterparts in the United States. While the presence of such issues does not suffice to define a specifically Jewish literature in Latin America, taken collectively, the creative articulation of such themes serves as a chronicle of the modern Jewish experience in Latin America and the struggles of these communities to retain their religious, ethnic, and cultural specificity despite the constant pressures to assimilate.

With the advent of totalitarian regimes in Latin America during the latter part of the twentieth century, numerous Jews were once again forced into emigration, along with thousands of other dissidents, terrorized, and persecuted. While some Jews sought refuge in Europe and Israel, paradoxically, many joined their fellow countrymen emigrating into the US, the same nation that had closed its doors on them during World War II.[6] This last link in a chain of exiles has had enormous effects on the literature of Jewish-Latin American writers who operate from beyond their former national borders.

While political and economic exile has been an experience shared by many Latin Americans, whether Jewish or not, Jewish intellectuals were particularly targeted by right-wing dictatorships for their perceived ties with international communism. Paradoxically, as Marjorie Agosín explains in her essay 'Through a field of stars, I remember', some were also the subject of threats during the

---

[4] Excluding 'converso' and crypto-Jewish presence during colonial times.

[5] While Argentina boasts an older Jewish community than other Latin American countries – thanks to the efforts of the Jewish Colonization Association and official efforts to boost 'white' immigration to repopulate the Pampas – this is certainly true of Jewish communities in regions that received the largest influx of immigrants after the 1924 Immigration and Naturalization Act restricted large-scale immigration into the United States.

[6] This subject has been addressed by numerous Jewish-Latin American writers, among them, Cuban Ruth Behar and Chilean Marjorie Agosín.

Socialist government of Salvador Allende for alleged ties to US imperialism (194), and, in the case of Cuban Jews, they have been deemed 'doubly-*gusanos*' for rejecting not once, but twice, their 'Jewish-Communist ideals'.[7]

This last experience of 'expulsion' has been represented in the literature of Latin American Jews in exile as a profound disillusionment with their communal past – at least from a national perspective. It shattered the myth of a shared national history and, as Leonardo Senkman has pointed out, it painfully erased all rhetorical illusions about a 'national destiny' (280).[8] Furthermore, this last exile forced those Latin American Jews who had left their homeland to confront the anti-Semitic image of 'stateless Jew', over which victory had been claimed a mere generation before. Suddenly, the teleological view of Jewish history so forcibly rejected by the previous generation would have to be reevaluated when, in the face of exile and homelessness, the State of Israel presented them with a viable alternative to the vast secularism of the United States.

Yet Jewish writers from Latin America in the United States have found a third way, a floating platform that is 'neither here nor there' from where to write. While these writers could have been easily claimed for Latino and Jewish-American literatures – and such inclusion would have definitely broadened the scope of these literatures – they remain fiercely identified with their respective Latin American countries and claim that cultural identity for their literary oeuvre. Nevertheless, issues that in their respective countries seemed to pertain exclusively to Jewish identity – such as exile, immigration, assimilation, language-based identity, and xenophobia – once in the US, pertain to the whole Latino experience. Ironically, the very insistence of Jewish-Latin American writers in the US on a cultural specificity that would differentiate their experience from that of Latino and Jewish-American writers has the potential of relegating their literature to the realm of autoethnography and self-referentiality.

Sufficiently aware of such a threat, Jewish-Latin American writers in the US have devised a series of narrative and poetic strategies to circumvent the autoethnographic trap while still alluding to their Jewish and Latin American cultural traditions. Humor, irony, parody, and sarcasm are among the tools most

---

[7] 'Worm' or 'Gusano' is a designation favored by the Castro government for those Cubans who have turned their backs on the Revolution and have sought exile, predominantly in the United States. Ruth Behar explains the 'double-worm' designation in 'Juban América', citing also Margalit Berjarano's 'The Deproletarianization of Cuban Jewry': the Cuban Jews in the United States were doubly 'wormy': not only had they abandoned the Revolution, as earlier, in the 1940s and 1950s, many had abandoned their Jewish-Communist ideals when they ceased being peddlers and became deproletarianized members of the Cuban middle class (Berjarano), but they had also made their way into the US body politic as Cuban refugees (206). Incidentally, Cuban Jews who leave the island for Israel are not considered 'gusanos', but 'repatriados'.

[8] Jewish Latin-American writers had learned from their nation's official history to represent the common, collective, past in a chronological, continuous, and homogeneous time, and remained, for a long period, hopeful with the optimistic portrait of such narratives in which the future of all citizens would be inextricably linked to their nation's past.

often used by these writers when reconstructing the past for their creative texts, for they allow allusions to a national past and to a national literary tradition while simultaneously disrupting its official posture and pretensions of continuity and homogeneity.

Autobiographical texts present yet another narrative strategy that instills a critical posture in the reconstruction of the past even while highlighting their subjective character: an insistence on the unreliability of memory and the relevance of the cultural and historical context of the act of remembering. Leo Spitzer elaborates on this subject in *Hotel Bolivia: The Culture of Memory in a Refuge from Nazism*:

> Transmitting the past through memory is problematic in another way: the recollection of any event or 'experience' – as well as 'forgetting it' – is a socially constructed act undertaken from the perspective of a 'present'. Factors like the 'where' the remembering takes place, its cultural context, the social and political background of the rememberer, his or her gender, age, economic situation, and perception of future – as well as narrative strategies and the discernible and invisible influences of ideology – all these affect recollection and the shapes of memory. (191)

Thus, by attempting to reconstruct the past not only from a temporal, but also a geographic distance, these writers successfully disrupt the unidirectional official discourse of their former countries by inserting a forking narrative: the narrative of exile, of the 'where' the remembering takes place. This ancillary narrative can also act as a bridge between the 'here' and 'there', the 'now' and 'then', a two-way street that inserts the experience of exile into national narratives, forging a continuity despite the disruption of departure.

There is yet another strategy present in the work of these writers: the device of a poetic 'no-place' where signifiers intermingle to suggest readings independent of national, geographic, ethnic, or biographical demarcations, but without negating their existence. In its struggles to avoid such referents, this poetic time-space concerns itself with exile, language, and the status of the word, elements of a poetry of displacement obsessed with the proposition of meaning.

## Marjorie Agosín (Chile, 1955)

Marjorie Agosín has been widely recognized for chronicling and denouncing human rights violations in Latin America, and using her poetry to lend a voice to the victimized, the tortured, and the disappeared. Her critical and creative texts are rooted deeply in feminist thought, which, along with her strong voice in human rights advocacy, have gained her considerable prestige among Latin American letters in the United States.

Although actually born in Bethesda, Maryland, and having spent a considerable part of her life in the US, Agosín considers herself a Chilean, for it was there where she spent most of her childhood and adolescence. Her grandparents had emigrated from Austria and Odessa, and had settled in Chile during the 1920s and 1930s, predating the large influx of Jewish immigrants during World War II. Agosín, a second-generation Chilean, grew up with Spanish and Hebrew, as she attended the Hebrew Institute in Santiago – after a brief and unhappy interlude at the English 'Union School', where she first experienced the painful stabs of anti-Semitism ('Through a Field', 190–1). Her education at the Hebrew Institute exposed her not only to a comprehensive Jewish religious education, but also to a rich literary tradition, which she – very early – claimed for her own writings. Having grown in the protected environment of the Institute – but after having experienced the xenophobia of the outside world – helped instill in young Agosín not only a great respect for her Jewish heritage, but also an acute sense of justice and empathy for the oppressed.

Agosín's family left Chile a second time in 1972 and settled in the Southern state of Georgia, where Agosín reportedly felt even more isolated than she had ever been in Chile. The mark of difference had manifested itself again, this time even within the confines of the Jewish community of Georgia: 'Now in our new home in North America, I was not only a Jew but a Latin American Jew, which implied to others, less dignity' ('Through a Field', 195). Feeling marginalized by the outside community as a Jew and a Latina, and also rejected by the Jewish community for her Chilean background, made her look to writing as her 'homeland', a place where she could revisit at leisure her places of memory and the nostalgia of belonging.

Her earlier poems are devoted to Jewish places of memory (*Conchalí*, 1980) and already show an incipient interest in the work of women writers and the relationship between women and language (*Brujas y algo más / Witches and Other Things*, 1984). Her texts, poetic and testimonial, have also served to chronicle the women's resistance to the military dictatorships of the 1970s and 1980s in Chile and Argentina, especially the 'Mothers of the Plaza de Mayo', which inspired *Circles of Madness* (1992). In 1994, Agosín published *Dear Anne Frank*, a collection of poems that establishes a dialogue with Anne Frank's diary and serves as testimony of the young woman's courage and hope. Through her poetry, Agosín draws parallels between the horrors of the Shoah and the reigns of terror during the military dictatorships in South America, once again lending her voice to the voiceless and forcing the reader to, at the very least, acknowledge their suffering.

In recent years, Agosín has turned to the genre of memoir for creative expression, reconstructing her family and communal past and writing the stories behind their succession of exiles (*A Cross and a Star: Memoirs of a Jewish Girl in Chile*, 1995; *Always from Somewhere Else: A Memoir of My Chilean Jewish Father*, 1998); and *The Alphabet in My Hands: A Writing Life*, 2000). Agosín continues this exploration of memories in her most recent poetry, *El ángel de la memoria (The Angel of Memory)* and *Entre los ángeles de la memoria (Among Angels of Memory)* (2005), both of which recover fragments of her past and reconstruct memories as if from pieces of shattered glass.

## Ruth Behar (Cuba, 1956)

Ruth Behar's family emigrated to the US in 1962, and although Spanish was retained as the domestic language, the language of her education, and of her later professional and creative writing, is English. As an anthropologist, her texts have explored the crossing of cultural borders and the relevance of a common historical past to identity-formation. She has advocated actively for a continued cultural dialogue between Cubans in the island and Diaspora Cubans, and has translated her poetry into Spanish in an effort to establish a readership in Cuba, where some of it has been published bilingually (*Poemas que vuelven a Cuba / Poems returned to Cuba*) (1995); (*Todo lo que guardé / Everything I Kept*) (2001).

Behar has explored documentary filmmaking as an alternative mode of expression, and has gained wide recognition through her documentary *Adio Kerida / Goodbye Dear Love: A Cuban Sephardic Journey* (2002). In this film, Behar documents her own search for memory and communal identity in Cuba, where she finds a healthy one-thousand strong Jewish community, almost exclusively Sephardic. Much to her surprise, she is met with a diverse group of individuals, who have grown accustomed to the gaze and camera lenses of the many Jewish-American tourists who flock to their gathering places in search of a certain exoticism and ethnic pride that would perhaps reinvigorate their own Jewish communities.[9]

Behar's autobiographical essays and documentary projects are concerned with cultural crossings and 'mestizajes', having found in the improbable mix of cultural ingredients that inhabits within herself the material for the creative exploration of identity-construction. Born of an Ashkenazi mother whose family came from Byelorussia and a father from a Turkish-Sephardic family, Behar represents both halves of the Jewish-Cuban experience. Her texts – both critical and creative – are rooted in autobiography and ethnography. In her essay 'Juban América', Behar expresses her longing for 'Juba', a mythical 'mestizo' Cuban-Jewish land that she could reconstruct from family histories and community memories:

> This essay has been a first effort on my part to begin to imagine Juba, a Juba that I want to build, salt pillar by salt pillar, from both family stories and my own struggle to reclaim all the little forgotten villages of my mestiza identity. Villages, *pueblos*, mean a good deal to me. . . . Then there are the cities –

---

[9] Ilan Stavans has often noted that American (US) Jews who came of age during the 1950s and 1960s had indeed sacrificed their ethnicity in order to assimilate into mainstream society; yet nowadays their children find themselves looking to other ethnic groups with envy and nostalgia. See Neal Sokol, *Ilan Stavans. Eight Conversations* (Madison: University of Wisconsin Press, 2004), 184–5. Stavans further quotes their increasing admiration for 'crypto-Jews' as emblems of nostalgia and a possible vehicle for re-ethnicization, a statement that could also be used to describe the Jewish-American tourist's fascination with 'Castro's Jews'.

Havana, New York, Miami Beach, Ann Arbor. In my Juba, there is room for all these villages and cities, and many other places for which I do not yet have names. (216–17)

Her texts are, therefore, rooted in a topography of memory, of places collected from old photographs and letters, suspended in time, which, as such, remain still unnamed.

Behar also explores women narratives in her writing, chronicling their vital role as family and community archivists and master weavers of stories from incongruous threads. In addition to poetry, essays, and documentary film-making, Behar has been working on a novel, *Nightgowns from Cuba*, which will narrate her family's multiple exiles, from Europe to Cuba to the US, but from the perspective of the Afro-Cuban woman who took care of her as a child before the 1959 Revolution. Such a structure will allow her to explore the ongoing dialogue between Jewish-Cuban and Afro-Cuban traditions and the deep 'mestizaje' of her wandering Jubans.

## Ariel Dorfman (Chile, 1942)

Ariel Dorfman stands alone among this group of Jewish-Latino writers, as his fiction forcefully resists the categorization of 'Jewish', and he has devoted very few pages to pondering his family history and Jewish background.[10] His fiction is rooted, however, in the experience of exile and the denunciation of human rights violations, which, for some, suffices to claim him for Jewish literature.

Although born in Argentina, Dorfman spent his early childhood in New York, where his parents had emigrated after the military ousted the constitutional government in 1943. A decade later, McCarthyism would force them once again into exile; this time they took permanent residence in Chile in 1954. It was in Chile that Dorfman spent his adolescence and early adulthood, and where he threw himself wholeheartedly into socialist politics during the years of Salvador Allende. In 1973, he was forced once again into exile, owing to his visibility during Allende's presidency and his outspoken resistance to the government of Augusto Pinochet.

Dorfman's first novel, *Moros en la costa* (1973; *Hard Rain*, 1990) depicts the political situation in Chile during the last months of Salvador Allende's government through a collage of fictitious short forms such as newspaper articles, scripts, book reviews, and encyclopedia entries, that question the authority of official texts and denounce the political and aesthetic despotism of the time.

His fiction deals with the horrors of war, the politics of power, the temptation of torture and betrayal, and the justice of revenge. Although several of his texts

---

[10] A notable exception is his essay 'The Discovery of Life and Language at an Early Age', excerpted from his memoir *Heading South, Looking North: A Bilingual Journey* (New York: Farrar, Straus & Giroux, 1998), in which he traces his family history through language(s) and translations.

are set in Europe, right before Nazi occupation (*Viudas*) (Widows) (1981); and *Konfidenz* (1994), the presence of such universal themes allows for alternative readings, as pertaining to the Shoah experience and the civilian 'disappearances' during military dictatorships in Latin America. The same holds true for his successful play, *La muerte y la doncella* (Death and the Maiden, 1992), a psychological thriller about power, torture, and revenge in which a woman confronts her torturer from fifteen years earlier and is determined to take revenge although his identity is never clearly confirmed. Its conflict could easily be taken from South America to post-Nazi Europe, or even to the Middle East, as a subtle commentary on the Arab-Israeli conflict.

Despite the recurring presence of such themes in his fiction – and their relevance to the Jewish-Latin American experience – Dorfman has seldom meditated on his personal experience of exile and its consequences for the construction of identity, with the notable exception of his memoir, *Heading South, Looking North: A Bilingual Journey*, an elegant and complex narrative in which he explores – albeit briefly – his Jewish background.

## Isaac Goldemberg (Peru, 1945)

Isaac Goldemberg was born in Chepén, in northern Peru, where he spent the first half of his childhood among his mother's Catholic family. When he was eight years old, he moved with his father to Lima, where, suddenly '5,700 years of Judaism' fell upon him 'like a ton of bricks' ('Life', 145). This first exile from Catholicism in rural Peru to Jewish life in the capital city marks the beginning of a lifelong questioning of identity. His texts, narrative and poetic, are concerned with such questions as 'What are the components of identity?', 'To what extent does ethnicity and religious heritage contribute to our perception and construction of identity?', 'Does one give equal weight to maternal and paternal heritages?', 'Does one identify with the majority or the minority – when one could, potentially, have equal access to both?', 'Or to neither?' ('Life', 145–6).

Goldemberg spent a great part of his early life trying to reconcile his Jewish and Peruvian heritages, as he expressed in his meditative essay 'Life in Installments':

> But in order to become a Jew I must erase my past. Thus my second exile: from myself. I have to stop being in order to be. In my new environment, that of the Jewish community in Lima, I begin to discover that its members are living a marked schizophrenic existence. My new Jewish friends feel Peruvian, but also something else as well, something that in time I myself learn to feel. It so happened that we found ourselves, my friends and I, vacillating back and forth between Jewish and Peruvian culture. For that reason, a large part of my work deals with an attempt to reconcile both of these roots and histories. ('Life', 146)

Not surprisingly, his writing seems to oscillate between these two cultural poles, as a great part of his creative fiction is highly autobiographical. Not unlike other

Jewish-Latin American writers, his texts explore the issues of exile and marginalization, but also, the question of legitimacy.

Other, smaller, exiles marked Goldemberg's early life, as he left in 1962 to study agronomy in Israel, and in 1963 to study medicine in Barcelona, returning to Peru two years later. Then, married to a New Yorker he had met in Israel, they emigrated to the US in 1964, where he pursued studies in literature and began his literary career. Jewish themes begin to emerge in *De Chepén a La Habana* (From Chepén to Havana), his second book of poems, published in New York in 1973. Its verses already evidence a tendency towards the marginal, and some critics begin to call attention to a 'strange, exotic voice' in his poetry ('Life', 151). The questioning of the components of identity is already present in these early verses, and the literary figure of the wandering Jew emerges; this would soon become central to his writing.

His first novel, *La vida a plazos de don Jacobo Lerner* (1978), shattered many of the established patterns and expectations of Latin American literature at the time. Its English translation, *The Fragmented Life of Don Jacobo Lerner* (1976), which preceded the publication of the Spanish, received tremendous acclaim from critics in the United States and enjoyed commercial success despite its challenging structure. This ambitious text is an eloquent chronicle of displacement, which juxtaposes the relatively brief history of the Peruvian Jewish community, several centuries of the Peruvian national experience, and over five millennia of Jewish history. It tells the story of Don Jacobo Lerner, a Russian Jewish immigrant in Lima during the 1920s and 1930s, who tries to piece together what his life had been from his present deathbed. Paradoxically, the protagonist has no voice in the novel, and it becomes the task of the reader to reconstruct his identity from the narrations of other characters and from old clippings and chronicles of events from *Alma Hebrea* (Jewish Soul), a publication of the Jewish community in Lima. Don Jacobo's voicelessness throughout the novel can be read as evidence of his marginalized condition and the hostility of his environment to his foreignness, which is further suggested in the fragmented discourse of the narrative.

*Tiempo al tiempo* (Time to Time) (1984), his second novel, is perhaps even more autobiographical than the first. The protagonist, Marquitos Karushansky Ávila, is raised by his Peruvian mother until the age of 12, by which time he moves with his father to Lima, where he attends the very schools attended by Goldemberg in his youth, the León Pinelo Jewish school and the Leoncio Prado Catholic military academy. Marquitos is eventually expelled from the military academy, and later emigrates to Israel, where the reader finds him in the midst of the 1967 Arab–Israeli conflict. Once again, Goldemberg presents a voiceless protagonist, as Marquitos's ordeals are narrated by the distant voice (who mimics an announcer at a soccer game) and by the testimony of his classmates.

Goldemberg's poetry has also been an effective vehicle for the exploration of his multifaceted and multilingual identity. His *Hombre de paso* (Just Passing Through) (1981) features a collage of English, Spanish, Yiddish, Quechua, and Castilian words, and serves as a caravanserai for historical and contemporary figures, ranging from the Spanish *conquistadores* and Inca chieftains to Jewish peddlers and rabbis. Identity-construction returns as a major theme in *La vida al contado* (Life in Installments) (1992), after which Goldemberg undertook the monumental task of compiling *El gran libro de América judía* (The Big Book of Jewish America) (1998), a panoramic literary anthology of Jewish presence in Latin America, which encompasses the texts and testimony of over 150 writers and chronicles a continuous Jewish presence, old enough to counter any charges of exoticism in Jewish Latin American letters.

His later poetry exhibits a shift from the formal deconstruction of the elements of identity to a more abstract examination of the contradictions of the self. The poems in *Los autorretratos y las máscaras* (Self-Portraits and Masks) (2002) explore in a highly theological language the issues of silence and emptiness as the paradoxical evidence of God's presence, a question only subtly suggested in his earlier poetic texts.

### José Kozer (Cuba, 1940)

José Kozer is a poet's poet, dedicated with obsessive compulsion to his verses and finding in them a registry – or evidence – of a life lived. His poetry defies all thematic and formal classification, just as his persona evades all cultural, national, and ethnic identification. Kozer was born in Cuba, at the heart of an immigrant Jewish family from Eastern Europe. He grew up in Havana and lived there until August 1960, when he emigrated to the US, making him a 'one-generation Cuban':

> I am first- and last-generation Cuban. My parents, Jews from Eastern Europe, immigrated to Cuba and were nationalized citizens (legally and spiritually). They loved Cuba. I was born there, Havana, 1940, and from there, one day, I left, Cubana de Aviación a Miami, Miami a Nueva York in a Greyhound bus, one of those in which blacks still had to sit in the back, and as I think that my daughters, born and raised in the United States are Americans (legally and spiritually), and with my death my Cuban generation will come to an end. A short lineage. ('Natural Instincts', 92)

This initial (and, somewhat, voluntary) exile has become an obsessive element in Kozer's poetry – an anarchic force that, paradoxically, offers the reader a single stepping-stone in an otherwise chaotic poetic universe.

Although he often alludes in his poetry to having been 'expelled', exile is suggested not as the exclusive realm of the immigrant or the refugee, but as the ultimate human condition. In his poetry, a river of existential angst runs deep below layers of literary references, irony, and self-mockery. Just as he holds it 'scarcely possible' to be able to write serious love poetry now, five centuries after Garcilaso,[11] the reader may sense that the same irony that facilitates an

---

[11] 'Garcilaso had the good luck to find a territory of Eros still virgin for poetry, territory

approximation to romantic poetry in his verses allows him poetic access to the lost homeland of his youth.

His first collection of poetry, *Este judío de números y letras* (This Jew of Numbers and Letters) (1974), features a caravan of Jewish characters interacting in a Spanish marked by the particular cadences of Yiddish. Yet, at times, a Cuban-accented voice intervenes, which revels in the use of diminutives ending in *–ico* and in the Afro-Caribbean rhythms of the poet's native Cuba. However evocative Kozer's Jewish-Cuban *mestizaje* may be, it often appears tinged with irony, subtly disturbing the apparent harmony of the verses:

> Rey de reyes por las blancas juderías,
> Llegó aquel hombre de una Europa de tubérculos,
> Abrió una bodega de alimentos judíos,
> Ubicó su expendio del maná en una plaza con moscas,
> Sensatamente llamó a su negocio La Bodega Cubana.
> (*Este judío*, 17)

> (King of Kings in the white ghettos,
> he came from a Europe of tubercles,
> he opened a Kosher grocery store,
> located his manna distribution center in a square full of flies,
> and adequately called his business The Cuban Market.)

Kozer could very well have chosen English for his creative writing, yet his poetry boasts an exuberant Spanish, at times stubbornly Cuban, and others archaic, as if made up of remnants of Yiddish, Hebrew, and other languages the peddler-poet has picked up during his pilgrimage. Gustavo Pérez-Firmat has remarked that Kozer's Spanish is a sort of 'Spanish-Esperanto', copious, erudite, and ambitious, 'a symptom of his uprootedness and a shield against himself' (52).

Although Catholic and Jewish mysticism operate symbolically in his earlier poetry, Kozer has also explored Zen Buddhism, whose presence illuminates the poet's obsession with the production of meaning through questioning, parentheses, and the paradoxical juxtaposition of seemingly incongruent elements characteristic of the koan.[12] His later poetry boasts the simplicity and presence of the Zen poetic tradition, although it is also reminiscent of the austerity of the Jabèsian verse: 'Un maniquí no tiene vida, por cierto. / ¿Pero y su sombra?'

---

that he could contemplate from a rhetorical language that was not yet misrepresenting a position that was quite new and recent, it was still fresh . . . In the twentieth century, how to write of love if not through irony, including the impudence?' ('Natural', 96–7).

[12] Cuban-Jewish poet Carlota Caulfield facilitated an interview with Kozer, recorded as a *sanzen* or private interview between disciple and master, 'En el juego de los eslabones se extravió Kozer: bikkuni dialoga con roshi' (Kozer Lost His Way in the Game of Links: Bikkuni Talks with Roshi) which, in its playfulness, underscores the presence and relevance of Zen Buddhism in Kozer's poetry. See the interview in Jacobo Sefamí (ed.), *La voracidad grafómana: José Kozer* (Mexico, D.F.: UNAM, 2002), 101–8.

(A mannequin has no life, for sure. / But what about its shadow?) ('Monocromo' (Monochrome) *Mezcla* (Mixture), 137).

His enormous catalogue of verses is perhaps the best testimony to his wandering, one in which Jewish and Cuban identify with each other to the point of fusion and internationalism is but another symptom of uprootedness: 'Uno, es todos. Cuba se viró, es judía, es Europa Oriental. Pues al igual que ellos nos dividimos, nos repartimos por el mundo, el Cubano errante. Eso es' (One, is all. Cuba is upside down; it's Jewish; it's Eastern Europe. Just as they were, we were split, scattered around the globe, the wandering Cuban. That's it.) (Kozer, 'Esto (también)', 27).

These are just a few of the Jewish-Latin American writers who write in the United States and whose texts can be claimed under the hyphenated designation of Jewish-Latino, owing to the persistence of questions that relate to identity-construction, ethnic and religious identification, marginality and belonging, migration and language, and the presence of certain discursive strategies that separate them from Jewish-American and Latino writers. Given more space, this partial list would have included, among others, Víctor Perera (1934–2003), whose *The Cross and the Pear Tree: A Sephardic Journey* (1995) related his Guatemalan childhood and evidenced his triple-minority status as a Sephardic-Latin American in the US; critic, short-story writer, and playwright Nora Glickman (Argentina, 1944) whose work has explored the Jewish white slave trade in Argentina and whose plays thrive on a feminist platform; Mario Szichman (Argentina, 1945), a master of parody and satire with near-perfect comedic timing whose family novels treat the history of Jewish immigrants in Argentina along with Peronism and its discontents; Alicia Borinsky (Argentina, 1946), a renowned poet, novelist, and critic whose irreverent style transgresses boundaries and conventions of the genres and who has often turned to satire to reveal the darker sides of Argentine history and society; David Unger (Guatemala, 1950), whose *Life in the Damn Tropics* (2002) is a thrilling exploration of Guatemala City during the perilous 1980s through the eyes of a Jewish narrator; and highly prolific critic, novelist, editor, and philosopher Ilan Stavans (Mexico, 1961), who has worked incessantly to bring Jewish-Latin American letters to English-speaking readers through the Jewish Latin America book series (University of New Mexico Press), which he created and still edits, *Tropical Synagogues: Short Stories by Jewish-Latin American Writers*, which he also edited in 1994, and his numerous meditative essays on Jewish, Latino, and Latin American literature.

## Works Cited

Agosín, Marjorie. *Always from Somewhere Else: A Memoir of My Chilean Jewish Father.* New York: Feminist Press, CUNY, 1998.

—— *Brujas y algo más / Witches and Other Things,* trans. Cola Franzen. Pittsburgh: Latin American Literary Review Press, 1984.

—— *Circles of Madness: Mothers of the Plaza de Mayo / Círculos de locura: madres de la Plaza de Mayo,* trans. Celeste Kostopulos-Cooperman. Fredonia, New York: White Pine Press, 1992.

—— *Conchalí.* New York: Senda Nueva de Ediciones, 1980.

—— *A Cross and a Star: Memoirs of a Jewish Girl in Chile.* Albuquerque: University of New Mexico Press, 1995

—— *Dear Anne Frank: Poems.* Bilingual edition, trans. Richard Schaaf. Washington, D.C.: Azul Editions, 1994.

—— *El ángel de la memoria / The Angel of Memory.* San Antonio: Wings Press, 2001.

—— *Entre los ángeles de la memoria/ Among Angels of Memory.* San Antonio: Wings Press, 2005.

—— *The Alphabet in My Hands: A Writing Life.* New Brunswick, New Jersey: Rutgers University Press, 2000

—— 'Through a field of stars, I remember', in Stephen A. Sadow (ed.), *King David's Harp: Autobiographical Essays by Jewish Latin American Writers.* Albuquerque: University of New Mexico Press, 1999, 189–98.

Behar, Ruth. 'Juban América', in Stephen A. Sadow (ed.), *King David's Harp: Autobiographical Essays by Jewish Latin American Writers.* Albuquerque: University of New Mexico Press, 1999, 201–23.

—— *Poemas que vuelven a Cuba / Poems returned to Cuba.* Matanzas, Cuba: Ediciones Vigía, 1995.

—— *Todo lo que guardé / Everything I Kept.* Matanzas, Cuba: Ediciones Vigía, 2001.

Bejarano, Margalit. 'The Deproletarianization of Cuban Jewry', *Judaica Latinoamericana: estudios histórico-sociales,* ed. AMILAT. Jerusalem: Magnes, 1988, 57–67.

Caulfield, Carlota. 'En el juego de los eslabones se extravió Kozer: bikkuni dialoga con roshi', in Jacobo Sefamí (ed.), *La voracidad grafómana: José Kozer.* Mexico, D.F.: UNAM, 2002, 101–8.

Dorfman, Ariel. *Heading South, Looking North: A Bilingual Journey.* New York: Farrar, Straux & Giroux, 1998.

—— *Konfidenz.* Buenos Aires: Planeta, 1994.

—— *La muerte y la doncella.* Buenos Aires: Ediciones de la Flor, 1992.

—— *Moros en la costa.* Buenos Aires: Sudamericana, 1973.

—— 'The Discovery of Life and Language at an Early Age', in Stephen A. Sadow (ed.), *King David's Harp: Autobiographical Essays by Jewish Latin American Writers.* Albuquerque: University of New Mexico Press, 1999, 121–39.

—— *Viudas.* Mexico: Siglo Veintiuno, 1981.

Furman, Andrew. *Contemporary Jewish American Writers and the Multicultural Dilemma: The Return of the Exiled.* Syracuse, New York: Syracuse University Press, 2000.

Goldemberg, Isaac. *El gran libro de América judía*. San Juan: Editorial de la Universidad de Puerto Rico, 1998.
—— *Hombre de paso / Just Passing Through*, trans. David Unger. Hanover, New Hampshire: Ediciones del Norte, 1981.
—— *La vida a plazos de don Jacobo Lerner*. Hanover, New Hampshire: Ediciones del Norte, 1980.
—— *La vida al contado*. Hanover, New Hampshire: Ediciones del Norte, 1992.
—— *Los autorretratos y las máscaras / Self-Portraits and Masks*, trans. Stephen A. Sadow and J. Kates. New York: Cross-Cultural Communications, 2002.
—— *The Fragmented Life of Don Jacobo Lerner*, trans. Robert Picciotto. New York: Persea Books, 1976.
—— *Tiempo al tiempo*. Hanover, New Hampshire: Ediciones del Norte, 1984.
Goldemberg, Isaac, and José Kozer. *De Chepén a La Habana*. New York: Editorial Bayu-Menorah, 1973.
Kozer, José. *Este judío de números y letras*. Tenerife, Canary Islands: Nuestro Arte, 1974.
—— 'Esto (también) es Cuba, Chaguito', in Jacobo Sefamí (ed.), *La voracidad grafómana: José Kozer*. Mexico, D.F.: UNAM, 2002, 15–27.
—— *Mezcla para dos tiempos*. Mexico: Aldus, 1999.
—— 'Natural Instincts', in Stephen A. Sadow (ed.), *King David's Harp: Autobiographical Essays by Jewish Latin American Writers*. Albuquerque: University of New Mexico Press, 1999, 85–102.
Lockhart, Darrell, B. (ed.). *Jewish Writers of Latin America: A Dictionary*. New York: Garland, 1997.
Perera, Víctor. *The Cross and the Pear Tree: A Sephardic Journey*. New York: Knopf, 1995.
Pérez-Firmat, Gustavo. 'Lenguaje-de-nadie', in Jacobo Sefamí (ed.), *La voracidad grafómana: José Kozer*. Mexico, D.F.: UNAM, 2002, 147–71.
Rubin, Derek. *Who We Are: On Being (and Not Being) a Jewish American Writer*. New York: Knopf, 2005.
Sadow, Stephen A. (ed.). *King David's Harp: Autobiographical Essays by Jewish Latin American Writers*. Albuquerque: University of New Mexico Press, 1999.
Sefamí, Jacobo (ed.). *La voracidad grafómana: José Kozer*. Mexico, D.F.: UNAM, 2002.
Sokol, Neal. *Ilan Stavans, Eight Conversations*. Madison: University of Wisconsin Press, 2000.
Spitzer, Leo. *Hotel Bolivia: The Culture of Memory in a Refuge from Nazism*. New York: Hill and Wang, 1998.
Stavans, Ilan. *Tropical Synagogues: Short Stories by Jewish-Latin American Writers*. New York: Holmes & Meier, 1994.
Unger, David. *Life in the Damn Tropics*. Syracuse, New York: Syracuse University Press, 2002.

# 11

# US Latina Caribbean Women Poets: An Overview

## CARLOTA CAULFIELD

The poetry of Latina women in the United States incorporates a great variety of voices that speak in a great diversity of registers on crucial themes such as identity, border, memory, and exile, to mention just a few of the more important concerns that their poetry presents. The forerunners included: Gloria Anzaldúa, Lorna Dee Cervantes, Ana Castillo, Lucha Corpi, Angela de Hoyos, Pat Mora, Alma Villanueva, and Bernice Zamora. During the 1970s and 1980s, these Chicana writers created new poetic spaces that integrated ethnicity, class, gender, sexuality, and language in shaping what we know today as Latina poetry.[1] Though previously only women poets who wrote in English had been considered Latina poets, today this concept has expanded to include those Latin American women poets who reside in the US, write primarily in Spanish and have their work translated into English. As Bryce Milligan has pointed out, Latina writers of non-Mexican heritage began to publish in the US – women with roots in Puerto Rico, Cuba, the Dominican Republic, and South and Central America – each bringing with them elements of their own national literary traditions.[2]

Faced with the impossibility of including here the numerous representatives that stand out today in the Latina literary scene of the US, I am limited by cultural affinity and space to present a concise overview of Latina Caribbean women poets, highlighting in particular the work of Sandra María Esteves and Judith Ortiz Cofer (Nuyorican/Puerto Rican-American poetry), Magali Alabau and Carolina Hospital (Cuban-American poetry), and Julia Alvarez (Dominican-American poetry).[3] The seventeen entries included in this chapter represent

---

[1] An important analysis of the historical and literary development of Chicana poetry appears in Marta Ester Sánchez's *Contemporary Chicana Poetry. A Critical Approach to an Emerging Literature* (Berkeley: University of California Press, 1985).

[2] In the Introduction to *Floricanto Sí!*, edited by Bryce Milligan, Mary Guerrero Milligan, and Angela de Hoyos (New York: Penguin, 1998), xxi.

[3] Some studies devoted to US Latina poets have presented key authors to the reading public as well as to university communities. Most important among them is Stacey Alba D. Skar's *Voces híbridas: la literatura de chicanas y latinas en Estados Unidos* (Santiago de Chile: RIL editores, 2001), which discusses in depth the works of Chicana, Nuyorican, and

poets I have read or seen perform in readings and literary gatherings. These are poets who come from different cultural, literary, and personal backgrounds, who write in English, and Spanish, and who examine and articulate issues of cultural identity and gender.[4]

## Nuyorican/Puerto Rican American poets

The Nuyorican/Puerto Rican women poets offer, without a doubt, a unique contribution to US Latina Caribbean poetry, which is made evident in a multi-faceted poetry that highlights 'their struggle against the oppression of society and also (their) liberation from the Hispanic male-dominated culture, as they attempt to balance Hispanic and US cultures' (Luis, *Dance*, 72). Indeed, these poets create new poetic spaces that seek to integrate their national, cultural, and gender identity. Their style is diverse as is the way they express their perspectives. They have produced a body of poetry that speaks of a cultural identity that includes the reaffirmation of the Pre-Columbian roots in the construction of the myth of Borinquen (the name that the ancestral indigenous people used to refer to the island of Puerto Rico).[5] But it is also a poetry that talks about being bicultural, and of racial and cultural conflicts, and ancestors. On the one hand, Puerto Rican women poets come from a poetry of great oral tradition, in which some poets use colloquial language, integrating bilingualism and code-switching. On the other hand, many poets use standard English and/or standard Spanish in a lyrical way that affirms the woman's voice.[6]

Some of these women poets have become known thanks to the numerous

---

South American women poets. Carlota Caulfield's *Voces viajeras* (Madrid: Torremozas, 2002) is dedicated to the Cuban women poets of the Diaspora, studying some of the Cuban American poets, while Zulema Moret's *Mujeres mirando al sur: antología de poetas sudamericanas en USA* (Madrid: Torremozas, 2004) is the only book to date on South American women poets living and writing in the US.

[4] For a theoretically detailed analysis of US Caribbean literature, see William Luis, *Dance Between Two Cultures: Latino Caribbean Literature Written in the United States* (Nashville: Vanderbildt University Press, 1997). Also see John K. Roth (ed.), *Writers of the Caribbean and Central América* (New York & London: Garland Publishing, 1992), 'Voices of the People: Latino Writing and the American Experience', in *American Diversity, American Identity: the Lives and Works of 145 Writers Who Define the American Experience* (New York: Henry Holt and Company, 1995), and Cathy N. Davidson and Linda Wagner-Martin (eds.), 'Latina Writing', in *The Oxford Companion to Women's Writing in the United States* (New York: Oxford University Press, 1995).

[5] For an analysis of Chicanoism and the Puerto Rican nationalism in New York, see Skar, *Voces híbridas*, 119–24.

[6] See Efraín Barradas, 'De lejos en sueños verla . . .: Visión mítica de Puerto Rico en la poesía neoyorrican', *Revista Chicano-Riqueña*, 7 (1979), 46–56, Juan Flores, *Divided Borders: Essays on Puerto Rican Identity* (Houston: Arte Público Press, 1993), William Luis, *Dance Between Two Cultures*, 37–98, and Eliana Ortega, 'Poetic Discourse of the Puerto Rican Woman in the US: New Voices of Anacaonian Liberation', in Asunción Horno-Delgado, Eliana Ortega, Nina M. Scott, and Nancy Saporta Sterbach (eds.), *Breaking Boundaries: Latina Writing and Critical Readings* (Amherst: University of Massachusetts Press,

anthologies of Nuyorican literature that have been published in the last fifteen years, and also thanks to their participation in the creation of literary groups, like the famous Nuyorican Poets Café, in which they have held an outstanding place. Others received more attention from the general public once prestigious North American publishers published their works. The two most important of these poets are Sandra María Esteves and Judith Ortiz Cofer, whose works can be understood as responding to issues of identity.

*Sandra María Esteves*
Sandra María Esteves (b. 1948) is a well-known Nuyorican visual artist, poet, and performer. She is, as the poet always declares, a Puerto Rican-Dominican-Boriqueña-Quisqueyana-Taino-African-American born and raised in the Bronx. Esteves became known as a performance poet in the Nuyorican Poets Café and turned into one of the principal exponents of Nuyorican identity. She was one of the founding poets of the Nuyorican poetry movement, as well as one of the first Nuyorican women to publish a volume of poetry in the United States. She was formerly the producer-director of the African Caribbean Poetry Theater. Her poems have appeared internationally in numerous anthologies, magazines, and literary journals. As an active poetry advocate and cultural worker, she has conducted literary programs for Teachers & Writers Collaborative, the Caribbean Cultural Center, Bronx Council on the Arts, and El Museo del Barrio, among numerous others. In addition to producing and directing spoken word collaborations, she continues creating art, teaching workshops, presenting poetry readings, and lecturing at universities and cultural centers throughout the US.

Esteves' first volume of poetry, *Yerba Buena* (1980), was revolutionary in establishing an urban Latina's choice and aesthetic. Some of her most outstanding poetry collections are *Tropical Rains: A Bilingual Downpour* (1984), *Bluestown Mockingbird Mambo* (1990), *Undelivered Love Poems* (1997), *Contrapunto in the Open Field* (1998), and *Finding your Way* (2001). She is the recipient of numerous awards and fellowships including a Poetry Fellowship from the New York Foundation for the Arts (1985), The Edgar Allan Poe Literary Award from the Bronx Historical Society (1992), Arts Review Honoree from the Bronx Council on the Arts (2001) and The Owen Vincent Dodson Memorial Award for Poetry from Blind Beggar Press (2002).

One of her best-known poems is 'A Julia y a mí', a bilingual answer to 'A Julia de Burgos', a 1938 poem by Puerto Rico's most renowned twentieth-century woman poet, which rejects the victimization of women. In this poem, Esteves not only acknowledges the extraordinary importance of Burgos as a precursor of many Puerto Rican women poets like herself, but also presents

---

1989), 122–35. See also Faythe Turner (ed.), *Puerto Rican Writers at Home in the USA: An Anthology* (Seattle: Open Hand, 1991).

political and identity issues. Her often-anthologized poem, 'My Name is María Christina', talks about self-discovery and identity where the poet declares her pride in being a Puerto Rican woman from El Barrio. Esteves' work 'shares deep roots in community life and popular culture'.[7] One dominant theme in Esteves' writing is the issue of self-discovery and racial identity. In 'Not Either', Esteves skillfully blends Spanish and English into verse, reinforcing her bicultural heritage, her hybrid identity, and the marginalization that a Nuyorican woman experiences in relation to her cultural context.

> Born in the Bronx, *not* really jíbara
> *Not* really hablando bien
> But yet, *not* Gringa either
> Pero *ni* portorra, pero sí portorra too
> Pero *ni* que what am I?[8]

## *Judith Ortiz Cofer*

Among the Puerto Rican poets who have become well-known outside New York one finds Judith Ortiz Cofer (b. 1952). She was born in Puerto Rico and was raised in the United States after 1956, but she spent extended periods at her grandmother's house in Puerto Rico. An active poet and speaker, she stands out as one of the most-published Latina poets. Ortiz Cofer is among the most notable of the Puerto Rican authors writing in English and publishing in mainstream academic and commercial publishing houses. Her poems about cultural conflicts of immigrants to the US mainland have made Ortiz Cofer a leading literary interpreter of the US–Puerto Rican experience. Nicolás Kanellos has pointed out that this poet is

> the first Puerto Rican writer to express from a middle-class point of view, the disjuncture of migrating from island to mainland, and back again. Her poetry celebrates the perspective she has gained from seeing life through the prism of two languages and two cultures. She also comments on the gender roles in both cultures. (*The Hispanic Literary Companion*, 229)

---

[7] Nicolás Kanellos in *The Hispanic Literary Companion* (Detroit, New York, and London: Visible Ink, 1997), 75. See also Sandra María Esteves, 'A Julia y a mí', in *Yerba Buena* (New York: Greenfield Review Press, 1980), 50–5. In 1940 Julia de Burgos (1914–53) emigrated to New York. Except for sojourns in Havana (1940–42) and Washington, DC (1944–45), she remained in New York until her anonymous death at 116th Street and 5th Avenue. Esteves elaborates on Burgos as a symbol of the Puerto Rican woman migrant in 'The Feminist Viewpoint in Poetry of Puerto Rican Women in the United States', in Asela Rodríguez de Laguna (ed.), *Images and Identities: The Puerto Rican in Two World Contexts* (New Brunswick: Transaction, 1985), 171–7.

[8] Poem quoted from Lourdes Rojas, 'Latinas at the Crossroads: An Affirmation of Life', in Rosario Morales and Aurora Levins Morales, *Getting Home Alive*, in *Breaking Boundaries: Latina Writing and Critical Readings*, 176.

Even though Ortiz Cofer concurs with the Nuyorican poets on some of the themes related to Puerto Rican identity, including predominantly a feminist critical approach to Puerto Rican culture, she expresses them from a less marginal perspective. She includes more personal subjects in her poems, especially those related to family history. In her poetry, Ortiz Cofer offers an image of Puerto Rico as some sort of paradise, but she relates to this paradise from the perspective of someone who also belongs to other cultural landscapes, for example the landscape of Atlanta, where she resides. This is clearly expressed in her poem 'The Idea of Islands', where 'it is not the physical island that is important, but the metaphorical one, the island you carry within'.[9] This does not deny her tight ties with the island, as the poet says so well in her well-known poem 'Exile':

> I left my home behind me
> but my past clings to my fingers
> so that every word I write bears
> the mark like a cancelled postage stamp
> of my birthplace.[10]

It is necessary to view the poetry of Ortiz Cofer as a cultural dialogue between the island and the mainland (the United States). In this context it is also necessary to point out that the poet writes in standard English without the mix of Spanish and English that is frequent in the poetry of Esteves and other Puerto Rican American poets. And when she incorporates words in Spanish, they are used in a standard form. Contrary to other Nuyorican poets who link their work to other Puerto Rican writers, like Julia de Burgos, Ortiz Cofer considers Virginia Woolf, Tony Morrison, and Flannery O'Connor as some of her principal inspirations.

Ortiz Cofer is the author of the poetry collection *Peregrina* (1986), *Terms of Survival* (1987), *Reaching for the Mainland* (1995) and *A Love Story Beginning in Spanish* (2005). Her best known poems were published in *Silent Dancing: A Partial Remembrance of a Puerto Rican Childhood* (1991), a book that received the 1991 PEN/Martha Albrand Special Citation in Nonfiction and a Pushcart Prize. It was followed by *The Latin Deli* (1993), a combination of poetry, short fiction, and personal narrative. Among Ortiz Cofer's many distinguished awards are fellowships from the National Endowment for the Arts, the Witter Bynner Foundation for Poetry, the Florida and Georgia Councils for the Arts, and the

---

[9] See Luis, *Dance Between Two Cultures*, 97. For more on Ortiz Cofer, see Edna Acosta-Belén, 'A *MELUS* Interview: Judith Ortiz Cofer', *MELUS*, 18:3 (1993), 83–97, Rafael Ocasio, 'Ortiz Cofer, Judith', in *The Literary Encyclopedia* (20 June 2002), Carmen S. Rivera, *Kissing the Mango Tree: Puerto Rican Women Rewriting American Literature* (Houston: Arte Público Press, 2002), and Patricia Montilla, 'The Island as Mainland and the Revolving Door Motif: Contemporary Puerto Rican Literature of the United States', Chapter 3 of this *Companion*.

[10] Quoted from Judith Ortiz Cofer's *Terms of Survival* (Houston: Arte Público Press, 1987), 46.

Bread Loaf Writers' Conference. She has also been the recipient of the Pushcart Prize for Non-Fiction (1990) and the Anisfield-Wolf Book Award (1993). Ortiz Cofer is Professor of English and Creative Writing at the University of Georgia, Athens.

## Other Nuyorican/Puerto Rican poets

In addition to Sandra María Esteves and Judith Ortiz Cofer, other poets have a relevant place in the Nuyorican/Puerto Rican American literary scene. Today Giannina Braschi (b. 1961), a Puerto Rican-born New Yorker poet and performer, has a distinguished place in the Puerto Rican poetry scene of New York. She is the author of *Empire of Dreams*, translated by Tess O'Dwyer and published with great success by Yale University Press in 1994. Her poems are avant-garde, and marked by surrealism and humor, in which the poet's urban sensibility resonates. She is an observer of and active participant in New York City, as well as other cities that mix and combine with her poetry, forming a multiple stage. Her poetry is also hybrid linguistically and structurally. Her work was published in 2000 in Spanish by the University of Puerto Rico. In her poetic and experimental novel, *Yo-Yo Boing!* (1998), the poet also writes in the code-switching half-Spanish, half-English that is the daily language of Latinos in the US.

Nuyorican poetry has found a very original and young voice in María Teresa Fernandez Rosario, known as Mariposa (Butterfly). She continues the important work of performance poetry and recitation in which Sandra María Esteves was a forerunner. Mariposa is a poet from the Bronx, an active performance poet, actress, educator, visual artist, and human rights activist. She belongs to a new and powerful group of Nuyorican poetry of 'literary artists' who are unified in their formative relation to hip-hop and other forms of artistic association and diffusion, such as spoken word, open mic, and literary cafés and clubs. She is known for her powerful performances in major New York City venues like the Nuyorican Poets Café and the Joseph Papp Public Theater. Mariposa's poetry has been featured on the acclaimed HBO documentary 'Americanos: Latino Life in the US', produced by Edward James Olmos and Nick Athas for Time-Warner. Among the most heard poems by Mariposa are 'Ode to the Diasporican' and 'Boricua Butterfly' where the poet expresses pride in her Nuyorican identity.[11]

Also under the rubric of Puerto Rican American poetry it is important to mention Aurora Levins Morales and her mother, Rosario Morales. They are feminists and radicals, Puerto Rican, American, and Jewish. They have

---

[11] See Montilla's essay in this *Companion*. For a study of the New Nuyorican poetry, see Juan Flores and Mayra Santos-Febres' 'Introduction' to 'Open Mic / Micrófono Abierto. Nuevas Literaturas Puerto/Neorriqueñas/NewPuerto/Nuyor Rican Literatures', in *Hostos Review*, 2 (2005), viii–xxvii. In particular on Mariposa, see Mireya Navarro, 'The Poetry of the Nuyorican Experience', in the *Puerto Rico Herald* www.PuertoRico-Herald.org (2 January 2002).

poignantly captured in their poetry and prose collection *Getting Home Alive* (1986) the multiple borderland identities and struggles experienced by Puerto Rican women.

Another well-known poet is Luz María Umpierre, author of the collection of poems *En el país de las maravillas* (In the Country of Wonders) (1972), *Una puertorriqueña en Penna* (A Puerto Rican Woman in Penna) (1979), and *Y otras desgracias / And Other Misfortunes* (1985). Her best-known collection of poetry is *The Margarita Poems* (1987) in which she celebrates lesbian love. She adroitly combines themes related to sexuality, sex, gender, nation, and language. Umpierre achieves in her poetry a clever integration of bilingualism and code-switching, as well as bringing forth issues of culture shock and discrimination. Her poetry has been included in numerous anthologies of Latin American and Puerto Rican poetry.[12]

## Cuban-American poets

For the most part, the work of the Cuban-American poets does not emphasize a discourse of resistance towards the North American culture such as found in Nuyorican poetry, but tends to focus primarily on a nostalgia for Cuba, and is deep rooted in the reality of exile. Memory and fragmented identity are predominant themes in this poetry.[13] Another distinguishing characteristic in some of the poets' work is the feminine re-writing of classic myths, physical and spiritual journeys, political denunciation, and Aztec, Mayan and Afrocuban mythology.

Many of the Cuban-American poets write in Spanish and their work has become known to the English-speaking public thanks to translations that have appeared in literary magazines and anthologies. A poet such as Magali Alabau is known mainly within the Cuban and Hispanic communities in the US, although her poetry, which has been translated into English and included in various anthologies, has meant a rise in her popularity in the US.[14] Cuban-American Carolina Hospital is the best known of this group in the US as she writes in English and is one of the leading promoters of Cuban-American poetry.

### Magali Alabau

Magali Alabau (b. 1945) is one of the most original Cuban poets of the Cuban Diaspora. A resident of New York since 1967, in 1968 she founded with the playwright Manuel Martin the 'Duo Theater' dedicated to experimental theater. She also founded in 1974, with Ana María Simo, the women's theater company

---

[12] For a study on the poetry of Luz María Umpierre, see Elena M. Martínez, *Lesbian Voices from Latin America: Breaking Ground* (New York: Garland, 1996).

[13] For a study on the Cuban literature of exile, see Silvia Burunat and Ofelia García (eds.), *Veinte años de literatura cubanoamericana: Antología 1962–1982* (Tempe, Arizona: Bilingual Press, 1988), and Isabel Álvarez Borland, *Cuban-American Literature in Exile. From Person to Persona* (Charlottesville: University of Virginia Press, 1998).

[14] See Caulfield (ed.), *Voces viajeras*.

'Medusa's Revenge', although she abandoned acting in 1985. Her published works include *Electra, Clitemnestra* (1986), *La extremaunción diaria* (The Daily Extreme Unction) (1986), *Ras* (1987), *Hermana* (1989), *Hemos llegado a Ilión* (We've arrived at Ilion) (1992), *Hermana/Sister* (1992), and *Liebe* (1993). She is the recipient of many awards, such as the Cintas fellowship (1990) and the New York Latin American Writers Institute Poetry Prize (1992) for *Hermana*. Alabau writes primarily in Spanish and her work has been translated into English by Anne Twitty. Her poetry has been included in many anthologies of Cuban and Latin American poetry as well as anthologies of Latina women poets and lesbian poetry.

Within the body of Alabau's work, most notable is *Electra, Clitemnestra* in which the poet rewrites the classic myth from an erotic lesbian perspective. *La extremaunción diaria* and *Ras* show the nonconformity of the poet in the alienating daily reality of New York City. What stands out in these collections of poetry are the themes of splitting and fragmentation of the individual, cultural duality, and exile. In *Hermana/Sister* the poet writes about the fear of the memory that binds her to a past of chaos and pain. Contrary to the nostalgia for the Island that appears in other Cuban poets of the Diaspora, there is no idealization of Cuba in the poems of Alabau. Her poetic voice is a careful observer of her past, which she considers dangerous. The poet does not want her memories, in spite of being very present, to usurp her present. As Librada Hernández has pointed out 'the discourse of exile meets (in these poems) the discourse of autobiography'.[15] For the poet:

> Cuba es un baúl amarrado
> lleno de prohibiciones.
> una caja que no abro
> porque salen todas, una a una,
> maldiciones.[16]

> (Cuba is a trunk bound with straps,
> full of the forbidden.
> A box I don't open
> because from it, one by one, emerge
> maledictions.)

## Carolina Hospital

The theme of memory is also found in great force in the poetry of Carolina Hospital (b. 1957), who has lived in the US since she was four years old. She is a

---

[15] 'Introduction' to Magali Alabau, *Hermana /Sister*, trans. Anne Twitty (Madrid: Betania, 1992), 9. See also Felipe Lázaro (ed.), *Poetas cubanas en Nueva York/Cuban Women Poets in New York* (Madrid: Betania, 1991), Caulfield, 'Texturas de caos o La extremaunción diaria de Magali Alabau', *Monographic Review/ Revista Monográfica*, 13 (1997), 384–93, and *Voces viajeras*, 13–14 and 46–51, and Elena M. Martínez, *Lesbian Voices*.

[16] Quoted from Magali Alabau, *Hermana/Sister*, 31.

poet and editor who has been 'on the forefront in the development of a Cuban-American aesthetic in Literature. Her poetry demonstrates the particularly bilingual-bicultural nature of the Cuban literary sensibility in the United States' (Kanellos, 138). Known for her work as an editor and promoter of Cuban-American culture, Hospital is also a novelist and essayist who published the ground-breaking anthology *Cuban American Writers: Los Atrevidos* in 1988. She lives in Miami and writes primarily in English.[17] In spite of publishing poetry in many anthologies and literary magazines, her recent work, *The Child of Exile: A Poetry Memoir* (2004), is her first collection of poetry.

Her poems include the theme of exile and the denouncement of the Cuban dictatorial regime. They also reflect on her double cultural identity, her Cuban roots, and her Cuban-American identity. One of the best-known and representative poems of Hospital's poetry is 'Dear Tía' (Dear Aunt), also included in *The Child of Exile*, where Cuba is a familiarly foreign land. In this poem, the poet expresses her feeling of alienation due to an inability to remember the past:

> The pain comes not from nostalgia
> I do not miss your voice urging me to play,
> your smile,
> or your pride when others called you my mother.
> I cannot close my eyes and feel your soft skin;
> listen to your laughter;
> smell the sweetness of your bath.
> I write because I cannot remember at all.[18]

## Other Cuban poets

Among Cuban women poets writing in the United States is Alina Galliano (b. 1950). Galliano has lived in New York since 1968. Her poetry is highly introspective and includes, among her most important themes, Aztec mythology and Sufi philosophy. The book that stands out in her body of work is *En el vientre del trópico* (In the Belly of the Tropics) (1994), which is fundamentally a denouncement of Cuba's socio-political crisis from inside the Afro-Cuban pantheon, with significant epic dimensions. The poet expresses critical intentions as well as conciliatory ones for the future of the Cuban nation. Her other books are *Entre el párpado y la mejilla* (Between Eyelid and Cheek) (1980), *Hasta el presente (Poesía casi completa)* (Until the Present Time (Almost

---

[17] Carolina Hospital has skillfully pointed out that the Cuban American writers who write principally in English 'have not substituted one cultural legacy for another. On the contrary, they have appropriated for themselves more, rather than less.' And she adds: 'Most writers today, especially in the United States, cannot be pigeonholed into a single national identity.' *Cuban American Writers: Los Atrevidos* (Princeton: Ediciones Ellas/Linden Lane, 1988), 16–17.

[18] Cited from Hospital's *Cuban American Writers: Los Atrevidos*, 169. See also William Luis in *Dance Between Two Cultures*, where he makes a detailed analysis of this poem, 172–5.

Complete Poetry)) (1989), and *La geometría de lo incandescente. (En fija residencia)* (Geometry of the Incandescent. (In Permanent Residence)) (1992). Galliano's poetry has been included in many anthologies of Cuban and Latin American poetry.

Another relevant Cuban poet is Lourdes Gil (b. 1951), who left Cuba at a young age, and grew up within the Cuban and North American cultural worlds. She writes in English and Spanish, and her work has been influenced by Cuban and North American literary traditions. Her better-known poetry collections are: *Neumas* (1977), *Manuscrito de la niña ausente* (Manuscript of the Absent Child) (1980), *Vencido el fuego de la especie* (The Defeated Fire of the Species) (1983), *Blanca aldaba preludia* (White Prelude) (1989), and *Empieza la ciudad* (The City Begins) (1993). Her poetry is characterized by a rich metaphorical language.

A poet who goes beyond the Cuban-American experience is Maya Islas (b. 1947), a resident of New York since 1965. Islas's poetry moves away from the traditional themes of Cuban poetry of the Diaspora, and is interested in exploring correlations between the creation and the expansion of the conscience. The influence of painting, in particular the Surrealists, is evident in her poems. Her outstanding books include: *Sola. . . Desnuda. . . Sin nombre* (Alone. . . Nude. . . Nameless) (1974), *Altazora acompañando a Vicente* (Altazora Accompanying Vicente) (1989) and *Merla* (1991). Another poet who deserves attention is Iraida Iturralde (b. 1951) who has resided in the United States since 1962.[19] She is an educator and translator as well as a poet. Among her best-known poetry collections is *La Isla Rota* (The Broken Island) (2002).

An internationally known voice among Cuban women poets writing in the United States is Juana Rosa Pita (b. 1939). She left Cuba in 1965. Pita is the author of a considerable output, including *Pan de sol* (Bread of Sun) (1976), *Las cartas y las horas* (Letters and Hours) (1977), *Mar entre rejas* (Sea Behind Bars) (1977), *El arca de los sueños* (The Ark of Dreams) (1978), *Manual de magia* (Manual of Magic) (1979), *Eurídice en la fuente* (Euridice at the Fountain) (1979), *Viajes de Penélope* (Penelope's Journeys) (1980), *Crónicas del Caribe* (Caribbean Chronicles) (1983), *Grumo d'alba / Grumo de alba* (Clot of Dawn) (1985), *El sol tatuado* (The Tattooed Sun) (1986), *Aires etruscos / Arie etrusche* (Etruscan Airs) (1987), *Plaza sitiada* (Besieged Plaza) (1987), *Sorbos de luz / Sips of Light* (1990), *Florencia nuestra. (Biografía poemática)* (Our Florence) (1992), *Transfiguración de la armonía* (Transfiguration of Harmony) (1993), *Una estación en tren* (A Season in the Train) (1994), *Tela de concierto* (Concert's Canvas) (1999), *Cadenze* (2000), the anthology *Cantar de isla* (Island's Canto) (2003), and *Pensamiento del tiempo* (Thought of Time) (2005). Her work is better known in Latin America, Spain, and Italy than in the US and she seldom appears in anthologies of Latina women poets. She writes in

---

[19] For a study of the poetry of Alina Galliano and Maya Islas, see my *Voces viajeras*, 15–18, 52–60, and 71–80. For a review of the poetry of Lourdes Gil and Iraida Iturralde, see *Cuban-American Writers: Los Atrevidos*. Also Lázaro (ed.), *Poetas cubanas en Nueva York*.

Spanish, and often collaborates with her son Mario Alejandro Pita in the translation of her poetry into English. Another of her translators was the late Donald D. Walsh. Her poems have been published in literary magazines in Latin America, Spain, the US, Germany and Italy. She has received many international poetry prizes. She identifies culturally more with the Hispanic-speaking world than with the US. The major themes of Pita's poetry are love and exile. In creating her own mythology, she forges an insular mythology. The intimate and the collective merge in her work.[20]

## Dominican-American poets

With the Cuban poets of the Diaspora, the Dominican poets also use the exiled word to refer to their condition in the US and they situate themselves, in this way, more closely to their country of origin than to their adopted country. The Dominican poets essentially develop themes pertaining to cultural identity, the celebration of Caribbean heritage, displacement, and marginalized beings. The race issue is fundamental in the poetic discourse of some, and the tribute to feminine literary figures and forerunners, as in the work of some of the Nuyorican poets, is of great importance in their work. Thanks to anthologies, such as Daisy Cocco de Filippis's and Emma Jane Robinet's *Poems of Exile and Other Concerns / Poemas del exilio y de otras inquietudes*, published in New York in 1988, Dominican-American poetry has expanded its readership in the US. Also through the support of Scherezada (Chiqui) Vicioso, the founder of the *Círculo de Mujeres Poetas* (Circle of Women Poets) in New York in 1980, many new poets, like Julia Alvarez, had their poems published.[21]

### *Julia Alvarez*
Julia Alvarez is the most successful and popular US Dominican woman writer. She was born in New York City (1950), but her parents brought her home to their native Dominican Republic when she was less than a month old. Her family left the Dominican Republic in 1960, as political exiles, and resettled in New York. Alvarez is better known as a fiction writer than as a poet, thanks to the extraordinary success of *How the García Girls Lost Their Accents* (1991). Like her fiction, her poetry also refers to her family, childhood memories, and her identity. Her double identity as a Dominican and as a North American is apparent in her writing style through her bringing the rhythm of Spanish to

---

[20] For a detailed study of the work of Juana Rosa Pita, see Jesús J. Barquet, *Escrituras poéticas de una nación: Dulce María Loynaz, Juana Rosa Pita y Carlota Caulfield* (La Habana: Unión, 1999), and Caulfield, *Voces viajeras*, 10–12 and 28–36.

[21] According to William Luis, the term 'exile' in the case of the Dominican writers refers more to a 'political position that prevents Dominicans from assimilating into the North American environment' (237); and see Elisabeth Coonrod Martinez, 'Between the Island and the Tenements: New Directions in Dominican-American Literature', Chapter 6 of this *Companion*.

English. Alvarez clearly defines her relation to Spanish and English when she states: 'I don't hear the same rhythms in English as a native speaker of English. Sometimes I hear Spanish in English . . . I'm mapping a country that's not on the map, and that's why I'm trying to put it down on paper.'[22]

Alvarez's first book of poems, *Homecoming: Poems*, 1984, revised and expanded in 1996 (as *Homecoming: New and Collected Poems*, 1996) has an intimate tone. These poems celebrate daily life as part of poetic and personal self-expression. In these poems, which are deeply autobiographical in nature, Alvarez returns to the world of her childhood in the Dominican Republic. She observes and comments on the patriarchal traditions inside Hispanic culture from a sharp female perspective. Heritage, identity, and linguistic concerns are central to much of her poetry. One of her best-known poems is 'Homecoming', where she describes her return to the Dominican Republic to attend a cousin's wedding and finds herself more an observer than a participant, not always feeling at ease in what she once considered a familiar environment.

Another collection of poetry that presents her intimate poetic style is *The Other Side / El otro lado* (1995), where Alvarez skillfully captures the experience of exile, love, and language. Her 'Bilingual Sestina' shows the interplay of two languages and cultures:

> Some things I have to say aren't getting said
> in this snowy, blond, blue-eyes, gum-chewing English:
> dawn's early light sifting through *persianas* closed
> the night before by dark-skinned girls whose words
> evoke *cama, aposento, sueños* in *nombres*
> from that first world I can't translate from Spanish . . .[23]

In *The Woman I Kept to Myself* (2004), she continues exploring themes of cultural identity, race, language, and women's traditional roles. Alvarez has received many distinctions including grants from the National Endowment for the Arts and The Ingram Merrill Foundation. Since 1988 she has been teaching English and Creative Writing at Middlebury College in Vermont.[24]

## *Other Dominican poets*

Of the Dominican women poets writing in Spanish in the US, Marianela Medrano (b. 1954) is finding a place in US Latina Caribbean literature. Some of her poems show a sharp irony when talking about the influence of North American culture in her family life. Her best-known books are *Oficio de vivir* (The

---

[22] Quoted from Julia Alvarez, *Something to Declare* (Chapel Hill: Algonquin Books, 1998), 173.
[23] Quoted from Julia Alvarez, *The Other Side / El otro lado* (New York: Dutton, 1995), 3.
[24] The bibliography of Julia Alvarez is very extensive. For that reason we refer the readers to the author's website at http://www.alvarezjulia.com/ It contains a list of books, articles, and interviews, scheduled appearances and biographical information.

Craft of Living) (1986) and *Los alegres ojos de la tristeza* (The Happy Eyes of Sadness) (1987). Some of her poems have been published in *Alba de América* and *Brooklyn Review*. Like Medrano, Miriam Ventura (b. 1957) is another Dominican poet known in the US who offers a female perspective in Dominican poetry. She is the author of *Poemas de la noche* (Poems of the Night) (1986) and *Trópico acerca del otoño* (Tropic Concerning Autumn) (1987).

Another poet highly deserving of attention is Sherezada (Chiqui) Vicioso (b. 1948). She is a poet, literary critic, and educator. She lived in New York for seventeen years, where she attended Brooklyn College and Columbia University; she has lived in the Dominican Republic since the 1980s. She prefers to write poetry in Spanish and has a good readership in the Dominican Republic as well as in the United States. Among her most outstanding books are: *Viaje desde el agua* (Journey from the Water) (1981) and *Un extraño ulular traía el viento* (The Wind Brought a Strange Howl) (1985). In 1987, she published the poetic biography of *Julia de Burgos, la nuestra* (Julia de Burgos, One of Ours). She is also a playwright – and this is obvious in the way that she builds her poetry, as scenes where a poetic voice observes the events. One of Vicioso's major themes is the issue of race, which does not always appear in Dominican literature, and, as seen in her often-anthologized poem 'Perspectives', Vicioso's poetic voice becomes an observer of the lives of working Dominican women who tried to find a place in North American society, particularly in New York City.[25]

## Coda: A Personal Note by way of conclusion

In 1994 I received an invitation from William Luis to be part of an anthology of Hispanic-Caribbean poetry written in the United States. I accepted it and found myself, one year later, included in an special issue of *Boletín de la Fundación Federico García Lorca* dedicated to Caribbean poets writing in Spanish and English.[26] This issue of the *Boletín* was my key to further readings of US Caribbean poetry. Later on, Luis's *Dance Between Two Cultures. Latino Caribbean Literature Written in the United States*, published in 1997, became and remains the best overview of Latino Caribbean literature in the US, studying several representative women poets who also appear in this chapter.

US Latina Caribbean women poets have produced and continue to create a significant body of work. They occupy a central position in the US Latino literature and continue to leave a mark on the multicultural US literary scene. I am

---

[25] For a comprehensive study of the poetry of Sherezada (Chiqui) Vicioso, see William Luis, *Dance Between Two Cultures*, 255–60. He studies her poems 'Perspectives', 'Reports', 'Wo/men', and 'Haiti'. For an analysis of Vicioso's issues of race and color identification in the Dominican Republic, see Coonrod Martínez's chapter in this *Companion*. See also 'An Oral History (Testimonio)', in Asunción Horno-Delgado et al. (eds.), *Breaking Boundaries*, 229–34; and Lizabeth Paravisini-Gebert and Consuelo López-Springfield (eds.), *Callaloo*, 23:3 'Dominican Republic: Literature and Culture' (Summer 2000).

[26] William Luis, 'Poesía hispano-caribeña escrita en los Estados Unidos', *Boletín de la Fundación Federico García Lorca* (Madrid: Fundació García Lorca, 1995), 19–93.

proud to be a part of this group of women writers who are constantly mapping new territories in the contemporary literary scene and are architects of bridges that link the Caribbean to a plurality of poetic expressions.

## Works Cited

Acosta-Belén, Edna. 'A *MELUS* Interview: Judith Ortiz Cofer', *MELUS*, 18:3 (1993), 83–97.
Alabau, Magali. *Electra, Clitemnestra*. New York, Concepción, Chile: Ediciones del Maitén, 1986.
—— *Hemos Ilegado a Ilión*. Madrid: Betania, 1992.
—— *Hermana*. Madrid: Betania, 1989.
—— *Hermana / Sister*, trans. Anne Twitty. Madrid: Betania, 1992.
—— *La extremaunción diaria*. Barcelona: Rondas, 1986.
—— *Liebe*. Coral Gables, Florida: La Torre de Papel, 1993.
—— *Ras*. New York: Medusa Editions, 1987.
Alvarez, Julia. *Homecoming*. New York: Grove Press, 1984; rev. edn, Dutton, 1996.
—— *How the García Girls Lost Their Accents*. Chapel Hill, North Carolina: Algonquin Books, 1991.
—— *The Other Side / El otro lado*. New York: Dutton, 1995.
—— *Something to Declare*. Chapel Hill: Algonquin Books, 1998.
—— *The Woman I Kept to Myself*. Chapel Hill, North Carolina: Algonquin Books, 2004.
Álvarez Borland, Isabel. *Cuban-American Literature in Exile. From Person to Persona*. Charlottesville: University of Virginia Press, 1998.
Barquet, Jesús J. *Escrituras poéticas de una nación: Dulce María Loynaz, Juana Rosa Pita y Carlota Caulfield*. La Habana: Unión, 1999.
Barradas, Efrain, 'De lejos en sueños verla . . .: Visión mítica de Puerto Rico en la poesía neoyorrican', *Revista Chicano-Riqueña*, 7 (1979), 46–56.
Braschi, Giannina. *Empire of Dreams*, trans. Tess O'Dwyer. New Haven: Yale University Press, 1994.
—— *Yo-Yo Boing!* Tempe, Arizona: Bilingual Review Press, 1998.
Burunat, Silvia, and Ofelia García (eds.). *Veinte años de literatura cubanoamericana: Antología 1962–1982*. Tempe, Arizona: Bilingual Press, 1988.
Caulfield, Carlota, 'Texturas de caos o *La extremaunción diaria* de Magali Alabau', *Monographic Review / Revista Monográfica*, 13 (1997), 384–93.
—— (ed.). *Voces viajeras. Poetisas cubanas de hoy*. Madrid: Ediciones Torremozas, 2002.
Cocco de Filippis, Daisy, and Emma Jane Robinet (eds.). *Poems of Exile and Other Concerns / Poemas del exilio y de otras inquietudes*. New York: Ediciones Alcance, 1988.
Davidson, Cathy N., and Linda Wagner-Martin (eds.). *The Oxford Companion to Women's Writing in the United States*. New York: Oxford University Press, 1995.
Esteves, Sandra María. *Bluestown Mockingbird*. Houston: Arte Público Press, 1990.
—— *Contrapunto in The Open Field*. New York: No Frills Publications, 1998.
—— *Finding Your Way, Poems for Young Folks*. New York: No Frills Publications, 2001.
—— 'The Feminist Viewpoint in Poetry of Puerto Rican Women in the United

States', in Asela Rodríguez de Laguna (ed.). *Images and Identities: The Puerto Rican in Two World Contexts.* New Brunswick: Transaction, 1985, 171–7.
—— *Tropical Rain: A Bilingual Downpour.* New York: African Caribbean Poetry Theater, 1984.
—— *Undelivered Love Poems.* New York: No Frills Publications, 1997.
Flores, Juan. *Divided Borders: Essays on Puerto Rican Identity.* Houston: Arte Público Press, 1993.
—— and Mayra Santos-Febres, 'Introduction' to 'Open Mic / Micrófono Abierto. Nuevas Literaturas Puerto/Neorriqueñas/NewPuerto/Nuyor Rican Literatures', *Hostos Review*, 2 (2005), viii–xxvii.
Galliano, Alina. *En el vientre del trópico.* New York: Serena Bay Books, 1994.
—— *Entre el párpado y la mejilla.* Bogotá, Colombia: Unión de Escritores Colombianos, 1980.
—— *Hasta el presente (Poesía casi completa).* Madrid: Betania, 1989.
—— *La geometría de lo incandescente (En fija residencia).* Miami: University of Miami, 1992.
Gil, Lourdes. *Blanca aldaba preludia.* Madrid: Betania, 1989.
—— *Empieza la ciudad.* Coral Gables, Florida: La Torre de Papel, 1993.
—— *Manuscrito de la niña ausente.* New York: Giralt, 1980.
—— *Neumas.* New York: Senda Nueva de Ediciones, 1977.
Horno-Delgado, Asunción, Eliana Ortega, Nina M. Scott, and Nancy Saporta Sterbach (eds.). *Breaking Boundaries: Latina Writing and Critical Readings.* Amherst: University of Massachusetts Press, 1989.
Hospital, Carolina. *Cuban American Writers: Los Atrevidos.* Princeton: Ediciones Ellas / Linden Lane, 1988.
—— *The Child of Exile: A Poetry Memoir.* Houston: Arte Público Press, 2004.
Islas, Maya. *Altazora acompañando a Vicente.* Madrid: Betania, 1989.
—— *Merla.* Madrid: Betania, 1991.
—— *Sola . . . Desnuda . . . Sin nombre.* New York: Mensaje, 1974.
Iturralde, Iraida. *La Isla Rota.* Madrid: Editorial Verbum, 2002.
Kanellos, Nicolás, *The Hispanic Literary Companion.* Detroit, New York, London: Visible Ink, 1997.
Lázaro, Felipe (ed.). *Poetas cubanas en Nueva York / Cuban Women Poets in New York.* Madrid: Betania, 1991.
Luis, William. *Dance Between Two Cultures: Latino Caribbean Literature Written in the United States.* Nashville: Vanderbilt University Press, 1997.
—— 'Poesía hispano-caribeña escrita en los Estados Unidos', *Boletín de la Fundación Federico García Lorca.* Madrid: Fundación García Lorca, 1995, 19–93.
Martínez, Elena M. *Lesbian Voices from Latin America: Breaking Ground.* New York: Garland, 1996.
Medrano, Marianela. *Los alegres ojos de la tristeza.* San Juan: Editorial Búho, 1987.
—— *Oficio de vivir.* Santo Domingo: Colección Separata, 1986.
Milligan, Bryce, Mary Guerrero Milligan, and Angela de Hoyos (eds.). *Floricanto Sí!* New York: Penguin, 1998.
Morales, Rosario, and Aurora Levins Morales. *Getting Home Alive.* Ithaca, New York: Firebrand Books, 1986.
Moret, Zulema (ed.). *Mujeres mirando al sur: antología de poetas sudamericanas en USA.* Madrid: Torremozas, 2004.

Navarro, Mireya, 'The Poetry of the Nuyorican Experience', *Puerto Rican Herald*, 2 January 2002. www.PuertoRico-Herald.org.
Ortega, Eliana. 'Poetic Discourse of the Puerto Rican Woman in the US: New Voices of Anaconian Liberation', in Asunción Horno-Delgado, Eliana Ortega, Nina M. Scott, and Nancy Saporta Sterbach (eds.). *Breaking Boundaries: Latina Writing and Critical Readings*. Amherst: University of Massachusetts Press, 1989, 122–35.
Ortiz Cofer, Judith. *A Love Story Beginning in Spanish*. Athens: University of Georgia Press, 1995.
—— *Peregrina*. Golden, Colorado: Riverstone Press, 1986.
—— *Reaching for the Mainland & Selected New Poems*. Tempe, Arizona: Bilingual Review Press, 1995.
—— *Silent Dancing: A Partial Remembrance of a Puerto Rico Childhood*. Houston: Arte Público Press, 1991.
—— *Terms of Survival*. Houston: Arte Público Press, 1987.
—— *The Latin Deli*. Athens: University of Georgia Press, 1993.
Paravisini-Gebert, Lizabeth, and Consuelo López-Springfield (eds.). *Callaloo*, 23:3 'Dominican Republic: Literature and Culture' (Summer 2000).
Pita, Juana Rosa. *Aires etruscos / Arie etrusche*. Cagliari, Italy: GIA Editrice, 1987.
—— *Cadenze*. Foggia: Bastogi Editrice Italiana, 2000.
—— *Cantar de isla*. La Habana, Cuba: Editorial Letras Cubanas, 2003.
—— *Crónicas del Caribe*. Miami: Solar, 1983.
—— *El arca de los sueños*. Washington, Buenos Aires: Solar, 1978.
—— *El sol tatuado*. Boston: Solar, 1986.
—— *Eurídice en la fuente*. Miami: Solar, 1979.
—— *Florencia nuestra. (Biografía poemática)*. Miami, Valencia: Arcos, 1992.
—— *Grumo d'alba / Grumo de alba*. Pisa: Giardini Editori, 1985.
—— *Las cartas y las horas*. Washington: Solar, 1977.
—— *Manual de magia*. Barcelona: Ámbito Literario, 1979.
—— *Mar entre rejas*. Washington: Solar, 1977.
—— *Pan de sol*. Washington: Solar, 1976.
—— *Pensamiento del tiempo*. Miami: Amatori, 2005.
—— *Plaza sitiada*. San José, Costa Rica: Libro Libre, 1987.
—— *Sorbos de luz / Sips of Light*, trans. Mario de Salvatierra. New Orleans, San Francisco: Eboli, 1990.
—— *Tela de concierto*. Miami: Zunzún Viajero, 1999.
—— *Transfiguración de la armonía*. Coral Gables, Florida: La Torre de Papel, 1993.
—— *Una estación en tren*. Miami: Instituto de Estudios Ibéricos, 1994.
—— *Viajes de Penélope*. Miami: Solar, 1980.
Rivera, Carmen S. *Kissing the Mango Tree: Puerto Rican Women Rewriting American Literature*. Houston: Arte Público Press, 2002.
Rojas, Lourdes, 'Latinas at the Crossroads: An Affirmation of Life in Rosario Morales and Aurora Levins Morales' *Getting Home Alive*, in Asunción Horno-Delgado, Eliana Ortega, Nina M. Scott, and Nancy Saporta Sterbach (eds.). *Breaking Boundaries: Latina Writing and Critical Readings*. Amherst: University of Massachusetts Press, 1989, 166–77.
Roth, John K. (ed.). *American Diversity, American Identity: the Lives and Works of*

*145 Writers who Define the American Experience.* New York: Henry Holt and Company, 1995.
—— (ed.). *Writers of the Caribbean and Central America.* New York, London: Garland Publishing, 1992.
Sánchez, Marta Ester. *Contemporary Chicana Poetry: A Critical Approach to an Emerging Literature.* Berkeley: University of California Press, 1985.
Skar, Stacey Alba D. *Voces híbridas: la literatura de chicanas y latinas en Estados Unidos.* Santiago de Chile: RIL editores, 2001.
Turner, Faythe (ed.). *Puerto Rico Writers at Home in the USA: An Anthology.* Seattle: Open Hand, 1991.
Umpierre, Luz María. *En el país de las maravillas.* San Francisco: New Earth, 1972.
—— *The Margarita Poems.* Berkeley: Third Woman Press, 1987.
—— *Y otras desgracias / And Other Misfortunes.* Berkeley: Third Woman Press, 1985.
Ventura, Miriam. *Poemas de la noche.* Santo Domingo: Editora Webber, 1986.
—— *Trópico acerca del otoño.* Santo Domingo: Editora Huellas, 1987.
Vicioso, Sherezada (Chiqui). *Julia de Burgos, la nuestra.* Santo Domingo: Editora Alfa y Omega, 1987.
—— *Un extraño ulular traía el viento.* Santo Domingo: Editora Alfa y Omega, 1985.
—— *Viaje desde el agua.* Santo Domingo: Ediciones Visuarte, 1981.

## 12

# The Latino Film Experience in History: A Dialogue Among Texts and Collaborators

### DARIÉN J. DAVIS

The complexity of the Latino experience has yet to be adequately explored in film. As in Latino literary texts, most themes and characters in Latino films have emerged from the sensibilities of a community's insertion into the North American reality. From these national experiences, filmmakers have been able to explore issues relevant to the broadly constructed 'Latino' community. As film production relies on a collaborative series of complex and symbiotic relationships between scriptwriters, editors, and directors, the cultural and ethnic backgrounds of those who have contributed to the Latino image in film in the United States have shifted over time. Film's dual nature as 'mass media' and 'cultural text', which emerges out of what Theodor Adorno has called the culture industries, underscores its political and social relevance in the construction of Latino realities.[1]

### Introduction

At the beginning of the twentieth century, US films quickly emerged as one of the most important cultural products in influencing the way that North Americans viewed themselves and how they viewed others.[2] Hollywood, the undisputed center of North American film production since the post-World War I era and for most of the twentieth century, not only controlled what films were produced but where and how they were distributed and exhibited. As the pre-eminent actor in the film culture industry, Hollywood films often reflected North American social values and also played a role in shaping them. Moreover, over the last century, Hollywood production has evolved as it engages with new and emerging social realities, changing ethics, and shifting aesthetic values.

In its representation and construction of minority communities, Hollywood followed and perpetuated widely practiced social conventions from segregation

---

[1] Theodor Adorno, *The Culture Industry* (London: Routledge, 1991).
[2] Robert Sklar, *Movie-Made America: A Social History of American Film* (New York: Random House, 1975).

to stereotyping and exploitation of gender roles, violence, and sexuality. But Hollywood also documented early attitudes towards Jews, working classes, and the social change from the 1950s' civil rights movement, the emergence of Chicano consciousness in the 1960s, and immigrant rights in the 1970s and 1980s. These social movements, which called for individual rights and representation, also influenced the emergence of an independent film industry beyond the traditional Hollywood nucleus. Advances in technology since the 1970s and the wider distribution of international films have also influenced the ethical and aesthetic forms of representation in the US. Many of the early stereotypes remain etched in North American collective consciousness despite the heightened awareness of the importance of Latinos to the North American mainstream culture. Images that cast Latinos as 'outsiders' also divide Latinos between 'those who see themselves as part of the American mainstream' and 'those who live on the margins'. Thus, cinematic stereotypes of Latinos, like symbols and labels elsewhere, often provide the dominant mainstream white culture in the US with a sense of security of itself and perpetuate a static vision of Americanness. Ironically, contemporary Latino filmmakers often feel obliged to dialogue with (and in some instances claim), utilize or manipulate these early images as they create new narratives, impressions, and images.

'Latino films', which emerge from the Latino community in the US, are a relatively new phenomenon, and a result of Latino empowerment and shifting paradigms of representation in the American cultural industry. The Latino *presence* in North American films, on the other hand, dates back to the early twentieth century. This representation, like that of other ethnic films, must be understood in its proper historical context. Although non-Latino directors and producers often constructed their Latino *mise en scène* based on stereotypical and one-dimensional representations of *Latinidad*, the talent of early Latino actors *within* the industry, nonetheless, paved the way for more nuanced representations later on. This chapter explores the changes and development of filmic representation of the Latino experience from the 1910s to the present day by focusing on three major themes: the early construction of *Latinidad*, 1910–1950; civil rights and social dramas, 1950–1990; and the celebration of Latino literature, culture and icons, 1980s–present.

Latino feature films, like film production in general, fall under a variety of genres including fictional dramas, historical epics, shorts, comedies, biopics, and docudramas made for Hollywood studios, for film festivals and for independent companies or television. Documentaries have played a critical role in bringing knowledge and insight of Latino communities despite the fact that distribution of documentaries lags far behind mainstream feature films and thus they are not as widely seen outside university circles and other educational forums. Given the variety and number of films, it is useful to examine the development of Latino films historically.

## The early construction of Latinidad in the United States, 1910–1950

In the early years, Hollywood barred many minorities from depicting themselves, even if the roles were not complimentary. Those films that featured Latin American actors and actresses tended to oversimplify and stereotype people from Latin America and the region as a whole. Ironically, many national Latin American film industries and many Latin American producers and directors followed similar practices in their homelands when it came to their indigenous and black populations.[3] The film industry *wants* to make a profit and thus produces feature films starring a given actor or actress who will help bolster its returns. In many cases, even when foreign peoples are present, they serve as an exotic backdrop to the central plot, as Ella Shohat has so ably illustrated in her essay on feminism and empire.[4]

When Hollywood turned its camera towards the Latino population in the US, its creations were *no less stereotypical*, although Hollywood did not recognize a Latino community in the US *per se* but rather used terms such as 'Latin' and 'Latin American' interchangeably. This strategy located Latin-ness in a foreign geographical territory despite the fact that by the 1920s many Americans of Mexican descent had lived in the US for generations. Mexico's loss of its southwestern territories in the Mexican-American war of 1846–1848 and the signing of the Treaty of Guadalupe Hidalgo meant that thousands of individuals who claimed Mexican identities would be given the option of becoming American citizens and creating the first major populations of Latin American background. Other Latin Americans, particularly Cubans and Puerto Ricans displaced by the 1898 Cuban-Spanish-American war, joined them.[5] One cannot forget the anti-Hispanic and anti-Catholic sentiments against the Spaniards that swept the US at the end of the nineteenth century. These attitudes surely influenced the images of the charming but inept or anachronistic Latins.

Hollywood filmmakers relied first on actors and images from Mediterranean Europe and then from white Latin Americans, mostly from Mexico and Brazil, to construct non-threatening one-dimensional images of *Latins* who were distinct from 'Americans' but who would, nonetheless, be easily recognized. From the 1920s to the 1950s, US filmmakers forged on-screen *Latin* identities based on the political and economic relationships of the US to its backyard, a term that reflected how many white North Americans viewed the entire region

---

[3] Emilo Fernández, *María Candelaría*. Mexico, 1942. Consider the Hollywood feature films in which top actors and entertainers played exotic roles (Elvis Presley in *Harum Scarum* or the many films on Cleopatra played by white American stars). A good article on this phenomenon is Ella Sohat's 'Gender and Culture of Empire: Towards a Feminist Ethnography of the Cinema', *Quarterly Review of Film and Video*, 13:1–3 (1999), 45–85.

[4] See any of the Indiana Jones films: *Indiana Jones and the Temple of Doom* (1984), *Indiana Jones and the Last Crusade* (1989), or *Romancing the Stone* (1984), for example. Shohat, 'Gender and the Culture of Empire.

[5] Today there are more people who identify themselves as Puerto Ricans living on the mainland than on the island of Puerto Rico.

'south of the Rio Grande'. *Latin* (the precursor term to *Latino*) applied to exotic lands that begged for US direction in the wake of the Roosevelt Corollary that reinforced the US image as the regional police. Images in the mainstream press reinforced this. Comic strips and political critics as well as satirists depicted Cuba, Puerto Rico and the region as a whole as a woman in need of protection, or as a young child or baby, and even utilized the image of the black *sambo* to personify the region.[6]

The Mexican Revolution of 1910 was a major watershed of the early twentieth century, sparking interest in the US press, as well as in the small film industry created in Hollywood in 1909. Hollywood brought together independent filmmakers who would be instrumental in shaping images of Mexico for the US audiences. Two main images emerged that helped transform *Latins* from innocent and helpless populations at the turn of the century to rebellious peoples, who nonetheless merited a paternalistic attitude from the US. Mexicans were violent and, as one commentator asserted, the Mexican was 'a mixed blood' and could not be trusted. This image coalesced with the *greaser* prototype, essentially a Mexican *mestizo* and bandit present in a plethora of films, including *Tony the Greaser* (1911), *Bronco Billy and the Greaser* (1914), and *The Greaser's Revenge* (1914).[7]

Pancho Villa, the Mexican revolutionary who opposed the Mexican dictator Porfirio Díaz, and a US ally from the 1870s to 1910, received much media attention. Villa, only one of five revolutionary leaders and perhaps the least politically organized of those who opposed Diaz, became the most sensational. He even signed a $25,000 contract with the Mutual Film Corporation, allowing them to follow his exploits. This agreement resulted in the creation of *Life of Villa* (1915). This film became one of the first feature-length movies, introducing American audiences to the horrors of the Mexican Revolution and depicting war scenes and violence never before seen on screens in the US. Although it was released the same year as D. W. Griffith's *Birth of a Nation*, an overtly racist and violent film about life during and after the American Civil War, *Life of Villa* nonetheless propagated the notion of a violent Mexican nature. Reactions to the film clearly demonstrated that many Americans felt that violence was non-American. So one-dimensional and derogative were the images that, in February 1922, the Mexican government decided to ban all offensive films produced by US companies.

In many respects, North American filmmakers have been more comfortable

---

[6] George Black, *The Good Neighbor: How the United States wrote the History of Central America and the Caribbean* (New York: Parthean Books, 1988) provides us with a few examples.

[7] Allen Woll, *The Latin Image in American Film* (Los Angeles: UCLA Latin American Studies, 1980), 6–29. In their book *Hispanics in Hollywood: An Encyclopedia of Film and Television* (New York: Garland Publishers, 1994), 4, Luis Reyes and Peter Rubie document the changing use of the term 'greaser' from the 1855 law that bore its name to its use for the dark-skinned working class *mestizos* of the 1880s to its 1950s use for delinquent teenagers.

exploring their taboos through minority realities. In the late 1920s, sex became a part of the Latin image with the rise of the 'Latin lover' epitomized by Rudolph Valentino. Valentino stood for a Latin male ethic and aesthetic: tall, dark (but not too dark), and handsome with an appetite for American women. The *Latin lover* began as a distinctly Mediterranean model, however. Italian-born Valentino perfected the role.[8] Ramon Navarro, of Mexican descent, who starred in *Where the Pavement Ends* (1923), was an example of an early Latin lover from Latin America. The production scenes in *Where the Pavement Ends* (shot mostly in Cuba with Cuban extras) give us a hint as to why the Latin Lover is always lover and never husband or partner and remained an outsider.[9]

The characters played by Brazilian actor Raul Roulien often met the same fate. In 1931, Roulien moved to the US to star in two Hollywood films, *Delicious* and *Flying Down to Rio*, but would later appear in a string of others including *Careless Lady* (Fox, 1932) set in Singapore, the detective thriller *State Attorney* (1931), and *It's Great To Be Alive* (1932). Roulien was a white *carioca* who played the eternal Latin playboy or suave and handsome gentleman, and was fundamental in cementing the stereotype associated with *Latinidad* and the 'exchangeability' of national types across national and linguistic barriers.[10]

The period beginning in the 1930s and proceeding to the beginning of the Cold War saw some improvement in Latin images, although characters of Latin American backgrounds remained distinctly foreign, depicted by specific cultural practices, heavy accents, broken or incorrect English, and a host of other signifiers that described *Latins* as outsiders. 'The Good Neighbor Policy' (1933–1947), inspired by President Roosevelt and carried out under Eisenhower, helped transform the southern neighbors from aliens and foreigners to friends and allies against the evil empires of World War II (Germany and Japan), or at least that was the intention. *Latin-ness* was virtually indistinguishable from Latin America, although films about the Latin population in the US began to be explored.[11] The *Latin* population in the US remained largely marginalized and had little impact on the forging of the cinematic images. Indeed, around the same time, the US was actively trying to displace the Mexican-American population from the southwest and to 'return' them to Mexico. Thus, the 'Good Neighbor Policy' was an economic and political initiative with significant strategic consequences.

The US wanted to strengthen relations with Latin America's largest country, which also occupied a strategic geographical position in the Atlantic. Brazilians made their way to the US in record numbers, although the overall total relative to

---

[8] Born in Castelleneta, Italy in 1895, Rudolph Valentino left Italy for Paris in 1912, eventually emigrating to the US. In Hollywood he became a giant of the silver screen for his type-cast role as a seductive, dark, and handsome Don Juan type. Like many of the Latin lovers, rarely does he succeed in winning the leading woman's heart and securing commitment from her.

[9] Woll, *Latin Image*, 24–5.

[10] Reyes and Rubie, *Hispanics in Holywood*, xx.

[11] Black, *The Good Neighbor*.

Mexicans and Puerto Ricans was negligible. The sheer talent and charisma of Brazilian performers such as Carmen Miranda and Aurora Miranda and musicians such as Aloysio de Oliveira and Ari Barroso awakened North American producers to the vibrancy of Latin American popular culture and its potential impact on the US. In addition, producers sensed irresistible opportunities in the talent of performers, and soon began to utilize Brazilian idioms to shape Latin-ness. The vivacious, ever-smiling, and charming Carmen Miranda made a series of films, including *Down Argentine Way* (1940), *That Night in Rio* (1940), and *Copacabana* (1948), which pleased North American audiences but outraged Brazil and Argentina. Her sister Aurora followed in her path, with movies such as *The Phantom Lady* (1944), *Brazil* (1944), and *The Three Caballeros* (1945), a movie in which she made animation history. The Mirandas' screen characters were either temperamental spitfires or vivacious entertainers who spoke (or sang), often committing comedic cultural *faux pas* and dressed consistently in outrageous costumes often covered in fruit. Carmen Miranda embodied *Latinidad* and forged an association with Latin America as an agricultural land filled with shallow, inferior, albeit fun-loving people. Reactions from South of the border did not put a stop to these types of constructions.[12]

Miranda's performance, which represented the Brazilian experience, also came to represent 'Latin-ness'. With few forums for shaping their cultural products, Brazilians adapted to a US mainstream gaze that might have understood what 'Latin-ness' meant in broad terms but certainly did not take the time to distinguish between national cultures, as they would, for example, between Europeans. These stereotypes mesmerized many audiences, and have continued to dominate the press. On the other hand, some in the North American press approached the new *Latin* presence critically. On 28 January 1940, Lucile Neville sarcastically noted: 'Any story with a plot about revolutions, tamale workers or the love of a *marimba* player for a beauteous senorita sounds fine to producers just now.'[13]

The creation of a 'Latin type' in the US market meant that individual countries and cultures were not distinguishable, a blunder that was not without its benefits for Brazilians who could play a wider number of roles representing Mexicans, Argentines and other South American characters, and vice versa. In the Republic film *Brazil*, for example, Mexican actor Tito Guizar played the Brazilian lead Miguel, singing tunes in English and Portuguese composed by Ari Barroso. Guizar and Dolores del Río, also a Mexican, appeared in *Flying Down to Rio* (1933) to play Brazilian characters. Disney was not far behind with its creation of the parrot Joe Carioca and Uncle Samba, combining Mexican, Colombian, and Brazilian sounds into a potpourri called 'Latin Music'.

---

[12] Born in Lisbon, Carmen Miranda grew up in Rio where she became known as a singer and actress. She made her US debut in New York City in 1939 in a play called *The Streets of Paris*.

[13] 'Now That Hollywood Has Discovered Latin America, Anything Can Happen', *Washington Post*, 8 January 1940.

Despite the cultural homogenizing practices, Hollywood produced several savvy and engaging pictures on Latin American themes, although almost always Americanized or promoting American political values. William Dieterle's 1939 *Juárez*, in honor of Mexican independence hero Benito Juárez, is a case in point.[14] *Juárez* dramatizes the triumphant resistance of President Benito Juárez and his followers against the attempt by Louis Napoleon to install Maximillian von Habsburg as Emperor of Mexico while giving Juárez anachronistic democratic traits.

Other films continued in this tradition of focusing on fictional or real personalities of Hispanic background (i.e. proto-Latino) but presented by Hollywood stars. Both *The Mark of Zorro* (1940) and *Captain from Castile* (1947) featured the talent of leading man Tyrone Power. While Zorro (a character from Johnston McCulley's *The Curse of Capistrano*) fought for personal and community justice in *The Mark of Zorro*, in *Captain from Castile*, the male protagonist nobleman Pedro de Vargas escapes persecution in Spain and uses his sword to aid Cortez in his 'expedition'. The historical representation of Latin American personalities by American stars continued with Marlon Brando playing Emiliano Zapata in the 1952 production of *Viva Zapata!* Despite the social progress since the 1930s and the availability of a number of talented Latino actors from Latin America, Hollywood continues to rely on selected stars to represent Latin or Latin American personalities and to promote and sell their films. These 'stars' can now be drawn from the broader Latino populations but do not necessarily aim to match the actors or actresses to specific national types. Consider Antonio Banderas as Pancho Villa and Javier Bardem as Reinaldo Arenas, for example. This practice, which is not necessarily problematic for Latino communities, is consistent with industry trends in which 'starring' white performers represent a wide range of European and American white characters and where African Americans represent personalities from Africa, the US and the Caribbean.

After World War II and during the first two decades of the Cold War, the geopolitical relationship between the US and Latin America shifted. New images accompanied these changes. Latin American republics were potentially good neighbors but also potential enemies, but the growing presence of immigrants from Latin America would slowly begin to shape more nuanced Latino characters. Actors in Hollywood such as Ricardo Montalban and Ricardo Llamas continued the perfection of the Latin lover, but Latin husbands also emerged in the era that saw the consolidation of television as a mass media. Ricky Ricardo provided millions of Americans with laughs in the syndicated television situational comedy *I Love Lucy* in which he played actress Lucille Ball's husband. Desi Arnaz, a white Cuban who was married to Ball in real life,

---

[14] William Dieterle, *Juárez* (Warner Brothers, 1939). The film is sympathetic to the Mexican independence cause. Woll arrived at similar conclusion in *The Latin Image*, 60–62.

succeeded in areas where many Latinos had failed.[15] In 1940 he made his debut appearance as Manuelito, a Latin football player, in *Too Many Girls*, the film version of a George Morrison play. Arnaz's early career borrowed much from the earlier Latin stereotypes. He frequently played the fun-loving Latin male musician who often did not understand American customs. But both Arnaz and Ball utilized and manipulated existing comedic forums and perceptions about Latins to give simple lessons about culture, family life, love, and human relations. The *I Love Lucy* Show, which began as a television program in 1951, played off the relationship between a Latin immigrant (musician) in the US with a strong Spanish accent and a regular white American girl played by Lucille Ball. Arnaz also frequently used the show to parade his musical talent, and the show remains one of the most endearing sitcoms in US television history.[16]

Stereotypes continued on the silver screen and in television with the reprisal of the stereotypical greaser-like images from the 1930s and 1940s movies based on the *Cisco Kid*. The *Cisco Kid* came to television in 1950 and ran for five years. According to Luis Reyes and Peter Rubie, the television series based on the Cisco Kid portrayed a classic hero with added Latin gentility who became a popular icon for thousands of Americans. In a dialogue with the earlier film versions, Luis Valdez produced a more nuanced comedic *Cisco Kid* for television in 1994 with a Latino cast. The earlier Cisco Kid, who was an unscrupulous gun-toting 'Mexican or Mexican-American' in his first appearance in 1914, evolved first into a more digestible good bandit and then into the Quixote-like character of the 1940s in search of justice with his sidekick Pancho.[17]

## Civil rights and social change: growing pains in Latino film, 1950–1990

John Wayne's 1960 *The Alamo* followed many stereotypical depictions of the previous decades. Viewed today, the portrayal of Mexican soldiers is so one-dimensional that the film borders on unintentional comedy. The *Latina* stereotype of the World War II era musical was not yet laid to rest, although she had been transformed. In *The Alamo*, for example, the *Latina* is able to win over North American soldiers.[18] These gendered dynamics will shift in later films such as *Dance With Me?* (1998) with Puerto Rican singer Chayanne and the African-American performer Vanessa Williams.

In the post-civil rights era four major types of films about Latinos have emerged – (1) the social drama, often presented as theater or as musical, and focusing on Latino injustices; (2) tales of family life and struggles and joys, or

---

[15] Audrey Hingley, ' Life with Lucy', *Saturday Evening Post,* 266:2 (1994), 46–50. Wendy Smith, review of '*Desilu: The Story of Lucille Ball and Desi Arnaz*', *Variety* 350:3 (15 February 1993), 103. See also Desi Arnaz, *A Book* (New York: William Morrow and Co., 1976).
[16] Other Desi Arnaz movies include *Four Jacks and a Jill* (1941), *Bataan* (1943), and *The Escape Artist* (1982).
[17] Reyes and Rubie, *Hispanics in Hollywood*, 333–44.
[18] John Wayne and John Ford, *The Alamo* (1960).

as the film version of the *bildungsroman*; (3) urban tales of violence and survival; and (4) the biopic – although these four genres were not necessarily mutually exclusive. We will examine them in turn.

*Social dramas*
By the 1960s, Puerto Rican immigrants and their children born on the mainland had already begun to change demographics in some cities on the East Coast, particularly New York. Their demographic presence and diversity also affected Latino film production. In 1961, *West Side Story*[19] provided a musical portrayal of the difficulty that the Puerto Rican faced in the attempt or failure to assimilate into North American society. The debate on the level of assimilation and participation in the American dream, however, was overshadowed by the violence and ethnic tensions caused presumably by the new Caribbean presence. The conflict in *West Side Story* (1961) centers on inter-ethnic relations in the tradition of Romeo and Juliet: the inability of the Puerto Rican and white communities to allow the union of a Puerto Rican woman with a 'white' North American. Ironically, Tony, the modern Romeo, is of Italian ancestry and in former decades constituted part of the 'Latin imaginary'.

The *West Side Story* musical format succeeds as entertainment and as social commentary at the same time. It is an American story that highlighted the early problems of young people and delinquency in the inner cities but it also documents the frustrations of the Puerto Rican community in New York. The performance of the scene and song 'America', which showcased the singing and dancing talents of a group of Puerto Rican women led by Rita Moreno (Anita) against a number of Puerto Rican men headed by her boyfriend Bernando (played by the Greek-American actor George Chakiris), represents one of the most powerful renditions of the Latino immigrant conflict on the US mainland. The story of Puerto Rican immigrants to New York City is also at the center of Rick Carrier's 1962 *Strangers in the City*. While not as well known as *West Side Story*, Carrier's story deals candidly with economic marginalization through the struggles of two children fighting to survive in a hostile city.

The 1960s would bring a number of social melodramas that focused explicitly on prejudice, exclusion, and the inability to pursue the American dream. Many of these types of films, which first emerged in the 1930s, focused on social problems in North American society and were didactic in nature, according to Peter Roffman and Jim Purdy. Roffman and Purdy's study focuses on the films that feature Chicano issues in the 1950s such as *Bordertown* (John Sturges, 1950), *Salt of the Earth* (Sturges, 1950), *Right Cross* (Sturges, 1950), *My Man and I* (William Wellman, 1952), and *The Lawless* (Joseph Losey, 1952).[20]

Although Roffman and Purdy examine the first half of the twentieth century,

---

[19] Robert Wise and Jerome Robbins, *West Side Story* (1961).
[20] Peter Roffman and Jim Purdy, *The Hollywood Social Problem Film: Madness, Despair, and Politics from the Depression to the Fifties* (Bloomington: Indiana University Press, 1981).

social melodramas continued to constitute a mainstay of Hollywood lore and a forum through which Latino stories gained currency. Moreover, 'Latino' and 'Latin American' continued to be treated as one and the same, and one-dimensional Latin-ness remains situated south of the Rio Grande even in the work of astute North American filmmakers. Orson Welles's *A Touch of Evil* (1958), for example, which occurs in a Mexican border town, is full of 'gringo' and Mexican stereotypes but has very little to do with exploring Mexican culture or providing a Mexican worldview.

After the Cuban Revolution of 1959, the fear that Latin America was a breeding ground for revolutionaries surfaced in comedies, features, and documentaries. Che Guevara, Fidel Castro's partner in the Sierra Madre Mountains of Oriente, Cuba, became a universal cult hero, for example. Feature films such as *Che* (1969), *Duck You Sucker* (1972), *Viva Max* (1970), and *Bananas* (1979) emphasize the rebel image, sometimes in comedic ways, adding another layer of stereotypes, although not necessarily replacing previous ones. The rising flow of immigrants from Latin America, which began in the 1960s and continued to the end of the century, would have an impact on film production.

The 1969 *Popi*, directed by Arthur Hiller, is an unappreciated film that many Latino filmographies ignore. Graced by the talents of Alan Arkin and Rita Moreno and a host of others, *Popi*, which comes from the English spelling and pronunciation of 'papi' (or father), centers on the hardships of a Puerto Rican father (Abraham) and his two young sons in Spanish Harlem. Although the film was billed as a comedy, its humor is intimately interconnected with serious urban problems of poverty, child labor, parental inadequacy, and crime. At the same time, the film alludes to the differences among Latinos, particularly Puerto Ricans and Cubans, and the unequal treatment the latter receive based on US foreign policies. Abraham concocts a plan to send his poor Puerto Rican sons out to sea in the hope that they will be rescued and treated as Cuban refugees, and eventually be adopted by a rich family.[21]

The social and civil rights movements of the 1960s, including the Black civil rights movement and the Chicano movement, were turning points in North American consciousness and had a discernible impact on the film industry. Emerging Latino writers and their stories provided important raw material for screenwriters, directors, and actors in shaping contemporary Latino cinematographic texts in the 1980s and 1990s. Finally, Latino directors would emerge on the cultural landscape with a multiplicity of film genres. Nuanced film representations often appeared side by side with familiar stereotypes and static representations. Moreover, film continued to explore the ambiguous place of Latinos in US society as it drew on and conflated Latinos with Latin Americans in general. At the same time the fluidity or transnational identities and liminality of the immigrant experience have received more sophisticated treatments. Leon Ichaso's 1979 *El Super* provides a case in point.

---

[21] Arthur Hiller, *Popi* (1969).

*Family portraits: Exile, dislocation, and celebration*

*El Super* is the story of Roberto, a superintendent, who dreams of his tropical island homeland and refuses to assimilate into the new culture. Ichaso's film provided a deeply moving portrait of an immigrant's struggle with his new cultural reality, a theme that not only reverberates in the literary texts explored in this volume but also in other films about immigrants.

The 1980s and 1990s yielded a host of films on exile, cultural adjustments and life in the US from a number of cultural perspectives and genres. *La Cuidad (The City)*, 1998, directed by David Riker in collaboration with the New York Latino immigrant communities, tells the story of illegal immigrants from Latin America in New York. Four stories explore the diverse but similar struggles of homelessness, poverty, and attempts at forming community. Angel Muñiz's comedic *Nueba Yol* (1995) tells the not so funny story of Balbuena, as a modern Dominican immigrant *pícaro* in a strange land, while *Raising Victor Vargas* (2002) is as much a coming-of-age story as it is of Latino immigrants' generational conflicts and expectations in New York.

Gregory Nava's *El Norte* (1983) and Robert Redford's *The Milagro Beanfield War* (1988) are perhaps the two most critically acclaimed Latino films of the 1980s. *El Norte* provides more bitter political commentary on the Latino experience in the US by focusing on the life of two poor Guatemalans. At the beginning of the film, viewers are confronted with myths and perceptions of the US before the two protagonists Pedro and Josefita cross the border. Josefita reports that, 'There (in the United States) even the poorest people have toilets exactly like Don Rodrigo. You flush it and everything vanishes. You can really pee with style there.' Enrique adds, 'There's a lot of money there. Look at everyone who has friends or family who has gone. All of them say things and you can see on TV how it is.'[22] The film documents the transformation of an awestruck 'Latin American' into a poor unknowing 'Latino' who is exploited at every turn.

In many ways, the 1980s represented a coming of age for Latino filmmakers one generation after the civil changes of the 1960s and a decade after terms such as 'Hispanic' and 'Latino' had entered the mainstream vernacular. The 1970 Census was the first one that asked specifically whether a person was of 'Spanish/Hispanic origin', and listed six possible responses: 'Mexican', 'Puerto Rican', 'Cuban', 'Central or South American', 'Other Spanish' and, 'No. None of these'. More nuanced questions appeared in the 1980 Census, although no range of questions will ever be able to account for the multiple ways that Latinos identity themselves.

Directors such as Greg Nava would go on to produce a number of films that resonated deeply with Latino audiences, including *My Family, Mi Familia* (1995) and *Selena* (1996). According to Nancy de los Santos, Nava's work is a labor of love for the diverse Latino community. He portrays grown men,

---

[22] The original text is in Spanish with English subtitles. These translations, however, are the author's.

working-class men, white-collar men, and little boys and wives, sisters, and families in all their complexities.[23] Indeed, in *Mi Familia* Nava serves up a complex family and community story over three generations utilizing a host of talented Latino actors, including Jimmy Smits, Esai Morales, Eduardo López Rojas, Jenny Gago, Elpidia Carrillo, Lupe Ontiveros, Jacob Vargas, Jennifer Lopez, Maria Canals, Leon Singer, Michael D. Lorenzo, Jonathan Hernandez, Constance Maria, and Edward James Olmos.

Issues of civil rights, marginalization, and justice continue in a number of other films. The 1982 made-for-TV movie *The Ballad of Gregorio Cortez* is one such example. Based on a novel by Américo Paredes and directed by Robert M. Young, *The Ballad* takes place in Gonzalez, Texas in 1901. Gregorio Cortez is a Mexican on the run after being 'involved' in three different murders. He does not speak English and comes face to face with prejudice in society and racism in the justice system in the US. The film presents a nuanced Cortez who is not necessarily innocent. Luis Valez's groundbreaking *Zoot Suit* (1981) focuses on similar themes and was released one year earlier. Valdez's film is essentially a musical film adaptation of his original play, and included various theatrical shots so that the audience would understand the roots of his film as a theatrical production. *Zoot Suit* follows the story of four men (three of them Chicano), who were put on trial for murder at the height of the racial tensions and rioting that plagued Los Angeles during World War II. *Zoot Suit* documented and in some instances glorified various aspects of Chicano culture while highlighting the injustices that Chicanos faced in a racist justice system. Valdez is careful to avoid one-dimensional views of Chicano culture. He avoids clichés by presenting rich and conflicted characters who demonstrate generational conflicts within the Chicano family, *machismo*, and issues of friendship, class and inter-ethnic romance – themes he had already developed in the Chicano theater movement at whose center was El Teatro Campesino.

Subtle and literary representations in films continued into the 1990s with the emergence of other Latino directors, although many of them were first contracted to make films for television. Severo Pérez's adaptation of Tomás Rivera's *And the Earth Did Not Swallow Him* (1995) recounts the story of Marcos, a Mexican-American boy living in Texas in the early 1950s and presents a complicated American family portrait: migrant farm workers, sibling rivalry, child labor, and a plethora of other social issues. Directors such as Pérez portray Latino characters who, despite often desperate situations, rise above their difficulties and celebrate their lives through music and culture. Music production and cultural celebration have always constituted important forums for affirmation and self-acceptance. They have also provided mechanisms through which Latinos engage with the broader American society. We see this in other stories such as *La Bamba* (also by writer-director, Luis Valdez, 1986) and *Crossover Dreams* (Leon

---

[23] Nancy de los Santos, ' "The Conversation" Tribute to director Gregory Nava', 14 February 1999 (article was originally published in the 1999 festival souvenir program of the San Diego Latino Film Festival) http://www.sdlatinofilm.com/trends17.html.

Ichaso, 1985). The former tells the story of Ritchie Valens's rise to rock 'n' roll stardom, while the latter chronicles the ways of a New York salsa singer who wants to cross over into pop. *The Mambo Kings* (1992) also celebrates the contribution of Latino musicians while showcasing diverse Latino icons such as Celia Cruz and Tito Puente.

*Urban (and borderland) tales of assimilation and exclusion*
The diversity of Latino contemporary film is astounding given its one-dimensional and limited beginnings. Yet it is hardly reflective of the actual diversity of the Latino community. Films such as *Born in East L.A.* (1987) have succeeded in highlighting the North American nature of the Latino experience as distinct from the Latin American. Writer/director Cheech Marin here created a story in which the main character is accidentally deported to Mexico without official identification. He does not speak Spanish but neither can he convince US authorities to let him return home. This situation highlights the Latino's comedic/tragic liminal situation even when individuals insist on their American-ness. US-born or -raised directors such as Marin have played important roles in illustrating the geographical rather than linguistic definitions of Latino-ness. While some Latin American immigrants readily adopt the *Latino* label over time, others continue to hold on to defining themselves along national lines. Still others utilize a number of labels depending on context. The US Department of Census has not been able to address these nuances. This is particularly true for the growing number of Brazilians who may or may not see themselves as Latinos, and certainly do not view themselves as 'Hispanic'.

Despite its comedic value, Marin's character's experience in urban North America portrays social and economic problems that other directors have treated in other films. Ramón 'Ray' Meléndez's *Stand and Deliver* (1987) is an inspirational story of triumph against the odds. Jaime Escalante, a math teacher at East Los Angeles' Garfield High School, refuses to allow the students in his class to fail or meet the low levels in math that many expect of them. When his dedication and their hard work pay off, school officials and national authorities raise suspicions about cheating, diminishing their hard work. Based on a true story, *Stand and Deliver* is a part of a tradition that explores racism and bigotry but ultimately celebrates community spirit and Latino success. Other filmic depictions have been more sobering, including those that treat urban violence such as *Colors* (1988) by Dennis Hopper; or witty, as in the 1991 *Hanging With the Homeboys*, about two African Americans and two Latinos in the South Bronx. Ivan Dariel Ortiz's *Heroes from Another Country* (*Héroes de otra patria*, 1998) focuses on two Puerto Rican soldiers in the Vietnam War, while the stories of family life and generational conflict in the Dominican community take center stage in *Manito* (2002). Other urban tales include *Smile Now, Cry Later* (2001), a story of two brothers trying to survive in the urban streets of their *barrio*, and *Undefeated* (2003), John Leguizamo's story of a Latino boxer in Queens.

Mexican director Sergio Arau's satire *A Day Without a Mexican (Día Sin Mexicanos)* (2004) highlights US economic dependency on Latinos, particularly in California. Stories of Latinos on the East or West Coasts figure prominently in the cinematographic imagination, as compared to experiences in the South or the Midwest. Worthy of mention are the works of independent filmmaker Robert Rodríguez, who ironically is one of the more important Latino directors in Hollywood. His action films, such as *El Mariachi* (1992) and *Desperado* (1995), center on the life and troubles of a mariachi singer, although the focus is clearly on action, suspense, and entertainment consistent with his other Hollywood films.

Stories that feature Latinas have figured prominently in Latino films whether as a part of the main drama or in works that highlight the female characters, as in the work of Gregory Nava, Mira Nair, Natatcha Estebanez, and Patricia Cardozo. Nair's *The Perez Family* (1995) centers on Dottie Perez, who has left Cuba for the US. Based on the novel by Christine Bell, the film's light tone stems from the mistakes of an overworked immigration officer, dating it as a pre-September 2001 comedy-drama. Estebanez's *The Blue Diner* tells the story of a Puerto Rican mother and daughter living in Boston and their ordeal as Elena, the daughter, becomes aphasiac and mysteriously loses her ability to speak Spanish in a film that the director has called 'truly bilingual'. Estebanez, nonetheless, sees her work as a human story, an attempt not to recreate stories about Latinos as boxers, or with guns and drugs, but simply as she put it: 'What is special about the film is the story, precisely. It's an attempt to say, "Hey, we are just like you guys".'[24] *Real Women Have Curves*, based on a book by Josefina López, and directed by Patricia Cardozo, focuses more specifically on Latina women and the female body by examining the choices and options of 18-year-old Mexican-American Ana one summer.

Latino filmmakers, like their literary counterparts, remain interested in issues from Latin America and the Iberian peninsula and in recreating them in English for a North American and international market. These 'translations' or reinterpretations from within the US may or may not be well received by national audiences, particularly if they deal with critical issues that offend national sentiments or go against prevailing political currents. Films about Cubans and Cuban-Americans such as *Azúcar Amarga* (1996), for example, have yet to be released in Cuba, just as *Romero* (1989), about the assassinated Salvador archbishop, was not released in El Salvador until the end of the civil war. Although some cinematographic representations of literary texts or of Latin American issues or of historical personalities, such as *Frida* (2002), have benefited from the work and views of Latino authors, this has not necessarily resulted in successful film adaptations.

In many cases talented white, African American, and Latino actors and actresses, producers, and filmmakers have successfully told Latin American stories in English, capturing the subtleties and 'truths' of given realities. William Hurt, Raul Julia, and Sonia Braga successfully brought Argentine author Manuel Puig's *Kiss of the Spider Woman* to life for Hollywood under the artful

---

[24] http://www.identitytheory.com/ people/birnbaum16.html [Accessed 16 June 2005].

direction of Hector Babenco in 1985. The same was not true of the 1994 production of Isabel Allende's acclaimed book *House of the Spirits* or for the film adaptation of Julia Alvarez's *In the Time of the Butterflies*. Although both productions relied on well-known talented actors living in the US, they suffered from a number of critical mistakes in casting, editing, and direction that had little to do with the original texts.

Two Brazilian movies are worthy of note. *A Fronteira* (2004), written and directed by Roberto Carminati, is the only feature film to date that discusses the crossing of Brazilians into the US through the Mexican border. The film looks at immigration through the lens of two Brazilian families who put everything at risk to enter the US in pursuit of a better life, and the unexpected obstacles and challenges they face. In addition to the discrimination and exploitation they experience once they arrive, the Brazilians miss their homeland in ways they had never expected. *A Fronteria* dialogues most obviously with *El Norte* but also with a number of Brazilian and *Brazuca* literary texts discussed by Antonio Luciano de Andrade Tosta in this volume. It is also a precursor of the 2005 Globo International Brazilian *novela America*.

The same might also be said of *Dois Perdidos Numa Noite Suja* by Brazilian director José Joffily. Joffily places the 1970s play by Brazilian playwright Plínio Marcos into a New York setting and provides a dark and tragic tale of two Brazilians in New York. The two main characters, Paco and Tonho, are illegal Brazilian immigrants in the city. While Tonho dreams of being successful and attaining the illusory American dream, he misses his family and Brazil. Paco, a female rapper and performer, is more indifferent about Brazil but also dreams about success there: for her it should be in the music industry. The film is about the relationship of the two as illegal immigrants, their life in the New York underground and about what they have to do to survive.

A number of Brazilian filmmakers are based in New York, including Helena Soldberg, who directed the docudrama about Carmen Miranda, *Bananas is My Business* (1996). Other filmmakers based in New York such as Karim Ainouz (*Madame Satã*, 2002) continue to make films on themes in Brazil. Well-known filmmakers, such as Walter Salles, who lead transnational lives in Brazil and the US, have been able to navigate both systems in interesting ways. Salles's *Motorcycle Diaries* (2004), about the early years of Ernesto 'Che' Guevara and his travels with his friend Alberto Granado before his time as a revolutionary leader in Cuba, was produced by Robert Redford. In many ways, given the privileges and access to media and markets that Latinos and Latin Americans working in the US have, they are in better positions to make regional connections that promote Pan-Latino or Latin American connections than their counterparts living in Latin America or in local communities who struggle with local issues.

Films such as *The Motorcycle Diaries,* produced in the US in Spanish for the overseas and national market, are indicative of the changes in the US market and the widespread understanding of Spanish as a first or second language. Similar dynamics are at play in *Maria Full of Grace* (2004). In reality, movies have been made in Spanish in the US for decades, although marketing to the national markets is a recent phenomenon. One of the pioneers in this endeavor has been John Sayles, with movies such as *Lone Star* (1996) and *Men with Guns* (1997). In addition, Mexicans have produced a number of 'Border films' in Spanish (such as Alejandro Springall's *Santitos*) that treat if they do not specifically target issues related to the border.

*Latino hagiography: the biopic*
While screen writers, actors, and filmmakers such as Salles have played an important part in denouncing injustice on the one hand and in portraying the complexities of the multinational, multicultural Latin American and Latino communities on the other, films have also celebrated the community's heroes and icons. Latino community leaders, activists, musicians, artists, and other cultural producers have been memorialized in a number of cinematographic representations, not always without controversy. The best of these biopics, like other films about Latinos, have not necessarily only come from Latino directors but from directors with strong and meaningful ties with the Latino communities. A number of film biographies have treated their subject critically such as *The Wonderful Horrible Life of Leni Riefenstahl* (1995) or provocatively such as *Love Is the Devil: Study for a Portrait of Francis Bacon* (1998), but many more are hagiographies. This is especially true for communities such as the Latino or African-American that do not necessarily have extensive filmographies with which they may dialogue.

Isaac Artenstein's *Break of Dawn* (1988), based on the life of Pedro J. Gonzalez, highlights the importance of activists who have struggled on behalf of Latino communities. Gonzalez championed the cause of Mexican-Americans in California during the Depression years and worked for the reform of the California penal system. Although the film suffers from budget constraints, viewers receive an intimate interpretation of the Mexican radio performer and activist and his role in opposing the mass deportation of Mexicans and Mexican-Americans between the wars.

*Selena: The Movie* retells the story of the rise and tragic death of Selena Quintanilla-Pérez, who was quickly becoming one of the most popular Latina singers of the 1990s. This is a homage to the memory of a young woman who so many fans clearly loved. As a biopic Gava's film falls clearly within the hagiography camp and does not attempt to critically address issues of class and gender or the entertainment business in general. Nor does the film give us a great deal of insight into Selena's private life. The film begins in Texas, where Abraham Quintanilla's dreams of singing English-language pop are dashed by racist white Americans and intolerant Mexican-Americans. Later, we understand how the immigrant father, like so many fathers before him, deposits his dreams in the talents of his ten-year-old daughter.

Selena's life illustrates the continuing tensions between 'American culture' and English, and her Latino identity. The film shows Selena's rebellious attitude towards Spanish and her pop cultural influences when she was a teenager. 'I don't want to learn to sing in Spanish! I don't even like Spanish music. I like Donna Summers,' she tells her father. With his response, her father articulates the Latino ambivalence and duality present in so many films: 'The Americans jump all over us because we don't speak perfect English, and then the Mexicans jump all over us because we don't speak perfect Spanish.' Interestingly, her father chooses the term 'Americans', rather than whites or Anglos, a rhetoric that situates him and his family as outsiders even though they are American citizens. In the end, the film shows how Selena successfully navigated the various worlds that she inhabited. The biopic helped spread the news about Selena's life and death, but it also catapulted Jennifer Lopez into national attention. While some Mexican-Americans protested that a Puerto Rican actress and singer was playing a Mexican-American, Hollywood was following a tradition that audiences, including Latinos, had accepted for decades.

On the East Coast, two film biographies illustrate how cultural icons need not necessarily be models seen in a positive light, although Latinos, like other ethnic groups in the West, tend to idolize their heroes after they have died. Film biographies can also simply give us windows on the lives or the art of Latinos whether they are immigrants such as Reinaldo Arenas or native-born such as the Nuyorican Miguel Piñero. Arenas grew up poor in the eastern Cuban province of Holguín, and he supported Fidel Castro and the guerillas in the Sierra Maestra mountains against the dictatorship of Fulgencio Batista (1952–1959). After the triumph of the Revolution, Arenas moved to Havana and would soon afterwards begin to have serious problems with Cuban censorship and the military revolutionary ideals, after which his sexuality became a major problem for the Revolution. Arenas eventually left the island for the US in the *Mariel* boatlifts of 1980. He moved briefly to Miami before settling in New York, where he continued to write until his death from AIDS (although it was officially called a suicide) in 1990.

With the completion of *Before Night Falls* (2000), director Julian Schnabel created an ambitious homage to this singular Cuban writer. The film relies on many of Arenas's writings, including his memoir (1993), from which the film takes its title. It depicts many human rights violations in Cuba and his life as a writer in New York before his death. As with Selena, who was born in the US, Arenas experiences the duality of the immigrant and the exile, longing for Cuba and happy to have the freedom to long. The film ends with a Spanish and English version of the poem 'Yo soy', which emphasizes Arenas's belief that he would forever be that child 'of always', located far from American shores.

Feelings of alienation also abound in the creative world of Miguel Piñero presented in another Ichaso production, *Piñero* (2001). Piñero became many things to many people, and the director exploits this ambiguity on many levels. He is victim of the system, a junkie, an artist and poet, an adventurer, a bad boy, a bisexual and deeply committed to his community. He was also involved in the founding moments of one of the most important Nuyorican cultural forums, the Nuyorican Poets Café. Ichaso provides an intimate portrait of his protagonist and his film seems like a series of vignettes woven together. He neither condemns nor praises Piñero's lifestyle or his habits but he downplays his bisexuality and the fact that he died of AIDS.

*Piñero* may not be as deeply fleshed out as it might have been, but this is a shortcoming of many biopics of artists including Selena and Arenas. Piñero's visit to Puerto Rico serves to highlight his biculturalism, his ambivalence about his identity and the way in which he utilized two languanges, three issues that have been constant in films about Latinos since the 1930s. A number of other biographical films on Latinos in the US made for television might be added here. Some are excellent, others not so successful. The biopic, like the social drama and urban tales, will continue to expand Latino consciousness in the years to come.

## Conclusion

Latino films have evolved in positive ways since the decades of limited access and stereotypes. Latino literary voices have provided materials for more nuanced scripts, and culturally astute non-Latino producers, filmmakers, and actors have dialogued with the Latino community in many ways that would have been impossible prior to the 1960s. These changes reflect social and political advances in North American societies as a whole. At the same time historical stereotypes continue to appear in films although they are also issues of contention, manipulated by Latinos and others. As Latinos continue to ask 'who are we?', multiple answers will emerge. 'Latin-ness', like 'American-ness', cannot cease to be a contested identity.

If we object to Carmen Miranda representing a Latina in her 1940s fashion, do we also reject Sonia Braga or Jennifer Lopez representing a Mexican-American? What do those rejections say about Latino expectations? Like the US population in general, the Latino population is a diverse one, and constructing images to represent it is no easy feat. Migration continues to engender a complex status that has transformed Latino demographics, forging class, racial, and generational distinctions among national communities (Cubans who arrived in the 1960s and 1970s, Cubans from the *Mariel* boatlifts, Cubans arriving in the 1990s and second-generation Cuban-Americans, for example). To bring these communities under one umbrella for a celebration of culture does not necessarily mean that Latinos unite across national origin lines to secure collective political programs that demand more space, resources, and attention. We must ask the historical questions of the film adaptation of Isabel Allende's *House of the Spirits*. Is it really, as one critic said, 'the 90s version of Hollywood projecting false Latinos', or is it more in the spirit of one Colombian friend's assertion: 'I don't care who's in it. It's a Latino story.'

## Works Cited

Adorno, Theodor. *The Culture Industry.* London: Routledge, 1991.
Arenas, Reinaldo. *Before Night Falls: A Memoir,* trans. Dolores M. Koch. New York: Penguin Books, 1993.
Arnaz, Desi. *A Book.* New York: William Morrow & Co., 1976.
Black, George. *The Good Neighbor: How the United States Wrote the History of Central America and the Caribbean.* New York: Pantheon Books, 1998.
Davis, Darién. 'The Brazilian-Americans: Demography and Identity of an Emerging Latino Minority', *The Latino Review of Books,* 3:1–2 (1997), 8–15.
De los Santos, Nancy. ' "The Conversation": Tribute to director Gregory Nava', 14 February 1999. http://www.sdlatinofilm.com/trends17.html. [Accessed 16 June 2005.]
Hingley, Audrey. 'Life with Lucy', *Saturday Evening* Post, 266:2 (1994), 46–50.
Neville, Lucile. 'Now That Hollywood Has Discovered Latin America, Anything Can Happen', *Washington Post,* 28 January 1940.
Reyes, Luis, and Peter Rubie. *Hispanics in Hollywood: An Encyclopedia of Film and Television.* New York: Garland Publishers, 1994.
Roffman, Peter, and Jim Purdy. *The Hollywood Social Problem Film: Madness, Despair, and Politics from the Depression to the Fifties.* Bloomington: Indiana University Press, 1981.
Sklar, Robert. *Movie-Made America: A Social History of American Film.* New York: Random House, 1975.
Smith, Wendy. 'Review of *Desilu: The Story of Lucille Ball and Desi Arnaz* by Coyne Steven Sanders and Tom Gilbert', *Variety,* 350:3 (1999).
Sohat, Ella. 'Gender and Culture of Empire: Towards a Feminist Ethnography of the Cinema', *Quarterly Review of Film and Video,* 13:1–3 (1999), 45–85.
Woll, Allen. *The Latin Image in American Film.* Los Angeles: UCLA Latin American Center Publication, 1980.

# FURTHER READING

## Books and essays on US Latino literatures

Abalos, David T. *Latinos in the United States*. Notre Dame, Indiana: University of Notre Dame Press, 1986.
Aparicio, Frances R. 'La vida es un spanglish disparatero: Bilingualism in Nuyorican Poetry', in *European Perspectives on Hispanic Literature of the United States*. Genvieve Fabre (ed.), Houston: Arte Público Press, 1988, 147–60.
Aparicio, Frances R., and Susana Chávez-Silverman (eds.). *Tropicalizations. Transcultural Representations of Latinidad*. Hanover and London: Dartmouth College, 1997.
Barradas, Efraín. 'Puerto Rico acá, Puerto Rico allá!' *Revista Chicano-Riqueña*, 7:4 (1979), 46–56.
Benmayor, Rina. 'Getting Home Alive: The Politics of Multiple Identity'. *Americas Review*, 17:3–4 (1989), 107–17.
Castillo, Ana. *Massacre of the Dreamers: Essays on Xicanisma*. Albuquerque: University of New Mexico Press, 1994.
Darder, Antonia, and Rodolfo D. Torres (eds.). *The Latino Studies Reader. Culture, Economy & Society*. Malden, Massachusetts and Oxford: Blackwell Publishers, 1998.
Davis-Undiano, Robert. 'The Emergence of New World Studies: Anaya, Aztlan, and the New Chicana'. *Genre: Forms of Discourse and Culture*, 32:1–2 (1999), 115–40.
Habell-Pallan, Michelle, and Mary Romero (eds.). *Latino/a Popular Culture*. New York: New York University Press, 2002.
Heyck, Denis Lynn Daly (ed.). *Barrios and Borderlands: Cultures of Latinos and Latinas in the United States*. London: Routledge, 1994.
Hiraldo, Carlos. *Segregated Miscegenation: On the Treatment of Racial Hybridity in the US and Latin American Literary Traditions*. New York: Routledge, 2002.
Monge Rafuls, Pedro R. (ed.). *Lo que no se ha dicho*. New York: OLLANTAY Center for the Arts, 1994.
Muñoz, José Esteban. *Disidentifications: Queers of Color and the Performance of Politics*. Minneapolis: University of Minnesota Press, 1999.
Ortega, Julio (ed.). 'La otra orilla del español: las literaturas hispánicas de los Estados Unidos'. *Insula*, 667–68 (2002), 13–16.
Quintana, Alvina E. (ed.). *Reading US Latina Writers. Remapping American Literature*. New York: Palgrave Macmillan, 2003.
Sánchez, Marta E. *Contemporary Chicana Poetry. A Critical Approach to an Emerging Literature*. Berkeley: University of California Press, 1985.
Singh, Amritjit, Joseph Skerrett, and Robert Hogan (eds.). *Memory and Cultural*

*Politics: New Approaches to American Ethnic Literatures.* Boston: Northeastern University Press, 1996.
Skar, Stacey Alba D. *Voces híbridas: la literatura de chicanas y latinas en Estados Unidos.* Santiago de Chile: RIL Editores, 2001.
Taylor, Diana, and Juan Villegas (eds.). *Negotiating Performance: Gender, Sexuality and Theatricality in Latin/o America.* Durham, North Carolina: Duke University Press, 1994.
Vázquez, Francisco H., and Rodolfo D. Torres. *Latino/a Thought: Culture, Politics, and Society.* Lanham, Maryland: Rowman & Littlefield, 2003.

## Anthologies of US Latino literatures

Aguenbaum, Harold, and Margarite Fernández Olmos (eds.). *The Latino Reader: An American Literary Tradition from 1542 to the Present.* Boston: Houghton Mifflin, 1997.
Aguenbaum, Harold, and Ilan Stavans (eds.). *Growing Up Latino: Memoirs and Stories.* Boston: Houghton Mifflin, 1993.
Algarín, Miguel, and Bob Holman (eds.). *Aloud: Voices from the Nuyorican Poets Café.* New York: Henry Holt, 1994.
Carlson, Lori M. (ed.). *Cool Salsa: Bilingual Poems on Growing Up Latino in the United States.* Introduction by Oscar Hijuelos. New York: Henry Holt, 1994.
Castillo-Speed, Lillian (ed.). *Latina: Women's Voices From the Borderlands.* New York: Touchstone / Simon & Schuster, 1995.
Caulfield, Carlota (ed.). *Voces viajeras. Poetisas cubanas de hoy.* Madrid: Ediciones Torremozas, 2002.
Caulfield, Carlota (ed.). *Web of Memories. Interviews with Five Cuban Women Poets.* Hot Springs, Arkansas: Eboli Poetry Series, 1997.
Cortina, Rodolfo (ed.). *Hispanic American Literature: An Anthology.* Lincolnwood, Illinois: NTC Publishing, 1997.
De Jesús, Joy L. (ed.). *Growing Up Puerto Rican: An Anthology.* New York: William Morrow, 1997.
Fernández, Roberta (ed.). *In Other Words: Literature by Latinas of the United States.* Houston: Arte Público Press, 1994.
Flores, Juan, and Mayra Santos-Febres (eds.). *Open Mic /Micrófono abierto. Nuevas Literaturas Puerto /Neorriqueñas / New Puerto / Nuyor Rican Literatures. Hostos Review / Revista Hostosiana,* 2, 2005.
González, Ray (ed.). *After Aztlan: Latino Poets of the Nineties.* Boston: David R. Godine, 1992.
González, Ray (ed.) *Mirrors Beneath the Earth: Short Fiction by Chicano Writers.* Willimantic, Connecticut: Curbstone Press, 1992.
González, Ray (ed.). *Without Discovery: A Native Response to Columbus.* Seattle: Broken Moon Press, 1992.
González, Ray (ed.) *Currents From the Dancing River: Contemporary Latino Fiction, Nonfiction, and Poetry.* New York: Harcourt Brace, 1994.
Hernández Cruz, Victor, Leroy V. Quintana, and Virgil Suárez (eds.). *Paper Dance: 55 Latino Poets.* New York: Persea, 1994.
Hernández-Gutiérrez, Manuel de Jesús, and David William Foster (eds.). *Literatura Chicana, 1965–1995: An Anthology in Spanish, English, and Caló.* New York: Garland, 1997.

Heyck, Denis Lynn Daly (ed.). *Barrios and Borderlands: Cultures of Latinos and Latinas in the United States.* New York: Routledge, 1994.
Hospital, Carolina (ed.). *Cuban American Writers: Los Atrevidos.* Princeton: Ediciones Ellas / Linden Lane, 1988.
Hospital, Carolina, and Jorge Cantera (eds.). *A Century of Cuban Writers in Florida: Selected Prose & Poetry.* Sarasota, Florida: Pineapple Press, 1996.
Hoyos, Angela de (ed.). *Mujeres Grandes. Anthology One.* San Antonio: M & A Editions, 1993.
Hoyos, Angela de (ed.). *Mujeres Grandes. Anthology Two.* San Antonio: M & A Editions, 1995.
Johnson, Rob (ed.). *Fantasmas: Supernatural Stories by Mexican-American Writers.* Introduction by Kathleen Alcalá. Tempe, Arizona: Bilingual Press / Editorial Bilingüe, 2001.
Kanellos, Nicolás (ed.). *Short Fiction by Hispanic Writers of the United States.* Houston: Arte Público Press, 1993.
Kanellos, Nicolás (ed.). *The Hispanic Literary Companion.* Detroit, New York, and London: Visible Ink, 1997.
Lázaro, Felipe (ed.). *Poetas cubanas en Nueva York / Cuban Women Poets in New York.* Madrid: Betania, 1991.
López, Tiffany Ann (ed.). *Growing Up Chicana/o: An Anthology.* New York: William Morrow, 1993.
Luis, William (ed.). 'Antología: Poesía hispano-caribeña escrita en los Estados Unidos'. *Boletín de la Fundación Federico García Lorca*, 9:18 (1995), 17–93.
Martín-Rodríguez, Manuel M. (ed.). *La voz urgente: antología de literatura chicana en español.* Madrid: Editorial Fundamentos, 1995.
Milligan, Bryce (ed.). *Corazón del Norte: A Selection of North Texas Latino Writing.* San Antonio: Wings Press, 1996.
Milligan, Bryce, Mary Guerrero Milligan, and Angela de Hoyos (eds.). *Daughters of the Fifth Sun: A Collection of Latina Fiction and Poetry.* New York: Riverhead Books, 1995.
Milligan, Bryce, Mary Guerrero Milligan, and Angela de Hoyos (eds.). *Floricanto Sí!: A Collection of Latina Poetry.* New York: Penguin Books, 1998.
Noriega, Chon A. (ed.). *The Chicano Studies Reader: an Anthology of Aztlán, 1970–2000.* Los Angeles: UCLA Chicano Studies Research Center Publications, 2001.
Olivares, Julián, and Evangelina Vigil Piñon (eds.). *Decade II: A Twentieth Anniversary Anthology.* Houston: Arte Público Press, 1993.
Poey, Delia, and Virgil Suárez (eds.). *Iguana Dreams: New Latino Fiction.* New York: Harper Perennial, 1992.
Poey, Delia, and Virgil Suárez (eds.). *Little Havana Blues: A Cuban-American Literature Anthology.* Houston: Arte Público Press, 1996.
Rebolledo, Tey Diana, and Eliana S. Rivero (eds.). *Infinite Divisions: An Anthology of Chicana Literature.* Tucson: University of Arizona Press, 1993.
Santiago, Robert (ed.). *Boricuas: Influential Puerto Rican Writings – An Anthology.* New York: One World / Ballantine, 1995.
Santiváñez, Roger (ed.). 'Destellos Digitales. Escritores peruanos en los Estados Unidos 1970–2005', *Hostos Review / Revista Hostosiana* 3, 2005.
Simmen, Edward (ed.). *North of the Rio Grande: The Mexican-American Experience in Short Fiction.* New York: Penguin, 1992.

Soto, Gary (ed.). *Pieces of the Heart: New Chicano Fiction*. San Francisco: Chronicle Books, 1993.
Stavans, Ilan (ed.). *New World: Young Latino Writers*. New York: Delta / Dell, 1997.
Tashlik, Phyllis (ed.). *Hispanic, Female and Young: An Anthology*. Houston: Arte Público Press, 1994.
Tatum, Charles M. (ed.). *New Chicana / Chicano Writing.* Tucson: University of Arizona Press, 1993.

# INDEX

Acosta, Iván, 80
Acosta, Oscar 'Zeta', 23
Adorno, Rolena, 168
Adorno, Theodor, 208
Agosín, Marjorie, 178, 180–181
Ainouz, Karim, 222
Alabau, Magali, 91, 197–198
Albues, Tereza, 145
Alcántara Almánzar, José, 102
Alfonso, Paco, 89
Allende, Isabel, 222, 225
Allende, Salvador, 179, 183
Alonso, Dora, 90
Alurista, *see* Urista, Alberto Baltasar
Alvarez, Julia, 101–110, 201–202, 222
Álvarez Borland, Isabel, 69–70, 73–74, 78
Amoretti, María, 127–128, 130
Anaya, Rudolfo, 21–22, 121
Anzaldúa, Gloria, 28, 45, 191
Aranda, José F., 30
Arau, Sergio, 220
Arce, Manuel, 80
Arenas, Reinaldo, 69–70, 72, 74, 214, 224, 225
Arkin, Alan, 217
Arlt, Roberto, 170
Arnaz, Desi, 214–215
Artenstein, Isaac, 223
Athas, Nick, 196
Athayde, Roberto, 145

Babenco, Héctor, 222
Ballagas, Emilio, 96
Banderas, Antonio, 214
Barbosa, Livia Neves de H., 146, 154
Barquet, Jesús J., 74, 201
Barradas, Efraín, 52–53, 192
Barros, Zeca, 144
Barroso, Ari, 235
Bashevis Singer, Isaac, 168
Batista, Silvana, 145
Behar, Ruth, 67, 68, 70, 81–82, 178–179, 182–183
Bellessi, Diana, 167–168, 171

Bellow, Saul, 168
Benítez Rojo, Antonio, 74
Beserra, Bernadete, 141, 151
Bianciotti, Héctor, 170
Bicalho, José Victor, 145
Blanco, Richard, 84
Bolaños, Aimée G., 73
Borges, Jorge Luis, 165, 169–171
Borgia, Lucrezia, 73
Borinsky, Alicia, 160–161, 167, 188
Borrero, Juana, 73
Boscana, Gerónimo Fray, 15
Braga, Ana Cristina, 146, 168
Braga, Sonia, 221, 225
Braschi, Giannina, 196
Bráz, Júlio, 145
Brecht, Bertolt, 20
Brene, José Ramón, 90
Bretas, Angela, 144–146, 150–151, 153–154
Bruce-Novoa, Juan, 14
Burgos, Julia de, 193–195, 203
Busch, Juan Daniel, 38

Cabeza de Baca Gilbert, Fabiola, 18
Cabeza de Vaca, Álvar Núñez, 14
Cabrera, Lydia, 88, 96
Camby, Vincent, 80
Campa, Román de la, 67, 71, 74
Canals, María, 219
Candido, Antônio, 143
Cantú, Norma Elia, 24
Capó, Bobby, 39
Cárdenas, Raúl de, 90, 95–96
Cardozo, Patricia, 221
Carminatti, Roberto, 144–145
Carpentier, Alejo, 80
Carrier, Rick, 216
Carrillo, Elpidia, 219
Cartagena Portalatín, Aída, 103
Casal, Julián del, 70
Castañeda, Omar, 120, 122, 132–133, 135, 137
Castellanos, Isabel 89
Castillo, Ana, 39, 191

Caulfield, Carlota, 73, 187
Chakiris, George, 216
Chase, Cida S., 126, 129
Chávez, César, 20
Chávez, Denise, 25
Chayanne, 215
Chejfec, Sergio, 160, 164–165
Chen Sham, Jorge, 126–127, 129–131
Cisneros, Sandra, 22, 27, 37–40, 45–49, 116
Clifford, James, 68
Cocco de Filippis, Daisy, 103–104, 201
Columbus, Christopher, 107, 109
Connor, Anne, 113
Contreras, Hilma, 103
Corpi, Lucha, 24, 191
Corrales, José, 90, 95–96
Cortázar, Julio, 159, 171
Cortez, Gregorio, 15, 219
Cortez, Hernán, 214
Cosme, Eusebia, 96
Cota-Cárdenas, Margarita, 24, 109
Cruz, Angie, 101, 109, 111, 113–116
Cruz, Celia, 220
Cuadra, Pablo Antonio, 122, 124–125
Cuauhtémoc, 20
Cujec, Carol, 46–47
Cullen, Jim, 147–148, 153

DaMatta, Roberto, 146, 152, 154
Díaz, Roberto Ignacio, 168–170
Díaz, Junot, 101, 109, 111
Díaz Parrado, Flora, 89
Dorfman, Ariel, 183–184
Doyle, Jacqueline, 40
Duany, Jorge, 70
Duchesne Winter, Juan, 142

Eire, Carlos, 71
Eliott, Gayle, 46
Espinosa, Carlos, 70
Estebanez, Natatcha, 221
Esteves, Sandra María, 103–104, 191, 193–196
Estorino, Abelardo, 90
Estrada, Noel, 58

Felipe, Carlos, 90
Fernández, Damián, 67, 70
Fernández, Roberto G., 80–81
Fernández, Macedonio, 170
Fernández Rosario, María Teresa (Mariposa), 196
Ferreira Moura, Ricardo, 149
Fitts, Alexandra, 39, 43–44

Florit, Eugenio, 68
Fornet, Ambrosio, 67, 70
Fowler Calzada, Víctor, 70, 76, 81
Fulleda, León, 90

Gago, Jenny, 219
Galliano, Alina, 96, 199–200
Galvão, Heloisa Maria, 145
García, Cristina, 74, 78, 116
García-Obregón, Omar, 125
García Ramos, Reinaldo, 74
Gaspar de Alba, Alicia, 29
Gil, Lourdes, 200
Glickman, Nora, 160–162, 188
Goldemberg, Isaac, 184–186
Gombrowicz, Witold, 170
Gómez de Avellaneda, Gertrudis, 71, 73
Gonzáles-Berry, Erlinda, 24
Gonzáles, Myrna-Yamil, 38
González, Jovita, 18
González, Rodolfo 'Corky', 20
González Goyri, Roberto, 135
González Viaña, Eduardo, 10
Guajardo, Paul, 37
Guillén, Nicolás, 68, 88
Guillot, Olga, 96
Guimarães, Norma, 145
Guizar, Tito, 213

Hanashiro, Maria Alice, 149
Henfil, 140–141
Henríquez, Pedro, 104
Heredia, José María, 71
Hernández, Jonathan, 219
Hernández Catá, Alfonso, 82–84
Hernández Cruz, Victor, 53–56
Hernández Espinosa, Eugenio, 90
Herrera, Andrea O'Reilly, 69, 70, 79–80
Herrera-Sobek, María, 27
Hijuelos, Oscar, 74, 121
Hiller, Arthur, 217
Hinojosa, Rolando, 22, 24
Holz, Édel, 144, 146, 152
Holz, Fernando, 144
Hospital, Carolina, 191, 197–199
Hoyos, Angela de, 191
Hudson, W. H., 170
Huidobro, Vicente, 170
Huizinga, Johan, 69, 71
Hurston, Zora Neale, 18
Hurt, William, 221

Ichaso, León, 80, 217–219, 224
Ilarregui, Gladys, 160–161, 167

Islas, Arturo, 22
Islas, Maya, 200
Iturralde, Iraida, 200

Joffily, José, 222
Joyce, Rosemary A., 135–136

Kahlo, Frida, 73
Kanellos, Nicolás, 158, 194, 199
Kozameh, Alicia, 160–161, 163
Kozer, José, 186–188

Laviera, Tato, 53, 56, 61
Leal, Luis, 14–15
Leal, Rine, 89–90
LeGuin, Ursula K., 168
Leguizamo, John, 220
Leon, Thales de, 145, 150
Levins Morales, Aurora, 59, 196
Lezama Lima, José, 72
Llamas, Ricardo, 214
Lockhart, Darrell, 177
Lopez, Jennifer, 219, 224–225
López, Josefina, 29, 45, 221
López Rojas, Eduardo, 219
Lorenzo, Michael D., 219
Losey, Joseph, 216
Loveira, Carlos, 68
Luis, William, 144, 203
Lupe, La, 96

Magalhães, Valéria Barbosa de, 145
Mansilla de García, Eduarda, 169
Marcos, Plinio, 222
María, Constance, 219
Marin, Cheech, 220
Martes, Ana Cristina Braga, 146, 151
Martí, José, , 70–71, 82–84, 108
Martín-Rodríguez, Manuel, 90, 92, 95
Martínez, Tomás Eloy, 160–161, 163, 168
Martínez, Victor, 29
Martínez Furé, Rogelio, 89
Masiello, Francine, 164, 167–168
Medrano, Marianela, 202–203
Meléndez, Ramón 'Ray', 220
Mena, María Cristina, 16–18
Mendes, Lucas, 143, 145
Méndes Sosa, Tomás, 39
Méndez, Miguel, 21
Millián, José, 90
Milligan, Bryce, 191
Mir, Pedro, 102
Miranda, Aurora, 213
Miranda, Carmen, 141, 213, 222, 225

Mistral, Gabriela, 73, 108
Mitchell, Christopher, 140–141
Mohr, Nicholasa, 60–62
Molloy, Sylvia, 160–161, 165, 168, 171–172
Monge Rafuls, Pedro R., 77–78, 90
Monroe, Marilyn, 148
Montalbán, Ricardo, 214
Montaner, Rita, 92, 96
Monteflores, Carmen de, 60
Montes Huidobro, Matías, 74, 81, 89–92
Mora, Pat, 191
Moraes, Reinaldo, 145
Moraga, Cherríe, 28–29, 45
Morales, Alejandro, 26
Morales, Ed, 47
Morales, Esai, 219
Morales, Rosario, 52, 59, 196
Moreno, Rita, 216–217
Moret, Zulema, 160–161, 167, 192
Moro, César, 170
Morrison, George, 215
Morrison, Toni, 116
Mota, Kátia, 151
Muñiz, Angel, 218
Murrieta, Joaquín, 15, 21

Nair, Mira, 221
Napoleon, Louis, 214
Nascimento, Milton, 152
Nava, Gregory, 219, 221
Navarro, Mireya, 196
Navarro, Ramón, 212
Negrín, María Luisa, 122
Negroni, María, 160–161, 167, 171
Neto, Belchior, 145–146
Niggli, Josefina, 17–18, 24, 29
Nolasco, Sonia, 142, 145–146
Novaes, Carlos Eduardo, 140, 142, 145, 147–148, 152–154
Novás Calvo, Lino, 74
Nuez, Iván de la, 74

Ocampo, Victoria, 169
Olivares, Julián, 38
Oliveira, Aloysio de, 213
Olmos, Edward James, 15, 196, 219
Ontiveros, Lupe, 219
Oñate, Juan de, 14
Ortega y Gasset, José, 76
Ortiz, Ivan Dariel, 220
Ortiz Cofer, Judith, 60, 62–63, 191, 193–196
Otero-Warren, Nina, 18

Padilla, Genaro, 15
Palacios, Conny, 120, 122–126, 137
Paredes, Américo, 15, 219
Partnoy, Alicia, 160–161, 163
Perdigão, Paulo, 140, 142, 148
Pereiras García, Manuel, 90, 95–96
Perera, Hilda, 74
Perera, Víctor, 188
Pérez, Loida Maritza, 109
Pérez, Severo, 19, 219
Pérez de Villagrá, Gaspar, 14
Pérez-Firmat, Gustavo, 67–68, 70, 72, 74, 78–79
Piglia, Ricardo, 160–162, 165–166, 168, 170–171
Pinochet, Augusto, 183
Piñera, Virgilio, 70, 90, 170
Piñero, Miguel, 104, 224–225
Pita, Mario Alejandro, 201
Ponce, Mary Helen, 23
Ponce de León, Néstor, 70
Portillo-Trambley, Estela, 22, 29
Power, Tyrone, 214
Pratt, Mary Louise, 147, 158
Prida, Dolores, 90
Puente, Tito, 220
Puig, Manuel, 160, 165–66, 168, 171, 221
Purdy, Jim, 216

Quintanilla, Abraham, 223
Quintanilla-Pérez, Selena, 223

Rawlings, Norberto James, 103
Redford, Robert, 218, 222
Rheda, Regina, 145
Riker, David, 218
Río, Dolores del, 213
Rivera, Edward, 52, 58
Rivera, Tomás, 19, 21–22, 28
Rivero, Eliana, 69, 72, 76, 81
Robinet, Emma Jane, 201, 204
Rodríguez, Luis Felipe, 68
Rodríguez, Richard, 38, 47
Rodríguez, Robert, 221
Rodríguez de Laguna, Asela, 194
Roffman, Peter, 216
Rojas, Lourdes, 194
Rojas, Rafael, 67, 70, 74, 83
Rosario, Nelly, 101, 109, 113, 116
Rosas, Manuel, 162
Roth, Philip, 168
Roulien, Raul, 212
Ruíz de Burton, María Amparo, 16
Rushdie, Salman, 73, 76–77, 82

Saer, Juan José, 159, 170–171
Safran, William, 68
Said, Edward, 161, 164
Saldívar, Ramón, 30, 47
Sales, Teresa, 140–141, 152
Salles, Walter, 222–223
Sánchez Lamouth, Juan, 103
Sand, George, 73
Santa Cruz y Montalvo, Mercedes de, 71
Santana, João, 145
Santiago, Esmeralda, 52, 60–61
Santiago, Héctor, 90
Santiago, Silviano, 145
Sarduy, Severo, 72
Sarmiento, Domingo Faustino, 162
Sayles, John, 223
Schnabel, Julian, 224
Scotto, Luis Alberto, 145
Sebe Bom Meihy, José Carlos, 141–142
Senkman, Leonardo, 179
Silvestre, Edney, 143, 145
Singer, León, 219
Smith, Bessie, 92
Smits, Jimmy, 219
Soldberg, Helena, 222
Soto, Gary, 28
Spitzer, Leo, 180
Springall, Alejandro, 223
Stavans, Ilan, 182, 188
Stozek Filho, Carlos, 145
Strejilevich, Nora, 160, 163–164
Sturges, John, 216
Suárez, Virgil, 71, 75
Summers, Donna, 224
Svich, Caridad, 90
Szichman, Mario, 160, 163, 168, 188

Tedlock, Dennis, 133, 135
Thomas, Piri, 52
Timerman, Jacobo, 160–161, 163
Torres-Saillant, Silvio, 112, 116
Trauer, Valeria, 151
Triana, José, 90
Tristán, Flora, 73

Umpierre, Luz María, 197
Unger, David, 188
Ureña Henríquez, Salomé, 102, 106
Urista, Alberto Baltasar, 21

Valdez, Luis, 20–21, 215, 219
Valentino, Rudolph, 212
Valenzuela, Luisa, 160, 161, 167, 168, 171
Vallbona, Rima de, 120, 122, 126–128, 137

Ventura, Miriam, 203
Vera León, Antonio, 69
Viau Renaud, Antonio, 103
Vicioso, Sherezada 'Chiqui', 104–105, 201, 203
Victoria, Carlos, 74
Vilas Boas, Sergio, 142, 145
Villa, Pancho, 211, 214
Villanueva, Alma Luz, 25, 191
Villanueva, Tino, 23
Villarreal, José Antonio, 21
Villaseñor, Victor, 25
Viramontes, Helena María, 27, 44

Von Arx, Regina, 153

Walsh, Donald D., 201
Welles, Orson, 217
Wellman, William, 216
Whitman, Walt, 102
Wilcock, Juan Rodolfo, 169
Woolf, Virginia, 170, 195
Wyatt, Jean, 44

Zamora, Bernice, 191
Zapata, Emiliano, 20, 214
Zimmerman, Marc, 37, 48, 101

www.ingramcontent.com/pod-product-compliance
Lightning Source LLC
Chambersburg PA
CBHW070336240426
43665CB00045B/2121